US Politics, Propaganda and the Afghan Mujahedeen

US Politics, Propaganda and the Afghan Mujahedeen

Jacqueline Fitzgibbon

I.B. TAURIS
LONDON • NEW YORK • OXFORD • NEW DELHI • SYDNEY

I.B. TAURIS
Bloomsbury Publishing Plc
50 Bedford Square, London, WC1B 3DP, UK
1385 Broadway, New York, NY 10018, USA
29 Earlsfort Terrace, Dublin 2, Ireland

BLOOMSBURY, I.B. TAURIS and the I.B. Tauris logo are trademarks
of Bloomsbury Publishing Plc

First published in Great Britain 2020
This paperback edition published in 2021

Copyright © Jacqueline Fitzgibbon, 2020

Jacqueline Fitzgibbon has asserted her right under the Copyright,
Designs and Patents Act, 1988, to be identified as Author of this work.

Series design by Adriana Brioso
Cover image: Members of an Afghan Mujahideen group at a camp at Jegdalay
in Kabul Province, Afghanistan, 28th May 1988. (© David Stewart-Smith/Getty Images)

All rights reserved. No part of this publication may be reproduced
or transmitted in any form or by any means, electronic or mechanical,
including photocopying, recording, or any information storage or retrieval system,
without prior permission in writing from the publishers.

Bloomsbury Publishing Plc does not have any control over, or responsibility for,
any third-party websites referred to or in this book. All internet addresses given
in this book were correct at the time of going to press. The author and publisher
regret any inconvenience caused if addresses have changed or sites have ceased
to exist, but can accept no responsibility for any such changes.

A catalogue record for this book is available from the British Library.

A catalogue record for this book is available from the Library of Congress.

ISBN:	HB:	978-1-7883-1277-6
	PB:	978-0-7556-3725-6
	ePDF:	978-1-8386-0400-4
	eBook:	978-1-8386-0401-1

Typeset by Integra Software Services Pvt. Ltd.

To find out more about our authors and books visit www.bloomsbury.com
and sign up for our newsletters.

Contents

Introduction		1
1	US foreign policy and Afghanistan: History, context and Carter	13
2	The Reagan administration: Foreign policy influences and the importance of propaganda	33
3	The Reagan Doctrine, propaganda and the Afghan conflict	53
4	Justifying escalation in Afghanistan	71
5	The Afghan Media Project	87
6	'The road to Geneva and beyond': The superpower summit, public diplomacy and the Afghan conflict	105
7	The beginning of the end: The Geneva Accords and national reconciliation	125
Conclusion		147
Notes		154
Selected bibliography		217
Index		223

Introduction

The Soviet invasion of Afghanistan on 24 December 1979 rekindled Cold War antagonisms between the United States and the Soviet Union. It also afforded hard-line anti-communists in the United States an 'opportunity' to embroil Washington's superpower foe in a 'Vietnam-like quagmire'. This goal was pursued along dual tracks, both shaped by America's own Vietnam experience. One track is well documented – the arming of Afghans resisting the Red Army and the Kabul government. The other strategy less so; this involved the deployment of propaganda and public diplomacy centred on the Afghan conflict to undermine the Soviet Union internally and internationally and justify a more assertive and militant America. This book documents and analyses the programmes, people and policies associated with this second strategy. Alongside this, it investigates private organizations in the United States that supported the *mujahedeen*'s struggle for various reasons and the influence they brought to bear on government policy through their public advocacy. The result is a fresh perspective on American foreign policy on the Afghan conflict in the 1980s and on the use of propaganda to facilitate US aims and shape policy.

The Soviet invasion of Afghanistan and subsequent occupation coincided with an era of expansion and growth in news media and, initially at least, received widespread international coverage. Interest in the conflict soon waned and such indifference threatened effective aid to the Afghan resistance – a central plank of the Reagan Doctrine. It also threatened the conflict's potency as an instrument of US foreign policy propaganda. To counter this, an alliance of the American allies of the *mujahedeen* in private voluntary organizations (PVOs), Congress and, from 1981, within the Reagan administration turned to public diplomacy and propaganda to re-ignite public interest.

Propaganda is the selective use of information to intentionally shape opinions, attitudes and behaviours to promote the goals of the propagandist. This book explores the relationship between propaganda and the development and implementation of US foreign policy from 1979 to 1989 in relation to the conflict in Afghanistan. The propaganda emanated from the administrations of Presidents Carter and Reagan, committees of Congress, PVOs and conservative think tanks. Target audiences included the US public, international publics, the US congress along with the administrations themselves. Propaganda is enabled by barriers limiting the free flow of information. In the case of Afghanistan, its remoteness, inhospitable terrain and other dangers constituted just such a barrier to Western media allowing information on the conflict to be shaped by biased sources. Propaganda was used in an attempt to manufacture consent sometimes successfully (the supply of Stinger missiles to the *mujahedeen*) and sometimes unsuccessfully (the Reagan administration's bid to regenerate the US chemical weapons programme). It involved the deliberate omission of information which would have cast the *mujahedeen* in a negative light and the use of emotive language and atrocity stories to evoke outrage against the Soviet Union.

While the protagonists of this study may have had common cause, their agendas and target audience often differed. *Mujahedeen* supporters in Congress and the PVOs sought to manipulate public opinion and to influence the executive branch to increase aid to the resistance. In some instances this was effective and public diplomacy and propaganda by these groups did help shape the foreign policy environment on Afghanistan.

The Reagan administration also used the conflict to bolster its attempts to undermine the Soviet position in arms treaty negotiations and to impose political and economic costs on the USSR. It pointed to events in Afghanistan to justify the assertion of American military might and to evoke American exceptionalism, which it believed was undermined by the legacy of the Vietnam War and emasculated by the Carter administration. However, while Afghan propaganda helped further the Cold War objectives of the Reagan administration, it also constrained its ability to pursue a negotiated settlement. The administration's own harsh rhetoric created a 'credibility trap' that limited officials' ability to negotiate a settlement on the Afghan conflict or restrict the flow of arms to the *mujahedeen*.

Propaganda generated by the US supporters of the Afghan *mujahedeen* presented them as noble 'freedom fighters' representative of the Afghan people and struggling against a repressive superpower. However, divisions and tensions arose about the manner in which the rebels should be assisted by the United States. The Carter administration, particularly President Carter and his National Security Advisor, Zbigniew Brzezinski, reacted to the invasion with steely rhetoric but only a modest amount of military aid to the rebels. However, the Reagan administration's ascent to power just one year later promised more vigorous support for the insurgency.

Hard-line anti-communists energized by neo-conservative and New Right philosophies were ascendant in the nascent administration. They agitated for a more assertive American foreign policy posture towards Moscow and quickly identified assistance to the Afghan insurgency as a means to pursue this agenda. However, the administration was often divided on how far it was willing to provoke the Soviets with its Afghan programme. As a result, the more militant hawks or 'bleeders' in the administration turned to propaganda and public diplomacy to generate the necessary pressure to promote their policies.[1] Afghanistan would provide ample material for this strategy to influence the formulation of foreign policy.

These 'bleeders' had a number of objectives which could be facilitated by effective propaganda. Chief amongst these was the desire to 'raise the costs' in blood and treasure of the intervention to the Soviet Union by embroiling them in a protracted conflict – reminiscent of America's own debacle in Southeast Asia just a few years beforehand. Aiding the *mujahedeen* could also help realign the United States with Islamic and Third World states, where Washington felt its reputation was tainted by the Iranian Revolution, its ignominious retreat from Vietnam and Soviet propaganda. Propaganda and public diplomacy had a pivotal role to play in ensuring the conflict extracted a high political toll from Moscow. It also offered the opportunity and means to reassert American exceptionalism. Washington framed its endorsement of the *mujahedeen* as advocacy of liberty, self-determination and religious freedom. Its public diplomacy contrasted these virtuous motives with the Soviet's alleged foreign policy doctrine of militaristic imperialism. This investigation outlines how informational strategies were developed and deployed by the Reagan administration as instruments to achieve Cold War pre-eminence. It details their impact on Afghanistan which was largely negative as they impeded negotiation and resolution.

The Reagan administration's commitment to strengthening the US propaganda infrastructure was evident from its earliest days in office. The administration drafted National Security Decision Directives (NSDDs) to enhance the informational/public diplomacy apparatus for foreign policy applications.[2] This reflected a widespread conviction in conservative and neo-conservative foreign policy circles that Vietnam had been lost in the living rooms of America.[3] This 'lesson' was internalized by those seeking to shape a more assertive US posture on the international stage and vigorously applied during the Reagan years in support of the Reagan Doctrine particularly in the case of Afghanistan. NSDD 75 'US Relations with the USSR' – the 'strategic rationale of the Reagan Doctrine' underlines this argument as it pinpointed Afghanistan as a specific vulnerability of the 'Soviet Empire' ripe for exploitation.[4] CIA director, William Casey, identified the Afghan conflict as the quintessential anti-communist insurgency, which could serve as a template for US intervention by proxy in other Third World regions.

The Reagan Doctrine strove to affect this policy of intervention by aiding insurgencies in Nicaragua, Cambodia, Mozambique and Angola. In its lifetime, unlike Nicaragua, the Afghan strand of the doctrine provoked little controversy, instead enjoying a 'peaceful consensus' in political circles and this remained largely the case up to 11 September 2001.[5] As a result, the Afghan insurgency was chosen by Washington to dominate the public narrative around the doctrine. This conflict was used to rationalize US policies as a reaction to Soviet aggression and expansionism and legitimize US interference in the internal political evolution of these states. Since 9/11 there has been a re-evaluation of the 'success' of the doctrine's military and political imperatives in Afghanistan but not of the propaganda which was an intrinsic element of the strategy and so vital to its execution. This research investigates this neglected aspect of the Reagan Doctrine's application in Afghanistan, which had such significant long-term consequences for both America and Afghanistan, and its wider role in 'selling' the doctrine domestically and internationally.

The propaganda and public diplomacy around this strategy involved the development of a number of motifs about the conflict and its protagonists. The *mujahedeen*'s war with the Red Army was framed in David versus Goliath terms or, alternatively, as a struggle between 'holy warriors' and aggressive, godless communists. The insurgents' values and goals were equated with those of Americans. The rebels were allegedly fighting for 'freedom' and the reality of their corruption and suppression of minority and women rights was ignored. The oblique term 'self-determination' was used, as 'democracy' did not feature in many *mujahedeen*'s political lexicon. The

Islamic fundamentalism of some insurgent groups was sold to the American public as a deep piety with parallels in American Christianity while studiously avoiding any comparison with Iranian fundamentalists. This narrative justified US support for the rebels. However, it ignored the reality of the violent and complicated civil war between various tribal, religious and political factions being prosecuted within Afghanistan and the reactionary and anti-American nature of some of the protagonists. This skewed narrative empowered those willing to fight the Soviets and emasculated those willing to negotiate. This deepened divisions in Afghan political and social circles and made post-conflict peace harder to achieve.

US support for the *mujahedeen* was not solely rooted in the Reagan administration but stemmed too from congressional supporters and PVOs. Often even more ardent advocates of the rebels than the administration, their aim was to increase military, financial and political support to the insurgents. To achieve this, these groups also turned to public advocacy and propaganda to press their agenda. This created an environment, which, on occasion, left the administration, particularly the State Department, with little room to manoeuvre on negotiations.

By the late 1970s, conservative activism had developed and grown in strength and sophistication. As a result, the Reagan administration did not need to create 'cut-outs' or front organizations to promote its foreign policy agenda on Afghanistan though future document releases may prove they did do so in some cases. Instead, advocacy groups were created by private organizations and individuals dedicated to promoting a hard-line anti-communist US foreign policy. However, there was a web of connections between these 'private' organizations, members of Congress and the administration, which facilitated access to the corridors of power for the PVOs and, at times, enabled them to influence decision-making on Afghanistan. This state-private network also reinforced or amplified the policies of the administration via this civil or private advocacy as it was more potent with the public due to its non-official origins. This granular 'bottom-up' examination of how this network worked in the case of advocacy for the Afghan *mujahedeen* in the United States has been absent from scholarship on the conflict so far. Interestingly, it demonstrates that the lines between private and administration advocacy were often blurred. At times, these PVOs solely aligned with the belligerent policies proposed by the administration's 'bleeders', thus strengthening their positions by magnifying their public impact.

PVOs like the Committee for a Free Afghanistan and Afghan Relief Committee held dinners, conferences, gave testimony at congressional hearings, distributed literature, wrote opinion pieces in newspapers and appeared on television news shows to raise funds and awareness. The Heritage Foundation, a conservative think tank, regularly issued strongly worded analysis pieces denouncing Soviet actions and endorsing an expansion in aid to the rebels.

These pro-*mujahedeen* advocates publicly campaigned for the supply of US-made anti-aircraft missiles (Stingers) to the rebels and for a USIA (United States Information Agency) programme to increase media coverage of the conflict (the Afghan Media Project). They vociferously denounced the Geneva peace process, thus constraining the administration's ability to negotiate on a resolution and the Red Army's withdrawal from Afghanistan. Congressional supporters, many with connections to the PVOs, met with *mujahedeen* visiting the United States, visited the rebels' camps in Pakistan and organized hearings to publicize the conflict. These propaganda and public diplomacy campaigns helped shape administration policies and programmes, which further militarized the conflict, undermined attempts at national reconciliation in Afghanistan, encouraged intransigence amongst the rebels and delayed a settlement. The methods and motivations of these private and congressional supporters and their effectiveness in generating attention for the conflict in order to influence policy are explored in detail in this book. Fred Halliday held that the privatization of support for the Nicaraguan *Contras* increased the 'degree of political commitment, participation and sense of importance felt by right-wing activists' in relation to Central America whilst also inhibiting domestic criticism. This was true too for the Afghan supporters, who were often one and the same as the pro-*Contra* advocates. The ties and tensions between these private activists, the administration and congressional supporters of the *mujahedeen* are revealed along with their impact on the public discourse and administration policy.

Both assisted and challenged by these domestic US supporters of the *mujahedeen*, the administration often walked a tightrope. It sought to undermine the Soviet Union on the international stage with strident rhetoric and visceral accounts of wrongdoing and war crimes in Afghanistan while, at the same time, engaging in delicate negotiations with Moscow on a number of issues from arms control to the Strategic Defense Initiative (SDI). Congressional and private *mujahedeen* supporters operated under no such constraints however, and often formed the vanguard in the push for increased political, military and financial support to the Afghan rebels. Untangling these relationships reveals the web of forces seeking to influence US foreign policy in this instance and the essential role of propaganda and public diplomacy in doing so.

Propaganda legitimized the political credentials of the *mujahedeen* leadership, even those known to be corrupt, reactionary and violent. It shaped the public discourse on the conflict and ensured widespread consensus on the morality of supporting the rebels. While at the time seemingly justified within America's Cold War worldview, this strategy subjugated the political, economic and social stability of Afghanistan to the US struggle with its superpower rival. This would have long-term consequences for Afghanistan, the United States and international stability.

There is a rich seam of literature on the Afghan conflict and US foreign policy towards it which this book has referenced for background and context, in particular, Steve Coll's *Ghost Wars*, Oliver Roy's *Islam and Resistance in Afghanistan* and Diego Cordovez and Selig Harrison's *Out of Afghanistan: The Inside Story of the Soviet Withdrawal*.[6]

As well as more contemporary works discussed later, a number of seminal studies on the development and uses of propaganda including Walter Lippmann's *Public Opinion*, Harold Lasswell's *Propaganda Techniques in the World War* and Edward Bernays's *Propaganda* provided useful insights into the conditions necessary and means and techniques required for successful propagandizing.[7] Lippman argues that without some degree of censorship, propaganda is impossible and certainly the dangerous conditions in Afghanistan created a barrier to widespread coverage of the conflict creating conditions akin to censorship. As a result, information often filtered through to the media and the public from sources that had an agenda. Writing in the aftermath of the First World War, Lasswell describes propaganda as a co-equal branch of operations against an opponent alongside military and economic actions. This thinking is reflected in the Reagan administration's prioritizing of propaganda some sixty-odd years later. Lasswell also outlines the need to 'fortify the mind of the nation with examples of insolence and depravity' by the enemy and provides a list of propaganda techniques including 'atrocity stories' of rape, torture or the alleged use of chemical weapons all of which are evident in the US propaganda swirling around the Afghan conflict. While delivery methods might have been updated by the 1980s, the basic techniques had remained the same. Lasswell describes them as 'old standbys [that] can be relied upon'. Similarly, Bernays's chapter on propaganda and politics provides a list of instruments for delivering political messages from the obvious like radio and newsprint but extending also to exhibitions and the co-operation of educational institutes warning of the need not 'to put all one's eggs in one basket'. This message was well-heeded by Reagan's propagandists.

While a number of other researchers have explored US foreign policy and propaganda, these tend to concern the early Cold War period or before and often focus on government agencies.[8] This book adds to this body of literature but extends its reach into the late 1980s but, more than that, it offers a new perspective by illuminating the role played by private organizations. Propaganda on the Afghan conflict produced and propagated by conservative think tanks, especially the Heritage Foundation, is put under the spotlight. Jason Stahl's recent publication *Right Moves* examines the influence of right-wing think tanks on US politics. It outlines how Heritage became the 'go to conservative voice' in the 1980s.[9] Stahl's work is mostly concerned with the domestic policy arena which this study will augment by examining the influence of Heritage and others on foreign policy formation in relation to the USSR and Afghanistan during the 1980s. Along with the examination of think tanks, this work provides the first detailed investigation of private conservative lobby groups advocating for support to the Afghan *mujahedeen* enriching our understanding of the function of propaganda in US foreign policy in this era.

But how is propaganda used to benefit US foreign policy and what exactly is public diplomacy? The historiography of propaganda and public diplomacy in US foreign policy offers a wide range of interpretations of these expressions and their ambiguous definitions. An examination of the literature in this area illuminates the shifting terminology used to frame US official and unofficial information strategies since the 1960s. Public diplomacy, propaganda, public relations, information management, psychological warfare are all phrases used to describe the US foreign policy establishment's information strategies. These are variously designed to shape domestic (both public and congressional) and foreign (public, state and international organizations) opinion. All evoke differing connotations; as a result, some terms are privileged over others.

The term 'public diplomacy' came to prominence in the mid-1960s when the USIA (1953–1999) adopted it to define its mission to generate support for US foreign policies internationally. It was co-opted as an acceptable alternative to propaganda – a term shunned in the United States due to its associations with the Nazi regime in Germany and later with the Soviet Union. Consequently, phrases such as public diplomacy, psychological operations and information warfare gained favour.

However, America's issue with the term 'propaganda' has deeper cultural roots too. The US 'exceptionalist' ideology precludes any consideration that its dialogue with the wider world could be propagandistic. This exceptionalist justification for American propaganda is evident in the writings of Reagan administration officials such as Kenneth Adelman and Carnes Lord about proposed information strategies, which affected the Afghan conflict as well as the rhetoric and policies of the administration.[10]

In the post-Second World War period the CIA blurred the boundaries between propaganda and public diplomacy by orchestrating or funding 'private' cultural organizations and citizens groups which articulated 'Western' ideologies and challenged Soviet communism in the battle for international 'hearts and minds'.[11] This was possible due to a developing Cold War consensus in the public and political sphere around the threat posed by communism.

Over time, US public diplomacy strategies developed to engage with more two-way, marketing-based initiatives designed to create a dialogue with an audience and encourage cultural exchange. Under Reagan, however, public diplomacy was harnessed to more propagandistic purposes. It was utilized under the guidance of officials who saw little difference between it and propaganda other than its more acceptable inference to the public. Nicholas J. Cull states that the term was taken 'in vain' by Reagan's White House. Others agree and highlight dubious practices. Peter Kornbluh points out that Walter Raymond, Jr – transferred to the National Security Council as Public Diplomacy Co-ordinator from the CIA – was a propaganda and psychological warfare expert rather than a public diplomacy practitioner.[12] Historian and former diplomat, Raymond Garthoff described the administration's NSDD 77 on public diplomacy as unveiling 'a new intensified ideological propaganda campaign'.[13] Nancy Snow also questions the propagandistic nature of 'public diplomacy' campaigns conducted by the Reagan administration such as Project Truth and later Project Democracy, concluding the USIA, under Reagan, was a 'propaganda agency'.[14] USIA official Alan Snyder described USIA Director Charles Wick as the agency's most successful propagandist and Reagan himself declared his determination to win 'the propaganda war' with the USSR. Contravening the spirit of the 1948 Smith-Mundt Act, films on Afghanistan produced by the USIA in 1980s for foreign distribution were distributed within the United States.[15] Ultimately, the public diplomacy practised by the Reagan administration and its agencies involving the Afghan conflict often better fits the description provided by Jowett and O'Donnell on propaganda – 'the deliberate, systemic attempt to shape perceptions, manipulate cognitions, and direct behaviour to achieve a response that furthers the desired intent of the propagandist'.[16]

Writing in the 1960s, the French philosopher Jacques Ellul argued that for propaganda to be effective it must reflect the psychological and sociological worldview of its audience. In the West during the Cold War, people were conditioned to accept that Soviet intentions were invariably malign and those of the West virtuous. This pre-disposed Western publics to believe official propaganda as it reflected their cultural frame of reference. Andrew L. Johns argues that US presidents use 'the ideological language of American exceptionalism, freedom, and democracy' to justify involvement in a conflict and frame a conflict within a Manichean 'good versus evil' context.[17] Historical analogies are evoked to provide a simple and simplistic frame of reference. The Afghan conflict offers an excellent example of this tendency.

The Reagan administration was aware of the potential of propaganda and conscious of the 'lessons' of Vietnam in its relation with the media. Officials like Lord and Adelman evoked an ideological mission emphasizing the 'national desire to exalt America's virtues' and 'bring the message of freedom to today's gloomy regions of despotism'.[18] Robert Parry and Peter Kornbluh's investigation into the Iran-*Contra* affair describes the administration's dedication to propaganda as 'a "new art form" in foreign policy' informed by America's defeat in Vietnam, which it blamed, at least partially, on Soviet and North Vietnamese disinformation.[19]

Noam Chomsky identifies dependence by the media on government and other 'expert' sources as one of the 'five filters' of news which marginalize dissent.[20] In the case of the Afghan conflict, the US media was largely dependent on the administration and other pro-*mujahedeen* advocates for information, as Afghanistan was too distant and too dangerous for most journalists to visit. This distance between the war zone and the media resonates with Lippmann's conviction that propaganda needs just such a 'barrier' to flourish.[21] The administration's propaganda was enabled not only by the 'barrier' of distance and danger but also by the ideological barrier to delineating the Soviet side of the story amongst Western journalists. Over the years, the declassification of documents from Soviet-era archives has allowed an exploration of Soviet motivations and, with the collapse of the Cold War duality, a less ideologically coloured appraisal. This throws US propaganda into greater relief as it is apparent that, contrary to the stated beliefs of Western Cold War warriors, Moscow's aims were not expansionist. Details have since emerged of the Soviet military's disagreement over the decision to invade, the Politburo's fear of the spread of Islamic fundamentalism and political instability and its sense of vulnerability due to the basing of cruise missiles in Western Europe.

US foreign policy and the Afghan conflict: From Carter to Reagan

The Soviet invasion of Afghanistan took place on President Jimmy Carter's watch and this book looks back to that era to explore the genesis of US propaganda policies on the conflict. Many of the post-9/11 books written on the subject recognize Carter's early policies and their contribution to subsequent events, though the earlier 'triumphalist' literature, which followed the demise of the USSR, minimized Carter's contribution. Reagan escalated US involvement for sure, but Carter and his National Security Advisor Zbigniew Brzezinski's initial contribution, particularly the propaganda element, was influential. Brzezinski was determined to seize the 'opportunity' afforded by the invasion of Afghanistan to stir up Muslim dissatisfaction with the USSR. He admits this in his memoir *Power and Principle*, published long before the 'blowback' from these policies became evident.[22] Gates argues that Carter's contribution to the downfall of the Soviet Union is underappreciated. He regards administration propaganda to 'keep alive the heritage of ethnic minorities in the Soviet Union' as significant. The significance of

Carter's role in the Afghan conflict is clarified by gathering together his administration's propaganda and public diplomacy initiatives and situating them within the larger context of Washington's engagement with the conflict over the subsequent decade. While Carter's policies on handling the Soviet invasion of Afghanistan have been reassessed as more important than initial post-Cold War literature acknowledged, this undoubtedly represents a poisoned chalice in the light of 9/11. Unquestionably, the true damage in Afghanistan was done under the Reagan administration when support for the *mujahedeen*, both financial and rhetorical, reached its zenith laying the seeds for unrest in the region for future decades.

Reagan administration policy on Afghanistan was largely informed by the Reagan Doctrine, which promised US support for anti-communist 'freedom fighters' mainly in the Third World. According to Fred Halliday, the doctrine consisted of five components of which a new theory of war, Low Intensity Combat (LIC), was one. LIC consisted of a number of elements including a policy to mobilize support for the doctrine's objectives within the United States via propaganda and 'privatize' political and financial support for insurgents through right-wing pressure groups.[23] This book reveals how these elements were central to the administration's policy towards the Afghan conflict.

In *Speaking My Mind*, President Reagan described the doctrine as 'our often controversial policy of supporting those fighting for freedom and against communism wherever we found them'. Administration officials like CIA Director William Casey were quick to realize that the benefits offered by the Afghan conflict to the promotion of the doctrine's objectives were singular. The *mujahedeen* enjoyed widespread public and congressional approval and could be used to promote less popular insurgencies. Following Reagan's State of the Union address in 1985, conservative commentator Charles Krauthammer described the policy as 'overt and unashamed American support for anti-Communists revolution' rooted in 'justice, necessity, and democratic tradition'. Krauthammer's language reflected the aspirations of the New Right conservatives for a resurgent, proactive United States and a belief that the United States was entitled to discern which revolutions were worthy of support. However, the *mujahedeen*'s political values did not reflect those of Western democracies necessitating public diplomacy, which cloaked these discrepancies.

Reagan's foreign policy not only reflected the aspirations of his New Right and neo-conservative supporters but was also shaped by them. Much has been written of their efforts to influence a more assertive US posture towards the Soviet Union ever before the invasion of Afghanistan.[24] This research shows how their propaganda efforts centred on the conflict facilitated these objectives. It analyses the programmes devised to achieve these aims, and details the individuals involved in the conception and implementation of these propaganda schemes.

Jerry Wayne Saunders, writing of the Committee on the Present Danger (CPD), points out that for hard-line anti-communists Afghanistan provided the justification for a much sought after military build-up similar to the way the Korean War enabled the implementation of NSC 68.[25] Scott Lucas documents how the CPD in an earlier iteration had been involved in the campaign to promote NSC 68.[26] As well as a devotion to the projection of American power, these militarists were convinced of the importance of shaping public perceptions to ensure support. Paul Nitze, a member of the CPD, writing in *Foreign Affairs* in 1980, outlined the significance of Afghanistan and the need to challenge Soviet propaganda. While claiming consternation at Soviet aggression, in fact, they saw the invasion as an opportunity to advance their militarist agenda and, as a result, machinated for the conflict's continuance. Members of these elites had access to the corridors of power following Reagan's election but other conservative anti-communists in the PVOs also played an active role in the Afghan conflict.

This privatized application of the Reagan Doctrine both challenged and promoted administration policies. Whereas once public diplomacy was assumed to describe only the activities of states and their agencies instead, scholars like Cull now talk of 'international actors' and extend its preserve to NGOs. These more expansive interpretations of the term embrace the initiatives of the PVOs described in this book whose propaganda efforts aimed to influence domestic US political and public circles. There was interplay between congressional supporters of the *mujahedeen*, their public diplomacy initiatives and their relationships with PVOs too. George Crile's *Charlie Wilson's War* offers a detailed, entertaining account of one Congressman's pivotal role in arming the *mujahedeen* and highlights the links between some pro-*mujahedeen* PVOs and members of Congress.[27] However, as this book shows the network in Congress supporting the Afghan rebels ran wider and deeper than one Congressman and was driven by more than adventurism.

The arc of US engagement with the Afghan conflict extends over the decade from 1979 to 1989. Although the most significant propaganda and public diplomacy programmes were developed during the Reagan administration, the roots of US involvement (governmental, congressional and private) lay in the Carter era. The Saur Revolution in Afghanistan occurred in 1978 precipitating the Soviet entanglement in Afghanistan and leading to its civil war being recast in a Cold War light. As a result, this study's starting point is the late 1970s and the domestic and geopolitical considerations which underscored the US reaction to events in Central Asia. From there, it examines Reagan's commitment to re-asserting American military might on the international stage and the role of propaganda initiatives and public diplomacy programmes on the Afghan conflict had in justifying this politically and morally.

Afghanistan stood out as the quintessential Reagan Doctrine programme – effective, popular and uncontroversial at the time – and the Reagan administration wanted it to stay that way. In order to maintain the *mujahedeen*'s popular support in the United States, the administration developed and disseminated propaganda and public diplomacy that drew parallels between the political and religious values of the rebels and those of Americans. This, in turn, enabled the decision to escalate US support for the *mujahedeen* under NSDD 166. The administration considered the Afghan conflict crucial to its efforts to 'roll back' Soviet 'expansionism' and opened up the possibility that the United States could finally shake off 'the Vietnam Syndrome'.

However, the United States faced setbacks, not least its troublesome image in the eyes of other countries. Washington needed to challenge the 'moral equivalence', which underwrote this attitude, and the Afghan conflict provided an opportunity to do just this. NSDD 166 not only provided for military escalation to facilitate US objectives in Afghanistan but increased propaganda pressure too. The Afghan Media Project, created by the USIA, would train *mujahedeen* in Peshawar, Pakistan, as print, video and photographic journalists. The material gathered by them would then be relayed worldwide via a news agency funded by the programme to address the dearth of international news coverage on the conflict.

Around the time the Reagan administration was preparing to escalate its support for the *mujahedeen*, Mikhail Gorbachev was elected to lead the Communist Party of the Soviet Union and thus the state. As preparations for a superpower summit in Geneva got underway, Gorbachev flagged his intention to scale back military spending in the Soviet Union. This was viewed with suspicion by Washington, which, in any case, was committed to developing the Strategic Defense Initiative. The administration's 'Road to Geneva' public diplomacy programme, of which the Afghan conflict was a cornerstone, was developed to counter Moscow's stance.

Geneva was also the venue for the stop-start peace negotiations between Kabul and Islamabad on the Afghan conflict. In their final phase, the Soviets sought to introduce a national reconciliation programme to prepare Afghan's warring parties for the post-conflict period. The US State Department looked favourably on facilitating an orderly withdrawal by the Red Army but US *mujahedeen* supporters in Congress and the PVOs were outraged that the agreement might allow the USSR to withdraw peacefully and deny the *mujahedeen* a triumphant victory. Furthermore, NSDD 270 outlined how the administration too sought to undermine national reconciliation plans but endeavoured to conceal this with public diplomacy. This ultimately led to delays in reaching a final agreement and, in the interim, efforts at national reconciliation were scuppered with long-term and widespread consequences.

The public diplomacy and propaganda programmes and initiatives of the Carter and especially the Reagan administrations were wide-ranging, multi-agency with varying goals. Ultimately, they served the overarching objective of gaining pre-eminence in the Cold War both militarily and ideologically. PVOs and members of Congress unwavering advocacy of the *mujahedeen* demonstrated that a 'cultural consensus' shaped by Cold War imperatives existed around the virtue of supporting the rebels. These actors had a complicated and not always complementary relationship with the administration. Their actions sometimes constrained the executive's negotiating options in relation to Afghanistan or undermined the CIA as with the Stinger missiles debate. The implications of this for the people of Afghanistan were given little consideration.

1

US foreign policy and Afghanistan: History, context and Carter

American foreign policy towards Afghanistan underwent a volte-face in the latter half of President Jimmy Carter's term. This was triggered ostensibly by the Soviet invasion but an equally important factor was the 'loss' of Iran, a geopolitical catastrophe for Washington. Domestic forces such as a looming presidential election further contributed. These factors coupled with pressures from the virulently anti-communist New Right and neo-conservative movements impelled Carter towards a more belligerent foreign policy which would have considerable implications for Afghanistan.

Just four years after the fall of Saigon, direct US military action over the Soviet invasion was out of the question and would remain so throughout the Reagan administration. Washington needed to counter Moscow's intervention while avoiding military engagement. The US response included the well-documented covert action programme to aid the Afghan *mujahedeen* in their fight against their government and its Soviet mentors. Less well-documented are the propaganda efforts, initiated under Carter, albeit tentatively, to exact the maximum cost to Moscow's international reputation. These included attempts to radicalize Muslims and the public diplomacy debacle that was the Olympic boycott.

These efforts not only ensured that Afghanistan remained a thorn in the USSR's side but they also served to prolong the conflict with disastrous results for Afghan society and politics and, ultimately, international stability. Carter's policies provided a template for the Reagan administration's strategy on Afghanistan making the Georgia politician's administration a natural starting to explore how propaganda became one of the most powerful weapons in the Afghan conflict.

To understand this, it is necessary to examine the historical, geopolitical and domestic circumstances informing the US entanglement in the Afghan conflict. These contexts are vital to clarifying the motivations for US foreign policy in the region. They provide a framework for analysing US propaganda on the conflict by enabling the juxtaposition of strategic and political aims with public assertions of the administration. They demonstrate how and why propaganda became an intrinsic pillar of Washington's strategy on the Afghan conflict.

The 1978 coup orchestrated by Afghanistan's small communist party triggered deeper involvement from Moscow in Afghan affairs driven largely by security imperatives. While Washington was well aware that Soviet motivations were grounded in localized security concerns, US propaganda contended that the invasion was part of an aggressive Cold War strategy hatched by Moscow to control the Persian Gulf. This elevated tensions internationally and fashioned Afghanistan as a theatre for confrontation between 'freedom' and 'communism'. However, US foreign policy towards the region demonstrates Washington's indifference to Afghanistan before the 'loss' of Iran and the Soviet invasion. These circumstances sharpened Afghanistan's significance to the United States but not, as its propaganda insisted, due to any concerns about Afghan self-determination. Instead, Carter was motivated by geostrategic imperatives that were driven by domestic influences. Within the United States, the Afghan invasion seemed to validate the uncompromising anti-Soviet stance of New Right organizations like the Heritage Foundation. It seemed to vindicate neo-conservative politicians' and intellectuals' ominous warnings about Soviet intentions and ideology. Carter was compelled to take these views seriously, as they gained traction with the public. These constituencies were adept at using the media to promulgate their ideas in an effort to influence US foreign policy. As a result, when it came to Afghanistan, propaganda was an instrument not solely of US foreign policy but also of domestic forces seeking to shape it. This would continue to be the case throughout the lifetime of the Reagan administration.

The Saur Revolution, Soviet intervention and US foreign policy

In Kabul during the spring of 1978, the Saur (April) Revolution brought the People's Democratic Party of Afghanistan (PDPA) to power. This coup would spark a series of events leading to the Soviet invasion to prop up the PDPA and US actions to undermine it. The PDPA consisted of two factions: the Khalq (led by Nur Mohammed Taraki) and the Parcham (led by Babrak Karmal). In response to Soviet pressure, the party had maintained an uneasy alliance under the republican regime of Mohammed Daoud Khan (1973–1978). Moscow feared instability in bordering Afghanistan and, to this end, had advised patience in pursuing political and social change in Afghanistan.[1] While the PDPA's Parcham faction sought moderate political reforms, the Khalq were more radically Marxist. Following the coup, Taraki assumed the presidency and initiated reforms, which the tribal societies of rural Afghanistan considered an affront to their traditional ways.

Popular unrest stirred. An uprising in Herat on 15 March 1979 resulted in the death of a number of Soviet advisors. The Afghan Army division garrisoned in Herat decamped to the insurgents' side. Taraki found the rebellion increasingly impossible to suppress and persistently requested Moscow's assistance. The Soviet leadership was alarmed by events and suspected outside interference. On 17 March 1979, Foreign Minister Andrei Gromyko informed the Politburo that 'bands of saboteurs and terrorists' sponsored by the United States, China, Iran and Pakistan had infiltrated the insurgency and reduced Herat to 'chaos'.[2] He warned that 'under no circumstances may we [the USSR] lose Afghanistan'.[3] Dating back to Stalin's leadership, the Soviet Union feared the re-emergence of a threat similar to the one posed historically by Germany and, as a result, considered the security of its periphery of vital strategic importance.

The NATO deployment of cruise missiles in Western Europe had heightened Soviet insecurity, and the 'loss' of Afghanistan could bring US missiles within range of key strategic assets in the USSR. Furthermore, Afghanistan could become the 'new Iran', that is, a listening post for the United States into Soviet Central Asia.[4] The Politburo agreed to military aid for the Taraki regime but refused to send in troops, which they quite rightly believed would provoke an unfavourable international response and worsen the situation within Afghanistan.[5] By September 1979, President Taraki was usurped by his even more radical Prime Minister Hafizullah Amin. Within weeks, Taraki was murdered. Soviet leader Leonid I. Brezhnev had personally assured Taraki of his support and worried about the implications of the assassination for Soviet credibility.[6] Moscow watched with disquiet the self-destructive policies of the PDPA and the growing unrest in Afghanistan. They nursed fears that Amin was courting the United States or that he was a CIA agent.[7] Soviet concerns grew that the revolution would fail amidst in-fighting, outside interference and overzealous application of Marxist doctrine in the under-developed, traditional society of rural Afghanistan. Reflecting these fears the Politburo made the fateful decision, against Soviet military advice, to intervene to maintain the Afghan revolution.[8]

International condemnation ensued. President Carter, already reeling from other foreign policy setbacks that year, including the 'loss' of Iran and the continuing Tehran hostage crisis, reacted angrily. Responding to events in his State of the Union address in January 1980, he outlined the 'Carter Doctrine'. In it, Carter promised a more assertive US posture to protect against any further Soviet encroachment on US 'interests' in this region.[9] Within the United States, an outspoken coalition of New Right and neo-conservatives commentators insisted that détente was dead and the Soviets were on the march across the Third World. According to this constituency, the Brezhnev Doctrine cemented Soviet gains in perpetuity. As this perspective gained ascendency, a chill descended upon superpower relations heralding a new era in the Cold War.

While Afghanistan was important to the Soviet Union for obvious geostrategic reasons, US interests in the state were ambiguous, at least until the Iranian revolution. Afghanistan's present was circumscribed by the region's imperial past. Following the Second World War, the crumbling British Empire limped away from its colonial possessions on the Indian subcontinent, and the Indian Independence Act of 1947 partitioned the former colony into India and Pakistan. Pakistan inherited British India's 1,500-mile border (approximately) with Afghanistan – the Durand Line. However, Kabul never recognized this border contending that lands beyond it in North Pakistan were part of Afghanistan. It registered its discontent by voting against Pakistan's admission to the United Nations in 1947. Over the course of the following decades, the Cold War further divided the region. The United States established security relations with Pakistan under Eisenhower. Along with Iran, the state became an intrinsic element of a 'northern tier' containment strategy for the region. Pakistan was also a member of the Southeast Asia Treaty Organization. On the other hand, Washington considered Afghanistan strategically unimportant and refused Kabul's requests for military assistance. This allowed the Soviet Union to establish some influence in the state via considerable aid and assistance.[10] Moscow invested heavily in the modernization of the Afghanistan military, and Soviet training personnel were stationed there.¹¹ US indifference to Soviet involvement in the state was evident when Eisenhower visited Kabul in 1959 and his plane was escorted in to land by Afghan-piloted Soviet MiG jets, to little public comment in America.¹² China's split with the Soviet Union in 1960 and subsequent border wars with India in 1962 meant, by default, China was allied with Pakistan and the United States within the context of regional politics. Non-aligned India accepted military aid from the USSR signing a friendship treaty in 1971. These lingering imperial-era animosities and Cold War alliances would become entangled in the programme to aid the *mujahedeen*'s fight against the PDPA in the 1980s.

The United States did provide some development aid to Afghanistan and educational assistance from the 1950s. These early educational programmes emphasized the compatibility between Islamic and Western values in an attempt to contain Soviet influence, though not in any determined way.¹³ Afghanistan was ostensibly non-aligned prior to the Saur Revolution but even following the communists' ouster of Daoud an initial assessment of the coup by the US Ambassador Theodore Eliot downplayed Soviet involvement.¹⁴ Eliot described the leaders as 'young, leftist and nationalistic' and his initial meeting with Taraki as friendly.¹⁵ This was soon to change. By June 1978, less than two months later, the Kabul embassy, now under the stewardship of Ambassador Adolph 'Spike' Dubs, characterized the new regime as 'overwhelmingly dependent on the Soviet Union'. In a telegram to Washington, the ambassador added that Afghanistan's foreign policy was likely to be shaped by this relationship. Furthermore, Moscow would continue to strengthen its influence in Afghanistan if it did not negatively affect Soviet international relations.¹⁶ Hardliners like Brzezinski went even further by contending that the security of Iran, the Persian Gulf and Pakistan was under threat from increased Soviet involvement in Afghanistan. The view in the Carter administration that the Soviets had legitimate security concerns informing its policy towards Afghanistan was losing ground to a more 'hawkish' analysis. Still, on 1 December 1978 Secretary of State Cyrus Vance remained hopeful 'that a constructive US-Afghan working relationship could still emerge'.¹⁷

However, 1979 would prove a turbulent year for US foreign policy in the region casting Afghanistan in a new strategic light. In January, following over a year of popular unrest, the Shah of Iran fled into exile leaving the reactionary anti-American Ayatollah Khomeini to assume the leadership of the state. The Shah had been a key ally of the United States, dating back to his installation following the US-British orchestrated ouster of Iranian Prime Minister Mohammed Mossadeq in 1953. The 'loss' of Iran was a significant factor in provoking US engagement in a new 'great game' on the Afghan playing field.¹⁸ Robert Gates, at the time a NSC analyst, characterized Washington's perspective as follows: 'In the global competition, the US loss of Iran was in itself an important strategic gain for the USSR.'¹⁹ Brzezinski framed it even more dramatically stating that the loss of Iran 'would be the most massive American defeat since the beginning of the Cold War, overshadowing in its *real consequences* the setback in Vietnam'²⁰ (emphasis in original). Furthermore, instability in Iran could precipitate a Soviet intervention, summoning up ghosts of the earlier Cold War standoff in 1946. This 'loss' and its strategic implications profoundly shaped US reaction to the invasion of Afghanistan later in the year.

As the Carter administration dealt with the fallout from events in Iran, its relations with Afghanistan were strained by the murder of Ambassador Dubs in Kabul. Dubs was kidnapped by anti-government rebels on 14 February 1979 seeking the release of an imprisoned associate. In the subsequent negotiations, the Afghan authorities excluded US embassy staff while the Soviet embassy's chief security advisor assumed an advisory role. During the ensuing gun battle between the kidnappers and the Afghan security forces, Dubs was shot dead. The United States immediately blamed the Soviet as well as the Afghan authorities for his death though both protested their innocence. Afghan Foreign Minister Amin insisted that 'the actions of the Afghan authorities were completely aimed at releasing the ambassador unharmed, and were inspired by friendly relations between the two countries'.[21] Nevertheless, the Carter administration suspected a Soviet conspiracy surrounding the ambassador's death. *Time* magazine judged events more dispassionately stating, 'the perverse tragedy of Spike Dubs was that guerrillas fighting a pro-Soviet regime had picked an American to show the world their rebellion'.[22] Instead, the administration ignored this manifestation of the rebels' attitude towards any outsiders, not just Soviet ones. Rumours persisted in the United States that the kidnappers were Soviet or Afghan government operatives and the attack was orchestrated to discourage US aid to the insurgents.[23] Within days the White House drastically cut back development aid and planned military assistance to Afghanistan.[24] In May, the Senate passed a resolution halting any new ambassadorial appointment to Afghanistan until its political leaders apologized for Dubs's death and assured the safety of US officials in the country.[25] The Kabul embassy would remain open with a skeleton staff but no ambassador for the duration of the Afghan conflict. The killing of Ambassador Dubs precipitated a rapid deterioration in US-Afghan relations which coincided with Carter's decision during the summer of 1979 to support the Afghan resistance.

By March 1979, the United States had not yet aided the insurgency, contrary to Soviet beliefs, but CIA proposals to do so were under consideration. At a Special Co-ordination Committee meeting on 30 March 1979, officials discussed the possibility of 'sucking the Soviets into a Vietnamese like quagmire' by assisting the Afghan rebels.[26] US National Intelligence Officer Arnold Horelick advocated covert action to inflame Muslim public opinion against the Soviets.[27] While propaganda designed to incite discontent between Muslims and the Soviet Union was a persistent theme of American propaganda during the Reagan era, its genesis under Carter is evident. The President signed a 'finding' on 3 July 1979, which authorized, amongst other actions, covert propaganda and psychological operations against the Taraki regime.[28] Soon after, President Carter ordered the administration's analysis of the situation in Afghanistan to be publicized marking the beginning of the administration's overt public diplomacy strategy around the Afghan conflict.[29] Although committed to making political capital out of Soviet interference in the state, the administration had little actual knowledge of the domestic complexities at play or whether the Soviets were masterminding events.[30] Nonetheless, the NSC concluded, 'whatever, the Soviets role in this, they should be made to look as if they had a hand in the operation,' concluding that Amin was 'the Stalin of the drama and the Soviets should have him hung prominently around their necks'. The administration would not let its superficial understanding of the Afghan situation stymie an opportunity to castigate the Soviets publicly, regardless of the ramifications. This would be a recurring feature of US propaganda on the Afghan conflict.

Within a few days of the invasion Carter signed a new 'finding' which authorized the shipment of arms to the Afghan insurgency to 'harass' the Soviets.[31] The President was startled by the geopolitical implications of the invasion but recognized immediately that the Soviet Union 'had made a tragic miscalculation' which he intended to capitalize on.[32] Carter met with congressional leaders and the media to ensure 'the American people understood the strategic ramifications of the Soviet invasion'. Washington gave little consideration to Soviet security concerns or Afghan agency in events. Acknowledging such nuance did not serve American interests though it may have facilitated an earlier resolution to the conflict, which certainly would have served Afghan interests. Newspapers rushed to promote Washington's interpretation of the invasion and its alleged roots in a centuries-old Russian desire to access the warm water ports of the India Ocean via South Asia – a region Moscow allegedly considered within 'its proper sphere of influence'.[33] The *Washington Post* framed Soviet actions as a 'shrewd move on the world geopolitical chess board' that would provide it with a 'staging area for direct leverage deep inside Central Asia'.[34]

In the light of Moscow's actions, Carter now accepted his National Security Advisor's analysis of Soviet intentions observing, 'my opinion of the Russians has changed most drastically in the last week'.[35] Brzezinski still worried that Carter would see the Afghan intervention as an isolated incident rather than part of a greater Soviet strategy. He continued to press upon the President the wider strategic implications, warning that the United States now faced 'a regional crisis' involving Iran, Afghanistan and Pakistan.[36] Emphasizing the propaganda potential, Brzezinski stated that 'world public opinion will be outraged at the Soviet intervention. Certainly, Moslem countries will be concerned, and we might be in a position to exploit this'.[37] He alleged Soviet expansionism claiming that Afghanistan was 'the *seventh* state since 1975 in which communist parties have come to power with Soviet guns and tanks, with Soviet military power and assistance' (emphasis in original).[38] Brzezinski's characterization of events was reflected in Carter's address to the nation on 4 January 1980, which stated 'we must recognize the strategic importance of Afghanistan to stability and peace. A Soviet-occupied Afghanistan threatens both Iran and Pakistan and is a steppingstone to possible control over much of the world's oil supplies'.[39]

Brzezinski believed that ensuring 'a Soviet Vietnam' required a proactive policy. The *mujahedeen* needed military and financial assistance, and Pakistan and China had to be encouraged to provide it.[40] Achieving these objectives hinged on portraying the Soviets as aggressive and expansionist – a representation the Soviets did not let go unchallenged.

The Soviets hit back at the US condemnation of the invasion. They argued that Washington was seeking to sabotage détente and, due to the loss of Iran, destabilize Afghanistan. Moscow accused Washington of trying to gain control of the region's oil resources and overthrow the revolutions in both Iran and Afghanistan.[41] This fed world opinion already sceptical of US motives and deeply concerned about any escalation in tensions between the superpowers.[42]

To counter this, the Carter administration needed to recast the narrative around the Afghan crisis arguing that it was not a civil war but an attack on Afghans (and by extension on all Muslims) by the Soviet Union. Soviet motivations were not rooted in security concerns but part of a geostrategic Cold War master plan. And US interest in the state's 'freedom' following decades of indifference was genuine. However, along with international opinion Carter also had to convince domestic critics.

Domestic influences on Carter's Afghan policy

President Carter's opponents long considered foreign policy one of his major vulnerabilities, ripe for exploitation during the upcoming election. The invasion of Afghanistan provided a welcome boon to their propaganda efforts. Republican activists ran election campaign television advertisements asking, 'do you think the Soviets would have invaded Afghanistan if Ronald Reagan had been president?' showing Soviet tanks rolling through the state. However, the administration was well aware of the public perception of incoherence and division in its foreign policy decision-making and was determined to challenge it.[43] Afghanistan offered an opportunity to affect a tougher stance without fearing the consequences, unlike Iran where the United States still hoped to re-establish relations and so had to tread more softly.

Carter faced a formidable foe in the resurgent conservative movement that had gathered momentum during the 1970s culminating in a swing to the right in the national mood by the dying days of the decade.[44] Traditional Republican conservatism was refreshed by a more radical New Right movement and, in the foreign policy arena, by disaffected conservative Democrats calling themselves neo-conservatives. Voluntary groups with conservative links and anti-communist agendas sprung up to advocate the Afghan insurgents' cause. This diverse movement gathered together a wide-ranging agenda, reflecting conservative thought on domestic social and economic issues, but on foreign policy all were staunchly anti-communist and, for them, Afghanistan would become a *cause celebre*. The neo-conservatives would prove particularly damaging for Carter as their disaffection reflected internal Democratic Party disarray on foreign policy.

In the early 1970s, an alliance of disillusioned conservative Democrats, led by Henry 'Scoop' Jackson, formed the Coalition for a Democratic Majority (CDM) to 'win back' the Democratic Party from its left-wing. The CDM also had a foreign policy agenda. It believed that US military muscle and resolve were weakened by Vietnam and sought to reassert US power and prestige in the international arena. Members developed a hyperbolic analysis of Soviet military capability and its accompanying doctrine. The CDM established the bipartisan Committee on the Present Danger (CPD) as a foreign policy interest group to widen its political base and agitate for policy change.

The CPD was home to many of the early neo-conservatives following its formation in March 1976 by Paul Nitze, Eugene Rostow and James Schlesinger amongst others.[45] Anti-détente and anti-SALT (Strategic Arms Limitations Talks), the organization was committed to alerting the public to the real nature of the Soviet Union, which it considered more dangerous than Nazi Germany.

Nitze provided the intellectual framework for the group's thinking and argued that the Soviet Union possessed a 'grand strategy' which the United States lacked.[46] This theory posited that the Soviets awaited, in both war and peacetime, an international 'correlation of forces' to align which, once in place, would offer the optimum conditions to export communism. To implement this strategy the Soviets used all resources at their disposal – military, economic, political or psychological. Nitze contended that Moscow had continually undermined détente and looked to further its strategic aims, one of which – controlling access to the Persian Gulf – was significantly advanced by the invasion of Afghanistan. To counter this, Washington needed to adopt a long-term strategic view of foreign and defence policy. The Soviets had built up their military might and expanded (again Nitze offered Afghanistan as evidence of this) throughout the 1970s. The United States needed to redress this but not just militarily. According to Nitze, it was just as important that America counteracted the Soviets' 'powerful and effective propaganda line' and gained control of public opinion.[47]

Nitze's arguments echoed the findings of the 'Team B' analysis of the National Intelligence Estimates in 1976 of which Nitze was a part, along with other CPD members.[48] Challenging the CIA's ('Team A') assessment of Soviet military capability and intentions, 'Team B' argued that a 'window of vulnerability' existed in US defence through which the Soviets could launch a first strike. The necessary response was a massive arms build-up by the United States. The findings of 'Team B' were leaked in December 1976, following Carter's election victory in the hope of influencing the new administration. The newly formed CPD quickly sought to publicize its analysis to a wide audience, holding its first press conference just days after Carter's election. However, Carter selected mostly 'doves' for national security positions in his administration, side-lining Nitze.

Events in Afghanistan would help promote the CPD's national security framework much as Korea did for NSC 68.[49] Initially, the CPD approved of Carter's reaction to the Soviet invasion of Afghanistan. His confrontational posture and acceptance of the need to check Soviet power closely mirrored the CPD's perspective. As his re-election campaign loomed and given his new tougher stance on the Soviets, Carter hoped to establish common ground with neo-conservatives. A meeting was arranged to exchange ideas on 31 January 1980. However, far from drawing the neo-conservatives closer, this meeting pushed them further away and into the arms of the future Reagan administration.[50] Fifty members of the CPD would go on to take up positions in the Reagan administration.[51] The CPD worldview would have a significant impact on US support for the Afghan *mujahedeen*. However, the neo-conservatives, while influential within elite circles, did not have the far-reaching impact of other New Right organizations like the conservative think tank, the Heritage Foundation. Heritage circulated its ideas around Congress and the media, actively seeking to shape the national debate on many issues including Afghanistan. It was scathing of Carter's foreign policies.

The co-founder of the Heritage Foundation, Paul Weyrich, was one of the chief architects of the New Right movement. Funded by Joseph Coors and Richard Mellon Scaife, Weyrich established an organization that described and promulgated an intellectual framework for conservative ideology.[52] Ed Feulner, Heritage co-founder, outlined the foundation's combative agenda; thus, 'we conduct warfare in the battle of ideas'.[53]

The Heritage Foundation critique of Carter's defence and foreign policy stemmed from the earliest days of the administration. Providing the media with analysis and commentary 365 days a year, the Heritage Foundation advocated powerfully and publicly for its policy perspectives. In the case of foreign affairs, these were anti-détente and anti-communist. It offered free delivery of its analysis/opinion pieces to journalists and members of Congress; its aggressive marketing served to smooth over its questionable scholarly credentials.[54] The think tank issued short reports or 'backgrounders' agitating against SALT II and characterizing Carter's policies as a form of appeasement. Afghanistan would provide Heritage with a locus for its propaganda.

Like Nitze, Heritage warned of Soviet first strike capability. It asserted that the Soviet 'worldview' would interpret defence cuts by Carter as a 'lack of resolve'.[55] It insisted that Moscow sought nuclear superiority – a view Senator Daniel Patrick Moynihan observed had 'gone from heresy to respectability, if not orthodoxy'.[56] According to the foundation, the United States was 'strategically vulnerable' and SALT was reinforcing this.[57] Heritage claimed Carter's decision to cut military aid to Ethiopia for human rights abuses had pushed it into the Soviet sphere of influence. This undermined the United States in the strategically valuable Horn of Africa and allowed the USSR access to the Indian Ocean and, potentially, control of the Red Sea and the West's oil supply.[58] US inaction on Iran and the Horn of Africa compounded this and unsettled America's allies.[59] The PDPA coup in Afghanistan was evidence that Soviet influence had spread 'at an alarming rate' and could infiltrate revolutionary Iran next.[60] This would result in the loss of vital CIA listening posts, making monitoring SALT II compliance difficult. The fact that the United States lost influence in Iran without any communist interference did not feature in Heritage's analysis. Afghanistan would provide ample justification for its narrative on world affairs.

According to Heritage, 'the geopolitical key to unravelling the existing order in South Asia [was] Afghanistan'.[61] Alongside Soviet gains in South Yemen and Ethiopia, a pro-Soviet Afghanistan would complete 'a giant pincer movement designed to encircle Gulf oil reserves'. This would allow the Soviets to sever the 'petroleum jugular vein of the West'.[62] Entrenched in Kabul, the USSR could then incite separatism in Iran and Pakistan. Once the region was Balkanized, the breakaway states would turn to Moscow for protection extending basing and port facilities around the Indian Ocean in return.[63] The 'correlation of forces' would then be in the Soviets' favour, creating a 'domino effect' where the rest of the Gulf States would fall in line with the USSR. But it was a 'domino that could fall either way'.[64] There was an opportunity to entrap the Soviets in Afghanistan and slow this process.[65] Heritage recommended Carter imitate 'Soviet policy in Southeast Asia' (Vietnam) and arm the Afghan insurgents to create an 'Afghan tarbaby'.[66] While Afghanistan was a stepping stone into the 'Northern tier' for the USSR, it could also function as a stepping stone for Islamic fundamentalism back into the Soviet Muslim states of Central Asia, fomenting unrest there with US assistance.[67] This notion of using Islamic fundamentalism as a weapon against the Soviets was already under consideration by Brzezinski. However, unlike Brzezinski's contention of compatibility between the West and Islam, Heritage was more wary. According to its analysis, Arabs despised the West, dating back to the crusades, so much so that they embraced its enemy – the USSR. As a result, Muslims could not be trusted to check Soviet expansion.[68] Instead, the West had to project its military power into the region to counter it.[69]

Heritage criticized Carter's sanctions over the invasion as 'limited in scope, symbolic in nature'. Unchecked, the Afghans could well become the 'Cubans of Asia' fostering unrest throughout the region.[70] While there had been comparisons between the Afghan and Vietnamese insurgency, Heritage saw a vital difference – North Vietnam was aided by China and the Soviet Union while Afghan rebels were receiving little outside assistance. The rebels needed military aid to 'complicate Soviet efforts to suppress the insurgency' and the United States should provide it.[71]

The Heritage Foundation belittled Carter's overtures to Pakistan.[72] The United States had cut off aid to Pakistan a year earlier, over its nuclear weapons' programme and, according to Heritage, Carter's new offer followed inadequate consultation with Pakistan's military dictator, Muhammad Zia ul Haq. The think tank described Brzezinski's visit to Pakistan in February 1980 to discuss a US aid package as a 'three-ring media circus'.[73] It argued that Pakistan's rejection of this package made the United States appear unreliable and such 'unpredictability' eroded the confidence of US allies worldwide. Heritage believed propaganda was vital to exploiting Soviet economic and psychological vulnerabilities. The foundation denounced the USICA's (United States International Communication Agency) policy to 'stop short of trying to stir up unrest inside the Soviet Union' with its output on the Afghan invasion.[74] Instead, the United States should target anti-Soviet propaganda at 'Soviet minorities, such as Jews and Moslems, dissident intellectuals and frustrated, dissatisfied workers' along with Islamic and Third World states. International organizations and forums such as the UN should be utilized to propagate 'pro-American values' of freedom and capitalism. While Carter came in for heavy criticism, Heritage approved of Congress' plans (now with a Republican-majority Senate) to appropriate an extra $2.1 million for the USICA for increased broadcasts to Islamic nations.[75]

The Heritage Foundation was not the only conservative think tank that sought to exert influence on US Congress, government and public opinion. In what the *Washington Post* described as a 'recent drift to the right in the country's intellectual climate', the American Enterprise Institute, the Hoover Institute and the Center for Strategic and International Studies (CSIS) at Georgetown University all grew rapidly during the late 1970s. This offered a new face of conservatism fronted by East Coast professionals and intellectuals – a 'New Right counterestablishment'.[76] This counter-establishment would become integrated into the establishment upon the election of Ronald Reagan with many members of conservative think tanks appointed as foreign policy and defence advisors. However, 'Heritage was President Reagan's favorite think tank', which elevates the significance of its policy prescriptions on the Afghan conflict.[77] The think tank provided Reagan with a 1,100-page document 'Mandate for Leadership' which, amongst other things, helped Reagan realize 'his vision of a world free of communism'. However, domestic influences on Carter's Afghan policy, and subsequently Reagan, extended beyond elite foreign policy hawks in the CPD and the pugilistic Heritage Foundation.

Soviet action in Afghanistan prompted the formation of a myriad of private advocacy organizations focused on generating publicity and funds for the Afghan resistance.[78]

These ranged from church groups holding cake sales to buy boots for 'freedom fighters' to bigger organizations with political connections hosting celebrity dinner parties in the capital. While many NGOs, American and international, provided much-needed aid to Afghan refugees, this book concentrates on a specific few who focused on generating public support for the *mujahedeen* and lobbied the executive and Congress to increase aid via the media and public events.[79] These groups played an important role in keeping the Afghan conflict in the limelight, campaigning for the rebels and shaping the public debate. As well as fundraising, they published newsletters, posted advertisements in major newspapers, wrote articles and lobbied Congress on legislation. Furthermore, they supplied information to journalists, brought *mujahedeen* to the United States and hosted lectures and conferences on Afghanistan. Such organizations were responsible for pressing Carter to proclaim the first week of the Moscow Olympics 'Afghanistan Relief Week' and persuading President Reagan to declare 22 March 'Afghanistan Day' in 1982.[80] They campaigned for Congress to pass the 1984 Tsongas-Ritter Resolution and agitated for the supply of Stinger missiles to the insurgency. They sought to influence US foreign policy, at times complementing administration efforts, at other times frustrating them. Many of these groups were linked to a network of other Afghan PVOs and neo-conservative/New Right individuals or organizations. Some had links to congressional representatives and government officials. Although focused ostensibly on the Afghan conflict and the need for increased military aid to the insurgency, these organizations' politics and propaganda demonstrate that the conflict served to facilitate their wider anti-communist agenda.

One of the first of these NGOs was the Afghan Relief Committee (ARC) formed in 1980 by former US ambassador to Afghanistan Robert Neumann and Mary Ann Dubs, Spike Dubs's widow. ARC had close connections to the State Department. Its membership roll included many former ambassadors. Dubs had also been the editor of the *Congressional Quarterly Daily Digest* until late 1980 when she left to join the Foreign Service. Neumann served on Reagan's transition team, briefly holding the post of ambassador to Saudi Arabia.[81] Unusually, information for ARC relating to various funds and fundraising was passed via State Department telegrams to posts. Consul Staff administrated ARC bank accounts and raised funds locally.[82] Given that, it's understandable that Moscow believed the committee to be a CIA front for smuggling arms to the insurgents.[83]

ARC also had links to other conservative organizations. Neumann was associated with the conservative think tank the CSIS. From 1983, he was director of Middle East Programs at CSIS where he worked with Michael Ledeen, a leading figure in the Iran-*Contra* affair.[84] In 1980, ARC began fundraising for humanitarian aid to the Afghan refugees. Its anti-communist credentials were evident at its events where 'Free Afghanistan' T-shirts, featuring a Russian bear attacking an Afghan hound, were on sale and speakers were openly critical of the Carter administration. At one such event, fundraiser, anthropologist, Afghan expert and sometimes CIA consultant, Dr Louis Dupree advocated for military aid to the insurgency. Dupree was deported from Afghanistan in 1978 amid accusations of spying and would testify before Congress on many occasions on the Afghan conflict.[85] ARC concentrated on Washington and elite decision-makers in its efforts to influence Afghan policy. To this end, it organized cheese and wine parties, sold calendars, met with Senators, held press conferences on Capitol Hill and organized Smithsonian lectures on the conflict. Another ARC founder member, Rosanne Klass at Freedom House, also actively worked to shape public opinion on the conflict by establishing the Afghan Information Center as 'a clearinghouse for information on the conflict' for the US media.[86] At the time, Freedom House had links to neo-conservative activism.[87] Like Dupree, Klass would testify before Congress on the Afghan conflict a number of times offering a pro-*mujahedeen* analysis of the situation.

The American Friends of Afghanistan (AFA) was established by Dr Thomas Gouttierre in 1979. Gouttierre was the director of the Center for Afghan Studies, University of Nebraska at Omaha (UNO), which had longstanding connections with Afghanistan. The centre later provided controversial educational material (which encouraged *jihad* against the Soviets) to Afghanistan, largely funded by the USAID.[88] Neumann of ARC was involved with this organization along with three other former US diplomats to Afghanistan – Theodore L. Eliot Jr., John M. Steeves and Leon B. Poullada – who served on the AFA board.[89]

Another organization, the Committee for a Free Afghanistan (CFA), received its start-up funding from the Heritage Foundation and was connected to the World Anti-Communism League (WACL).[90] It was led by a former army officer, Karen McKay, who had previously worked for Accuracy in the Media – a conservative media watchdog. The Federation for American-Afghan Action (FAAA) was also linked to the Heritage Foundation and to the neo-conservative lobby group, Free the Eagle. It pressed Congress to keep a check on military aid to Afghanistan, which it suspected the CIA and/or the Pakistani Directorate of Inter-Services Intelligence (ISI) of diverting for their own ends.[91]

These advocacy organizations were a diverse bunch, activated by the Soviet invasion for sure, but serving agendas that both preceded and transcended the Afghan crisis. They were fiercely anti-communist and linked to New Right or conservative groups. All were seeking to influence, by lobbying and public critiques, US policy on Afghanistan with the aim of increasing aid to the insurgency. Some confined themselves largely to raising awareness (albeit from an anti-communist, anti-Kabul viewpoint only) and funds; others were more extreme in the actions they were prepared to undertake to promote their cause. All adeptly used publicity and propaganda to further their aims and persuade Congress and the American public of the legitimacy of the Afghan cause.

These domestic influences overwhelmingly urged an aggressive response to perceived Soviet adventurism. They shared a militant anti-communism making them particularly formidable in the arena of foreign policy where their interests merged. They lobbied Congress, Carter and later the Reagan administrations in an attempt to influence policies towards Afghanistan. They faced little challenge to their Manichean worldview within the United States, and their anti-Soviet arguments gained credibility following the Afghan invasion. Their influence would reach its zenith under the Reagan administration and help to shape foreign policy towards Afghanistan. These organizations would prove to be powerful advocates for the *mujahedeen* cause, pressuring the US government and Congress to increase aid dramatically over the course of the conflict and stymie efforts to negotiate a settlement.

However, anti-Soviet sentiments following the Afghan invasion were not solely the preserve of neo-conservative or New Right organizations, elite or otherwise. The invasion hardened Carter's attitude towards the USSR but his options for action were constrained by the American public's wariness of military intervention abroad following Vietnam. As a result, the administration channelled its resources and energy into anti-Soviet propaganda to exact a political cost from Moscow with varying success.

Carter's propaganda on Afghanistan

The administration and the USICA recognized the propaganda opportunity afforded by the Afghan conflict. However, Afghanistan was not on the agency's 'Program Design' for 1980. Therefore, nothing was prepared, nor in the pipeline, which could be readily disseminated to US embassies around the world for local placement.[92] The USICA also struggled to cope with increasing its public diplomacy output while facing personnel and budget cuts. This meant that Carter's public diplomacy strategy on Afghanistan, in as much as he had one, was *ad hoc* and harried. It focused on three main objectives. It sought to provoke anti-Soviet sentiment amongst Muslims to undermine Moscow. It endeavoured to rally international interest in Afghanistan, to unsettle the Soviets and raise the political costs of the invasion. Lastly, it hoped to champion America as the more virtuous superpower, repairing the damage wrought to its image by Vietnam and the Iranian revolution.

The administration faced a number of obstacles in promoting its narrative on Afghanistan. Internationally, many states saw the United States as much as a threat to world peace as the Soviet Union and were wary of any action that could ignite a superpower conflagration or undermine détente. There was a widespread belief that the United States was no longer the world's leading power, creating concern in Washington that countries were 'hedging their bets' in not condemning the Soviets.[93] Carter was perceived to have overreacted rhetorically for electioneering purposes, and the US response was seen as hypocritical in the light of its involvement in Vietnam.[94] Some even thought it possible that America had provoked the Soviet invasion in the first place by arming the rebels, beefing up its naval presence in the Indian Ocean and the NATO deployment of Theatre Nuclear Forces in Western Europe. In the Middle East there were suspicions that US actions were designed to secure access to oil or produce a 'Yalta-type' agreement with the Soviets to carve up the region. Most publics though were more concerned with domestic and economic issues, especially the high cost of oil, which one USICA report suggested could be linked to the Afghan conflict for propaganda purpose.[95] Events in far-flung Afghanistan were of little interest particularly after initial coverage of the invasion abated.[96] There was also a divergence between public and elite opinion. General publics showed scant support for military counter-measures like strengthening NATO. The USICA believed a 'public education effort' was necessary to counter negative perceptions of US motives and win back some semblance of moral authority over the Soviet Union. To this end, much of the US propaganda aimed to highlight Soviet wrongdoing.

Long before the December 1979 invasion, Brzezinski was convinced that the Soviets were ideologically expansionist and nursed a historic desire to access ports on the Indian Ocean.[97] According to Brzezinski this important region was inherently unstable, an 'arc of crisis' where 'political chaos could well be filled by elements hostile to our values and sympathetic to our adversaries'.[98] In Iran, this 'chaos' had undermined US interests – the *Time* cover of the issue containing the Brzezinski article depicted a large bear (symbolic of the Soviet Union) ominously hovering over the region. In Afghanistan, Brzezinski was determined that this volatility would serve US interests. In fact, he had been preparing propaganda to provoke such an opportunity. In 1977, Brzezinski had set up the inter-agency Nationalities Working Group headed by academic and spy Paul B. Henze to examine how the multi-ethnic nature of the Soviet Union might be exploited.[99] Literature on Soviet ethnic histories and cultures was smuggled into the USSR to seed disaffection.[100] By January 1979, the importance of the Soviet nationalities question was 'whetted' by the situation in Iran and the chance that the USSR could use its Islamic nationals to gain a foothold there and in Afghanistan.[101] A superpower race was on for the allegiance of these minorities. However, while the Soviet Union increased its broadcasting to the region to deliver its propaganda, the United States lacked experts with suitable linguistic skills to compete.[102] To counter this, the USICA needed to develop a network of academics and professionals with such skills and nurture a future generation of regional specialists. To this end, the State Department organized a conference of Middle East academics on 16 February 1979 to consider how the United States should mediate its public diplomacy with Muslims and assess the impact of Islamic fundamentalism on relations. The participants concluded that fundamentalism represented an outlet for political dissatisfaction rather than a religious resurgence but warned that many Arabs saw the United States as a defender of the status quo.[103] So it seemed that US foreign policy was a major obstacle to redefining America's image with this constituency but rather than change its policies, Washington instead chose to improve perceptions of the United States by denigrating the USSR.

In January 1979, as Shah Mohammed Reza Pahlavi fled Iran, Brzezinski requested the CIA to conduct a global survey of Muslim religious movements in order to gauge the influence of Islamic fundamentalism on possible crisis points in Afghanistan, Pakistan, Egypt and the Philippines.[104] While another report judged communism of little influence in the 'arc', Brzezinski was still concerned that Islamist states could tilt towards the USSR much as Libyan dictator Muammar Gaddafi did. There were real concerns that US policies on Iran had made it appear 'anti-Islamic, anti-nationalist' and 'imperialist' while, according to Brzezinski, 'the Soviets, who have been viciously oppressing Islam in their own territories for 60 years, aim to emerge from the present commotion in the Middle East with an enhanced image as protectors of Islamic nationalism'.[105] Brzezinski was determined to challenge these perceptions.

This image of American foreign policy as anti-Muslim was further reinforced by its position on Israel and Palestine, which was seen as pro-Israeli by Arab states. Brzezinski believed that the United States should counter this and appeal to Muslims by emphasizing America's moral values and commitment to social justice and by highlighting Soviet actions in Afghanistan. US diplomatic outposts needed to 'get our story across in every way possible'.[106] A Cold War propaganda battle for the hearts and minds of Muslims was underway and Washington believed the Afghan conflict had a central role to play.

As early as September 1979, Brzezinski recommended using public diplomacy to expose Soviet actions in Afghanistan.[107] Covert propaganda methods were also used. On 4 July, the day after Carter signed the initial 'finding' authorizing propaganda and psychological operations, Afghan 'students' were on the streets of New Delhi protesting outside the Afghan and Soviet embassies.[108] In September, the CIA station in New Delhi funded and organized demonstrations by the 'Islamic Association of Patriotic Afghan Students in India' outside the Soviet embassy in the city, which generated widespread coverage in India and further afield. Further demonstrations were arranged for Denmark, the United States, Iran and Germany.[109] Mostly, however, the administration orchestrated overt propaganda or public diplomacy targeting Muslim publics to 'cast the Soviets as opposing Moslem religious and nationalist expressions'.[110] Brzezinski wanted Soviet actions publicized to mobilize Muslims and allow the United States to demonstrate its 'sympathy for the Afghan freedom fighters'.[111]

Over the spring and summer of 1979, as revolution raged across Iran and the Soviets became increasingly entangled in Afghanistan, Brzezinski worked hard to raise tensions between Islam and communism while emphasizing its affinities with Christianity.[112] He argued that the 'Islamic renaissance' was 'a religious phenomenon rooted in certain basic values which are not alien to the Christian tradition'.[113] On 2 August 1979, he warned the Soviets against imposing 'alien doctrines on deeply religious and nationally conscious peoples'.[114] Brzezinski saw Afghanistan as the Soviets' Achilles heel which could, with effective propaganda, be manipulated to US advantage. Facing into an election year, Carter badly needed this foreign policy edge. This strategy intensified following the invasion. A memorandum entitled 'Response to the Soviets regarding Afghanistan: A Menu of Possible Actions' on 28 December outlined its thrust:

> The Soviet Union is atheistic by doctrine and has published enormous amounts of anti-religious and anti-Muslim literature. The US, on the other hand, firmly believes in religious freedom and enshrines it in our Constitution. Three million Muslims practice their religion freely in the US.[115]

To this end, increased propaganda aimed at the Muslim world was vital.[116] It was also vital to recast the widely held perception that Soviet moves on Afghanistan were part of a 'superpower chess game' as a USSR versus Third World/Muslim world confrontation.[117] Such machinations would be more effective if distanced from Washington so Brzezinski recommended the United States work with Islamic states 'both in a propaganda campaign and in a covert action campaign to help the rebels'.[118] A 28 December memorandum suggested Muslim and non-aligned countries should be encouraged to criticize the USSR publicly.[119] Another memorandum days later argued that the United States 'should be able to count on tactical allies in many different quarters, *particularly among the Moslem countries. We should exploit this tactical* advantage to the hilt' (emphasis in original).[120] It stated that 'the aim should be to isolate Soviets within Moslem world'.

Brzezinski's efforts were reflected in the US media. A *Washington Post* article on 27 December 1979 headlined 'Moscow versus Islam' called the Soviet invasion a 'gratuitous power grab'.[121] Brzezinski continued his propaganda offensive in an interview on 31 December on *US News & World Report*, where he contended:

> We [the United States] do not have any imperial designs on the Moslem world. We, in fact, encouraged the colonial powers to terminate their domination of the Moslem world. In contrast, the Soviet Union exercises direct physical domination over several tens of millions of Moslems. It denies them their religious rights. It has also traditional designs on the independence of Moslem countries.[122]

Department of State spokesman Hodding Carter re-iterated this narrative the next day stating, 'the true enemy of Moslem independence and of the Islamic region is not the United States or Washington'.[123] Carter's State of the Union address towards the end of the month also further contributed by stating, 'the Moslem world is especially and justifiably outraged by this aggression against an Islamic people' adding the United States believes 'that there are no irreconcilable differences between us and any Islamic nation. We respect the faith of Islam, and we are ready to cooperate with all Moslem countries'.

One of the USSR's objectives in invading Afghanistan was to quell the flames of revolutionary Islamism fearing its spread to Soviet Central Asian satellite republics. However, the Carter administration's propaganda strategy around the invasion quickly identified this as a vulnerability of the Soviets, and efforts to kindle Muslim resentment became a central theme. Whilst originally a Brzezinski initiative, this approach would prove an enduring leitmotif of US propaganda over the following decade. Although the United States made strenuous efforts to gain support from the Muslim world and undermine the Soviets' relationship with Islam, its propaganda strategy also had other targets.

To reach a greater audience the administration needed to articulate its vision of the wider strategic implications of the Soviet action. In his 1980 State of the Union address, Carter claimed that 'Soviet-occupied Afghanistan threatens both Iran and Pakistan and is a steppingstone to possible control over much of the world's oil supplies', which endangered the 'peaceful balance of the entire world'.[124] The President compared Soviet actions to Nazi aggression, adding that it needed to be stopped before it became 'a contagious disease'. He described the invasion as 'the most serious threat to the peace since the Second World War'. Brzezinski, for his part, warned Iran, where the embassy hostage crisis continued, that 'Tehran could be next' implying that the leaders of that state should realize that the United States was its true ally not the Soviet Union.[125] The administration worked to keep Afghanistan in the public eye by issuing worldwide demarches, distributing daily circulars in the UN and initiating UN debates.[126] Voice of America (VOA) and Radio Liberty increased their output to the region though hampered by their inability to broadcast in either Dari or Pashto – the two major Afghan languages. The State Department urged the UK, France and West Germany to increase their programming to Muslim and Soviet Central Asian states.[127] However, notwithstanding these efforts, interest in the conflict waned.[128]

From an early stage, the administration, and others, saw parallels between Soviet involvement in Afghanistan and the US experience in Vietnam. The United States sought to mine the 'lessons' it had learnt about the corrosive effect of negative media coverage during that conflict and applied them to increase Soviet discomfort over Afghanistan. However, there were important differences, which needed to be addressed to guarantee continued media coverage. A National Security Council memorandum for Brzezinski on 31 December 1979 outlined the disparities between the two conflicts:

> Vietnam was a 'media event' and this had a major impact on US domestic and international opinion, turning much of it against the war and US involvement. This will not be the case in Afghanistan. The Soviets will restrict access to the war by the press, and there will be few film clips of Soviet soldiers setting fire to Afghan huts or mopping up Moslem villages being flashed across TV screens into Soviet living rooms – or for that matter across TV screens anywhere. This will minimize Soviet domestic and international criticism, after the initial furor dies down.[129]

It was certainly true that the Afghan government acted to keep foreign reporters out of Afghanistan at this time and that, in any case, Afghanistan was too remote and dangerous for most Western journalists. While the newspapers reported the diplomatic standoff, there was little television footage of the actual conditions within Afghanistan. However, in late March 1980 *CBS* reporter Dan Rather and a film crew travelled to the Afghanistan-Pakistan border crossing into Afghanistan disguised in traditional attire. Rather was disparaged for his melodramatic tone but his report that the *mujahedeen* 'desperately' needed weaponry had a portentous impact. Representative Charles Wilson (D-Tx), who would be instrumental in appropriating congressional funds for the *mujahedeen* during the 1980s, was particularly affected by the programme which sparked his interest in the Afghan rebels' cause.[130] Still, there was little incentive for media outlets to send reporters and camera crews, at great expense and danger, to a conflict of marginal interest to most of the US public. In order to guarantee coverage of the conflict the administration would have to generate its own publicity, and the Olympic Games due to take place in Moscow that year was an obvious candidate for such an initiative. The threat to boycott the Olympics would keep Afghanistan in the public consciousness that spring and summer. It certainly irritated the Soviets but did not prove a triumph for US public diplomacy as it ratcheted up tensions between the United States, its Olympic athletes and its allies.

During his 1980 State of the Union address, Carter announced to the nation that he had 'notified the Olympic Committee that with Soviet invading forces in Afghanistan, neither the American people nor I will support sending an Olympic team to Moscow'. According to the President, the Soviets viewed the Moscow games as 'a triumph for communism'.[131] He was determined that the United States would not participate in this display of Soviet power and prestige. The decision to withdraw from the Olympics though supported by the US media and public was resisted by US athletes and the US Olympic Committee (USOC), which described the proposal 'inappropriate and gauche'.[132] The State Department, that proposed the action, recognized that it would exact a heavy toll from the athletes while unlikely to affect Soviet policies.[133]

Nonetheless, US Olympic athletics' hopes were to become a pawn in a Cold War propaganda battle.

The President understood the boycott as a 'serious step', which initially he was only willing to undertake in concert with other states. He was wary of sports fans believing that 'Jimmy Carter killed the Olympics' – especially in an election year.[134] As the proposal gathered momentum within the administration during early January 1980, the idea of participating in the games while Soviet troops were still in Afghanistan became 'unconscionable'.[135] On 20 January 1980, the United States announced it would not participate unless there was a Soviet withdrawal within a month 'even if [the United States] had to stand alone among nations'. And, for a while, it looked like this may very well be the case as Olympic committees around the world balked at the US stance and even the USOC had to be strong-armed into compliance.

The proposed boycott quickly ran into trouble as the United States and various European national Olympic committees railed against entangling sport with politics.[136] National Olympic committees are private organizations so ultimately it was their decision whether to participate or not – a factor not given due consideration by the administration. Carter's authority and credibility were challenged by the possibility that the USOC would participate in Moscow.[137] However, Congress backed the President's proposal putting irresistible pressure on the organization. This pressure was compounded when the USICA publicized a Soviet pamphlet produced for the Olympics entitled 'Little Handbook for Party Activists', which suggested that awarding the games to Moscow was an endorsement of Soviet foreign policy and a recognition of its contribution to world peace.[138] If the Soviets saw the games as a political reward, this justified the United States using them to exact a political punishment. The USOC eventually endorsed the boycott on 14 April 1980 following threats by the administration to cut its federal grants and to impose taxes on the organization's other revenue streams.[139] Carter had also threatened to confiscate the passports of any athletes who attempted to travel to Moscow.

Some US allies were unwilling or unable to use such coercive tactics on their Olympic committees. While the Conservative government of Margaret Thatcher supported the boycott, the British Olympic Committee refused to bow to its demands and was backed by British public opinion.[140] Only 10 per cent of the French public approved of the boycott and Carter had to personally apply considerable pressure on West Germany to stay away.[141] By April 1980, 66 per cent of Australians opposed the boycott rising from 48 per cent in February.[142] These attitudes were partly inspired by a cynicism amongst many Europeans about Carter's motives.[143] There were fears that the United States had 'rhetorically over-reacted' and was jeopardizing SALT negotiations and ultimately détente.[144] US failure to inform or consult on the boycott before announcing it angered allies.[145] The US refusal to back an African-led boycott of the games four years previously meant particular efforts were needed to bring this constituency onside. And Washington seriously misjudged what was required to ensure this.

In what *Time* magazine described as 'the most bizarre diplomatic mission in recent US history', Carter sent the world champion boxer Muhammad Ali to Africa as his special representative to persuade the leaders of Tanzania, Nigeria, Liberia, Senegal and Kenya to support the boycott. Ali's ignorance of US and Soviet foreign policy in the region and the US refusal to back the African boycott rankled with Africans. Ali was left flustered and angry stating, 'If I'd known what I know now, I maybe wouldn't be here'.[146] Some felt sending a sports star instead of a diplomat to Africa was racist and demeaning with one Tanzanian official asking 'would you send Chris Evert [a tennis player] to negotiate with London?'[147] Ali accused Carter of sending him to Africa to 'take a whipping' while an anonymous State Department official disclosed that the boxer's utterances were giving them 'a little heartburn'.[148] All in all, the mission was a disaster failing to bring Nigeria, Senegal and Tanzania onside.

Attempts to organize alternative games also fell by the wayside – the USOC-organized meeting of international Olympic committees had only twelve states' attendees as many states rejected any further political meddling in the world of sports.[149] The administration lobbied hard to bring enough states onboard to sabotage the Olympic spectacle in Moscow that summer and salvage American credibility. In the end, France and many other Western European states' committees voted to go to Moscow. Only states closely allied to the United States and Muslim nations sympathetic to the Afghan's plight joined the boycott. Brzezinski admitted that the drive to boycott the games achieved 'only partial success'. Although Lloyd Cutler said the administration was aware that it would have to 'fight the entire world sports lobby', Carter admitted in his memoirs that he 'had no idea at the time how difficult it would be for me to implement it or to convince other nations to join us'. However, the administration's lack of diplomatic sensitivity in their promotion of the boycott was at least partially to blame. With US public and congressional opinion backing the decision some backroom diplomacy could have ensured the USOC agreed to the inevitable more graciously. Furthermore, it was obvious that the boycott was devised to embarrass the Soviets and spoil their Olympic spectacle rather than achieve any concrete goals in relation to Afghanistan. When asked at a press conference about whether the boycott would encourage the Soviets to withdraw from Afghanistan, Lloyd Cutler, who was Carter's right-hand man on the Olympics issue, stated laconically 'we don't'.[150] As a result, athletes who had dedicated their lives to training for such events felt aggrieved at being forced to sacrifice their efforts purely for propaganda purposes. Many US allies felt the same and this increased cynicism about the whole exercise. The boycott undoubtedly undermined Soviet hopes for an international showcase of their power and prestige but it proved a double-edged sword for Carter. The administration underestimated the practicalities of such a move and, as a result, was constantly embattled in defence of its proposal. It had to strong-arm other nations and its own athletes into acquiescence eroding the strong, multi-national symbolic gesture it originally envisioned.

Conclusion

The Carter administration had been ambivalent to the Soviet Union's long-standing involvement in Afghan affairs even after the Saur revolution, but the 'loss' of Iran precipitated a radical change in tack in US foreign policy in the region and the Carter administration, particularly Brzezinski, now viewed Afghanistan in a new strategic light. This new attitude was evident in the decision to aid the Afghan insurgency in the months prior to the invasion. Washington watched increasing Soviet entanglement in Kabul's affairs determined to make political capital from it. Moscow was primarily driven by security concerns and Washington's indifference to Soviet involvement in Afghanistan over the preceding decades demonstrated its acknowledgement that it fell within the USSR's 'sphere of influence'. However, for Carter, the invasion demanded a firm response.

This was driven partly by domestic factors. Facing an election, Carter's reaction was necessary to bolster his shaky foreign policy credentials. The vocal New Right and neo-conservative former Democrats were gaining traction publicly and provided a constant and damaging critique of Carter's foreign and defence policies. Afghanistan would provide both justification and focus for their conceptualization of the struggle against communism. Newly founded pro-*mujahedeen* PVOs added pressure with intimate, sympathetic portrayals of 'god-fearing' warriors struggling to free their country – something with which many Americans could empathize. However, many of these groups had ideological agendas and links to other hard-line anti-communist causes and organizations.

Carter's belligerent rhetoric and the pseudo-military posturing of his doctrine sought to disguise the fact that the United States was not going to engage militarily over the invasion. The still weeping wounds of Vietnam constrained Carter's options. Instead, American retaliation was routed through propaganda efforts as well as covert military aid. The lessons of Vietnam, particularly the power of negative media coverage to undermine a state's policies, infused Washington's reaction. This provided a template that served throughout the Reagan engagement with the conflict, albeit writ large. However, the government's propaganda apparatus was largely unprepared for such a dramatic turn of events, obvious in the ill-prepared, inept Olympic boycott. Other schemes such as that to set Muslims in Central Asia and elsewhere against communism had been under consideration by Brzezinski and others for a number of years. The outcome envisioned was far-reaching and Machiavellian. As well as inciting unrest and discontent amongst Muslims, these policies sought to improve perceptions of America in Third World and Islamic states and to present US foreign policy as supportive of self-determination. This propaganda aimed at meddling with the worldview of Muslims for US geopolitical ends would prove particularly insidious and destructive over time. Its ability to damage the Soviet Union, however, proved too tempting to resist, demonstrating clearly that Cold War imperatives and their domestic political drivers underwrote US actions not Afghan 'freedom'.

The Reagan administration would embrace and enhance the hawkish policies of the dying days of the Carter administration. It would co-ordinate, strengthen and institutionalize propaganda strategies to form a coherent and fundamental pillar of their 'rollback' policy centred on Afghanistan.

2

The Reagan administration: Foreign policy influences and the importance of propaganda

In November 1980, Ronald Reagan roundly defeated Jimmy Carter in the race for the US presidency. Reagan's manifesto promised to prioritize national security, reflecting the concerns of neo-conservative and New Right supporters about Soviet 'imperialism'.[1] In his first State of the Union address, Reagan warned the nation that 'since 1970 the Soviet Union has invested $300 billion more in its military forces' than the United States. To allow this to continue was 'a threat to national security'. Reagan believed that American military might was the only true guarantor of peace, views that were shaped by his experience of the Second World War.[2] Armed with a significant electoral mandate, though struggling against a straitened economy, Reagan was determined to bolster US military defence and 'roll back' perceived Soviet political gains, particularly in the Third World. As a result, in the administration's program for economic recovery, Defense was the only department not to face sweeping cuts. As well as projecting American military might, the administration sought to confront the Soviet Union ideologically, challenging it for world leadership, seeking to regain American prestige and credibility lost following the Vietnam War.

The administration believed effective propaganda vital to the successful implementation of these policies. To this end, it restructured and strengthened the US public diplomacy infrastructure. USIA funding was substantially increased and the agency was given a seat at the cabinet table. The administration initiated programmes such as Project Truth and Project Democracy to rebut Soviet propaganda and challenge the USSR. The Afghan conflict was an intrinsic element of these programmes and initiatives. It afforded the United States an opportunity to regain some moral authority on the world stage, to get on the right side of history by backing 'freedom fighters' seeking 'self-determination'. The support generated by these initiatives strengthened the *mujahedeen* but discouraged reconciliation between Afghan's warring parties. However, the administration showed little regard for the impact such a propaganda offensive would have on the nascent Afghan peace process.[3] Rather, the continuation of the conflict served US interests.

The Reagan administration's bid to strengthen public diplomacy in support of its foreign policy had its ideological origins in key administration officials not least Reagan himself. An examination of the views of Reagan, his New Right and neo-conservative supporters and those involved in developing the administration's Afghan propaganda initiatives reveals a deep-seated conviction in the importance of shaping public perspectives – a 'lesson' distilled from Vietnam. Research on the early years of the first Reagan administration (1981–1983), when key NSDDs on public diplomacy and the Afghan conflict were formulated, shows that the invasion of Afghanistan provided a seemingly irresistible opportunity to damage the Soviet Union politically with propaganda.

Two specific examples of administration propaganda used to justify two particularly contentious policies to Congress, international allies and their publics demonstrate this. In both cases, Congress was the ultimate target as it held the power to approve appropriations or not. In both cases, the Afghan conflict provided the bulk of the content for these initiatives. The first was the administration efforts to rehabilitate Pakistan's reputation to facilitate the transfer of substantial military aid. Such a bilateral security arrangement with Pakistan would steady the US strategic footing in the South West Asia region shaken by the 'loss' of Iran and the invasion of Afghanistan. However, Pakistan's nuclear ambitions along with its abysmal human rights record and ongoing military dictatorship troubled many members of Congress and the public. Reagan administration officials needed to justify any assistance to Pakistan. These efforts were aimed primarily at persuading Congress to revoke the 1976 Symington Amendment.[4] This would allow the authorization of the military aid package and ensure its continuation thereafter.

The second propaganda initiative involved efforts by the administration to justify US chemical weapon re-armament to Congress, international allies and their publics. Replenishing the stocks of such weapons risked triggering international opprobrium and faced congressional disapproval. The propaganda programme deployed hinged on accusations that the Red Army had deployed 'yellow rain' (an alleged chemical agent) in Southeast Asia and Afghanistan. This initiative was greatly assisted by individuals involved in pro-*mujahedeen* PVOs who gathered what they alleged was evidence of the crimes and testified before Congress on the issue. An investigation into the background of these pro-*mujahedeen* supporters reveals links to some congressional members and the administration. For these individuals the 'yellow rain' controversy provided an opportunity to push for American support for the Afghan rebels to enable continued hostilities against the Kabul government and the Soviet army. This campaign to justify increased defence expenditure, in particular on Chemical and Biological Weapons (CBWs), ran parallel with Washington's efforts to rehabilitate Pakistan's image and both relied heavily on the Soviet occupation of Afghanistan for material. This focus on fortifying US defences reflected President Reagan's ideology of peace through strength, and his faith in propaganda was shaped by his personal journey from actor to politician.

The Reagan worldview: Militarism and the role of propaganda

Although a Democrat in his early days, Reagan's political views grew increasingly conservative during the 1950s, culminating in the termination of his Democratic Party affiliation in 1962. Reagan was ardently anti-communist and imbued with a belief that

America had an exceptional role to play in world affairs defending freedom as 'the last best hope of man on earth'. Coupled with these beliefs, Reagan intuitively understood the power of effective communications aided by his careers as a radio presenter and a successful Hollywood actor. During the war, Reagan had even completed his military service with the Public Relations section of the Army Air Force before moving on to its first Motion Picture Unit.

Reagan's eloquent 'A Time for Choosing' speech endorsing Barry Goldwater for president in 1964 illuminated the future president's mastery of rhetoric and shone a national spotlight on this rising star of the right. Although Reagan's endorsement did little to help Goldwater's cause, it did inspire some wealthy conservatives to back the charismatic former screen actor in his successful bid for the governorship of California two years later.[5] Following Goldwater's disastrous election campaign, Reagan assumed the mantle of the conservative Republican leadership and, sixteen years later, the party's presidential nomination. In November 1980, Reagan won the US presidential election and, along with that, a Republican majority in the Senate and gains in the House of Representatives.

Reagan's presidential bid had unified the energetic and diverse New Right movement and gained the backing of the neo-conservative elite whom Carter had failed to engage.[6] Sharing Reagan's visceral distrust of Soviet intentions, anti-communist hardliners argued for increased defence spending and helped to develop the Reagan Doctrine to counter perceived Soviet advances. They demanded persuasive public diplomacy to support such militarism and champion American ideals. These influential and persuasive advocates would precipitate a sea change in the application of propaganda in US foreign policy.

Reagan was a member of the CPD and had courted its membership. In turn, its members both influenced and endorsed his policies on national security and foreign affairs.[7] They were also proficient at promoting their worldview in the public sphere. Jeane J. Kirkpatrick's November 1979 article in *Commentary* magazine titled 'Dictatorships and Double Standards' had greatly impressed Reagan, and the author served as a foreign policy advisor on his election campaign. Kirkpatrick's thesis helped provide an intellectual, philosophical and political justification for the Reagan administration's support for right-wing autocracies and counterrevolutionary forces. In the piece, Kirkpatrick argued that Carter's human rights-based foreign policies had undermined US allies in right-wing autocracies though, she contended, these dictatorships were 'more compatible with U.S. interests'. Kirkpatrick became a strident, vocal supporter of the Afghan *mujahedeen* who as anti-communists were compatible with her doctrine.

Kirkpatrick was not the only neo-conservative striving to promote her militaristic ideas in the new administration. Others gaining administration posts included Richard Perle and Harvard academic and Team B leader Richard Pipes. Richard V. Allen assumed the position of Reagan's National Security Advisor and Edwin Feulner, president of the Heritage Foundation, served as chair of the President's Advisory Commission on Public Diplomacy. These anti-communist hardliners had consistently peddled their views to the public through the media prior to Reagan's election and continued to use public diplomacy to shore up support for foreign policies subsequently.[8]

Reagan also saw persuasive public diplomacy as crucial to effective foreign policy, warning that the United States needed to 'stop losing the propaganda war'.[9] The President's views reflected an enduring belief amongst administration officials like Carnes Lord, Richard Pipes and Kenneth Adelman that the United States had lost its way in Vietnam due to adverse public opinion, which had undermined American resolve. The blossoming of modern communication systems made this more vital than ever before as the media, and publics', access to information about world affairs and US foreign policies increased. This created a gathering momentum in the administration around the need for US public diplomacy to unashamedly espouse American values and views internationally.

Adelman laid out his perspective in *Foreign Affairs* in the spring of 1981 where he predicted that public diplomacy was set to become 'Washington's major growth industry'.[10] He claimed that the new president was 'a gifted professional communicator' and that public diplomacy had 'the makings of becoming a hallmark of the Reagan administration's foreign policy'.[11] Adelman believed that Reagan's talent for relating to an audience, technological advances in communications and the 'fiery pro-Americanism' provoked by the twin crises in Iran and Afghanistan had heightened the importance of public diplomacy. He pointed to how anti-American propaganda had provoked the destruction of the US embassy in Pakistan in 1979. This could not continue unchallenged. According to Adelman, while USICA had suffered falling budgets and a confusing 'duel-mandate' under the Carter administration, the Soviets realized that 'ideas are more fatal than guns' and had spent five times more than the United States on public diplomacy. A Heritage Foundation report backed Adelman's assertions calculating that Moscow spent more on jamming US radio broadcasts than the United States spent on producing and transmitting them.[12] Conservative magazine *Human Events* added its voice to the argument by targeting the Voice of America where it demanded new personnel who understood 'the harsh realities of the global struggle' against communism.[13]

Adelman advocated for US public diplomacy to promote US foreign policy and 'the message of freedom', which, as a neo-conservative, he believed synonymous. These opinions reflected wider conservative opinion and that of the US public, angry at and bewildered by growing anti-Americanism around the world. Reagan and his supporters believed it was time to seize the initiative and re-assert the idea of America as an exceptional exemplar of universal values, domestically and internationally. The time had come to bury the 'Vietnam syndrome' and re-build the US public diplomacy apparatus in preparation for an ideological confrontation with the 'evil empire'. To this end, the administration drafted policy directives to create a co-ordinated, inter-agency public diplomacy infrastructure and delineate the role propaganda would play as a central plank, not just a support, of the administration's ideological challenge to the USSR.[14]

Strengthening the public diplomacy infrastructure

The Reagan administration considered upgrading US communications and information capabilities an intrinsic element of its defence strategy.[15] The burgeoning role of media and communications in international affairs necessitated a comprehensive, robust public diplomacy apparatus with which to challenge communism and ensure support for US policies amongst its allies. However, Washington needed to harness propaganda policies and programmes more closely to foreign policy objectives. Three NSDDs in particular, all drafted in the first two years of the administration, illuminate these aims and the strategies and programmes put in place to implement them.

On 20 May 1982, the President authorized NSDD 32 'US National Security Strategy'. Although primarily concerned with Eastern Europe, NSDD 32 laid out the administration's objective to 'contain and reverse the expansion of Soviet control and military presence throughout the world'. This was a distinct change from the earlier US policy of containment towards the USSR. The directive outlined the administration's commitment to the role of propaganda in achieving this. It vowed to 'strengthen the influence of the US ... by a full range of diplomatic, political, economic, and information efforts'.[16] An extra $100 million was earmarked for public diplomacy to support this initiative.[17] Information management, propaganda and public diplomacy initiatives were now interchangeable, to be combined and co-ordinated to provide a cornerstone for the emerging Reagan Doctrine.

A significant offshoot of this new strategy, in essence a wide-ranging propaganda programme, titled 'Project Democracy' was soon launched. On 8 June 1982, President Reagan addressed the British Houses of Parliament and outlined a 'global campaign for democracy' that would leave the Soviet Union 'on the ash-heap of history'. Its remit was wide-ranging – 'to foster the infrastructure of democracy, the system of a free press, unions, political parties, universities' around the world. US democracy advocacy was little more than a public diplomacy initiative aimed at undermining its Cold War rival. However, the administration failed to convince Congress of the merits of the project. Instead, the bipartisan, privately administered National Endowment for Democracy (NED) was established to carry out the initiatives envisioned by Project Democracy. The NED would impact on the Afghan conflict by funding a number of propaganda programmes over the course of the war. These included school textbooks for Afghan children in the refugee camps, which would later prove contentious due to their violent content exhorting *jihad*.[18] The NED also supported the activities of *Médecins Sans Frontières* in Afghanistan, which at that time was committed to public advocacy against communist regimes.[19]

In the meantime, the administration continued to focus on restructuring the relationship between US public diplomacy and national security. Polls showed a divergence between the United States and its allies on a number of issues such as détente, arms control, INF deployment and the peace movement.[20] Europeans did not feel sufficiently threatened by the USSR to consider more military spending on NATO and felt that the United States was contributing to the risk of war rather than peace.[21] Washington urgently needed to re-orientate world public opinion in its favour, and a major restructuring of its propaganda apparatus was deemed imperative to affect this. On 14 January 1983, Reagan signed NSDD 77, 'Management of Public Diplomacy Relative to National Security', to do just that.

Drafted by Carnes Lord, this directive sought to 'strengthen the organization, planning and coordination of the various aspects of public diplomacy of the United States Government relative to national security'.[22] Lord's neo-conservative ideology permeated the document. Lord believed that America needed 'a better grounded set of general ideas to frame its official discourse – if you will, an "ideology"'.[23] Lord, a scholar of Aristotle and Straussian thinking, argued that during the 1970s America appeared in 'retreat and decline' and that an active strategy to promote the 'clear superiority' of Western values and their universal application was imperative.[24] He believed that the United States represented 'the best possible regime' and its values universal and beneficial to all. Lord set about his task based on these uncompromising ideological principles.

NSDD 77 established a Special Planning Group (SPG) at the NSC tasked with overseeing the planning, monitoring and execution of all government public diplomacy to support national security policy. This would offer an unprecedented level of co-ordination and coherence to US public diplomacy. The SPG would be inter-agency consisting of a number of permanent members: the secretaries of State and Defense, the President's National Security Advisor, the directors of the USIA and USAID and the assistant to the resident for Communications.[25] The directive had a wide-ranging agenda encompassing all aspects of public diplomacy in support of US foreign policy from international broadcasting to political action. Under the SPG, four inter-agency committees were established: the Public Affairs Committee, the International Information Committee (which would take over Project Truth),[26] the International Political Committee (which would oversee Project Democracy) and the International Broadcasting Committee. These committees reported regularly to the SPG which provided guidance and co-ordinated the committees' programmes to ensure all were complementary.

In line with this new policy architecture, the NSC formed an inter-agency Afghan Working Group to promote sympathetic media coverage of the Afghan *mujahedeen*'s struggle.[27] CIA Chief William Casey transferred CIA propagandist, Walter Raymond Jr., to the NSC where he was involved in the creation of the notorious Office of Public Diplomacy for Latin American and the Caribbean. He also set up the Afghan public diplomacy programme. Raymond believed that US foreign policy programmes in Afghanistan and elsewhere had suffered due to insufficient 'resources and forces [for] these efforts'. However, his concern was not rooted in the negative implications for Afghanistan but, rather, the negative impact for US foreign policy. He considered that public diplomacy should provide a 'central focus for insuring greater commitment of resources, greater concentration of effort in support of foreign policies: call it political action, if you will'.[28] Raymond was central to expanding the public affairs, political and psychological warfare element of the US Afghan programme.[29]

Domestic propagandizing was forbidden under the Smith-Mundt Act of 1948; therefore, such activities could not be overtly directed at a domestic US audience; however, this would not preclude Reagan and his officials giving statements, speeches or issuing press releases, which supported the foreign policy objectives of the administration. While this was usual practice in past administrations, the administration sought to ensure this was carried out in a manner that maximized its effects. The Public Affairs Committee set up under NSDD 77 was charged with 'the planning and coordination of major speeches on national security subjects and other public appearances by senior officials' and co-ordinating 'public affairs efforts to explain and support major US foreign policy initiatives'. Even the President's interaction with the press was carefully managed by his officials to ensure he kept in line with his own official policy.[30] NSDD 77 demonstrated the administration's conviction that presenting a unified, clear ideology was vital to rendering a more powerful and effective message. The directive blurred the boundaries between domestic 'public affairs', foreign 'public diplomacy' and 'psychological warfare' as all were co-ordinated by one overarching NSC planning group and designed to complement one another. This doctrine was aggressively applied to Afghanistan where, as another NSDD outlined, the administration believed the Soviets were particularly vulnerable to propaganda.

NSDD 75, 'U.S. Relations with the U.S.S.R', was also signed in January 1983.[31] This directive was drafted in 1982 by Richard Pipes and reflected his alarmist view that communism had 'metastasized' and George Kennan's containment policy was no longer adequate to counter it. The directive specifically identified Afghanistan as a weak link in Soviet armour and propaganda as fundamental to exploiting it. While confirming Washington's ultimate objective in Afghanistan as withdrawal, it recommended interim actions designed to inflict maximum military and political cost on the USSR and advance American influence. This required an 'ideological thrust which clearly affirms the superiority of US and Western values'. To achieve this, it advocated propaganda tactics or 'instruments of political action', including Project Democracy, radio broadcasting along with highlighting Soviet human rights abuses.[32]

By 1983, the infrastructure of US public diplomacy had been restructured and considerably strengthened but there had also been a reassessment of its ideological applications, aided by neo-conservative intellectuals. Furthermore, the conflict in Afghanistan had clearly been identified as a prime target for this propaganda. It would be used to demonstrate to allies (and adversaries) in Congress, in Europe and in the Third World the aggressive, expansive threat the Soviet Union posed. Afghan propaganda bolstered the administration's argument for a major military aid package to the dictatorship in Pakistan. The 'yellow rain' propaganda programme was marshalled to support proposed US CBW rearmament proposals. It justified the US tough stance on arms negotiations and burnished the US moral superiority as a champion of 'freedom fighters' around the world. The USIA was chief amongst the agencies tasked with developing and administering the Afghan public diplomacy programme advocated by these NSDDs, particularly Project Truth and Project Democracy.

As well as the government-wide reconfiguration of US public diplomacy, the USIA was subjected to an internal re-orientation under its new boss, Charles Z. Wick. This would have particular impact on the agency's engagement with propaganda on the Afghan conflict. Wick was an outsider to the organization, with glamorous show business interests and a flamboyant nature. He was a close friend of William Casey and had a reputation for scaring 'the hell out of people'.[33] As the director of the USIA, Wick was both successful and controversial, but, over the course of his tenure (1981–1988), managed to double the agency's annual funding.[34] The agency's mission statement no longer included the Carter era ban on propagandistic or covert activities; instead, the emphasis would be to 'unmask and counter hostile attempts to distort or to frustrate the objectives and policies of the United States'.[35] Wick's Hollywood connections enabled extravaganzas such as the television show 'Let Poland Be Poland' for which Congress waived its ban on domestic dissemination of USIA output. It would be persuaded to do the same for at least two Afghan propaganda films. However, controversy dogged Wick's tenure at the USIA. Reagan appointee Philip Nicolaides described the organization as 'a propaganda agency' and Wick's performance before Congress to procure funding for Project Democracy failed to impress.[36]

However, Wick was active and inventive in his role too. He was committed to involving private sector experts in USIA committees, in executive posts and in fundraising for various programmes.[37] This approach infiltrated USIA product too. The agency's output on Afghanistan featured many private individuals and groups involved in pro-Afghan advocacy. They appeared in or helped create documentaries, Worldnet shows, conferences and literature on the conflict. Furthermore, Wick developed Project Truth to rapidly rebut Soviet disinformation and propaganda plaguing America. The project, which sought to ensure the United States spoke 'with one voice', was lauded by the President as possibly 'the best weapon of them all'. Soviet propaganda accused the United States of spreading swine fever and dengue fever. It accused America of testing 'killer mosquitoes' on Pakistani citizens with the intention of 'exporting' them to Afghanistan.[38] The USIA programme would contest such allegations. Project Truth also sought to spread some propaganda of its own. It aimed to increase the publicity around Soviet actions such as the invasion of Afghanistan or its alleged use of chemical weapons. Under its remit, the Voice of America was instructed to stop calling the Afghan *mujahedeen* 'anti-government guerrillas' and instead use the term 'freedom fighters'. This characterization better fitted with American ideals and so helped justify American support. Project Truth involved a co-ordinated inter-agency effort encompassing the CIA, the State and Defense. This allowed it to circumvent the domestic ban on USIA output. Although initially led by the USIA later, after NSDD 77, it would fall under the jurisdiction of the newly minted International Information Committee.[39] It would be just one of the many USIA propaganda programmes that would involve the Afghan conflict.

Ultimately, the administration's multi-agency co-ordinated public diplomacy strategy offered a powerful instrument with which to re-assert American exceptionalism and challenge Soviet communism. Internationally, Afghanistan's status as a victim of the USSR was uncontested. This was also the case within US media and congressional circles making the Afghan conflict an ideal hook on which to hang the administration propaganda offensives. In practical terms, re-asserting America and challenging communism meant convincing Congress to sanction funds for increased military expenditure. However, Congress would prove more than a passive receptor of administration propaganda as the administration's struggles with it over aid to Pakistan and chemical weapon rearmament illuminated.

Afghan propaganda and military aid to Pakistan

Congress' relationship with the executive had become increasingly antagonistic throughout the 1970s. In the early part of the decade, the legislature had acted to rein in defence spending and military adventurism abroad as well as run investigations into CIA abuses. In later years, however, it adopted a more 'hawkish' stance on foreign affairs and military spending.[40] The Reagan administration's plan to re-assert US authority internationally included controversial elements such as its proposed military aid package to Pakistan. This aid programme would shore up the United States' geostrategic position in South Asia weakened following the Iranian Revolution by consolidating America's influence with Pakistan. The administration turned to propaganda centred on the Afghan conflict to justify this policy to Congress and a wider public sceptical of Pakistan's credentials as a US ally.

On 7 April 1979, just eight months before the Soviet invasion of Afghanistan, Congress had fractured the US relationship with Pakistan by invoking the Symington Amendment in reaction to Islamabad's nuclear ambitions.[41] Pakistan's military leader Muhammad Zia ul Haq's actions also contributed to heightened tensions – just days before he alienated Western public opinion by executing political rival and former Prime Minister Zulfiqar Ali Bhutto. He compounded this in November of that year with an unhurried response to the attack on the US embassy in Islamabad, which culminated in the mission being razed to the ground by an angry mob.[42] However, Pakistan's status as a US regional ally was soon elevated by the 'loss' of Iran and the invasion of Afghanistan.[43] To re-engage with a wary Islamabad, the Reagan administration promised a significant military aid package to Zia. This was potentially controversial though and required congressional sanction. The administration sought to ameliorate this by emphasizing the threat Pakistan was under following the Soviet invasion of Afghanistan.[44] Afghanistan did not divide Congress like Pakistan did and the *mujahedeen* enjoyed bipartisan support pre-dating the Reagan administration. However, Zia supported the insurgents and this was invaluable in generating support for Pakistan. A Republican-majority Senate would help the administration's cause too.

To this end, administration rhetoric emphasized the threat to Pakistan in front of congressional committees and hearings and in the media, in the hope of persuading Congress to waive the Symington Amendment and approve the military aid package. Secretary of State Alexander Haig Jr. warned that Pakistan was 'in a very difficult position' and 'under great pressure' due to its 'very courageous position' on Afghanistan.[45] The President emphasized Pakistan's geopolitical importance stating it was 'in a very strategic position now in view of what has happened to Afghanistan', adding 'I believe it is in our best interest to be supportive of Pakistan'.[46] Undersecretary of State, James Buckley, again evoked the Afghan conflict in a briefing before the House of Representatives' Foreign Affairs Committee (HFAC) on 24 June 1981 where he outlined the proposed aid package, particularly Pakistan's need for advanced F-16 military jets. Buckley argued that since the invasion of Afghanistan, Pakistan faced 'a serious Soviet threat' and consequently suffered from a 'sense of acute vulnerability'.[47] Queries about the state's nuclear proliferation programme were brushed aside, though the administration was well aware that Pakistan was already capable of producing a nuclear bomb.[48] Administration tactics proved effective as Congress agreed to a six-year waiver of sanctions facilitating the transfer of $600 million per annum in aid to Pakistan.

However, congressional support was tenuous and came with the tacit understanding that this would be rescinded should Pakistan ever test a nuclear device. As a result, the administration's rehabilitation agenda needed to be continuously reinforced when opportunities, such as Zia's December 1982 state visit to Washington, arose. Reagan's public commitment to democracy promotion during his Westminster speech just six months earlier was little in evidence on this occasion – the military dictator had cancelled elections just before leaving Islamabad. Concerns about Pakistan's human rights record similarly fell victim to the Kirkpatrick Doctrine. Instead, in a toast at the dinner, Reagan publicly underscored the 'shared visions and goals' of Americans and Pakistanis and emphasized Pakistan's role in sheltering Afghan refugees. Zia, for his part, drew parallels between the aspirations of Islam and those of the America's founding fathers and assured Congress of the peaceful nature of Pakistan's nuclear programme. The negative effects of flooding the region with weapons did not receive any public attention.

The military aid did not just unsettle the PDPA and the Soviets. It also boosted instability within Pakistan and watered the seeds of ethnic and tribal unrest along the Pakistan-Afghanistan borderlands. A CIA situation report from October 1982 warned of the threat to Pakistani policing posed by well-armed insurgents in refugee camps ready to settle disputes with firepower. Pakistan's territorial integrity was under threat from Afghan Pashtuns, now coached in sophisticated warfare techniques, seeking to carve out their traditional homeland of Pashtunistan from Pakistan's disputed boundary with Afghanistan.[49] Furthermore, tensions between Pakistan and India were ratcheted up while US allies in the region such as Israel watched with alarm. This new security arrangement also ensured that early attempts to resolve the Afghan conflict were stillborn as the United States sought to influence Pakistan's negotiation strategy with Afghanistan. However, the aid programme, enabled by Afghan-inspired propaganda, achieved its aim of shoring up the United States' geostrategic position in South Asia weakened following the 'loss' of Iran. An even more sophisticated propaganda programme relying on much more than administration rhetoric would next be deployed to justify the administration's rearmament strategy.

Justifying US rearmament

The continuation of the war in Afghanistan and the anti-Soviet propaganda it facilitated served more than US geostrategic ends. It also assisted the administration's policy of rearmament, which faced congressional resistance and ambivalence amongst US allies. From the Team B exercise in late 1976 on, Reagan and his neo-conservative allies had predicted a widening gap between US and Soviet military capability. In April 1982, Reagan had proclaimed his belief that the Soviets had 'a definite margin of superiority' over the United States. This was backed up by a Heritage Foundation report in October 1982 titled 'What Price Defense' that urged congressional approval of increased defence spending.[50] It argued that the Soviet Union was operating 'at a semi-war mobilized pace, grinding out weapons at a rate two and three times that of the United States'. According to Heritage, the CIA predicted this would continue apace and warned Congress that it would be 'extremely shortsighted' to hinder US rearmament.

The report highlighted the need for public diplomacy to prop up this policy contending that public support could be gained if 'the Soviet threat is forthrightly explained to them'. As one journalist remarked at the time 'events in Poland, Afghanistan, Central America, and other trouble spots may well determine whether the move to '"rearm America" proceeds'.[51] However, by early 1983, CIA analysis showed that Soviet military procurement had levelled off and, in fact, had probably not grown since 1976.[52] This was a worrying development for an administration dedicated to a rearmament strategy predicated on Soviet military superiority and locked in a struggle for increased funding with a Congress concerned with waste and 'gold-plating' in defence expenditure. Around this time, the administration increased its flow of arms to the Afghan *mujahedeen* ensuring that the conflict, and Soviet involvement, would continue and provide plenty of fodder for Washington's propaganda machine.[53]

Exaggerating the menace posed by the Soviets, as illustrated by the Afghan crisis, played a significant role in the administration's justification for increased military spending to Congress. Reagan's speeches on Afghanistan focused on Soviet aggression and Afghanistan's potential role in arresting it. In December 1982, on the anniversary of the Soviet invasion, Reagan warned Americans that 'Afghanistan is a struggle we must not forget'; that 'Afghanistan is important to the world, because the Afghan people are resisting Soviet imperialism'; and that their subjugation would have implications for 'the safety of free men everywhere'.[54] The administration initiated a campaign that accused the Soviets of chemical weapon use in Afghanistan. This propaganda proclaimed the Soviet's atrocious amorality and war criminality and the necessity of US chemical warfare preparedness as a counterfoil. The President claimed that the United States had 'convincing proof' that the Soviets were using chemical weapons in Afghanistan to deliberately destroy crops, homes and villages. Moscow issued a sharp rebuttal accusing the United States of underwriting unrest in Afghanistan, thus delaying Soviet troop withdrawal. However, this propaganda campaign was not solely designed to antagonize the Soviets. Highlighting Soviet aggression in Afghanistan was instrumental to the administration's bid before Congress and with the American public for increased defence spending in recessionary times. The case for replenishing controversial chemical weapon stocks required especial rationalizing.

The Pentagon identified an apparent 'gap' between the CBW capabilities of the United States compared to the USSR in the mid-1970s. However, it was frustrated in its efforts to redress this by the Carter administration and Congress whilst bilateral discussions on banning such weapons went ahead in the late 1970s.[55] In 1980, following the Soviet invasion of Afghanistan, these talks were suspended. Heightened Cold War tensions offered a lifeline to those wishing to upgrade US chemical weapons stocks. First, congressional approval was needed.[56] Concerned US allies in Europe had to be convinced of the programme's utility too, as any chemical arsenal would need to be housed in Western Europe to be deployable against the Soviet Union.[57] To this end, the Reagan administration developed a propaganda campaign centred on allegations of CBW use by the Soviets in Afghanistan and Southeast Asia to facilitate these aims though it had little substantive evidence.[58] The administration argued that while it desired a complete ban on such weapons, upgrading its own stocks was a necessary foil to Soviet CBW capability.

Allegations about the Soviet use of CBWs in Afghanistan began to circulate not long after the invasion and were soon being cited to support the regeneration of the Pentagon's CBW programme.[59] As talks on disarmament, including CBWs, got underway in Geneva on 3 February 1981, the annual State Department Human Rights report began the offensive by accusing the Soviets of chemical warfare in Afghanistan. Soon after, the Reagan administration requested congressional approval for a military budget that included funding for a renewed chemical weapons programme. The Senate was divided on the subject and the administration acted to shape its considerations with its accusations. Senators narrowly approved funding to build, but not equip, the requested chemical weapons facility. Throughout the rest of the year, administration officials reiterated these allegations publicly as appropriations for CBW rearmament needed further congressional sanction.[60] By the end of 1981, the USICA's newly minted Project Truth began orchestrating a propaganda campaign around the subject that its executive committee endeavoured to distance from the administration. To this end, Walter Raymond and Michael Ledeen[61] were tasked with 'identifying non-American experts, moral leaders, defecting Soviet scientists with CBW expertise to document and express outrage at Soviet use of CBW'.[62]

In early 1982, the administration sought a large increase in the military budget from Congress for its new CBW programme. As the administration continued to require congressional approval, its propaganda gathered pace. This posited that Washington abhorred such weapons but was forced by Soviet actions to replenish US stocks as a deterrent. CPD founder and Arms Control and Disarmament Agency Director Eugene Rostow's call for a complete ban on these 'inhuman weapons of war' on 9 February 1982, the day after the President requested Congress allow the United States to restart its chemical weapon programme, provides an example of this stance.

Appearing before the Senate Foreign Relations Committee (SFRC) that March, Deputy Secretary of State Walter J. Stoessel Jr. alleged that over 3,000 people had been killed in Afghanistan by CBWs. The following day, Reagan accused the Soviets of CBW use on the Afghans.[63] But, just a week beforehand, Pentagon officials had admitted they had no evidence of Soviet chemical weapon use in Afghanistan.[64] Testifying at a HFAC hearing in March 1982, another State Department official alleged that Moscow's chemical weapon stockpile was 'well beyond reasonable deterrence requirements' and added 'this threat to our security has been brought into sharper focus by the actual use of chemical weapons in Afghanistan and chemical and toxin weapons in Southeast Asia'.[65] However, the only evidence offered by the State Department report of 22 March 1982 to Congress was that of refugee and defector testimony, as samples collected and analysed from Afghanistan and Southeast Asia showed no evidence of 'known chemical warfare agents'.[66]

Scientists questioned the allegations and the administration's research; the media expressed scepticism, but, nevertheless, the propaganda continued. Other Western states remained unconvinced and concerns were raised by experts that the accusations were 'a mere smoke screen for the projected [US] poison-gas rearmament'.[67] A more effective strategy was needed to convince the sceptics and this came in the form of the 'yellow rain' allegations.

The 'yellow rain program' formed a central plank of the US propaganda output on chemical weapon use by the Soviets in Afghanistan over the following years.[68] It began in 1981 when Project Truth underwrote a speaking tour of Europe for author Sterling Seagrave. His book claimed to document the Soviet use of chemical weapons in Afghanistan, Yemen and Laos.[69] The book alleged that a poisonous 'yellow rain' (a mycotoxin) had been sprayed by the Soviets on insurgents and innocents alike. The USIA aired these allegations further on its Worldnet 'Afghan Digest' programmes. These featured clips on 'bio warfare' in Afghanistan with close-ups of 'victims' and, in one, Seagrave gave a statement on 'yellow rain'.[70] However, eminent scientists such as Harvard professor Dr Matthew Meselson contested these allegations arguing that samples analysed were more than likely naturally occurring and probably bee faeces.[71] Nevertheless, a combination of administration and private propaganda helped the accusations gather momentum. ABC ran a documentary titled 'Rain of Terror' urging greater administration action on the subject.[72] Following the publication of Seagrave's book, conservatives began to push the administration to publicize its evidence of 'yellow rain' use via the VOA and international fora.[73] However, as US credibility on such issues was questionable, the administration needed to persuade its international allies and international organizations to support its allegations.[74] To this end, the administration mobilized a web of private interests in support of its claims.

By late 1982, Walter Raymond was working alongside the State Department, the CIA and the USIA to 'get a multifaceted campaign launched worldwide, involving press, travelling shows, special envoys, possible tribunals and special collections efforts'.[75] Secretary of State George Shultz presented a report to the UN and Congress charging the Soviets with CBW use in Southeast Asia on 29 November; however, in the face of an 'equivocal' report on the subject by the UN, McFarlane felt a 'significant escalation of both public and private public diplomacy to garner greater support' was required.[76] Ensuring that these accusations were not solely emanating from the administration was vital to their credibility. According to McFarlane:

> Our ability to mobilize and encourage those countries that have independent evidence of the use of yellow rain must be undertaken. Such parallel reporting and support is essential if our case is to be made and the world is to view this as something larger than simply an element in US-Soviet bilateral.

Raymond wanted to add 'more clout to the public diplomacy campaign' by dispatching former ambassador to NATO, Robert Ellsworth, to visit Western allies to persuade them to put any evidence they had on the toxin into the public domain.[77] Former President of the American Academy of Sciences, Dr Frederick Seitz,[78] agreed to travel overseas to meet with scientific and government officials 'to use his prominent scientific position to help build world support for the conclusions [the administration] had reached'.[79] The administration sought to fund testing and analysis of 'yellow rain' toxins, while maintaining the illusory 'independence' of such research. The Institute of Foreign Policy Analysis – a think tank linked to the Tufts School of Diplomacy and funded by conservative organizations such as Scaife's – established, with Freedom House, a 'Chemical/Biological Weapons Information Project' which offered to do just this.[80]

The project's director, Stuart Schwartzstein, along with self-proclaimed 'cold warrior' Leo Cherne,[81] met with Raymond to discuss how the project could assist the Department of Defense in conducting analyses of victims of CBW.[82] Raymond approached the Pentagon on the subject emphasizing that Schwartzstein needed to 'maintain his independence so that he would be effective as a spokesman'.[83] When Schwartzstein appeared in the media or before Congress defending the 'yellow rain' allegations he was not linked to the administration. Cherne, along with Frank Barnett,[84] was also involved in discussions with Raymond and Casey about organizing a 'private' war crimes grand jury to 'try' the Soviets for CBW use. They hoped this public diplomacy initiative would generate a 'world climate of outrage' and carefully considered how to maximize this. They selected Paris as the venue as it was 'sufficiently "independent and socialist"' which would enhance credibility and, they believed, journalists enjoyed being assigned there which meant media coverage would be guaranteed. Raymond recommended 'Third World personages' should form the majority of this 'independent' grand jury. This would help set it outside a Cold War framework and instead place the conflict in a USSR versus the Third World context. Raymond reckoned that the publicity generated by the tribunal would put the Peace and Disarmament movements 'on the defensive' on issues of 'mutual trust', treaty verification, 'the symmetry of the morals of the superpowers'. Furthermore, it would undermine Soviet promises of 'no first use'.[85] Raymond outlined the plan's utility to the administration's CBW rearmament policy stating 'given congressional difficulties with the budget for CBW build up, the least we can do is to launch an all out effort to condemn Soviet violations'. Although there is no evidence such a tribunal was established, US PVOs did facilitate Afghan *mujahedeen* in appearing before the Permanent Peoples Tribunal in Paris (formally the Russell Tribunal that had negatively evaluated US intervention in Vietnam) in 1982.[86]

Although there was widespread scepticism about the veracity of the 'yellow rain' claims, some media outlets did relay the administration's story and 'experts' amongst the Afghan PVOs were often the source of information reported. Writing in the *Boston Globe* Theodore Eliot Jr. of ARC described the Soviet use of CBWs against Afghans was 'well documented'.[87] The CFA and other PVOs like Freedom House and the International Rescue Committee (IRC) were involved in propagating the allegations from early on and were instrumental in gathering witnesses to give evidence confirming the charges.[88]

The CFA was particularly active. According to their literature, '[Karen] McKay and the Committee played a critical role in assisting the government in obtaining new samples of biological toxins being used in Laos, Cambodia and Afghanistan'.[89] Sterling Seagrave was amongst their Council of Advisors. The CFA's genesis was in the hard-line anti-communist right and this was reflected in its advocacy. It leaned heavily on propaganda to raise awareness. The organization was conceived by the Council for the Defense of Freedom (formally the Council against Communist Aggression) and the American Security Council.[90] It was linked to Accuracy in the Media, where McKay worked before becoming the CFA's executive director, and was housed in Heritage Foundation offices.[91] The PVO was a member of the Coalition for Peace through Strength (a national security lobby group with alleged links to far-right Eastern European groups) and boasted of alliances with 'a number of influential interest groups'.[92] It counted John K. Singlaub – a former US Army major general and CIA operative, founder of the United States Council for World Freedom (a chapter of the World Anti-Communist League) and co-chair of the Coalition for Peace through Strength – as an advisor along with a formidable list of conservative hawks and individuals connected to the *mujahedeen*'s cause.[93] There were even allegations by other PVOs that it was a CIA front organization.[94] Singlaub was also involved with the Nicaraguan *Contras* and ultimately embroiled in the Iran-*Contra* affair. McKay, who described herself as 'somewhere to the right of Attila the Hun', was a foreign area operations officer with the US army reserves.[95] She was 'schooled in unconventional and psychological warfare' and worked in the Middle East for years as a military correspondent and so, presumably, was an able propagandist.[96] The CFA sought to co-operate with the administration to increase popular support for Reagan's policies on Afghanistan though its relationship with the administration, particularly the State Department, would prove rocky over time.[97]

Jim Coyne of *Soldier of Fortune* magazine, which was associated with the CFA, was involved in investigating the 'yellow rain' allegations too. The publication offered a $100,000 bounty for evidence of the toxin. Samples collected by the magazine were passed on to McKay who, in turn, gave them to Senator Leach for analysis. Although initial analyses 'proved disappointing', further tests in government laboratories eventually turned up traces of 'yellow rain' toxins.[98] The Senate committee hearing on this subject in November 1981 was stacked with these not very impartial PVO witnesses – McKay, Seagrave, Coyne, along with various US Army and administration officials and a number of 'Afghan Freedom Fighters'.[99] Chair, Senator Larry Pressler, acknowledged the impact of any findings on arms control negotiations and highlighted the inconclusive nature of the evidence. However, those testifying overwhelming presented the case for CBW being used in Southeast Asia – only Dr Matthew Meselson was present to offer testimony that questioned the evidence. The weight of this oral evidence proved influential as Pressler ultimately concluded 'a Holocaust' was underway in the region, contributing to the propaganda swirling around the allegations.

The CFA, Freedom House, ARC and the Heritage Foundation sponsored a trip for Afghan *mujahedeen* to give evidence before another joint congressional hearing in February 1983 and an accompanying press tour. The *mujahedeen* trip aimed for maximum publicity and featured a meeting with the President and a visit to New York and other US cities. Michael Barry – an American anthropologist, who was involved with ARC and Freedom House[100] – acted as their translator.[101] The Afghans accused the Soviets of using CBWs and of burning children to death.[102] During the trip, Representative Ritter, a *mujahedeen* supporter, again evoked the 'Holocaust' to describe Soviet actions in Afghanistan. The Heritage Foundation weighed in behind the accusations with similar inflammatory language. Two of the organization's reports outlined 'a brutal poison Holocaust' underway in Laos, Kampuchea and Afghanistan and included vivid descriptions of the effect of the chemicals.[103] Heritage distributed such reports to Congress and they were often relayed by the news media as well.[104]

The 'yellow rain' allegations featured in the *New York Times* and influential *Wall Street Journal* editor Robert Bartley authored a *Foreign Affairs* article on the subject.[105] This rehashed the administration's case arguing that it justified US CBW rearmament.[106]

Bartley met with William Clark to discuss the article and received official approval for his stance. The NSC's public relations advisor recommended that Clark 'keep the door open' for this journalist as his newspaper provided 'consistent support' to the administration's national security policies.[107] The administration was aware of the need to nurture such symbiotic relationships with certain media to ensure its propaganda initiatives received adequate coverage.

On 28 June 1983, *Parade* magazine ran an article on 'yellow rain', which Clark described as 'the product of a major US Government effort to invite individuals and nations to join us in examining the evidence'.[108] The article quoted Seagrave, Dr Amos Townsend,[109] Dr Bernard Wagner and Dr B. A. Zikria[110] whom Clark described as 'reputable individuals who have assisted the US'.[111] In October 1983, *Commentary* magazine featured an article by Italian journalist Lucio Lami and translated by Michael Ledeen.[112] It accused the UN, the American and European media and the International Red Cross of suppressing accusations of 'yellow rain' use by the Soviets.[113] United Nations High Commission for Refugees (UNHCR) vigorously denied the charges.[114] Reports continued to appear in some media about 'yellow rain' right up to late 1984 when they began to fizzle out.

The administration's propaganda centred on 'yellow rain' was conceived to facilitate the replenishment of US chemical weapons stocks. It worked to disseminate this information via 'independent' sources to bolster its credibility and was aided by certain media and private organizations. Although the propaganda was internationalized to create maximum embarrassment for the Soviet Union and offer the United States leverage in arms control talks, its ultimate target was Congress as it controlled the allocation of funding for CBW rearmament. Congress, as will be shown in the next chapter, was a driving force in the escalation of support for the Afghan insurgency in the United States and some members of Congress accepted the administration's allegations, even pre-empted them.[115] However, many were seriously concerned about the development of such controversial weaponry and the administration's propaganda campaign failed to convince and, consequently, between 1982 and 1984, Congress steadfastly refused to approve appropriations for revitalizing US chemical weapons production. Robert Gates, then Deputy Director of Intelligence, would later admit the allegations were baseless.[116] For the PVOs, the CBW accusations helped amplify their conviction that the Soviets were ruthless in their pursuit of supremacy. Pitted against this backdrop of CBW recriminations and increased military aid from the United States to Pakistan, proximity talks on a peace agreement between Islamabad and Kabul began in Geneva on 15 June 1982. Hard-line anti-communists within and outside the administration would seek to ensure the negotiations were stillborn.

UN proximity talks between Pakistan and Afghanistan

Following the UN General Assembly's condemnation of the Soviet offensive in Afghanistan on 20 November 1980, Moscow had begun to tentatively seek a political resolution.[117] As Reagan assumed the mantle of power in Washington, it was quickly made clear to Pakistan that the administration did not approve of the parameters for talks. Furthermore, Pakistan's public rehabilitation in the United States, and the military and economic aid that accompanied it, was dependent on its new role as a 'front-line state' in the 'second Cold War'.[118] The US media echoed this stance – the *New York Times* warned that direct negotiations between Pakistan and Afghanistan could serve to legitimize the Afghan government, disrupt aid to the rebels and hence 'sanitize' the Soviet presence there.[119] Alexander Haig had proposed 'expert level' talks on Afghanistan between the United States and the Soviet Union following discussions in Moscow in October 1981 when Ambassador Dobrynin told him 'the USSR has made a serious mistake in Afghanistan' and 'wanted to find a basis for getting out'.[120] However, there was resistance to any deal brokering with the USSR from inside and outside the administration.

Administration hawks agitated against negotiations with Moscow. In a memorandum on the proposed talks, Richard Pipes wrote, 'The Russians are taking a clobbering in Afghanistan ... Why let them off the hook?'[121] Pipes, along with Raymond, Geoffrey Kemp and Norman Bailey, urged an end to 'fruitless "talks" with the conquerors' and argued that 'every dollar spent to support the Afghan *mujahedeen* will save us tens if not hundreds of dollars in the future (not to speak of lives) when the Russians use their Afghan springboard to attack the Gulf'.[122] Not all administration officials agreed though; US ambassador to Pakistan Ronald Spiers contended that US material support for the *mujahedeen* was only 'politically and morally justified', if a political solution was attainable and urged engagement with the UN peace negotiations.[123] This would not occur however, given the consensus developing among some that the Afghan conflict's continuance was serving US interests.

Influential conservative voices outside the administration reinforced this stance. Leon Poullada advocated arming the *mujahedeen* as a proxy US Rapid Deployment Force, while Morgan Norval of *Political Gun News* (a Viguarie production) argued the Afghan rebels were 'eager to do our dirty work' and should be aided in doing so.[124] *Human Events*, of which the President was a fan, recounted a meeting of several dozen conservative organizations in Washington in January 1982 to review Reagan's first year in office.[125] At this, representatives accused the State Department of being 'staffed with remnants of the Kissinger regime and career officials' who pursued 'the illusions of détente, restrained demeanor toward our Communist opponents and cavalier treatment of our friends'. They called for 'maximum efforts to provide aid to freedom seekers everywhere, especially those in Afghanistan, Angola, Cuba, Nicaragua and Poland'.[126]

Soviet General Secretary Yuri Andropov, following his successful succession battle in late 1982, was keen to seek a resolution to Afghanistan that would allow withdrawal 'with honour'. In April 1983, following a year of indirect negotiations between Pakistan and Afghanistan, agreement on a settlement was within reach. Pakistan, facing a growing refugee crisis, fears over Pashtun nationalism and internal opposition to assisting the *mujahedeen* seemed willing to reach a compromise. However, doubts remained over whether the Soviets would follow through on the agreement and the United States was decidedly cool towards the idea of a settlement, which did not include the removal of the PDPA regime.[127] Around this time, Richard Perle was actively lobbying conservative congressional members and administration officials to upgrade arms to the Afghan rebels, and Casey and Reagan were contemplating extending the conflict into Soviet Central Asia.[128] In late May, the Soviets were openly talking of a timetable for withdrawal. Pakistan's foreign minister, Yaqub Khan, arrived in Washington to discuss the draft settlement before a renewed round of negotiations planned for June to US press reports that an increased aid package was being offered to the *mujahedeen*.[129] Khan was informed by the State Department that the agreement was unworkable. Ultimately, Reagan administration 'bleeders' won the battle by undermining negotiations as an early resolution to the conflict as it did not serve their Cold War strategy.

The administration's intransigence mirrored that of the PVOs who took to the public sphere to air their views. Robert C. Macauley, founder of charity AmeriCares, railed against the negotiations in the *Christian Science Monitor*. He decried the 'naiveté' and gullibility of Western journalists who believed 'that a peaceful Soviet withdrawal from Afghanistan is just around the corner' and offered his own spin on the conflict and negotiations. Macauley insisted that 'the Afghan freedom fighters are not the result of outside agitation', as Moscow claimed, but the Kabul government was describing it as a 'puppet regime' of the USSR. He characterized the peace talks as 'either a propaganda ploy or a blueprint for final Soviet victory' and predicted the Red Army would overrun Afghanistan again if provoked. US endorsement of the any settlement would mean it gave 'its tacit consent to a reinvasion'.[130] Freedom House called for more arms for the *mujahedeen* in a *Wall Street Journal* article in September 1983. The anti-negotiation sentiment emanating from the United States achieved its goal. Following his Washington visit, Khan sought to redefine Pakistan's position as the Soviets prevaricated over the timetable for withdrawal. Mired in recriminations, the talks lost momentum and any chance of an early resolution was lost. The United States was ambivalent. Some, particularly in the State Department, advocated for more diplomacy while the 'bleeders' remained committed to increased aid to the *mujahedeen* to block the Soviets negotiating a 'cheap' way out of Afghanistan.[131] Hardliners in the Politburo did not make finding a resolution any easier either.

Around this time, those within the Reagan administration seeking to increase assistance to the *mujahedeen* began to gain a definite edge over those promoting a diplomatic course. The continuous pressure by PVOs, congressional *mujahedeen* supporters and neo-conservative elements within an administration high on 'interventionist enthusiasm' after the invasion of Grenada began to have an effect. Coupled with evidence of the *mujahedeen*'s resilience and tenacity, hawks like Casey became convinced that Afghanistan could damage the Soviet Union much more than initially envisaged. The stage was set for the massive explosion in aid to the Afghan rebels that would follow over the next couple of years.

Conclusion

The Reagan administration came to office infused with the exceptionalist ideology of its New Right and neo-conservative supporters. This manifested in a determination to reinstate America's perceived rightful leadership of the international community and challenge communism. It was an ideological as much as a military mission and the Afghan conflict would play a central role in facilitating its objectives. The conflict roused conservative anti-communists who saw in it an opportunity to confront the Soviet Union and project American power. They identified propaganda as pivotal to achieving these goals. Those within the administration set about strengthening its infrastructure and encouraging more wide-ranging, co-ordinated application. Those without deployed it to full effect in the media and congressional hearings.

However, the vision for US public diplomacy aspired to more than being a prop for foreign policy. Instead, it would be an intrinsic element of foreign policy producing a co-ordinated and coherent ideological narrative of US virtue and Soviet brutality. Under the newly established inter-agency process US public diplomacy would range from presidential speeches and USIA output to democracy promotion.

Reasserting American power in South Asia following the 'loss' of Iran and the invasion of Afghanistan depended on an alliance with Pakistan. Pakistan's nuclear ambitions and human rights abuses had the capacity to undermine this, however. This provoked a public rehabilitation effort by the Reagan administration, which focused on Pakistan's new role as a 'frontline state' in the fight against Soviet expansionism across the Persian Gulf.

Re-arming America to assure its military supremacy had to be justified by the administration to a parsimonious Congress and sceptical international allies. CBWs were considered especially loathsome and could only be legitimized as a counterpoise to Soviet stockpiles and deployment. This necessitated a co-ordinated, sophisticated programme of propaganda. The 'yellow rain' campaign was ambitious involving PVOs, media coverage, Worldnet programmes and testimony before Congress and international tribunals. The administration developed a multi-faceted propaganda campaign, overseen by CIA propagandist Walter Raymond, and endeavoured to ensure that propaganda emanating from it was kept at a remove from its source to enhance its credibility.

While aid to *mujahedeen* remained at Carter levels for these first three years of Reagan's presidency, the administration quickly realized the public diplomacy gift the Soviets had handed it. It immediately began to ratchet up this element of their Afghan strategy to maximize Soviet discomfort. The conflict provided fodder for Project Truth and campaigns like 'yellow rain'. The Afghan conflict could and would inflict serious damage on the USSR in the global competition of ideologies envisaged by Project Democracy and the trickle down of information back into the Soviet Union itself contributed to domestic disenchantment. Without a Soviet withdrawal from Afghanistan, the United States would be justified in eschewing any early accommodation on arms limitation,[132] justified in seeking to replenish its stockpile of controversial chemical weapons and indulging in a military-aid spending spree involving former political pariahs like President Zia in Pakistan.[133] All the United States had to do was keep Afghanistan in the public eye and, of course, keep the conflict going as long as possible to inflict maximum damage.[134]

3

The Reagan Doctrine, propaganda and the Afghan conflict

Reagan's plans for national security involved a controversial strategy for assisting insurgents in the Third World conduct guerrilla war against their left-leaning governments that would be later identified as the Reagan Doctrine. Debate exists about whether the Reagan Doctrine represented a grand strategy on the part of the Reagan administration or was just an ad hoc series of foreign policy initiatives represented, in retrospect, as coherent, co-ordinated and committed to overturning the Soviet Union. Whichever the case, the Afghan programme was an example of these policies or this doctrine in its 'purest form'.[1] Many of the 'Reagan Doctrine' rebels were reactionary counterrevolutionaries utilizing brutality or illegal means to conduct their wars making it imperative for the administration to propagandize their support for them. The doctrine's advocates in the public and private spheres recognized from the outset that propaganda would be intrinsic to its successful application. To this end, in the case of Afghanistan, the administration contrived in its use of rhetoric to characterize the *mujahedeen* as having values and aspirations consonant with those of America and the West.

Political scientist James Scott describes this as the administration's 'declaratory strategy'.[2] It sought to emphasize parallels between Americans and the rebels by insisting they were fighting for 'freedom' – a cause perennially close to Americans' hearts. However, what this 'freedom' represented to Afghans was never explored beyond the need to end the Soviet occupation and the PDPA leadership. Such rhetoric sought to minimize the divergence amongst fundamentalists, conservatives, Afghan minorities and women about what freedom represented for these groups. US propaganda emphasized the *mujahedeen*'s unity and their alleged role as Afghan's leaders as a sop to democratic mores. It drew parallels between Western Christianity and Islam and declared incompatibility between Muslim faith and communism. And, most of all, it emphasized the Soviets' unbridled brutality in the conduct of their campaign in Afghanistan. This was primarily not only to damage Soviet credibility and integrity but also to justify any *mujahedeen* 'reaction' as reasonable and proportionate.

The administration looked to international institutions such as the UN and International Committee of the Red Cross (ICRC) to help legitimize and amplify this propaganda. The administration, along with the PVOs, established 'Afghanistan Day' as a public diplomacy event to generate propaganda opportunities. The USIA, with help from various conservative interests and PVOs, organized conferences and produced films and even 'facilitated' a visit by Hollywood actor Kirk Douglas to the camps of Peshawar and dinner with Zia ul Haq.

As well as working with the administration, the PVOs networked with Congress to promote the Tsongas-Ritter resolution (eventually passed in 1984) while others fundraised to establish a radio station – Radio Free Kabul – to help promote the resistance and publicize the conflict. All the while, the administration, PVOs and congressional supporters turned a blind eye to the problems associated with the *mujahedeen* in Peshawar and Afghanistan, its infighting, its corruption and repression, and its violence.

The propaganda generated to support the Afghan resistance by US supporters sought to incite religious unrest and justify *mujahedeen* actions which served to hinder the process of conflict resolution in Afghanistan. The war was prolonged to serve their virulent anti-communism and the aspirations of the Reagan Doctrine.

The Reagan administration and the Afghan public diplomacy weapon

Neo-conservative administration officials, like Kenneth Adelman, had quickly recognized the propaganda value of Afghanistan. In early 1981, he decried VOA delays in orchestrating 'effective' radio transmissions into Afghanistan following the Soviet invasion arguing that

> a splendid opportunity was thereby lost for America's information services to tell the Afghan people how the Soviets had reduced at least 60 Afghan villages to rubble and slaughtered their inhabitants, crushed student revolts in the capital, and committed a host of other atrocities. Lost was the opportunity to inform Soviet Muslims in Central Asia of their government's action against their fellow believers. And lost was the opportunity to tell the Afghan people how Americans sympathized with their plight.[3]

While Adelman lamented what he saw as America's lackadaisical approach to shaping the story of the invasion, he rightly contended that the Soviet Union had immediately recognized the importance of propaganda to winning over Afghans. It had quickly set to work conveying communist ideology and news of social and economic improvements under the PDPA government. Less than two months after the invasion, the Politburo laid out plans to initiate 'a pro-Soviet, anti-counterevolutionary media campaign, in Afghanistan'. This would seek to explain Soviet actions, 'unmask the anti-Soviet, anti-Afghan policy unleashed by imperialist circles and the Peking hegemonists' and help develop the Afghan mass media.[4]

Adelman was not alone in his beliefs and soon a consensus would emerge around the need to propagandize the Afghan conflict in the US favour. The Heritage Foundation argued that the 'current situation in Afghanistan and the growing significance of the Soviet Moslem nationalities' warranted increased investment in US radio transmissions into the region.⁵ CIA Director William Casey saw Afghanistan as a model for other administration interventions arguing 'we need half a dozen Afghanistans'.⁶ And this was not just militarily – in July 1981, the State Department recommended to Casey, in response to a request for ideas on Afghanistan, a 'sustained campaign' of propaganda. It vowed that 'the occupation can and will be raised with the press, in programs, and in private meetings with contacts' in US foreign missions. The memorandum emphasized the need for film and video footage to augment this and hold media interest – an assertion which would be re-iterated over the years by many pro-*mujahedeen* advocates and underpin the development of initiatives like the Afghan Media Project in 1985.⁷ Now, neo-conservative and New Right voices had a chance to shape US foreign policy rather than just critique it, and propaganda was identified as a powerful weapon in America's arsenal. The Afghan insurgency provided an ideal opportunity to launch an ideological offensive on the Soviet Union.

Around the same time, the Politburo was becoming increasingly sensitive to Soviet public perceptions of the war as it entered its second year. When considering the advisability of funding epitaphs on the gravestones of soldiers who had died in Afghanistan, it concluded that while burial 'with honors' was fitting 'perpetuating the memory' of the dead soldiers any further would be politically damaging. The Politburo was by then receiving many letters from people complaining of the death of their loved ones in Afghanistan.⁸ Just over a year and a half after the invasion internal discontent over the war was rumbling in the Soviet Union – a discontent that its US rivals were determined to exacerbate.

The Reagan administration had lifted a number of Carter's sanctions on the Soviets once in office, much to some supporters' annoyance; however, it also campaigned vigorously to drum up international condemnation of the USSR and impressed upon international institutions to join its chorus of disapproval. In July 1981, the US mission in Geneva began organizing a visit to Washington for Alexander May, president of the ICRC. Under Reagan, the United States began donating funds to the organization's prison visits programme and Elliot Abrams later described the US relationship with the ICRC under Reagan as never closer or more financially supportive.⁹ Kirkpatrick urged May to meet with the new Republican leadership of the Senate and with foreign affairs leaders in the House. The mission hoped to set up meetings for May with the President, vice president and other members of Congress.¹⁰ May was already acquainted with US Federal Reserve chair Paul Volcker and former chair Arthur Burns due to his former role as vice president of the Swiss Central Bank. Ambassador Gerald Helman recommended to Washington a 'high-level reception' to 'dramatize the kind of skilful, voluntary, quiet approach to international humanitarian problems' by the ICRC. The visit would serve to highlight US funding for Afghan refugees. It would emphasize the fact that the Soviets would not allow the ICRC to offer humanitarian assistance within Afghanistan. The State Department hoped to use the visit to discuss with May the forthcoming ICRC annual conference in November 1981 in Manila at which Afghanistan would be a topic presumably to seek to influence the conferences deliberations. Details of these discussions are not available but at the November conference that year the ICRC approved a resolution which, according to a telegram from the US embassy in Manila, 'for the first time ever named situations of armed conflict in which the ICRC [had] been denied access'. The organization had traditionally not done so at its conferences but agreed this time following May's 'strong plea for approval'. The regions cited were only those which had, or were alleged to have, Soviet ties – Afghanistan, Western Sahara and Ogaden – and, the telegram gloated, 'Soviet discomfort was obvious'.[11]

The Reagan administration also targeted the UN General Assembly to disseminate its propaganda about Soviet actions in Afghanistan. Addressing the UN General Assembly in November 1981, Ambassador Kirkpatrick emphasized two of the administration's main themes – Soviet brutality and the *mujahedeen*'s unity and representative nature. She accused the Soviets of deploying mines 'disguised as ordinary household items or toys' which attracted and, consequently, maimed or killed Afghan children.[12] Kirkpatrick's statement to the UN in late November 1982 re-iterated claims of the Soviet use of chemical warfare, 'butterfly bombs', booby-trapped toys and pens, and the targeted killing of civilians including children – claims which were at the very least unsubstantiated and would later be discredited. She characterized the Afghan resistance as 'a spontaneous, countrywide resistance movement' – another claim that manipulated the truth by presenting this movement as unified under the leadership of the Peshawar Seven.[13] Reagan also raised the subject of Afghanistan in his UN General Assembly every year of his presidency bar one echoing these same US propaganda themes about the conflict.[14] The State Department endeavoured to organize international conferences around the Afghan refugee situation in an effort to 'maintain a high level of international concern about this issue'. As one official outlined, such conferences would ostensibly be 'humanitarian in purpose, but would have the added benefit of focusing world attention on the responsibility of the Soviet Union for this continuing tragedy'.[15] NSC officials discussed how to encourage the UN Secretary General to dispatch an inspection team into Afghanistan similar to the one sent to the Iran–Iraq War. Yet again, this would be portrayed as humanitarian in concept and purpose, when in fact, this proposal was designed to open up new propaganda channels and reinforce existing ones. NSC documents outline the belief that such an action would 'offer a new avenue for engaging world opinion' and help 'sustain or improve' the UN General Assembly's vote condemning the Soviet occupation.[16]

Disseminating its propaganda about Red Army war crimes and *mujahedeen* unity via international organizations allowed the administration to reach a wide audience; however, it still needed to align the traditionalist and fundamentalist Islamic *mujahedeen* group's ideologies with those of Western publics. To this end, the administration sought to draw parallels between Christianity and the resistance's brand of Islam. Most importantly, US supporters needed to differentiate it from Ayatollah Khomeini's virulently anti-Western strain of the religion in Iran. Following Zbigniew Brzezinski's footsteps, the Reagan administration styled the Afghan rebels as God-fearing 'holy warriors'. According to Steve Coll, William Casey believed Muslims and Christians had joint interest as 'believers' in the struggle against atheistic communism.[17] Casey was not alone in this as much of the New Right's anti-communism was infused with religious eschatology identifying communism as evil, inspiring a common cause with other religions battling this 'godless' ideology. Reagan held similar beliefs telling the 'people of Afghanistan' via the VOA at the end of Ramadan in August 1981 that Americans shared with them 'a belief in God'.[18] He also infamously called the Soviet Union an 'evil empire'. During his trip to the Peshawar refugee camps in 1984, embassy officials in Islamabad advised Vice President Bush to commend the Afghans for defending their 'traditional way of life and religious convictions'.[19] This narrative appeared in the media too as *Christian Science Monitor*'s Edward Girardet called the Afghan rebellion 'a true Islamic revolution' bearing 'few if any parallels to Iran's'. He described its leaders as 'young and to an extent well-educated' and 'characterized by political moderation rather than the fanaticism Westerners tend to associate with the Islamic upheavals of today'.[20] The *mujahedeen*'s religious righteousness in the face of Soviet atheistic brutality was a theme repeated again and again in administration propaganda on Afghanistan. *Mujahedeen* supporters in the United States wanted more opportunities to promulgate these themes and raise the profile of the Afghan conflict than those afforded by the forums of international institutions or state visits to Afghan refugee camps. For this purpose, the administration set about orchestrating commemorations such as 'Afghanistan Day' to generate publicity and capture media attention.

The 'Afghanistan Day' propaganda programme

The European Parliament originally proposed the observance of 'Afghanistan Day' (21 March) in December 1981.[21] American members of the US Congress-European Parliament Action Group on Afghanistan then approached the Reagan administration about presenting a similar resolution in Congress.[22] The administration quickly recognized the contribution such an event could make to focusing public attention on Afghanistan and portraying Americans as 'champions of freedom, friends of the downtrodden, and enemies of oppression'.[23] Furthermore, it would be useful in reminding Congress of the 'burden' being borne by Pakistan in harbouring Afghan refugees, justifying continued US military and economic aid which remained a contentious issue.[24] The administration established a task force and joined forces with Congress, PVOs and other conservative interests to promote awareness of the day in the United States and internationally. The CFA was, yet again, deeply involved. It organized a letter-writing campaign directed at Congress and the administration, which pressed for a resolution recognizing Afghanistan Day. However, it seems that both branches of government were already committed to doing so.[25] Representative Don Ritter of the Congressional Task Force on Afghanistan was one of its primary sponsors in the House of Representatives, which unanimously endorsed the resolution.

In December 1981, the administration decided to adopt the European's proposal and develop a public diplomacy initiative around it. 'Afghanistan Day' would be celebrated on 21 March and so the administration needed to hastily set about establishing a task force to 'stimulate wide public participation' and generate and co-ordinate publicity around the day.[26] Ambassador Gerald Helman was tasked with talking to members of Congress and PVOs (the CFA was singled out) who would lend support to the programme. The Europeans were encouraged to take the lead and although members of the European Parliament had first proposed the idea there was scepticism within the State Department that 'their capabilities and motivations may be less than what might be optimum'. However, the administration was keen that 'Afghanistan Day' not appear 'US made'.[27] For this reason, officials encouraged Congress to delay their vote on recognizing the day until after the European Parliament's vote.[28] To counter perceived European apathy, Helman would travel to European capitals to rally support and liaise with British conservative *mujahedeen* supporter Lord Nicholas Bethell.[29] The administration hoped to further distance 'Afghanistan Day' from any Cold War context by presenting support for the initiative as ethnically, religiously and politically diverse. To ensure this the 'Afghanistan Day' proclamation signing ceremony in the White House was slated to feature 'representatives from all the ethnic groups' with an emphasis on 'those whose homelands are the victims of Soviet aggression'.[30] European sponsors would be invited along to 'demonstrate the international nature' of the day. The administration urged the Europeans (European Community 10) to encourage Muslim states to support the day to lend legitimacy and intended to approach the Saudis for their endorsement.[31] Messages of support and observance were sought from major religious denominations – Muslim, Jewish and Christian – on their respective holy days of Friday, Saturday and Sunday before the day ('Afghanistan Day' would take place on a Sunday in 1982).[32] Business, trade and labour organizations were called upon to advertise their support in major newspapers. Ensuring a bipartisan flavour to the initiative was prioritized with former presidents Nixon, Ford and Carter requested and acquiescing to publicly support the occasion as well as former Secretaries of State Henry Kissinger and Dean Rusk. Democrats as well as Republican members of Congress were invited to the signing ceremony. The administration was determined to fashion a propaganda campaign around 'Afghanistan Day', which drew in a wide selection of Americans as well as the international community in order to distance the event from its real roots in Cold War intrigues. However, they were also determined not to leave any element to chance and, to this end, sought to manipulate media interest and public involvement in the day.

The NSC enlisted Gray and Company, a public relations firm, to 'solicit media interest' in general though with an emphasis on the networks' evening news editors.[33] A concerted media onslaught was launched targeting selected print and broadcast media including *New York Times, Washington Post, Time, Wall Street Journal, Newsweek* and *US News and World Report*.[34] Events around the United States were co-ordinated by a private sector committee, created by the State Department but led by a private individual. The task force considered high-profile figures such as television evangelist Reverend Billy Graham and conservative commentator William Buckley for the role but in the end Nixon's former Secretary of State William P. Rogers was chosen.[35] Rogers's role was to orchestrate 'citizens' efforts' to mark 'Afghanistan Day' as well as co-ordinate the private sector's response. The administration would make officials available to testify at the congressional or European Parliament hearings on the 'Afghanistan Day' resolution to generate publicity. It would approach selected French and Dutch journalists and the 'French doctors' to gain 'impartial' testimony.[36] The President guaranteed further publicity for the day by mentioning it during his State of the Union address in January 1982.

'Afghanistan Day' provided 'an opportunity for global expressions of support for the principles of independence, self-determination, and freedom' but first administration rhetoric needed to ensure the public associated these traits with the Afghan resistance.[37] The President stressed these themes when he issued the proclamation. He spoke of *mujahedeen* heroism, fired by a passionate desire for freedom and self-determination, facing down Soviet brutality. Reagan praised Afghans as 'a nation of unsung heroes whose courageous struggle is one of the epics of our time'. He emphasized that the resistance's fight was for self-determination, distancing it from geopolitics, stating that 'the fire of resistance in Afghanistan is being kindled and sustained not by outside forces, but by the determination of the Afghan people to defend their national independence'. Rogers had arranged with James Beggs, the administrator of NASA, that the President would dedicate the launch of the space shuttle Columbia to 'the people of Afghanistan'.[38] Reagan took the opportunity to again highlight the *mujahedeen*'s noble desire for freedom stating:

> Just as the Columbia, we think, represents man's finest aspirations in the field of science and technology, so too does the struggle of the Afghan people represent man's highest aspirations for freedom. The fact that freedom is the strongest force in the world is daily demonstrated by the people of Afghan.

On the day of the signing ceremony, Reagan attended a gala ballet performance by the Joffrey Ballet in the Kennedy Center, Washington, which was to be dedicated to the Afghan resistance by the company's director, Robert Joffrey, who was of Afghan descent. Soviet Ambassador Anatoly Dobrynin had been due to attend too but declined upon hearing of the show's political agenda. The propaganda task force organized administration officials to be available for talk shows, press briefings and rallies around the United States on the day.[39] Yet another event was organized by the committee in the Kennedy Center on 'Afghanistan Day'. At this, Vice President Bush spoke in support of the Afghan insurgents before invited guests from the diplomatic, religious and various ethnic communities. Bush addressed the audience while holding a miniature 'butterfly' landmine, which he alleged the Soviets were using to attract and maim Afghan children.[40] Another speaker called them 'weapons of terror – disguised as children's toys'.[41] The fact that these landmines (PFM-1) were clones of a US army design, BLU-43 nicknamed 'dragon tooth', which were sown in Vietnam during the US engagement there, was not mentioned.[42] Other speakers used the platform to criticize the lack of press coverage of the war particularly as they alleged the US media was so ready to criticize US foreign policy. Don Ritter addressed this issue stating, 'the silence is deafening, broken by an occasional blip amid the din of El Salvador. The news teams have abandoned the most heinous rape of our time. Do we need criticism of the United States to get press attention?'[43] A slide show depicting the living conditions of the refugees in Pakistan was then shown, narrated by a former star of the silver screen, Joan Fontaine, herself a recent visitor to the camps. Outside, the CFA had organized a rally condemning the Soviet invasion. However, tensions between the CFA and the administration were evident as the rally organizers criticized the vice president for not coming out to address them and chided the administration for lifting the grain embargo.

The administration's propaganda proved effective as anti-Soviet demonstrations were held in the United States, India, West Germany and Pakistan some accompanied by chants of 'Death to Brezhnev'. Egypt mounted what US ambassador to the State, Alfred Atherton, called a 'major effort' in support of the day with rallies and speeches condemning the Soviets and praising Reagan and Congress. The day received widespread coverage on Egyptian television, which even played a thirteen-minute clip of a USICA video on Afghanistan released to coincide with events.[44] While 'Afghanistan Day' ostensibly marked the Afghan New Year, it also coincided with the start of the spring fighting season – a time when economic, political and psychological support for the *mujahedeen* was paramount – and the public diplomacy campaign developed by the Reagan administration to promote the commemoration served to facilitate this.

'Afghanistan Day' was not the only manufactured 'commemoration' developed by the administration to publicize the Afghan conflict. Each year, for the duration of the conflict, on the anniversary of the Soviet invasion (usually around 27 December), Reagan issued a statement to 'commemorate' this occasion. This generally involved familiar themes – lauding the 'Afghan Freedom Fighters' who 'because of the love of freedom of their countrymen, have been forced to flee for their lives' and promising the United States would always support the cause of a free Afghanistan. The Soviets were routinely denounced as imperialists who indiscriminately attacked civilians. The annual 'Captive Nations' proclamation was used to issue similar statements.[45]

The administration's rhetoric would continue to draw on Afghanistan to provoke the Soviets. Whilst calling for a meeting with Brezhnev, at the same time, the President was still repeating administration claims that the Soviets were using chemical weapons in Afghanistan and scattering mines disguised as toys.[46] On 3 June 1982, Casey outlined the role of the Afghan resistance in containing Soviet-backed terrorism:

> In the final analysis all these threats boil down to a struggle for the hearts and minds of men. The courage of the Afghan freedom fighters, supported by arms and training provided by other nations escalates the price and deters armed insurrection everywhere.[47]

George Shultz visited the Peshawar refugee camps in early July 1983 'to call world attention to the plight of these brave and hardy people'.[48] He met with *mujahedeen* and vowed publicly 'fellow fighters for freedom, we are with you' and later dined with Zia promising continued US aid for the Afghan programme.[49] However, while the President suggested the 'fire of resistance' had been lit by a desire in Afghans to 'defend their national independence' that was not quite the complete picture. Furthermore, Reagan's concern for the violation of 'basic human rights' in Afghanistan did not seem to extend to the rights of Afghan women, Prisoners of War (POWs) or minorities who suffered under the socially conservative, criminal and corrupt elements of the Peshawar Seven.

The *mujahedeen*: Reality versus rhetoric

The administration's propaganda campaign around the Afghan conflict guaranteed plenty of media exposure; however, the image presented of the insurgents did not always tally with the government's own intelligence on them. Reagan decried 'the brutal suppression of national sovereignty in Afghanistan' in his June 1981 'Captive Nations' proclamation speech calling for 'self-rule' to be extended to the peoples of the Captive Nations. However, an analysis of the Afghan resistance in a 'primer' prepared by the Peshawar Consul earlier that month described Afghanistan as largely tribal and illiterate and so not overly impressed by the nationalist ideologies put forward by the political parties in Peshawar.[50] An earlier CIA report confirmed this observing:

> The creation of a sense of national unity amongst the diverse peoples of Afghanistan has long been a challenging problem to its rulers. Afghanistan is a tribal society, composed of some 20 ethnic groups of widely varying backgrounds and cultures. About the only cohesive elements among these groups are their observance of Islamic law, martial tradition, and a distrust of government.[51]

In fact, the only one with any hope of unifying the Afghans was King Mohammed Zahir Shah who enjoyed support from many of the factions as well as representatives of the twenty-nine Afghan provinces, the nomads and expatriate former officials.[52] Nevertheless, the United States declined to engage with him bowing to Zia's concerns about the monarch's irredentist aspirations centred on the controversial Durand Line boundary between the two states.

Reagan's exhortation of the rebels as 'noble heroes', so deserving of Western support and compatible with Western political ideologies, did not reflect the reality on the ground. The CIA characterized the fundamentalists amongst the resistance as dedicated to 'turning back the clock on a number of social reforms' and disdainful of any 'aid from "superpower hegemonists" like the US'.[53] The *mujahedeen* were involved in drug smuggling with much of the heroin trafficked ending up in the United States and Europe but this was ignored by the administration. Resistance groups were suspected of summarily executing POWs.[54] While the administration graphically described Soviet atrocities, *mujahedeen* acts of appalling violence and infighting went unmentioned.[55] The CIA report described Hekmatyar's party, Hizb-i-Islami, as particularly effective politically and militarily with 'superb PR operations' but trailing a 'very bad reputation for strong armed-partisanship on both sides of the border'.[56] Nevertheless, the administration channelled the lion's share of US funding to Hekmatyar, cynically distancing itself from the warlord and his brutal tactics by implying that he was, in fact, in the pay of the KGB.[57]

Many Afghans viewed the rebel political parties in Peshawar as 'self-seeking and ineffective' and believed attempts at alliances only sought to 'simulate Afghan unity while preserving party jobs and power'.[58] Reagan lauded Pakistan for assuming the 'burden' of the massive refugee population fleeing the conflict across its borders. However, he paid no lip service to reports of the tensions this created locally or the violence and lawlessness in the Peshawar region as heavily armed *mujahedeen* groups fought one another for power and drug smuggling routes. They even engaged local Pakistani police in gunfights. The Politburo alleged that some refugees who wished to return home from the camps were forbidden to do so, sometimes forcibly, by the rebels as they were gaining financially from the continued crisis. The host governments of Pakistan and Iran were similarly benefitting from the inflow of aid.[59] Still, the administration would not let these flaws detract support or tarnish the public image of its newest Cold War surrogates. Instead, it ignored the more unsavoury aspects of the Afghan resistance and their Pakistani benefactors, particularly the treatment of Afghan women and girls who were voiceless within a resistance whose very spark had been the PDPA's challenge to Afghan's patriarchal culture.

The Afghan insurgency pre-dated the Soviet invasion and one of the chief aggravating factors precipitating it was the PDPA's efforts to improve the rights of Afghan women particularly in education – over 96 per cent of Afghan women were illiterate.[60] Decree Number 7, issued in 1978, outlawed both the payment of 'bride price' and forced marriage. Announcing the decree President Taraki stated it would end 'the sale of girls for good as hereafter nobody would be entitled to sell any girl or woman in this country'. When the voluntary literacy programme failed to take off as the family patriarch invariably chose not to allow 'his women' to be educated, the state sought to forcibly implement it. One man killed all the women in his family rather than suffer the 'dishonour' of seeing them receive a basic education. Afghanistan was one of the few countries at this time where female life expectancy was shorter than male due to a culture of 'widespread cruelty' towards women.[61] While in urban Afghanistan women gained equal rights under the communist regime, even becoming government ministers; in the Afghan refugee camps of Pakistan traditional patriarchy reasserted itself and was 'respected' by the mainly male aid workers from the UN and other voluntary organizations.[62] Afghanistan's communist-era school textbooks extolled women's heroic role in the 1978 revolution and called on them to 'become active participants in the social, political, and economic life of the homeland'.[63] Textbooks produced for the Peshawar refugee camps (with American aid) would promote a more chauvinistic and violent perspective for young Afghans to emulate.[64]

During the course of the insurgency, female schoolteachers and other educated women were intimidated and subject to targeted assassination by the *mujahedeen*. These human rights violations in Afghanistan garnered little attention in the West possibly because the anti-communist resistance perpetuated them. According to the Kirkpatrick Doctrine, the struggle against communism trumped the defence of human rights. It would become the silent story of the war although the CIA had documented such attitudes as far back as 1980.[65] The 'heroic struggle' lauded by the Reagan administration, the PVOs advocating for the *mujahedeen* and the media never addressed the position of women and how their systemic repression was accepted as part of traditional Afghan culture.

The Reagan administration relentlessly castigated the Soviet actions in Afghanistan and undoubtedly atrocities were committed and civilians suffered due to Moscow's military tactics. However, the Soviets also undertook a number of educational and social initiatives to benefit Afghanistan's people and culture – partly as a counterinsurgency strategy to 'win hearts and minds'. This involved creating athletic and cultural organizations for young Afghans, trips to summer camps in the USSR and other training and education opportunities in the USSR. Educational and cultural infrastructure was developed and Soviet museums bought Afghan art for display in the USSR. Discrimination against Afghanistan's Shi'a population was discouraged.[66]

Nevertheless, despite the unsavoury aspects of the Afghan resistance, and some of the positive Soviet/PDPA initiatives, or perhaps because of them, US propaganda continued to be deployed to generate support for their cause. And the USIA, as the public diplomacy agency of US government, had a particularly active role to play.

The USIA's public diplomacy campaign

Following on from Adelman's exhortations in *Foreign Affairs* a year beforehand, on 4 July 1982, the VOA began to broadcast into Afghanistan in Pashto – one of the country's major languages.[67] Carnes Lord, Walter Raymond and others urged the administration to allow the VOA to use 'stringers' (freelance journalists) to bolster the station's output on the conflict.[68] While increasing copy available to the VOA, it could also potentially undermine its providence by allowing reports generated from unknown or biased sources on air. This happened frequently in USIA documentaries, press conferences and film clips where sources linked to pro-*mujahedeen* organizations were interviewed or reported on the conflict but were presented to the viewer as impartial witnesses or experts. USIA output also reflected themes that the administration, various PVOs and members of Congress had continually emphasized in relation to Afghanistan – resistance unity, the Soviet use of chemical weapons and other 'terror tactics', and the 'poverty of means' available to the *mujahedeen* to fight back with.[69] In 'Afghanistan 1982: The Struggle for Freedom Continues' the unity of the Afghan people was stressed describing them as a 'rich mosaic of ethnic traditions'. It went on to declare that the 'entire country had risen, almost as a man, against the invader' as the Soviet invasion triggered a 'powerful collective will'. Contributors with links to PVOs such as Michael Barry appeared offering damning translations of *mujahedeen* allegations of Soviet atrocities – seeding Afghanistan with mines and using 'starvation tactics' to force people to flee their land, shooting innocents, raping women and girls, and destroying food stores and crops. Soviet bombs deliberately targeted hospitals.[70] Other contributors included Edward Girardet of *CSM* and Vladimir Bukovsky, founder of Radio Free Kabul – a CFA, and later Reagan administration, backed project.

USIA footage did not just rely on individuals from PVOs to generate suitable content but created its own news too. It orchestrated events such as Hollywood film actor Kurt Douglas's visit to the refugee camps in Peshawar from 23 to 27 November 1982, which generated 'very favorable' media reaction and garnered worldwide coverage.[71] While there, Douglas met with Zia and developed a 'warmly sympathetic relationship' with the dictator. This was further cemented when Douglas attended the State dinner given in Zia's honour during his visit to Washington a month later. Later, Douglas opined that Pakistan was less repressive of human rights than the Soviet Bloc and compared the state's Islamic-based law system as akin to Israel's privileging of Judaism.[72] While Douglas was instrumental in ending the 'Hollywood black-list', his lineage as the son of Russian-Jewish immigrants to the United States probably accounted for his strong dislike of the Soviet Union which seemed to be common amongst Soviet and Eastern Bloc exiles to the West. In Pakistan, Douglas reiterated administration propaganda that the Soviets were targeting Afghan children with 'toy bombs'. He shared a Thanksgiving Day meal with Afghan elders at a camp, demonstrating the administration's propaganda theme of the peaceful co-existence between Afghan and American traditions, and was then taken on the obligatory foreign dignitaries' visit to the Khyber Pass to gaze on the Afghan border.[73] Subsequently, Douglas appeared on the *Tonight Show, Good Morning America* and held a press conference (arranged by Gray and Company) on his visit attended by major international and US media organizations. Overall, the USIA considered it a great success and the film was produced and distributed with a title that conflated US traditions with Afghan hospitality – 'Thanksgiving in Peshawar'.[74]

Following NSDD 77 in 1983, the USIA's output on Afghanistan increased to include regular programmes which included the Afghan Digest, longer documentaries, 'Afghan weeks' at United States Information Service (USIS) posts and clips on TV Satellite File.[75] This created an almost-continuous stream of visual material infused with US anti-Soviet propaganda available for distribution internationally on the Afghan conflict. Much of this output was created in conjunction with, or featuring, conservative anti-communist organizations.

The USIA documentary 'Afghanistan: The Hidden War' was widely distributed to coincide with the Afghan Independence holiday in August. The hour-long programme, described as 'vivid and frequently horrifying', was made available to local television networks and dubbed in Arabic, Portuguese, English, French, Spanish, Bengali and Indonesian.[76] TV Satellite File clips alleged the Soviets machine-gunned livestock and burned crops as well as dropping 'toy bombs'.[77] 'Afghanistan: Caught in the Struggle' (1983) was produced by the Sarah Scaife Foundation, which funded many conservative causes including the Heritage Foundation and ARC.[78] It featured interviews with representatives from the pro-*mujahedeen* IRC, the CFA, controversial journalist Arnaud de Borchgrave and Ambassador Kirkpatrick.[79] It rehashed propaganda featuring 'toy bombs' in Afghanistan, the murder and maiming of children, and the use of chemical weapons by the Soviets. In it, de Borchgrave melodramatically attributes the *mujahedeen* with forming the only barrier halting the Red Army from storming the Persian Gulf – another long-standing propaganda theme of US Cold War hawks and pro-*mujahedeen* advocates.[80] In similar ominous tones, TV Satellite File clip warned that the Soviets could be in control of all of the Middle East and South Asia by the year 2000 if not stopped by the Afghan resistance, with some help of course from 'free' nations.[81]

'Afghan Digest: Number 2' (1983) featured AmeriCares for Afghanistan as did TV Satellite File: Number 75 (1984).[82] Zbigniew Brzezinski, who was involved with AmeriCares, appeared in TV Satellite Number 29 while 'We Are Afghanistan' featured Dr Robert Simon and *Medecins Sans Frontières (MSF)*, which was very active in Afghanistan at the time and had adopted a forceful anti-communist political ideology in its activism. During the 1980s, *MSF* membership underwent an ideological schism about the desirability of maintaining neutrality in conflict situations.[83] In 1985, *MSF* created a think tank – *Fondation Liberté Sans Frontières* – which reflected its anti-communist ideology and challenged 'Third Worldism'. Essentially, few of the contributors to these USIA programmes could be described as non-partisan. This output was largely propaganda masquerading as news stories.

The USSR reacted with outrage to USIA output and described it as 'blatant, unbridled forgery' featuring CIA-funded mercenaries and 'professional anti-Soviet writers'.[84] At this stage, Soviet public opinion was becoming increasingly hostile to the war leaving the Politburo more vulnerable to negative international opinion. Although official Soviet media reports gave little exposure to this discontent until increased press freedoms under Gorbachev's glasnost policies (post-1985), reports did begin to trickle out in 1983 undoubtedly creating disaffection amongst Soviet publics with the conflict.

As well as its visual output, the USIA sponsored 'conferences' on Afghanistan. Again, these featured speakers linked to PVOs or the administration such as the one held in California in November 1983.[85] The conference co-ordinator, Ralph Magnus, was also AmeriCares for Afghans' director and a former USIA officer in Kabul. Papers were presented by Robert Neumann of ARC, Thomas Gouttierre, director of the Center for Afghanistan Studies at the University of Nebraska and Harmon E. Kirby of the State Department amongst others. The introductory paper made no secret of its bias declaring that the conferences participants 'all shared the fundamental belief that the Soviet Union's actions in Afghanistan have constituted a dangerous and illegitimate use of force, even terror, against a hitherto independent and nonaligned state'. Furthermore, all agreed that 'there was little to be added to the free exchange of ideas by having Soviet representatives present (presuming they would have come in any case)'. Essentially, the conference was a public diplomacy exercise rather than an effort to promote discourse and debate. Similar 'conferences' would take place over the rest of the decade held by the USIA and PVOs to publicize a Cold War-tinted perspective on the war in Afghanistan. However, using PVOs to distance the US government from Afghan-related propaganda was not just a USIA ruse but extended more widely through the efforts of the Interagency Working Group on Afghanistan.

The Reagan administration, propaganda and the PVOs

As the Afghan conflict entered its fourth year private 'political action' initiatives by PVOs were already extensive and increasingly entangled with both the executive and the legislature. By spring 1984, the Interagency Restricted Working Group on Afghanistan was seeking to co-ordinate all 'political action' in support of the Afghan rebels. This would include 'covert, overt, public, private' programmes and projects such as setting up 'private' 'Friends of Afghanistan' committees as well as liaising with organizations such as ARC and AmeriCares and supporting initiatives developed by PVOs such as Radio Free Kabul.[86]

Radio Free Kabul was conceived by writer and Soviet dissident Vladimir Bukovsky aided by the French philosopher Bernard Henri Levy. Bukovsky was not solely concerned with Afghanistan but had a wider anti-communist agenda. He was a foundering member of Resistance International – an organization which sought to rally anti-communist 'freedom fighters' internationally – and was also involved with the pro-*Contra* group, PRODEMCA, as were a number of others *mujahedeen* advocates.[87] At this time, Bukovsky was living in London following twelve years of various types of imprisonment in the Soviet Union for dissident activity for which he was subsequently deported. From its early days, Radio Free Kabul was supported by the CFA as well as a British support committee led by conservative parliamentarian Winston S. Churchill.[88] Funded from Britain and America via the exclusive private bank, Coutts and Co., the radio station was run by the resistance groups in Peshawar.[89] Bukovsky set up Radio Free Kabul in 1981; however, by 1983 the station was shut down due to financial and technical problems.[90] At this stage, the Reagan administration committed to funding the project, which satisfied the administration's Afghan policies of engaging with 'private' interests and widening the distribution of its propaganda.

The ARC also had close connections to the administration. It mainly outsourced the distribution of its aid to voluntary agencies operating in the region such as the IRC.[91] Back in the United States, ARC worked to raise the profile of the Afghan refugee situation as well as funds via its many influential friends. In September 1981, ARC and IRC hosted a benefit dinner at the opening of the Second Annual Afghan Fair with guests including CIA Chief William Casey, Representative Don Ritter, ARC co-founder and former Ambassador Robert Neumann, former Assistant Secretary of State for Near East Affairs, Harold Saunders and Arnaud de Borchgrave. After dinner, guests watched a film titled 'Courage Is Our Weapon'. This was produced by Joanne Herring, a close friend of Charles Wilson who had inspired the Congressman's interest in Afghanistan, and Charles Fawcett, a well-connected adventurer who would go on to establish the International Medical Corps with Dr Robert Simon to set up clinics within Afghanistan. While filming on location in Afghanistan, Herring and Fawcett had met, and greatly liked, Gulbuddin Hekmatyar – the Islamic fundamentalist leader who would become notorious for his ruthlessness and virulent anti-Westernism in later years. Subsequently, Wilson would also have dealings with Hekmatyar. Later, Fawcett toured the film around the United States and internationally including a screening at CIA headquarters.[92]

The AmeriCares organization also provided aid to Afghanistan and had links that spanned Congress and the administration. Senator Gordon Humphrey was on the AmeriCares advisory committee, which was described as 'composed mostly of well-connected, politically conservative individuals, many with ties to presidential administrations or experience in intelligence of foreign affairs'.[93] In 1983, its honorary chairperson, Zbigniew Brzezinski, announced the foundation's plans to airlift medical supplies to the Afghan *mujahedeen* and refugees promising that this was 'not a political effort, it is not designed to advance any foreign policy objective'.[94] However, this was not an honest characterization of aid agency's mission. AmeriCares director, Robert Macauley, was an old friend of George H.W. Bush who, on occasion, accompanied him to meet arriving airlifts of aid.[95] Prescott Bush Jr. was amongst its advisory committee.[96] Macauley consulted with the vice president before setting up an AmeriCares' Afghan programme, and Ralph Magnus was assigned project director. The organization received numerous letters of appreciation/endorsement from the President and vice president. In May 1984, the administration made plans to arrange a humanitarian aid drop to the refugee camps in Peshawar to accompany the vice president's visit; however, the Department of State could not arrange this in time and AmeriCares and the Pentagon stepped in to ensure the supplies were delivered – hardly an apolitical act from the charity.[97] Following this, AmeriCares proposed working with the administration to provide humanitarian aid to the Afghans, and the Afghanistan Working Group enthusiastically endorsed this.[98] This would be private–public partnership whereby the administration would grant aid to AmeriCares to the tune of $2,775,000 who would then funnel aid to the 'French doctors' working within Afghanistan allowing the administration to remain at a remove from direct interference in the state. AmeriCares would undertake to privately raise funds of $1,600,000 that would be sent to the Afghan interior in cash, which the US government could not be seen to do.[99]

While some private organizations would co-operate and co-ordinate with the Reagan administration, others targeted or were closely aligned with members of Congress. These PVOs sought to further their aims of increased aid or political support for Afghan insurgency by lobbying Congress directly or via the media sometimes creating friction between the two branches of government over policy towards the resistance. Along with the CFA, the Federation for American-Afghan Action (FAAA) pursued this avenue of influence. Andrew Eiva, a former army officer based in Boston, established the FAAA and the Free Afghanistan Alliance following time spent in Pakistan training *mujahedeen*. He worked with Winston Churchill Jr. to develop Radio Free Kabul and with Bukovsky on 'Operation Bastille' that was involved with Soviet POWs and defectors within Afghanistan.[100] Eiva also supported other anti-communist organizations such as the Polish resistance, Solidarity, and sat on the Captive Nations Committee for New England. Eiva started out as the Afghan lobbyist for a conservative organization called Free the Eagle and continued to work from its offices while running the FAAA as did other insurgency lobby groups such as RENAMO and the American Angolan Public Affairs Council.[101] These offices were in the Heritage Foundation building near Capitol Hill that also housed the CFA – bitter rivals of the FAAA.[102]

Eiva claimed authorship of the 1984 Senate resolution for 'effective aid' to the *mujahedeen* and persuaded Democrat Senator Paul Tsongas to be its main sponsor. He was also close to Senator Gordon Humphrey – a committed *mujahedeen* supporter. Eiva described the resolution, which called for increased aid to the Afghans, as attractive to congressional members wishing to reduce defence spending as it represented a 'bargain basement approach to damage Soviet military power'.[103] Eiva believed it necessary to reframe the Afghan issue within the parameters of 'broad American idealistic and economic interests as opposed to narrow ethnic ones to avoid ethnic backlash'. Eiva had received financial support from Paul Weyrich, co-founder of the Heritage Foundation, and many other conservative, New Right lobby groups.[104] Later, Eiva would claim to Congress that not all the aid earmarked for the *mujahedeen* was reaching its destination but rather was being diminished by corruption along the pipeline. This would prompt unwelcome investigations by Congress into the CIA's operation and heighten tensions between the legislature and the intelligence agency.

Rosanne Klass, director of the Afghan Information Center at Freedom House, also appeared before a number of congressional hearings advocating the *mujahedeen*'s cause.[105] Writing in the *New York Times* in January 1982, she echoed Tsongas's appeal for 'effective aid' in the form of 'antiaircraft and antitank weapons, medical supplies, the guns and the bullets they need and lack'. She contended that although the *mujahedeen* in Pakistan lacked unity, within Afghanistan the people were united against the Soviets and more than willing to continue fighting. She detailed alleged Soviet atrocities and compared them to the Second World War massacres such as Lidice, Katyn Forest and Babi Yar. Klass emphasized parallels between the Afghan resistance's motivations and US political ideals recalling a *mujahedeen* commander who asked Klass 'do you think Americans are the only ones who care about freedom?'

In April 1982, Heritage commissioned a poll, relayed in the media, which found 52 per cent of Americans supported arming the *mujahedeen* and other resistance fighters. The PVOs contributed to this support for the Afghan resistance with propaganda efforts in the media and at congressional hearings. Their agenda was varied ranging from propping up administration foreign policy on Afghanistan to a larger anti-communist crusade gathering in any rebel group, of any provenance, challenging communist regimes. For those PVOs and individuals committed to the latter, Afghanistan was merely a means to an end.

Congressional *mujahedeen* advocates

While the pro-*mujahedeen* PVOs certainly sought to influence Congress, many members of Congress had been advocating on behalf of the Afghan resistance from its early days. While the administration had to convince Congress to support its plans for Pakistan or its CBW programme, in the case of Afghanistan some in Congress were pressing the administration to demonstrate its allegiance to the *mujahedeen* more forthrightly in public. Since mid-1980, Representative Charles Wilson had used his position on the Defense Appropriations Committee to secretly divert funds to Afghanistan; others sought to raise the Afghans' profile to encourage the administration to increase aid. On 14 April 1981, fifteen Congress members representing both houses wrote to the President. They urged him to send 'a high level mission to the refugee camps in Pakistan' to 'highlight the attention of the United States on the tragedy that is taking place in Afghanistan' and 'once again focus the attention of the entire free world on the brutality of the illegal Soviet invasion and the harsh occupation of Afghanistan'. Soon after, representatives Pritchard and Ritter joined a State Department delegation to the Pakistan refugee camps – a journey many Congress members would make over the following years. In 1983, the troop of US political figures to Pakistan continued with a bipartisan congressional party led by Representative Clarence D. Long, who, at Wilson's urging, met with Zia and visited the refugee camps. Zia outlined the *mujahedeen*'s desperate need for anti-aircraft weaponry, which encouraged Long to support Wilson's appropriation of Defense Department funds for the Afghans. Afghanistan would become a *cause celebre* for congressmen. For those in Congress who stymied administration efforts to support the Nicaraguan Contras, Afghanistan offered them an opportunity to assert their anti-communism credentials.

In 1982, Senator Tsongas set up the bipartisan Afghan Task Force to advocate for the *mujahedeen* and critique the administration's policies. While Congress frustrated the government's policy on Nicaragua, it urged increased assistance to the Afghans accusing the administration of a policy of 'fighting to the last Afghan'.[106] At a press conference on 30 September 1982, surrounded by *mujahedeen* leaders, Tsongas announced the introduction of the resolution (which had ninety-nine co-sponsors). He called on the administration to provide 'material assistance' to the Afghan resistance arguing it was 'indefensible to provide the freedom fighters with only enough aid to fight and die, but not enough to advance their cause of freedom'. The first Tsongas Resolution did not get passed, blocked by CIA opponents who were already providing material aid to the *mujahedeen* and who feared exposure of their operation and the implications of this for Pakistan.[107] Republican Senator Charles Mathias also resisted due to concerns about making binding promises to the *mujahedeen* and undermining the ongoing UN peace negotiations.[108] Ultimately, the administration acceded to congressional wishes, after much wrangling, and authorized an increase in aid to the *mujahedeen* in late 1982. Along with Democrats Tsongas and Wilson, Gordon Humphrey (R-N.H), Don Ritter (R-Pa.) and Orrin Hatch (R-UT) would be consistent supporters of the Afghan resistance.[109] Ritter sponsored Tsongas's resolution in the House and eventually the Tsongas-Ritter resolution was passed though following a wording change from 'material' to 'effective' aid. Not all conservative interests approved of the congressmen's actions though with the Heritage Foundation denouncing it as little more than 'congressional rhetoric', which, in any case, would have been unnecessary had the administration acted appropriately to support the Afghans.[110]

Conclusion

The Reagan Doctrine funnelled military, financial and rhetorical support to insurgents resisting what the administration believed to be Soviet-backed or -inspired governments. In Afghanistan, the government was clearly supported by Moscow and along with the Red Army's presence enabled this conflict, above all others under the Reagan Doctrine, to be presented as an unambiguous battle against Soviet imperialism. However, on closer examination it was apparent that the *mujahedeen*'s concept of freedom was a world away from that of Americans' as it sought to alienate or subjugate swathes of Afghan society. Their 'noble heroics' were shadowed by violence and corruption. The fundamentalist Islam practised by some of these 'freedom fighters' held no common cause with Christianity, or moderate Islam. Propaganda was not just desirable but essential to reframe these rebels as suitable representatives of Afghan society and to justify US support. In the Cold War great game between posturing superpowers, the Reagan administration considered international criticism as important in 'forcing a change of the Soviet position as battlefield losses'.[111] Such was Washington's belief in the power of propaganda that the administration and other *mujahedeen* supporters were unwilling to wait for opportunities to crop up instead creating them with manufactured occasions like 'Afghanistan Day'. The administration sought to distance itself from its own propaganda and thereby boost its credibility by engaging with the private sector. This accorded too with the wider Reagan administration ideology of privatization or outsourcing of government programmes wherever possible. However, while the PVOs and Congress reinforced administration actions they also had their own motivations for endorsing the Afghan resistance. Some members of Congress saw it as a way to establish anti-communist credentials in the face of their resistance to aid to the Nicaraguan Contras that had drawn conservative ire. Many in the PVOs supported an anti-communist agenda extending beyond the Afghan conflict and liaised with or were members of other anti-communist causes such as PRODEMCA. Again, for them, Afghanistan provided a perfect propaganda opportunity devoid of the ambiguities, which marred public perceptions of other Reagan Doctrine 'revolutions'. Strains were evident within and between these actors though – the FAAA distrusted the CFA, the CFA fell out with the administration and Heritage criticized Congress and the Tsongas Resolution. All in all, these interrelationships were tense and tentative beneath the surface. However, on the face of it an overarching narrative centred on the nobility, heroism and representative nature of the Afghan 'freedom fighters' facing unbridled Soviet brutality gathered momentum aiding the next project of the US *mujahedeen* advocates – the supply of Stinger missiles to the resistance.

4

Justifying escalation in Afghanistan

As the war dragged on into its fifth year, the objectives of the Afghan *mujahedeen*'s supporters in the United States crystallized and certain goals converged. In 1984, hawks in the administration began to believe that something greater than a policy designed to be merely 'tactically sufficient to make life miserable for the Soviets' was now possible and that, in fact, the Soviets could be 'rolled back' or forced out of the Afghanistan.[1]

Hawks outside the administration like Brzezinski characterized Afghanistan as a 'watershed event' in the Cold War, which would enable America to shake off its 'Vietnam syndrome' once and for all.[2] America's superpower status had slipped somewhat in the preceding decade and many allies saw US actions in the international arena as much a threat to world peace as those of the Soviet Union. To address this, some in foreign policy circles believed that American military might needed to be re-asserted and such 'moral equivalence' challenged.[3]

The Soviet engagement in Afghanistan would provide propaganda material that would help facilitate such aims. The Soviet invasion was described as expansionary necessitating a robust American foreign policy reaction, and a renewed military, to check it. Accounts of Soviet actions within Afghanistan would portray the communists as ruthless and disdainful of human rights or the conventions of war. This was contrasted with US supposedly selfless support for 'freedom' and 'self-determination' worldwide. Ultimately, such characterizations would be used to justify the administration's decision to radically upgrade the quantity and quality of armaments supplied to the *mujahedeen* and, for the first time, to supply US-made weapons to the resistance.

In 1984, Reagan's landslide election victory coincided with the Republicans' retaining the Senate and making inroads into the Democrats' House majority. Congressional Democrats needed a stronger, unified stance on foreign policy to re-align with public sentiment and Afghanistan would provide an unambiguous platform for this.[4] As Democratic Representative Charles Wilson pointed out, 'I don't know anybody who wants to be against backing religious Freedom Fighters against the atheistic hordes from the North – you just can't make a case against it'. In October 1984, the Afghan programme benefitted from a significant increase in funding, largely due to the efforts of Wilson. NSDD 166 – 'US Policy, Programs and Strategy in Afghanistan' signed in March 1985 – provided retrospective justification for this funding surge promising that 'everybody gets to do what everybody wants to do'.[5] This would prove a defining period in this latter-day imperial battle in Central Asia.

Propaganda was utilized by all those involved to advance the Afghan rebels' cause and, consequently, their own goals. The Reagan administration sought to convince its international allies and the American public that the *mujahedeen*'s cause justified support and was not just an opportunity for Cold War posturing. It needed Congress to continue to authorize Pakistan's military aid package to secure the arms supply route into Afghanistan and maintain its strategic foothold in the region.[6] Furthermore, the administration aspired to inciting domestic opposition to the war within the USSR in the hope of internally destabilizing its rival. For their part, congressional supporters formed the bipartisan Congressional Task Force on Afghanistan, which began to hold regular hearings aimed at highlighting the situation in Afghanistan. Meanwhile, the various PVOs and conservative think tanks were active in many differing capacities, sometimes bolstering administration policies by partaking in USIA initiatives and at other times agitating against the administration and the CIA for perceived inadequate action on Afghanistan.

From the alphabet soup of *mujahedeen* supporters and mixed bag of agendas, one issue gained precedence and became the focus of a concerted campaign – the Afghan rebels were militarily under-equipped and required more sophisticated weaponry, particularly anti-aircraft missiles such as the US-made Stinger. This argument reflected the 1984 Tsongas-Ritter Resolution demand that the rebels receive 'effective aid' and its implementation was pursued by an alliance of PVOs, congressional members and 'bleeders' within the administration.[7] The determination of the *mujahedeen*'s supporters that the rebels should be equipped with Stinger missiles helped to precipitate NSDD 166 and a new direction for the Afghan programme which, in turn, provided the authorization and funding for the supply of American-made weapons to the Afghan rebels. Various supporters of the Afghan resistance began to press for this objective while, at the same time, the administration sought to improve America's international standing by contrasting its own 'moral' foreign policies with Soviet's 'immoral' actions of which it offered Afghanistan as a prime example. Propaganda was intrinsic to achieving both aims.

Justifying American foreign policy

From late 1983 into early 1984, the United States had tarnished its credentials internationally and strained relations with its allies. This was largely due to the divisive decision to deploy Intermediate Nuclear Forces (INF) missiles in Western Europe: disagreement with its Western European allies over the Trans-Siberian gas pipeline, its aggressive stance towards Nicaragua and its intervention in Grenada.[8] Although popular in the United States, Reagan's decision to invade the small Caribbean island of Grenada in October 1983, ostensibly to rescue American medical students, resulted in widespread criticism from America's Western European allies (including its staunch ally, the UK) and the UN. Many believed that the United States was just as given to intervention in other states as the Soviets while some 40 per cent of Western Europeans judged the two superpowers as equally untrustworthy.[9] Such 'moral equivalence' outraged some within the administration and US conservative circles. Efforts were undertaken to redress these perceptions. However, these negative views were unlikely to be shifted easily by straightforward public diplomacy particularly as the United States was also suspected of a readiness to use disinformation to further its foreign policy aims.

Worryingly, US allies also began to doubt its military strength believing the two superpowers to be roughly on a par. This was informed, ironically, by the administration's and its supporters' own scare-mongering about a Soviet military build-up in the preceding years which had been used to justify the need for increased military expenditure. While some European allies believed such a balance of power helped keep conflict at bay, it did not fit easily with the Reagan administration's doctrine of peace through strength.[10] To remedy this, the Reagan administration wished to upgrade its INF in Western Europe, in the face of much public discontent.[11]

To defend the administration's military objectives as necessary and counter growing cynicism about US policies, officials orchestrated a public diplomacy campaign. This characterized the Soviet Union as an expansionary empire, threatening its neighbours, as evidenced in Afghanistan. In contrast, US policies were depicted as ethical and grounded in universal principles and again Afghanistan provided the example. One of the chief proponents of this public diplomacy posture was Ambassador Jeane Kirkpatrick. In an address before the Royal Institute of International Affairs in early 1984, she condemned the growing belief amongst European publics and media that there was little moral difference between the actions and objectives of the two superpowers.[12] Kirkpatrick contended that the United States used force to liberate Grenada whilst the Soviet Union used force to conquer and victimize Afghans. Private think tanks were brought on board to help shore up this portrayal of the conflicting characteristics of the two superpowers. The conservative Shavano Institute for National Leadership, at the request of the State Department, held a conference in May 1985 featuring Kirkpatrick and many other conservative thinkers and writers. Entitled 'Moral Equivalence: False Images of US and Soviet Values', the conference received widespread media coverage in the United States.[13] Such non-government forums enhanced the credibility of the administration's message. This reflected the objectives for communicating government information outlined in NSDD 130, from March 1984, which stated:

> It is important to recognise that information disseminated by private and commercial organizations is likely to have special credibility with many audiences. A high priority should be placed on improving liaison and cooperation with, and support of, appropriate private sector information efforts.

Presidential rhetoric on the Afghan conflict was another fundamental element of this propaganda campaign. At a welcoming ceremony for King Fahd of Saudi Arabia in February 1985, the President spoke of the shared American and Saudi Arabian 'deep moral outrage' at 'the continuing aggression and butchery taking place in Afghanistan'. In his State of the Union address a month earlier, Reagan had cautioned against American 'innocence' in a 'world that's not innocent'. He exhorted that 'freedom' was 'under siege' and American 'support for freedom fighters was self-defense'. In

December, the President used the Bill of Rights/Human Rights Day proclamation to denounce the Soviets for having 'slaughtered innocent women and children', deployed poison gas and used toy bombs to cripple Afghan children. By comparison, Americans were portrayed as proud 'champions of freedom and human rights the world over' whose belief in the 'dignity of man and government by the consent of the people lies at the heart of our national character and the soul of our foreign policy'. However, the President's idealized image of America as an 'empire of liberty' contrasted with its foreign policy which condemned the 1984 Nicaraguan elections, though widely accepted internationally as free and fair whilst propping up a homicidal regime in El Salvador. The administration was determined to convince sceptical international publics of America's moral and military credentials and a firm stand on Afghanistan. The campaign encompassed more than rhetoric though as USIA programming, 'a strategic instrument of US national policy', was deployed to bolster it.[14]

In fact, USIA programmes on the Afghan conflict were intrinsic to the US policy to undermine the Soviet Union and justify US foreign policies. 'Afghan Digest, Number Two' offers a striking example of the agency's propaganda output on this subject. The programme's opening sequence shows Russian/Soviet expansion from its origins as Muscovy in 1462 through Russia in 1533, 1646 and 1801, and in 1917, 1933 and 1945 as the Soviet Union. It culminates in 1979 with a dramatic drum roll and a question mark over Afghanistan.[15] USIA output presented the Soviet Union as operating solely in its strategic interests in Afghanistan and of committing horrendous atrocities. It accused the Soviet Union of acting 'immorally' while the United States only sought to guarantee freedom and self-determination in Afghanistan. USIA programmes were presented in various formats such as documentaries or 'news clip' compendiums and often used individuals connected to pro-*mujahedeen* PVOs to narrate, analyse or bear witness to events in Afghanistan.

The fifth anniversary of the invasion of Afghanistan fell on 27 December 1984 and the administration decided to use the commemoration to frame a propaganda initiative.[16] The Interagency Working Group on Afghanistan considered it ripe for exploitation as it could help

> focus US and world attention on the continuation of the Afghan struggle, the brutal Soviet occupation, the admirable stand of Pakistan, and our desire to reach a negotiated political settlement – in the context not only of our Afghanistan policy but of our Soviet policy.[17]

The propaganda programme was wide ranging involving USIA output, a Senate resolution and an effort to encourage the major television network news programmes to cover the anniversary. Allies were urged to issue strong-worded statements condemning the Soviets, and *mujahedeen* leaders would make an appeal for worldwide support for their struggle. Senior officials would make statements and speeches, attend media briefings and appear on news shows. The President made a statement which lauded the rebels' 'noble struggle' and linked it to US political ideals stating, 'the Afghan people are writing a new chapter in the history of freedom' and 'we cannot and will not remain silent on Afghanistan'.[18]

The administration sent diplomatic demarches to NATO nations, the Islamic conference and ANZUS and ASEAN treaty states calling for support and statements and hoped to time the arrival of its latest humanitarian aid package to the Afghans to coincide with the commemoration.[19] The Interagency Working Group undertook to 'place articles in the media' and brief 'friendly journalists'. It hoped to co-ordinate with outside groups and individuals on activities around the anniversary. The Interagency Working Group scheduled Afghan-born Dr Zalmay Khalilzad for appearances in Egypt, Saudi Arabia and England as part of their Islamic-focused public diplomacy campaign.

Khalilzad was connected to other Afghan advocates and organizations. He was acquainted with Thomas Gouttierre of ARC and the UNO since his youth and Brzezinski whom he had worked closely with at Columbia University.[20] He would later work for the State Department under the neo-conservative Paul Wolfowitz.[21] As far back as 1979, Khalilzad had advocated US intervention in the Afghan Civil War.[22] He was, along with Brzezinski and others, involved in a PVO called Friends of Afghanistan, which Rosanne Klass of Freedom House once described as a State Department front organization.[23] On 17 December, Khalilzad gave a foreign policy briefing at the Washington Press Center stating that the Soviets had no intention of compromising on Afghanistan and their military tactics deliberately targeted civilians and crops.[24] Khalilzad argued Soviet control of Afghanistan provided a platform for the USSR to project its power further afield and that nearby states saw the Soviet move as part of a 'struggle for the destiny of the region as a whole'.

The Soviet's alleged geostrategic intentions in the region and deliberate targeting of crops and civilians were echoed in media opinion pieces by pro-*mujahedeen* advocates such as Freedom House's Klass.[25] Another PVO member with government connections, Theodore Eliot, co-founder of ARC and dean of the Fletcher School of Law and Diplomacy, presented one of the USIA's 'Electronic Dialogue' programmes.[26] Eliot's monologue alleged geostrategic motivations for the Soviet invasion including its age-old desire for a warm water port and control of Persian Gulf oil. He contrasted these with US intentions in Vietnam, which he argued were rooted solely in the desire to protect democracy.[27] However US goals related to Afghanistan were also geostrategic as opposed to idealistic in nature as NSDD 147, 'US Policy towards India and Pakistan' from October 1984, demonstrates.[28]

NSDD 147 assessed that 'the Soviet expansionary thrust into Afghanistan and the collapse of the Shah in Iran [had] heightened the strategic significance of the South Asian region for US global interests'. Back in 1983, State Department official Thomas Thornton argued that the Soviet invasion of Afghanistan had alienated surrounding Muslim states. He believed that the invasion provided 'a vehicle for the reintroduction of American interests in South Asia (as well as the Persian Gulf)'.[29] The United States needed to dislodge Soviet influence in the region, retain Pakistan as a regional ally and increase international attention on Afghanistan. Yet again, the administration considered propaganda instrumental to achieving its foreign policy objectives. As a result, NSDD 147 recommended the preparation 'for SPG approval a more active and far-reaching public diplomacy strategy for improving foreign and domestic understanding of and support for US policy in South Asia and Afghanistan'.

US gains could be consolidated by propaganda, which provoked anti-Soviet sentiment in the USSR's 'Muslim belt' that William Casey, echoing Winston Churchill, described as the 'soft underbelly' of the Soviet Union. NSDD 166 advocated using Afghanistan to isolate the Soviets from Third World and Islamic states stating that achieving such 'interim objectives [would] be in the US national interest, regardless of the ultimate outcome of the struggle in Afghanistan'. USIA research estimated that by 2000 one quarter to one third of all children born in the Soviet Union would be Muslim.[30] However, the United States had some obstacles to its objective of seeding unrest amongst Soviet Muslims. Reports from the CIA and USIA showed that Soviet Muslims were largely content and 'unlikely to be politically disruptive'. It reported that over the years, Moscow had reached a 'modus vivendi' which involved turning a blind eye to Muslim practices, often permitting Islamic festivals to be celebrated under secular guises. The report stated that Islam's potential as a rallying point for opposition to Russian rule depended 'to a great extent on the identification with it by today's youth'.[31] To this end, Casey approached the Pakistanis about sending subversive propaganda into the Soviet Muslim republics via Afghanistan.[32] Korans and books detailing Soviet atrocities in Uzbekistan and encouraging Central Asian culture and nationalism were dispatched as the Reagan administration, yet again, cultivated a strategy on the Afghan conflict originally conceived by Brzezinski and Carter.[33] The State Department's Project Democracy allocated $60,000 to fund Muslim 'thinkers and writers' to develop and legitimize the links between Islamic and democratic principles and practices.[34] Project Democracy offered further funding of $585,000 to establish a 'Center for Afghan Democratic Studies'. This would seek to inculcate 'democratic procedures and concepts' amongst the Afghan refugee population in Pakistan to 'rebuild' Afghan democracy following the eventual Soviet withdrawal.[35] The United States was determined to undo the relatively successful relationship Moscow had fostered between Soviet Muslims and secular communism and ensure that such a relationship was undermined in Afghanistan too.[36]

In Pakistan, the strategic lynchpin of US foreign plans for the region,[37] public opinion polls showed distrust of the United States – a preference for neutrality and widespread support for the development of nuclear weapons.[38] These attitudes presented real obstacles to the congressional support vital for the continuance of Pakistan's aid package. By October 1985, US intelligence believed Pakistan had produced an atomic weapon with Chinese aid just two months after Congress had enacted the Pressler Amendment to the Foreign Assistance Act. This law required the President to certify annually that Pakistan did not possess nuclear weapons in order to activate Pakistan's aid.[39] Congressional suspicion along with press revelations about Pakistan's nuclear programme left the administration negotiating a legal and ethical tightrope to maintain support for its South Asian ally.

The administration sought to present its foreign policy as guided by high-minded ideals of freedom and democracy. Instead, as NSDD 147 and NSDD 166 demonstrate, it was motivated by geostrategic concerns not dissimilar to the Soviet Union. To this end, it was willing to incubate unrest in Soviet Muslim states and seek to isolate the Soviets from Islamic states. Meanwhile, the State Department's Project Democracy attempted to foster links between Islamic and liberal democratic philosophies. The

Soviet invasion of its neighbour was presented as part of a larger strategy targeting the Persian Gulf which justified renewed military spending by the United States to check. To facilitate this the administration was willing to deceive Congress about Pakistan's nuclear ambitions while presenting the United States, in speeches, news articles, international forums and USIA programming as solely concerned with supporting the Afghan 'freedom fighters' and their struggle against the 'evil empire'. Escalation of the conflict in Afghanistan would further promote these goals.

Justifying escalation in Afghanistan

In March 1984, Selig Harrison found Kabul quiet and posited in a *Washington Post* article that 'the Soviets [were] winning in Afghanistan'.[40] This validated the contention of some *mujahedeen* advocates that the rebels lacked effective, modern military hardware particularly anti-aircraft missiles and that the administration and the CIA were shying away from such support. In NSDD 147, the administration outlined its aim to reassure Congress about Pakistan's nuclear intentions to secure its aid pipeline to the Afghan rebels; however, a core group of senators and representatives were already dedicated to upgrading the military capabilities of the *mujahedeen*. Inspired by Charlie Wilson's exuberant tales an increasing number of congressmen began to visit Peshawar. A *Los Angeles Times* article titled 'Afghan Rebel Gateway; Peshawar: Many Lured by Intrigue' describes how such foreign visitors would be given the 'Peshawar Package Tour'. This consisted of a visit to a model refugee camp, a meeting with Afghan elders, a tribal dance display and finally the obligatory photo opportunity at the Khyber Pass. At one stage, the Peshawar consulate had to ask for a break following nine unbroken weekends of VIP visits from the United States.[41] Such adventures served to enhance congressional support for the Afghan rebels.

To justify increased military supplies to the *mujahedeen*, congressional supporters needed to characterize the rebel leadership in Peshawar as a unified expression of the Afghan people's political aspirations. To this end, the Senate Committee on Foreign Relations issued a press release on 27 March 1984 to highlight a recent report, which urged the US government to recognize an Afghan government-in-exile.[42] The committee asserted that the resistance had made 'considerable progress toward unification'. It recognized that the United States had to tread carefully and act in consultation with Islamic states to avoid justifying Soviet propaganda that cast US support for the rebels in a Cold War light. Nevertheless, a unified resistance could be recognized as a government-in-exile and would then be entitled to open US support. However, this unification was proving very difficult to achieve.

A CIA report from early 1984, 'The Afghan Resistance: The Struggle for Unity', stated 'the Afghan resistance is divided into hundreds of different groups. Significant disagreements exist even about what it means to defend Islam and to free Afghanistan from the Soviets'. It was not even possible to have certain tribes living together in the refugee camps. This situation made offering recognition to an Afghan government-in-exile fraught with difficulty. As well as being difficult for the United States and its allies to support, such recognition would then require them to shut their embassies in Kabul and, consequently, 'an international window on the war would close'.⁴³ However, supporters contested the roots of resistance rivalry disputing allegations of tribal, religious or ethnic differences and instead pointed to a deliberate strategy on the part of the Soviets. In a Rand report presented to the Senate Select Committee on Intelligence, Alex Alexiev argued that Soviet internal strategy encompassed 'exacerbating the traditional tribal and ethnic tension, promoting separatism and preventing the emergence of an Afghan nationalism'.⁴⁴ Externally, he contended, the USSR was striving to remove the Afghan conflict from the international political arena. Klass also argued that the *mujahedeen* were 'operationally unified' and that 'Washington should stop demanding the kind of political unity that is impossible during an occupation'.⁴⁵

In his statement to the Senate Select Committee, Alexiev also called for more sophisticated arms for the rebels pointing to the lack of 'a portable heat seeking' anti-aircraft missiles as the 'most glaring deficiency' in their arsenal.⁴⁶ Just weeks after, on 4 October 1984, Congress unanimously passed the Tsongas-Ritter Resolution promising 'effective aid' to the rebels – dialled down from the 'material aid' called for in its first iteration. Congressional members now hoped to convert increased funding into military materiel. Soon after, Paul Tsongas retired and Gordon Humphrey took over the chair of the bipartisan Congressional Task Force on Afghanistan. Humphrey represented a very public thorn in the side of the administration in relation to Afghanistan. In response to the President's fifth anniversary statement, Humphrey held a joint press conference with four visiting *mujahedeen* where he questioned the management of the aid programme to Afghanistan which, he argued, was 'leaky'. He stated the rebels were 'critically, tragically and scandalously short of the weapons and supplies'.⁴⁷ PVOs like the FAAA concurred contending that only a fraction of the weapons sent were reaching the rebels.⁴⁸ A *mujahedeen* representative alleged 'what we have received has been so pathetically inadequate and ineffective; it is a condemnation to slow death'.⁴⁹ While Congress and the PVOs agitated for more military aid to the rebels, some within the CIA were reluctant to accede to this triggering a battle of wills over the direction of the Afghan programme. This battle was also fought out in public forums – in Congress, in the media and via USIA programmes.

The Congressional Task Force on Afghanistan strongly advocated for the supply of anti-aircraft missiles to the rebels. The Task Force was established to ensure that the government fully complied with the spirit of the Tsongas-Ritter Resolution and to keep Afghanistan to 'the forefront of both congressional and international attention'.⁵⁰ Its membership included Humphrey, Wilson, Ritter and others from the Senate and House Foreign Relations Committees, Armed Forces Committees and Intelligence Committees. It held regular hearings to 'help to bring the message to the American people and to our colleagues in the Congress' about the situation in Afghanistan. The expert witnesses selected to give evidence were certainly committed to helping the Committee achieve this as many were pro-*mujahedeen* and involved in pro-*mujahedeen* PVOs.

The first hearing of the Task Force on famine in Afghanistan heard testimony from Kurt Lohbeck, a freelance journalist based in Peshawar who worked for all three major US television networks.⁵¹ He gave evidence of his recent trip inside

Afghanistan with the rebels who, he claimed, only had a few ineffective or defective anti-aircraft missiles to defend themselves against Soviet airborne attacks.[52] A clip was shown of an ABC World News Tonight report featuring Lohbeck and rebel commander Abdul Haq (who was also present at the hearing) which reiterated the *mujahedeen*'s aging arsenal and need for anti-aircraft weaponry. Lohbeck was an advocate of Haq and had introduced him to Charlie Wilson.[53] Soon after this testimony, Lohbeck and Haq met with the departments of State, Defense and the DIA, including McFarlane and Raymond, to brief them on the situation in Afghanistan. They were introduced to Saudi Ambassador Prince Bandar bin Sultan to seek funding for Haq's activities.[54] Lohbeck was also involved with an NGO called the 'Afghan Mercy Fund' that, amongst other things, ran a hostel in Peshawar for visiting Western journalists and arranged contact for them with *mujahedeen* (usually Haq). The Mercy Fund also produced a resistance news bulletin titled 'The Humanitarian News Service', which had a reputation for pro-*mujahedeen* propaganda and bias amongst some journalists.[55] Lohbeck also allegedly set up press conferences for Afghan rebels and briefed them on how to deal with Western journalists. Lohbeck would become the main source of reportage for the CBS network, which covered Afghanistan more extensively than any other and featured Haq a number of times.[56] Other Congressional Task Force (CTF) witnesses included Rosanne Klass, of Freedom House and ARC, and Jack Wheeler of Freedom Research Foundation who re-iterated the call for the rebels to receive anti-aircraft missiles such as 'Stingers'.[57] In her statement, Klass likened Soviet tactics in Afghanistan to those of Genghis Khan and accused them of acts of genocide,[58] deliberate destruction of crops, livestock and irrigation systems.[59] She offered research from other pro-*mujahedeen* advocates – a Michael Barry article in *Commentary* and John Train of ARC – to supplement her statement. Lord Cranborne (a British Conservative Party Member of Parliament) of Afghan Aid and the British Afghanistan Support Committee also gave evidence. He argued for aid to be channelled via private networks to circumvent 'political manipulation', presumably by the Soviets who could use evidence of administration aid to undermine the *mujahedeen*'s credibility.[60] According to Lohbeck, Afghan Aid received considerable funding from USAID, and several individuals involved in this NGO had connections to British and French intelligence services.[61] Cranborne was also acquainted with Joanne Herring and helped her convince Senator Ted Stevens of the Senate Defense Appropriations Subcommittee to support Charlie Wilson's bid to have Oerlikon weapons sent to the *mujahedeen*.[62] Klass acknowledged the need to distance the *mujahedeen* from US assistance. She stated the rebels requested that any voluntary personnel sent Afghanistan should be Europeans rather than Americans 'as the political cost' would be lower.[63] All concerned understood that it was not in the US interest, or the *mujahedeen*'s, to publicize American aid to the resistance. MSF personnel were regular contributors to these hearings and were amongst the 'Europeans' to which US aid was regularly channelled. However, during testimony they never mentioned the trouble they had with the Afghan rebels extorting and stealing from them, kidnapping their personnel and imposing gender segregation policies.[64] It was in no one's interest to cast the *mujahedeen* in a less than favourable light.

The Task Force's objective of increasing coverage of the conflict in Afghanistan and building pressure for increased military aid seemed to work effectively. *The Wall Street Journal* reported on the hearing and echoed its findings stating the rebels must be given

> effective enough anti-aircraft weaponry to force the Soviets into a more extensive ground war and we simply must increase the news coverage of the war and the public yelling about it to a point that forces the world to look day after day into the real Soviet face.[65]

Further Congressional Task Force hearings would be held over the course of the conflict on medical conditions and Soviet strategy in Afghanistan mostly featuring witnesses with a pro-*mujahedeen* bias, including Jeane Kirkpatrick, Alexiev, Gouttierre and various *mujahedeen* representatives.[66] However, congressional hearings were not the only forum for advocates of increased and improved military aid to the Afghan resistance.

USIA programming also publicized the calls for more sophisticated weaponry for the *mujahedeen* particularly on its new satellite television service Worldnet that had been recently inaugurated in response to the negative international reaction to the US invasion of Grenada.[67] The programme garnered widespread media attention across Europe which, director Wick observed, the United States could 'never have afforded to buy' and did seem to have a positive influence on subsequent international reportage on Grenada. Worldnet broadcasted regularly following this and invited journalists who would be served wine and offered cigarettes and cigars at a selected US embassy while posing questions to American officials via video link.[68] This new public diplomacy tool allowed the United States to sidestep the often-negative interpretation of its foreign policies by European newspaper analysts, railed against by Kirkpatrick, and speak directly to their publics instead.[69] Nonetheless, America's West European allies had little interest in the situation in Afghanistan and were reluctant to endorse anything more than diplomatic measures to confront Soviet behaviour.[70] The USIA strove to redress this by highlighting allegations of human rights abuses in Afghanistan by the Soviets and the PDPA.

A Worldnet conference with the recently retired Kirkpatrick in December 1985 focused on human rights violations in Afghanistan in the light of the recent UN Report on the subject. In it, Kirkpatrick emphasized alleged Soviet war crimes and deliberate targeting of Afghan children. As well as questions from journalists, it also featured questions from Afghan resistance supporters Michael Barry and Lord Cranborne. These supporters used the issue to advocate for military aid to the resistance. Barry, representing the International Federation for Human Rights, stated that Afghans felt that 90 per cent of the human rights violations discussed could be prevented if they had adequate protection from airborne attack. A question from the German Afghanistan Committee asked why the West does not show 'solidarity' with the Afghans by supplying more effective weaponry.[71] Kirkpatrick responded that the United States and West Germany, as democracies, will respond to the will of their citizens in relation to supplying upgraded arms to the Afghan rebels. In other words, public opinion was of paramount importance to realizing this goal.[72]

Other USIA programmes such as TV Satellite File, a weekly news magazine programme, also promoted the need for improved military hardware and anti-aircraft weaponry for the *mujahedeen*.[73] In one show, Brzezinski advocated overt US aid questioning whether it was still necessary to supply the rebels only with Soviet-type weaponry (designed to maintain plausible deniability). He urged allies to 'tangibly sustain' the resistance.[74] Another episode reported that *mujahedeen* were disappointed that their Western allies did not provide 'weapons to knock down planes and helicopters' and emphasized the old and dysfunctional weapons the rebels were forced to rely on. The same programme covered a protest rally in Washington against the occupation where one flag stated 'Mr. President, missiles not words will stop the genocide'.[75] Supporters of the *mujahedeen* did not consider that diplomacy would resolve the conflict and kept up the propaganda campaign for anti-aircraft weaponry.

In 'We Are Afghanistan', Soviet warplanes and helicopters unleashed their payloads while the narrator warned that for Afghans 'the greatest danger comes from the sky'. According to the programme, the rebels attacked ground convoys successfully but could not 'control the sky'. It claimed Soviet aircraft retaliated by bombing nearby villages 'whether the village helped the *mujahedeen* or not'.[76] Although under the Smith-Mundt Act USIA material was not to be disseminated domestically, Congress authorized this film to be distributed within the United States along with 'Afghanistan 1982: The Struggle for Freedom Continues' and 'Afghanistan: The Hidden War'.[77]

The campaign to secure anti-aircraft missiles for the resistance was articulated in the public sphere by the pro-*mujahedeen* PVOs. An Afghan Resistance Seminar was held at the annual World Anti-Communist League Conference (WALC) and its findings urged 'governments of the Free World' to supply the rebels with anti-aircraft and anti-tank weaponry and associated training.[78] American Aid for Afghans based in Oregon called on the administration to match its donation of boots for rebels with anti-aircraft missiles.[79] Fazle Akbar, a *mujahid* and head of the Afghan Information and Documentation Center in Peshawar, made a plea for anti-aircraft missiles on a visit to the United States sponsored by congressional supporters and the CFA.[80] Jack Wheeler, addressing a CFA-organized press conference, echoed this demand.[81] At another press conference organized this time by the FAAA, four *mujahedeen*, through interpreters, said there was an urgent need for anti-aircraft weapons amongst the resistance.[82]

The Heritage Foundation added intellectual weight to these arguments with its analytical pieces. One dating from February 1984 pointed out the *mujahedeen* was 'vastly out-gunned' resulting in insignificant casualties for the Soviets giving them

> little incentive to surrender the strategic benefit of occupying Afghanistan: a potential stepping stone to the Persian Gulf, bases from which Soviet tactical air power can dominate the strategic Straits of Hormuz, and staging grounds for the subversion or even invasion of neighbouring Pakistan and Iran.[83]

The article went on to recommend the supply of 'shoulder-fired anti-aircraft missiles' and 'light anti-tank weapons'; 'rocket launchers; recoilless rifles; and anti-tank mines' as well as mortars to the rebels. It pointed to 'bureaucratic resistance' in the US government stalling such assistance – an allegation which other PVOs would echo.[84] A May 1984 analysis piece stressed 'the [Panjsher] valley's defenders, roughly 5,000 to 7,000 strong, lack the anti-aircraft and anti-tank weapons needed to blunt the Soviet advance'. It warned that 'US policy makers should not be lulled into believing that, because a UN sponsored peace is allegedly at hand, American support for the Afghan resistance is not necessary. A just peace, in fact, requires increased support for the freedom fighters'.[85] Another report entitled 'Moscow Stalks the Persian Gulf' alleged that the USSR wished to ultimately control Saudi Arabia and that the politically tumultuous Iran was an obvious target for Soviet subversion too. However, a Soviet incursion into Iran would be unlikely if the 'military deadlock' in Afghanistan continued to bog them down.[86] A December 1984 report released by the Heritage Foundation urged the administration to aid anti-communist insurgencies in nine countries and denounced the administration's efforts to date as 'cautious' and 'limited'.[87] This public campaign by advocates of increased military aid to the resistance met with little media challenge; however, some officials within the US government preferred a cautious, limited engagement in Afghanistan and were blocking the supply of US-made Stingers to the *mujahedeen*.

Consequent to NSDD 166 in March 1985, the Afghan programme was flush with the funds necessary to supply expensive anti-aircraft missiles to the rebels but this was initially stymied by opposition within and between the bureaucracies involved. John McMahon, deputy director of the CIA, was soon pinpointed as the chief obstacle to sending Stinger missiles to Afghanistan.[88] The CIA feared losing control of what it considered a very successful covert operation to its bureaucratic rival – the Pentagon.[89] It wished to protect its principle of 'plausible deniability' in covert operations and, in any case, according to CIA reports, the *mujahedeen* were holding their own quite well in Afghanistan.[90] This cautious approach not only protected the CIA but also protected Pakistan from increased Soviet ire and the *mujahedeen* from the 'taint' of being supported by the United States. However, Jack Wheeler aired a view shared by many supporters of the *mujahedeen* – that the CIA was 'screwing up in Afghanistan' and such 'covert and paramilitary operations should be run by the Defense Department'.[91]

In an effort to change this dynamic, in October 1985, McMahon was subjected to a hostile public campaign ostensibly initiated by Eiva at the FAAA and Free the Eagle.[92] Free the Eagle sent one hundred thousand letters to their conservative supporters urging them to write to Donald Regan, the White House Chief of Staff. This led to between ten and twelve thousand letters being sent to Regan demanding McMahon's resignation for failing to carry out the President's wishes.[93] Eiva also held press conferences where he blamed McMahon for the CIA's reluctance to send Stingers to Afghanistan.[94] Free the Eagle's founder, Neil Blair, knew Regan from conservative social circles and would use such occasions to make known the organization's misgivings about McMahon. Other Free the Eagle activists used similar tactics.[95]

Conservative congressmen, such as Wallop and Humphrey, also publicized their dissatisfaction with the CIA's and White House's stance.[96] The Heritage Foundation described McMahon's position on Afghanistan as 'Carteresque' – the ultimate New Right insult.[97] In the Department of Defense, foreign policy hawks Fred Iklé and Michael Pillsbury were determined to ensure the rebels received sophisticated US military supplies. They undertook a concerted campaign to persuade the chief decision-makers in the Afghan inter-agency process to assent.[98] Pillsbury, at that stage an assistant to Iklé, had previously served as an aide to Gordon Humphrey and advised a number of other conservative congressmen including Wallop.[99] Eventually, McMahon resigned on 4 March 1986 amid much press speculation as to his reasons. Free the Eagle and Eiva lauded this as 'a great breakthrough'.[100] Later that month the President approved the Stinger proposal.[101] Just another month later Michael Pillsbury was fired for leaking the Stinger decision to the press.[102]

On 25 September 1986 the first Stingers were used in Afghanistan to bring down Soviet helicopters.[103] The episode was videoed and shown around the White House and to certain Congress members. Fittingly enough for a military aid campaign fired by propaganda, the question as to whether the footage shown in Washington was itself propaganda orchestrated by the Pakistanis with Inter-Services Intelligence (ISI) officers rather than Afghan rebels firing the Stingers is still subject to debate.[104] Nonetheless, this was the kind of action footage which would guarantee network news coverage if it could be got out of Afghanistan. Another objective of the *mujahedeen* supporters – to provide the *mujahedeen* with video equipment to film the conflict – would help realize this.

The Soviets were, by turns, concerned and outraged by American propaganda directed at them about Afghanistan. Railing against Radio Free Afghanistan one commentator alleged that 'ideological subversion has been raised to the status of state policy' in Washington while another accused the USIA of 'exporting counter-revolution'.[105] Worldnet was 'provocative', peddling 'shameless lies' and 'cultural imperialism'. The *mujahedeen* were described as a 'counterrevolutionary rabble'.[106] However, the Soviets also ran their own propaganda campaigns featuring pro-regime *mujahedeen* and kept a tight lid on media reporting of the war at home to quell dissent.[107] Whether American propaganda had any real effect on Soviet public opinion, as the Reagan administration hoped, is difficult to quantify as Gorbachev only loosened media controls under Glasnost from July 1985 allowing open reporting on Afghanistan.[108] However, there were reports of isolated demonstrations in reaction to returning Soviet army casualties and increasing cynicism about the Soviet role in Afghanistan.[109]

The Afghan people, however, were to suffer most in the escalation of its civil war and its entanglement with the Cold War. In 1985, UNESCO commended Afghanistan for its literacy programmes but the Afghan school system would soon descend into disarray due to the war.[110] Controlling Kabul was an all-important goal for the *mujahedeen*. This led to a terror campaign which consisted of constant long-range rocket fire and the ambush of supplies entering Kabul. The rebels targeted infrastructure providing water and electricity, assassinated Soviet and Afghan army and civil service personnel, including one case where a bomb was placed under a dining table in Kabul University which killed nine Soviets and a female Afghan professor.¹¹¹ The calm that Harrison reported in Kabul in early 1984 was now a distant memory. Increasing the arms to the resistance was only ever going to increase the chaos in Afghanistan.

Conclusion

The Reagan administration was determined to re-invigorate and re-establish America's international prestige weakened, it believed, during the Carter years. To do this it sought to reassert the American military might but sought to present this policy as a necessity – a reaction to Soviet aggression. Reagan administration public diplomacy characterized the United States as ethical, freedom-loving and pro-democracy arguing that it was merely seeking to check a Soviet Union that was deceitful, dishonourable and expansionary. Afghanistan provided an ideal platform upon which to base such claims. The administration exploited the conflict to create opportunities like the annual commemoration of the invasion to convey its message to the international community. These accusations of human rights abuses and unethical combat practices undoubtedly undermined the Soviets' international standing as desired.¹¹² Stung by the growing anti-Americanism amongst Muslims, showcased spectacularly during the Iranian Revolution, the United States endeavoured to use Afghanistan to sow similar discontent with the USSR among Soviet Muslims and the wider Islamic community. While it did undermine the USSR's position with Islamic and Third World states, ultimately, the remaining lifespan of the Soviet Union was too short for such a long-term policy to damage it and, instead, the consequences of manipulating such sentiments blew back to the only superpower left standing.

Undermining the USSR did not always equate to bolstering US credibility, however, and US rhetoric often rang hollow in the cold light of its own foreign policies.¹¹³ Realizing its credibility deficit the administration sought to mask its propaganda and public diplomacy behind non-government sources such as the PVOs that provided testimony for congressional hearings and USIA programmes and kept a steady stream of commentary up in newspapers and on television. Such a policy was only partially successful, however, as the pro-*mujahedeen* PVOs were not easily controlled and were often critical of administration policy on Afghanistan.

On the other hand, the campaign by pro-*mujahedeen* PVOs and sympathetic Congress members to publicly prevail upon the administration and the CIA to acquiesce to supplying American-made anti-aircraft to the *mujahedeen* was more successful. Public diplomacy was used to ratchet up pressure on the more moderate or cautious members of the administration by the 'bleeders' and the conservatives in the PVOs. Supporters of the Afghan rebels utilized every avenue and forum they could access to press home their message from congressional hearings, USIA output, public demonstrations, print media opinion pieces to TV news programme punditry. Supporters sought to justify increased military aid by presenting the *mujahedeen* struggling to unify while engaging in a David- and Goliath-type battle with a vindictive superpower. Unity would offer the resistance, and its supporters, more legitimacy when arguing that the *mujahedeen* groups represented the Afghan people though this was far from the case. Advocates also focused attention on alleged Soviet atrocities to stimulate sympathy and outrage. As the media were far removed from events in Afghanistan they relied on biased sources for information from people whose agenda was to generate support for the *mujahedeen* and continued fighting rather than to promote negotiations and a political settlement. And it worked; US-made Stingers, as yet untried in the battlefield by the US military, were sent to the *mujahedeen* and brought down the first Hind helicopter in September 1986. The effect of the Stingers on the course of the conflict is contested; Gorbachev already referred to Afghanistan as 'a bleeding wound' earlier that year and was actively seeking an exit strategy for the Soviets.[114] Nevertheless, they did put Afghanistan back in the news to some extent. However, getting the footage of the missiles in action still presented difficulties for the media and the *mujahedeen*'s US advocates. TV news programmes depended on just such visuals to attract and maintain the viewer's attention, and another NSDD 166-funded project, the Afghan Media Project, would seek to address this by providing just such coverage.

5

The Afghan Media Project

On 27 March 1985, President Reagan signed National Security Decision Directive 166, 'US Policy, Programs and Strategy in Afghanistan'. Amongst other things, this directive pledged to 'increase international political pressure on the Soviets through public diplomacy' in order to help promote the administration's policy objectives in Afghanistan.[1] Within months, the USIA would establish the Afghan Media Project (AMP) to seek to fulfil this mandate. Mired in controversy from its inception the programme set out to train *mujahedeen* based in Peshawar, Pakistan, in print, video and photojournalism. This would allow them to enter Afghanistan, gather news and relay it to the wider world.

Private and congressional *mujahedeen* backers considered increased media coverage of Afghanistan crucial to generating popular public support for the Afghan resistance and to putting pressure on the administration to maintain its support. They advocated for this relentlessly in public forums and were influential on the conception and development of the AMP. At the same time as these efforts, NSDD 166 was being drafted heralding a more proactive turn to the administration's approach to Afghanistan. Amongst other objectives, the directive endorsed the contention that more effective propaganda was critical. Essentially, the directive sought to bolster application of the Reagan Doctrine in Afghanistan and the AMP was designed to strengthen the propaganda pillar of this multifaceted strategy. The output from this programme had the potential to shape the perceptions of international publics, damage Soviet relations with Third World and Islamic states and influence Soviet public opinion on the Afghan conflict.

From its earliest days, the AMP was contentious. Within the United States, journalists and academics were concerned about the taint of propaganda on their professions and any media outlets using the project's produce. As a result, this media programme was media shy about its own operations. Within Pakistan and the refugee camps, the difficulties around launching the project were a microcosm of the difficulties of US relationships with the *mujahedeen* and Pakistani authorities. The objectives of those involved in the implementation of the project, from Boston University (BU) to administration officials, also reflected the struggle between hard-line anti-communists and more moderate elements over Afghan policy on a macro-level.

Advocacy for increased media coverage of the Afghan conflict

Keeping the Afghan conflict in the public domain had been a long-standing concern of American *mujahedeen* supporters. Public interest in Afghanistan, in the United States and internationally, had waned following the dramatic early days of the Soviet invasion and occupation. In a television news environment increasingly in thrall to video imagery, the lack of any live footage from inside Afghanistan further circumscribed the conflict's airtime. While in 1980, 204.7 minutes per annum per US television network were devoted to Afghanistan this had slumped to 17.1 minutes in 1982 and recovered somewhat to 28.2 minutes per network per annum by 1984, but this was still only equivalent to a monthly average per network of 2.4 minutes.[2] Furthermore, this was happening at a time when televised news coverage was greatly increasing due to the growth of cable companies. Senator Orrin Hatch summed up *mujahedeen* supporters' frustration with this lack of coverage in a *New York Times* article. He argued that while 'Vietnam was fought in our living rooms on the evening news, Afghanistan is largely out of sight, out of mind' and railed against what he described as the 'de facto blackout by much of the world's media'.[3] Similarly, Afghan expert and academic Louis Dupree contrasted the 'open war' in Vietnam with the Afghan conflict which was 'closed to correspondents, except those approved by the Soviet Union' leading to 'tainted' pro-DRA coverage.[4] Theodore Eliot (of ARC) featured in a USIA Electronic Dialogue programme where he contended that the lack of media attention meant that there was little pressure on the Soviets to pull out of Afghanistan.[5]

Officials in the Reagan administration agreed. The NSC's Walter Raymond argued in a March 1984 letter to Reagan's National Security Advisor, Robert McFarlane, on proposed increased political action to support the rebels, that 'one of the most important areas is the question of world-wide TV coverage of the Afghan war'.[6] Raymond's Restricted Inter-Agency Working Group on Afghanistan put together a list of suggestions to rectify this. Proposals included the supply of mobile microwave transmitters, mobile video recorders and support for Radio Free Kabul. 'Friends of Afghanistan' committees would be dedicated to media coverage of Afghanistan to 'provide information and analysis to opinion leaders' and 'provide assistance to enterprising young journalists in the form of information, funding, and channels to the resistance'.[7] This comprehensive strategy to manipulate coverage of the conflict included recommendations to increase press briefings, establish contacts with foreign journalists who covered the conflict and encourage the distribution of their articles in the United States. The Inter-Agency Group recommended that administration officials meet with US editorial staff of major newspapers to encourage more reporting on Afghanistan. It proposed that VOA reception should be strengthened within Afghanistan. The group's suggestions also contained the kernel of an idea that would spawn the AMP: help the resistance promote their own story by training young Afghans to record and report on the war.[8]

This idea that the Afghan conflict was not receiving enough media coverage was reiterated at congressional hearings on Afghanistan. Here, *mujahedeen* supporters castigated the mainstream media for the dearth of reporting and accused them of cowardice, apparently for not risking their reporters in the field. Thomas Gouttierre of UNO appeared before a House Subcommittee on Human Rights where he accused the 'establishment media' of not being 'courageous' enough to seek information from Afghanistan instead relying on freelance journalists. He went on to liken the 'inattentiveness' of the American media on the question of human rights abuses in Afghanistan to its 'inattentiveness' to the plight of the Jews in Europe in the 1930s.[9] At a Congressional Task Force hearing in February 1985, Jack Wheeler lambasted the 'big five of American media' for not having reporters in Peshawar. He urged the US embassy in Islamabad to assist correspondents to report from Afghanistan.[10]

The Congressional Task Force on Afghanistan held a hearing on 'Effective Public Diplomacy' in June 1985 at which Zbigniew Brzezinski, Ben Wattenberg of the Board of International Broadcasters and a founder member of the Coalition for a Democratic Majority, Dr Louis Dupree and Ralph Magnus gave testimony.[11] Senator Humphrey chaired the session.[12] Humphrey described public diplomacy as 'the most powerful weapon' at the US disposal to affect the course of the conflict in Afghanistan but one that had been used 'very ineffectually' to date.[13] Other participants seemed to consider the media as no more than an instrument of US public diplomacy, which should be pressed into more effective action. Brzezinski observed that the Soviet occupation of Afghanistan put 'at stake the geopolitical future of South-West Asia'. He argued that international condemnation would exact the 'highest political cost' from the Soviets and that it was more likely than military reversals to encourage the Soviets to re-evaluate their strategy in Afghanistan.[14] Brzezinski advocated for more direct reporting from the battlefield to affect this. In his testimony, Wattenberg described network news attitudes towards Afghanistan as 'irresponsible' as they blamed the lack of coverage on the expense involved, difficulties with access and the unreliability of the information provided by the *mujahedeen*. US media had covered the My Lai story, Wattenberg argued, without direct access to the scene. He speculated as to whether the US media would have questioned the reliability of unverified, inconsistent reports of atrocities emanating from Auschwitz in 1943, drawing analogies between the Soviets and the Nazis.[15] Wattenberg suggested to the chair that equipping *mujahedeen* with 'minicams' to film footage to provide to the media could, potentially, quadruple news coverage of Afghanistan.[16]

Dupree too evoked Vietnam's news coverage and contrasted it to Afghanistan, which he stated was 'closed to media other than those officially approved by the Soviet Union'.[17] To counter this, the anthropologist proposed the United States set up a media centre in Peshawar to train *mujahedeen* in photography and video techniques, the product of which could be distributed worldwide. The centre could also provide guides and interpreters to visiting Western journalists to improve accessibility and, hence, coverage. Dupree suggested soliciting private funds to commission American and European public relations firms to 'flood the media with newsworthy items'. He recommended the establishment of Afghan Action Committees on college campuses to raise awareness amongst students. Such committees could be fed information from the proposed media centre.[18] AmeriCares' Ralph Magnus agreed with Brzezinski (who was on that charity's board) that public diplomacy represented the best hope for influencing Soviet actions in Afghanistan. He argued that the media would take the conflict more seriously if the Reagan administration did.[19] Magnus charged that US public diplomacy had lacked coherent policy guidance and commitment in relation to Afghanistan. He suggested increased funding and the establishment of an inter-agency task force to guide public diplomacy on the conflict.[20] The propositions put forward during this hearing that the United States provide video cameras to *mujahedeen* and develop a media centre in Peshawar were ideas whose time had come. Just two months later, under the auspices of NSDD 166, the USIA invited tenders to establish a media project for Afghanistan.

In NSDD 166, the administration upped the ante in the Afghan conflict by significantly increasing funding, weapons and intelligence to the resistance. The directive also decreed that international pressure on the Soviets should be increased.[21] This new policy objective aimed to force the Soviets to withdraw from Afghanistan – this would be a major propaganda as well as strategic victory in the Cold War. However, notwithstanding its ultimate objective, it listed interim goals, which would 'be in US national interest, regardless of the ultimate outcome of the struggle in Afghanistan'. Amongst these interim goals were three in which propaganda would play a significant role. The first goal was to isolate the Soviets from Third World and Islamic countries. The second, to ensure the *mujahedeen*, kept fighting as the continuation of the conflict helped the portrayal of the Soviets as imperialists, not the allies many Third World countries perceived them to be. Finally the directive sought to bring news of the war to the Soviet people to 'reduce their confidence in the Soviet military and Soviet external policies'. It was under this mandate that the USIA received the funding to launch the AMP.[22]

Even while the AMP was getting underway, congressional and administration *mujahedeen* supporters continued to generate opportunities to bring the Afghan conflict to world attention. The Commission on Security and Co-Operation in Europe (the Helsinki Commission) held a hearing on 'Soviet Human Rights Violations in Afghanistan'. Its aim was 'to bring to the attention of the American public and the scrutiny of world opinion' to allegations against the USSR.[23] Afghan supporters, Senator Humphrey and Representative Don Ritter, were members of the commission as was Assistant Secretary of Defense Richard Perle. During the hearing, Congressman Gary Ackerman characterized the Afghans as a 'peace loving, freedom loving people' and hoped that the hearing would attract the attention of the world's media. Ackerman argued that Afghan refugees arriving in the United States believed they had reached 'the last hope for freedom' and America needed to affirm that belief publicly to remain true to its political ideals.[24] Journalist Kurt Lohbeck also gave evidence. He denounced the unfolding human rights situation in Afghanistan as 'a Holocaust' and, yet again, contrasted media coverage of Afghanistan with that of Vietnam. He concluded that Americans lacked 'the interest or desire for more information' as they were 'not constantly bombarded with this story' as a result of the difficulty and danger in covering Afghanistan.[25] Congressman D'Amato condemned a 'conspiracy of apathy and silence' while another 'Holocaust' and 'genocide' were underway in Afghanistan.[26]

At another Congressional Task Force hearing on Afghanistan, Ambassador Jeane Kirkpatrick also argued that the Soviets were able to bear the costs of the war in Afghanistan, unlike the United States in Vietnam, as it was not covered in the Soviet media. She urged more radio propaganda to counter this.[27] US Cold War warriors had learnt a vital lesson from the Vietnam War – that media coverage can significantly affect public opinion and thereafter the course of a conflict. They were determined to apply this lesson to Afghanistan. The idea that the United States was undermined in Vietnam by domestic media coverage animated a desire for an aggressive propaganda strategy to visit a similar fate on the Soviets.

The USIA also sought to address the lack of media coverage of Afghanistan with programmes such as TV Satellite File, which regularly featured Afghanistan characterizing it as 'the forgotten war'. One programme, the Afghan Digest, featured a clip titled 'The War and the Press' which followed intrepid British TV news crews as they transported their equipment on horseback across Afghanistan due to the inhospitable terrain, illuminating the inherent difficulties for reporters covering this conflict.[28] Another show reported on a State Department conference from January 1984 where Zalmay Khalilzad recommended that 'private citizen groups' should fund young journalists willing to cover Afghanistan.[29] While such a move could help circumvent the cautious network news producers, it also had the potential to create a conflict of interest between the agenda of such groups and those of journalists they funded to cover the conflict. Nonetheless, by March 1984, Raymond's Interagency Afghan Political Action Group was recommending similar engagement with the private sector via 'Friends of Afghanistan Committees'.[30] The administration obviously did not envisage any discordance between its aims and those of private sector groups involved with the Afghan conflict.

The Heritage Foundation added its voice to this debate by urging the administration to 'raise the cost of the Soviet occupation' with a more effective public diplomacy programme in one of its reports. The report recommended increased Voice of America and Radio Liberty broadcasts to the Soviet public to keep them informed of the Soviet army losses and atrocities. It advised the USIA to boost its public diplomacy efforts to keep the non-communist world informed of the war too.[31] A later report recommended the United States 'inject the Afghan issue into every multilateral conference, international forum, and bilateral meeting with Soviet-bloc representatives'.[32] It argued that 'US government officials, academic specialists, and policy makers should drive home the horrifying human rights situation in Afghanistan'. The report went on to propose that wounded Afghan and Soviet army deserters should be brought before Western media to detail atrocities.[33] This proved difficult to initiate as the *mujahedeen* tended to visit fairly horrible deaths on captives, reducing the temptation to defect to them. This information would have created a propaganda nightmare for the administration if reported. However, Freedom House and the IRC did manage to bring some Soviet army defectors to the United States where they gained a certain celebrity status speaking of atrocities in Afghanistan.[34]

According to Robert Gates, the CIA actively promoted the Afghan's cause by sponsoring 'demonstrations, protests, meetings, conferences, press articles, television shows, exhibitions, and the like to focus worldwide attention on the Soviet involvement in Afghanistan'.[35] For US *mujahedeen* supporters, however, administration actions never seemed adequate so they initiated their own strategies to promote the *mujahedeen*'s cause. At its conference in September 1984, the right-wing WACL advised that 'Free Afghanistan Committees' be set up in WACL member states 'to lead in a program of effective public relations which would publicize the Afghan cause'. This would include publishing and distributing literature; setting up a speaker's bureau and informing leaders of governments on the situation in Afghanistan.[36] Other PVOs sought to bring the war to the media by arranging publicity tours of the United States for *mujahedeen*.[37] Abdul Haq was a guest, along with Kurt Lohbeck, at the 1985 Conservative Political Action Conference, 'Creators of the Future', where the president, during his opening speech, addressed the Afghan commander stating 'Abdul Haq, we are with you'.[38] Haq's extensive high-profile public relations efforts in the United States led some in the CIA to label him 'Hollywood Haq'.[39] During this period, many other *mujahedeen* toured the United States to promote their cause and solicit funding. President Reagan met with the resistance leadership in June 1986 and the 'rebel lobby' was Washington's latest growth industry according to the media.[40]

The administration understood the value of increased media coverage of the Afghan conflict in eroding the Soviet's international standing. Writing in *Foreign Affairs* in 1985, Secretary of State Shultz attested that the 'free flow of information' was 'inherently compatible' with Western democratic structures and detrimental to communist states. Nevertheless, the administration still sought to manage this flow of information in America's favour repudiating the very democratic norms that Washington espoused.[41] Casey outlined the justification for this thinking arguing that there was an 'asymmetry' between the effects of disinformation on the two superpowers. The United States was at a 'disadvantage' because it tolerated a free press that sometimes relayed Soviet propaganda while the Soviet press did not or could not reciprocate.[42] This imbalance justified propaganda by the United States to establish a level playing field. In Afghanistan, the lack of live footage of the war meant the conflict failed to command the television news coverage desired by the *mujahedeen* and their US backers. This was mainly because Afghanistan was just too dangerous for Western journalists to risk life and limb to cover. Overcoming this practical obstacle would be beneficial to the United States in its ideological battle with the communists.

Congressional supporters, PVO advocates and Reagan administration officials all seemed to agree that the Afghan conflict was not receiving the coverage it deserved and needed if it was to inflict any serious damage on the USSR. In the 1980s, the advent of cable television not only increased news coverage but also created an appetite for visual imagery such as video clips to capture and hold viewers' attention. *Mujahedeen* advocates realized that delivering news in this format was vital if coverage was to be increased. The AMP was conceived to address this – if the media would not dare to go to Afghanistan to gather this news then the USIA would deliver it to them.

The Afghan Media Project: Origins and controversy

Reacting to calls by *mujahedeen* advocates in Congress, PVOs and the Reagan administration, the USIA developed the AMP to train selected *mujahedeen* as reporters, photographers and videographers. Additionally, the project proposed to set up 'a TV news syndication service', which, it hoped, would service a worldwide market for its product. The emphasis on visual imagery, both video and photographic, would prove a potent and irresistible source of material on the Afghan conflict for many international media outlets, and contracts were established by the programme's organizers with the BBC, ITN, Associated Press and Reuters amongst others.[43] The Smith-Mundt Act banned USIA material that targeted an American audience, which meant that output from the Afghan programme could not be sold directly to US media outlets, however, as Hearst, one of the grantees, outlined in its November 1986 progress report:

> Several times during research efforts, news organisations in the United States have indicated that if a good story or picture comes along, they certainly will try to secure and use the material, and I think they would succeed. While this project is strictly not a USIA project, but, rather one ordered up by Congress and administered by the USIA, perhaps some additional thought might be given to the matter of US distribution.[44]

However, once the project was established, became 'independent' of its political masters and the material produced was no longer directly linked to the information agency, then it could legitimately be distributed in the United States.[45] To this end, from the outset the USIA tried to distance themselves publicly from the project stating the 'true emphasis of the project is to train Afghans to tell their own media story'.[46] Nonetheless, it was prominently listed as one of the agency's public diplomacy programmes as late as May 1987[47] and even Senator Humphrey admitted the AMP was propaganda though 'in the best sense of the word'.[48]

The Soviets reacted sharply to the project describing it as an extension of United States meddling in Afghanistan. They suggested the USIA now provided a manual for the rebels on the operation of video cameras similar to the CIA's instruction of the *mujahedeen* 'in the art of murdering civilians and destroying schools and mosques'. Moscow queried the hypocrisy behind the non-reporting by the US media of *mujahedeen* atrocities, which included the destruction of libraries and schools and the targeting of teachers and clergymen.[49] It alleged that

> in the last few years the bandits have destroyed 2000 schools, 130 hospitals, 100 first-aid stations and 234 mosques. They have also destroyed 906 co-operative farms. On 4th September last a plane of the Afghan airline was brought down with an anti-aircraft missile near Kandahar airport. All its 52 passengers died. Enquiry revealed that the bandits had used an American-made missile.

The Kremlin characterized the project as an intensification of the US psychological warfare against the Kabul government arguing that the United States had 'no intention to give the problem impartial coverage'.[50] Evidence would suggest that this was true.

Though many *mujahedeen* supporters had advocated openly for greater publicity for the Afghan conflict, nonetheless, the origins of this project are murky and its intentions not too far removed from Soviet allegations. NSDD 166 provided the political authority for the USIA to implement the Afghan Media Programme and Senator Gordon Humphrey persuaded Congress to authorize $500,000 to initiate it.[51] However, according to some, Walter Raymond of the NSC first put the idea for such a project to Humphrey who then pushed the authorization through Congress.[52] Raymond was regularly updated on the project's progress by the USIA and it seems likely that the Inter-Agency Group instigated the AMP. Raymond was already involved in a similar propaganda and disinformation project – the Office of Public Diplomacy for Latin America – that targeted the Sandinista government in Nicaragua. A number of other individuals involved in the Afghan project were also connected to the anti-Sandinista, Nicaraguan *Contra* cause.[53] Humphrey, who, at the same time, was instrumental in establishing Radio Free Afghanistan, had taken a special interest in the progress of the media project and also received regular updates from the USIA on its progress.[54]

In August 1985, another inter-agency group was formed by the administration, this time to formulate an action plan to facilitate the congressional mandate to 'promote an independent Afghan media service' and 'train Afghans in media and media related areas'.[55] The USIA put together an 'Afghan Media Staff' under project director John Mosher to manage the project. The Department of State, the Department of Defense and the National Security Council briefed the group. The USIA commissioned a report by John O. Koehler, a former director of the World Services Division of Associated Press and friend of President Reagan.[56] His remit was to assess the 'media situation regarding Afghanistan' in Europe and Pakistan and draw up guidelines for concept papers which were then sought from private institutions and groups.[57]

The Senate amendment authorized up to 1 million dollars for the AMP. It also sought to influence the development of the project calling on the USIA to consider Khalilzad's PVO, Friends of Afghanistan, for the grant.[58] Other pro-*mujahedeen* PVOs invited to submit proposals included the ARC and the CFA. There was tensions in the application process and USIA's counsel, Merry Lymn, warned that 'several of the applicants [were] politically connected' and represented 'rival interests in this and other forums'. She recommended that all advice on the bids should be in written form to avoid any accusations of unfairness.[59] It seems that the disunity and internecine rivalry of the *mujahedeen* also afflicted their American supporters. The administration had to carefully negotiate these conflicting agendas as it developed its policies and programmes in conjunction with private interests.

Ultimately, the organizations listed were deemed unsuitable by the USIA and the grant was divided and awarded jointly to BU, to train the Afghan students, and Hearst/King Features Syndicate to set up the news agency. The NSC had advised the USIA that grantees should be 'culturally sensitive' and run an 'above board operation'; however, BU was awarded the contract though they had no area expertise on Afghanistan.[60] Thomas Gouttierre's Afghan Center at the UNO had also submitted a bid, which Steven Olsson, who eventually became director of the AMP in Peshawar, had helped to develop.[61] Olsson observed that while the UNO had a number of Afghan professors on exchange from Kabul, the BU trainers had little knowledge of Afghan culture and society.[62] He was surprised when BU won the bid.[63] The evaluation panel recommended that the three advocacy PVOs who were originally asked to submit bids should be consulted by the grantees for expertise and contacts, thus keeping them involved as Congress had desired.[64] A provision was then added to the grant to include consultation with area experts and the PVOs, possibly to address this shortcoming in BU's personnel.[65] Kings Features consulted with *mujahedeen* advocates Louis Dupree, Thomas Gouttierre, Zalmay Khalilzad, the CFA and the ARC as well as a number of expatriate Afghans based in the United States in the development of the press packet.[66] In his new role as Special Advisor with the State Department, Khalilzad was also to be kept updated on the project's progress by the USIA.[67]

BU's College of Communications had been an early frontrunner in the bidding process and the only journalism school to apply for the grant.[68] However, its proposal provoked bitter divisions within the college. Some of the faculty believed that facilitating the course in Peshawar 'would not be academically, fiscally or operationally sound to participate in'.[69] A number of the academic staff feared that 'the program would be seen by the outside world and by the American academic community as not an educational program at all but as a venture in propaganda and counterintelligence'.[70] They argued that as Afghanistan never had a functioning free press in the past, establishing one at this stage would be slow and difficult without the added burden of operating out of a refugee centre 'awash with secret agents, rival political factions, and intense emotions'.[71] Everette Dennis of the Gannett Center for Media Studies at Columbia University agreed stating 'I don't think that (the Afghan training program) is a proper role and function for a journalism school'.[72] Pat Holt, journalist and former Chief of Staff for the Senate Foreign Relations Committee, argued that 'if the Afghan project proceeds, it will mean that the US government is paying a foreign political-paramilitary movement to propagandize itself with the American people'.[73] The dean of the college, Bernard Redmont, soon withdrew the college's bid, though not all the faculty agreed with his decision.[74] One college professor in particular, H. Joachim Maitre, decided to go over Redmont's head and contact his friend and university president, John Silber, to see if a proposal could still be put forward.[75]

Maitre was a controversial character within the college and beyond. The former East German MiG pilot had fled the communist bloc in 1953 and settled in the West.[76] Maitre, as well as being ultra-conservative and anti-communist (the *New York Times* described him as having 'a resume peppered with conspicuous partisanship'), also had connections to the Reagan administration and actively supported the Nicaraguan *Contras*' cause.[77] The *Boston Globe* called Maitre 'Oliver North's favourite dean'.[78] He had previous contacts with Wick and Raymond in the White House Situation Room in March 1983 as a 'personal representative of Axel Springer'[79] – a West German publisher. That time, Maitre was there to discuss financial contributions to fund Project Democracy and efforts to shape 'European public opinion regarding missiles (INF) and the NATO alliance'. This meeting included other powerful media operators such as Rupert Murdoch, James Goldsmith and George Gallup, and both President Reagan and Vice-President Bush dropped in to meet the attendees.[80] In January 1984, Maitre travelled to Honduras with Elie Weisel who also taught at BU and sat on the board of the pro-*Contra* organization PRODEMCA.[81] Their trip sought to draw attention to the plight of Miskito Indians and allegations they had been forced to flee Nicaragua by a Sandinista terror campaign. The USIS and US embassy facilitated this visit and it was funded by the public relations firm International Business Communications, which channelled funds to the *Contras* and ran a pro-*Contra* advertising campaign.[82] This was Maitre's third trip to the region and whilst there the visitors dined with the US ambassador to Honduras, John Negroponte.[83] Maitre also produced a pro-*Contra* film for the National Endowment for the Preservation of Liberty, another *Contra* fund-raising organization.[84] He made himself available to the State Department's Office for Public Diplomacy for Latin America to give speeches, write op-eds and attend congressional meetings to generate support for the *Contras*.[85] Maitre's involvement with anti-communist rebels extended beyond the *Contras* and the *mujahedeen* – in 1987, he visited Angola to meet with the anti-communist UNITA leader and Heritage Foundation favourite, Jonas Savimbi.[86] In 1983, Maitre had joined BU, appointed by his friend, John R. Silber, the university's equally controversial and conservative president, and another PRODEMCA member.[87]

Like Maitre, Silber too had links to the Reagan administration and served on the National Bipartisan Commission on Central America (the Kissinger Commission) and the Presidential Advisory Board of Radio Marti (though the evaluation panel and task force which recommended BU for the contract denied they were aware of this).[88] The AMP Program Manager, Saul Gefter, had served as deputy director of Radio Marti.[89] Silber was a friend of Charles Wick and the idea of outsourcing such a programme to a university would have sat comfortably with Wick's agenda of involving the private sector in the agency's work.[90] Particularly one led by an individual steeped in similar anti-communist ideology. Silber was a divisive figure – at one stage, ten of the university's fifteen deans called for Silber's resignation along with hundreds of faculty members. However, he proved adept at raising BU's endowment and was supported by the board of trustees.[91] Though a Democrat, Silber disagreed with the party on a number of issues demonstrated by his support for the Nicaraguan *Contras* and his opposition to sanctions against apartheid South Africa. He awarded honorary degrees to controversial political figures such as Mangosuthu Gatsha Buthlezi of South Africa and El Salvadorian President Napoleon Duarte and invited the conservative Republican Chief Justice William H. Rehnquist to be commencement speaker for one year.[92] Backed by Silber, the university opened a centre for the study of disinformation run by a former Czech intelligence agent Lawrence Martin (Ladislav Bittman) to counter Soviet disinformation and examine, according to Silber, 'to what extent is the manipulation of news essential to America's national survival'. Similar to Shultz and Casey, Silber expressed concern that 'democracy may be undermined by its own principles in the face of totalitarian techniques'.[93] This 'concern' became a justification for the United States to use propaganda, ostensibly to remedy this disparity.

The USIA had invited BU and five other groups to submit detailed proposals following the evaluation of the initial concept papers but, ultimately, BU ended up submitting not just one but two proposals. The College of Communications' bid, prepared under Dean Redmont, outlined a training programme on campus in Boston.[94] A rival proposal, from the university's central administration and various faculty members from the College of Communications and the Center for International Relations, offered training in Peshawar, in line with USIA guidelines. During the course of the preparations of these bids, the atmosphere in the university between the conflicting parties became increasingly fraught. At one stage, Redmont – a respected foreign correspondent of long-standing – had accusations that he was a spy for the Soviet Union in his youth bandied about in the college press.[95]

Silber sent a covering letter and copy of both proposals to his friend Wick as well as the project director, Saul Gefter. He wrote that BU would be 'delighted to punch some holes in the blackout the Soviets have imposed on their criminal behaviour in Afghanistan.[96] BU's second proposal, based in Peshawar, prepared with the help of Rosanne Klass from Freedom House, secured the $180,000 training grant while Hearst/King Features Syndicate won the bid to set up an Afghan news agency worth $310,000.[97]

Along with Maitre, BU's proposal listed Kurt Lohbeck amongst the personnel who would be involved in training the *mujahedeen* reporters.[98] Maitre's connections with European media organizations would be mined to develop contacts for news distribution. The proposal also detailed BU's 'reliable, established networks' with the director of *La Nacion* and *Rumbo Centroamericano* – pro-*Contra* Costa Rican publications.[99] So the project, at least the BU section, was firmly in the hands of staunch anti-communist Cold Warriors who heartily endorsed the Reagan Doctrine objective of challenging the Soviet Union via informational campaigns. Maitre described the programme's role thus: 'Our major task is to develop propaganda' as a foil to Soviet propaganda about the Afghan conflict.[100] As trainees would be drawn from the *mujahedeen* forces, training would be timed to avoid the 'campaigning season' that re-started each year around about the end of March when the snows melted on the Khyber Pass allowing the rebels to enter Afghanistan again from Pakistan.[101] However, getting the project started on the ground in Pakistan proved more difficult than anticipated.

Implementing the Afghan Media Project

While the USIA announced that BU and King Features had been awarded the AMP grant in February 1986, it would be a full year before actual training began in Peshawar. BU and AMP staff visited Pakistan in January 1986 to lay the groundwork for the project; however, the project quickly ran into difficulties amidst the ragbag of conflicting, and often hidden, agendas simmering below the surface in Pakistan.[102]

The Pakistan government's agreement was needed to allow the project go ahead in Peshawar; however, according to the Koehler Report, Pakistan did not permit any Western journalists to base themselves in Peshawar, only in the capital Islamabad.[103] While Pakistan did not outwardly censor its press invariably, according to another report, the official media outlets could be relied upon to 'self-censor' their output.[104] How this would be 'encouraged' in *mujahedeen* reporters under American trainers was undoubtedly a cause of concern for the Pakistan leadership. This was hardly the ideal environment for creating a 'free press'. The Pakistan government relationship with the *mujahedeen* was fraught too. Although locked in an alliance, the Pakistanis and the *mujahedeen* were not natural or historic allies. The very Afghans seeking refuge in Pakistan's North West Frontier Province were the same ethnic Pashtuns, which claimed this land for their own, in a dispute that pre-dated the establishment of the Pakistan state. To allow rebels with irredentist aspirations for its territories to establish a news agency to sell their story, independently of Pakistan, was a difficult concession for Pakistan to make.[105] While the Reagan administration endeavoured to progress the project in their contacts with the Pakistan leadership, the Pakistanis continued to drag their heels over the appointment of a director for the news agency leaving the training project homeless and 'unofficial' initially.¹⁰⁶ By November 1986, the project was still seeking a 'certificate of non-objection' from the Pakistani authorities to allow it to commence operations such as renting premises, organizing bank accounts and hiring staff. The diplomatic post in Islamabad was asked to step in to encourage the Pakistan government to allow the news agency to commence.¹⁰⁷ The Pakistanis eventually acquiesced though not without insisting that a Pakistani trainer be included on the teaching staff presumably to keep them updated on the project's status.¹⁰⁸ It appears that the Pakistanis were not the only ones to blame for delays as disagreement amongst the Peshawar Seven over the selection of a suitable Afghan director for the resource centre continued. By March 1987, the project still had no director though the first tranche of students had completed their training and the *mujahedeen* parties were 'clamoring' to secure places for their members on subsequent courses.¹⁰⁹

As well as the political machinations of the *mujahedeen* and the delays generated by Islamabad, the project's implementation also faced domestic hurdles. Senator Humphrey and the Congressional Task Force on Afghanistan were agitating for answers as to the cause of the hold-ups.¹¹⁰ Then in October 1986, due to increasing concern provoked by negative publicity, King Features gave notice that it was withdrawing from the project.¹¹¹

At this stage money, as well as patience, began to run short. The project had received excess Department of Defense property (mainly office and audio-visual equipment) under the McCollum Amendment, which had already facilitated the transportation of up to $10 million dollars of non-lethal excess stock to support the Afghan resistance.¹¹² Cameras and typewriters were selected by the AMP staff for use in the training project and by other Afghan information groups.¹¹³ However, this along with the congressional appropriation of $500,000 and a matching USIA contribution was not enough to fund the training and the operational costs of the resource centre, in advance, for a full year, as stipulated by the Pakistanis as a prerequisite to official approval. A shortfall of $700,000 was predicted and the USIA sought funds from the NSC, USAID and Congress. Private sources were approached too including Muslims in the United States who could enable their 'brothers and sisters half-a-world-away in striving to regain their country'.¹¹⁴

As delays continued to hamper the project, and BU sought to expand its role, it pointed the finger of blame at the USIA. Some sourness began to creep into the relationship between the two organizations. Maitre stated publicly that the USIA should 'back off' from its involvement and allow BU complete control and Senator Humphrey alleged the agency was the cause of delays as it sought increased funding.¹¹⁵ Maitre said the USIA had approached the Department of Defense, the State Department, the NSC as well as private donors to procure additional money to make the project 'bigger and bigger' but questioned whether involvement of these agencies would threaten the AMP's creditability. There were even rumours that Maitre's friend Oliver North (then at the centre of the Iran-*Contra* affair) was to become involved.¹¹⁶

Meanwhile, BU sought to organize a consortium to facilitate its takeover of King Features' grant allocation.¹¹⁷ This consortium would include a PVO called The Mercy Fund, which was already based in Peshawar and run by Ann Hurd, Kurt Lohbeck's partner, and Antony Campaigne, a conservative activist.¹¹⁸ The Mercy Fund raised donations for its Afghan projects via direct mail pleas to Americans that were filled with sensationalist claims such as that Afghan babies were being burnt alive by Soviet soldiers.[119] It had an office in Washington run by Campaigne and a house in Peshawar where Hurd and Lohbeck lived. The fund offered accommodation and introductions to *mujahedeen* (invariably Lohbeck's friend Abdul Haq) for Western journalists visiting Peshawar from where Lohbeck covered the war for CBS.[120] The Mercy Fund participation was initially looked on favourably by the USIA staff as it fulfilled the congressional mandate that the project be given over to private interests as soon as possible.[121] Senators Humphrey, Wallop, Bradley, Dodd and Simon sat on the PVO's national advisory board along with the president of the German Afghan Committee and the president of the Afghan community in the United States.[122] The fund offered to house the project; however, it was felt by the US consul in Peshawar that this would be unacceptable to both the Pakistanis and the *mujahedeen* if the Mercy Fund was also housed there. This suggested existing tensions between these parties. Furthermore, Kent Obee, Chief Political Affairs Officer in the US embassy in Islamabad, following talks with the Pakistan government, recommended that the fund's role should be kept low profile and their own literature at a distance from the AMP, until they assumed control of the news service at a later stage.[123] Presumably, the fund's hyperbolic style would have damaged the AMP's aspiration to be taken seriously by the world's media. In any case, at this stage, the relations between BU and the Mercy Fund were strained.[124] BU's Nick Mills recommended rejecting the Mercy Fund's proposal to create a larger news agency. He believed it would be too costly and argued that any links to their Humanitarian News Service could 'dilute the effectiveness and credibility' of the AMP. A larger agency could also threaten the viability of existing local information agencies which would be counterproductive.[125] The post in Islamabad agreed pointing to the high administrative costs associated with the Mercy Fund proposal and 'a completely unnecessary Washington office'. Eventually, according to Olsson, the 'threat' from a Mercy Fund takeover 'withered away'.[126] Olsson did not have a good relationship with Lohbeck from the start and felt that the journalist's involvement in the AMP would have been detrimental to the project's integrity.[127] However, the Mercy Fund was not the only right-wing advocacy group seeking a slice of the congressional funding made available for the AMP.

A number of private European organizations and individuals made proposals to the US government hoping to access some of this money.[128] The USIA was approached by Laurent Marechaux of Guild Europeenne du Raid, a Paris-based NGO involved in sending cash aid to Afghanistan.[129] The Guild's Director Patrick Edel was a member of the Organisation of the Secret Army (OAS), which opposed Algerian independence from France in the 1960s with a campaign of terror.[130] Marechaux was himself a former member of a French right-wing terrorist organization called the Youth Action Group, which had targeted American business interests in France in the 1970s. He visited the AMP's Project Director John Mosher offering for sale films he had shot in Afghanistan. While not suitable as news output for the project, the USIA was interested in buying them to play at their diplomatic posts, though not at the $10,000 fee Marechaux requested. Marechaux had also requested funding for an information project the Guilde was undertaking; he was told by project staff member Richard Hoagland to maintain contact as funds may again become available at a later date.[131] The USIA obviously hoped to fund even more propaganda projects in Afghanistan regardless of the dubious political lineage of their instigators.

AMP staff was also in contact with a similar privately funded West German media project (to which Lohbeck also had connections)[132] that based its training in West Germany.[133] The option to collaborate and share personnel, training, technology and satellite services was discussed as was the option of relocating the USIA project to West Germany if the Pakistan authorities continued to prove intransigent.[134] The Americans were keen as 'international co-operation would bring valuable credibility to the project' and dilute US involvement.[135] Gerhardt Lowenthal of ZDF, 'the spark behind the German Media Project', was a prominent New Right figure in 1980s West Germany and a member of the exclusive German Afghan Committee (DAK).[136] The DAK had links to the Mercy Fund and received donations from the Schweizer Ost-Institut whose founder Peter Sager was involved with the WACL.[137] DAK, which eventually managed to alienate a number of *mujahedeen* factions due to its partisanship, was also connected to the CFA and received funding from the US Congress and the US State Department.[138] This proposed alliance, along with another French proposal, never came to fruition but it is interesting to note how knowledge of the project and its funding filtered out beyond the American New Right and anti-communist PVOs involved in Afghanistan to a network of similarly minded groups in Europe.[139]

In its early days, the media project was hindered by obstacles generated by Islamabad and the Peshawar Seven, both of whom sought to control the creation of a 'free press' in Pakistan for their own political ends. In the United States, right-wing PVOs with links stretching across Europe endeavoured to get involved hoping to access some of the significant funding available and to ensure it developed as an instrument of anti-communist propaganda. To some extent though the staff within the USIA, the US embassy in Islamabad and BU who were not so ideologically dogmatic managed to fend off these challenges which would have completely undermined the AMP's credibility as a news source before it even began. However, the project's credibility as a media operation was under siege from the US press from its inception as journalists railed against the USIA's encroachment into its industry and the associated taint of propaganda.

The USIA relationship with the media over the AMP could best be described as fraught. Whilst on the one hand the project's raison d'être was to encourage increased media coverage for the Afghan conflict, on the other hand, the Afghan Media Staff sought to avoid publicity for the project itself. This was mainly to distance the news service, once established, from taint of US government involvement and accusations of media manipulation. While arguing on the one hand that Afghans would control the content produced, the USIA sought to steer the type of media product (video) produced to plug a perceived hole in coverage. Furthermore, Afghan trainees were chosen by the Afghan Resistance Alliance parties guaranteeing a certain bias from the outset. The USIA sought to manage press interest in the project from the start.[140] In general, media interest was discouraged and a 'low-key, low profile approach' was requested from those determined to do a story on it.[141] The USIA feared that 'unwanted publicity' could 'blow the whole project out of the water' and BU trainers in Pakistan were discouraged from giving interviews.[142] Though some articles such as *Newsweek*'s 'Journalism School for Afghan Rebels'[143] were not critical, it seems that any publicity at all linking the project to the US government was problematic, particularly for Islamabad, where it could be expected to generate 'significant negative ramifications'.[144] Tensions between the United States and Pakistan were heightened during this period as news that Pakistan had achieved weapons-grade nuclear capability became public, threatening congressional approval of its aid package. Tensions between the Pakistanis and the Afghan *mujahedeen* were ever present.[145]

The battle for control of the AMRC

By March 1987, BU had taken over the Hearst element of the project (to develop a news agency and distribution network) alone. However, at this stage, it would seem there were concerns from the post in Islamabad on how BU was running the programme on the ground and whether it could effectively market the output of the news agency.[146] Nonetheless, training had begun in earnest in Peshawar in February 1987 and thirty-two Afghans were given instruction in the first phase: ten in print media; ten in photojournalism and twelve in videography.[147] Members of this first group were drawn mainly from existing Afghan information groups and resistance nominees.[148] The second group was drawn from Afghan resistance groups with 'some emphasis on persons associated with Afghan commanders in the field'.[149] Without a director the project was still 'unofficial' and, consequently, homeless, so the IRC provided it with a classroom but for afternoon use only.[150] According to BU, the training programme was proceeding successfully and the resistance parties were keen to secure places for their candidates in future sessions.[151] Some of the trainees had even started to train other *mujahedeen* who did not secure places on the programme and, by the end of April 1987, material was being transmitted to London for distribution.[152] A more hopeful note was now sounded by the USIA with one report stating:

> It has been slow getting off the ground, and there's been more than enough finger-pointing to go around between State, NSC, Senator Humphrey's office, USIA, Boston University, the Pakistan government and our USIS post there. The BU training of Afghans has started in earnest now, following the three professionals the Agency sent out on our own training program last year, and results on the ground should lessen (but not eliminate) the criticism. It was a difficult undertaking we've known this from the beginning, and USIA doesn't need to be overdefensive about it.[153]

The training aspect of the project ran until November 1987 by which time the Afghan Media Resource Center (a fully fledged news agency never came to fruition) was set up. At this stage, the USIA sought to end its relationship with Maitre and BU whose contract was due to run out at the end of December 1987, in any case. Olsson, a freelance documentary filmmaker, was hired to administer the AMRC in its initial transition period. However, the rapidly deteriorating relationship between the USIA and BU, and Maitre and Olsson, would leave 'blood on the carpet'.[154]

Another report by Jack Koehler on the AMP in November 1987, this time commissioned by BU, recommended that if the AMRC was to be taken seriously by the Western media, it needed to be run solely by Afghans, and USIA and BU involvement must cease.[155] However, contrary to the report they had themselves commissioned, BU did not feel the AMRC was ready to go it alone and looked to prolong its involvement. At this stage, Olsson, with Kent Obee's support, moved to wrestle control of the administration of the centre from Maitre. Maitre reacted angrily writing to the USIA stating that Olsson was 'not an appropriate candidate for this or any other leadership position in the AMRC'.[156] However, Koehler had praised the filmmaker's role in the centre pointing out that the development of the television department 'had been spectacular with major credit undoubtedly due to the professional ability and attitude of Stephen Olsson'.[157] Koehler recommended that Olsson remain on as a consultant to the AMRC.[158] Maitre wished to extend BU's contract into the first three months of 1988, arguing that an effective distribution network had not yet been established and the project required an experienced journalist with TV news expertise to lead it up. He lamented the tendency towards documentary (Olsson's area of expertise).[159] The USIA politely, but firmly, declined Maitre's offer. Instead, it accepted Koehler's counsel that the time had come to hand the project over to the Afghans.[160] In a last minute manoeuvre, Maitre moved to terminate Olsson's AMRC contract but the USIA terminated BU's contract before he could affect this.

While the AMP's American stakeholders struggled for control of the programme, those involved on the ground in Peshawar sought to sidestep the political machinations and create something, which would truly seek to reflect the reality of Afghans' existence and experience during this period, not solely 'newsworthy' war footage. While Maitre had focused on teaching students to identify military hardware for strategic reasons, this was alienating some Afghans.[161] Olsson, along with the AMRC's Afghan Director Haji Sayed Daud, strove to take the project in a different, less politicized direction. They focused on documenting Afghans' lives and culture rather than just warfare and quietly developed a project which would tell Afghans' story to the world and not just the chapter concerning its pivotal role in a late Cold War proxy war. The project was renamed the Afghan Media Resource Center in June 1987.[162] Olsson's role as project manager (Maitre was the project director but only visited every six months or so) meant he was already effectively in charge of the programme on the ground. Along with Duad, he sent the newly trained Afghan journalists and cameramen out across all twenty-nine provinces of Afghanistan to document the lives and living conditions, traditions and culture of the land so many Westerners had fallen in love with in the 1960s and 1970s. However, it was not all plain sailing, even with BU out of the picture, Peshawar remained a very dangerous place to operate a news outlet, despite Rosanne Klass once describing it as safer than Boston.[163] At one stage, the school had to close down for a week due to running street battles.[164] Daud faced a litany of threats from the Soviet and DRA security forces, as well as *mujahedeen* opposed to US interference in Afghanistan, or unhappy with a perceived bias.[165] Duad was also constrained from hiring women for fear of incurring the wrath of the more fundamentalist *mujahedeen* groups.[166] So although the USIA's stated public diplomacy themes included highlighting the impact of the war on Afghan women and, initially, women trainees were suggested by the

O'Reilly report to reflect the modernization and secularization which had redefined their role, particularly in urban areas, since the 1950s, with the USIA's blessing women were barred from the AMRC.[167]

Olsson left in February 1988 but continued to liaise with the AMRC, which stayed open until 1992. The centre did leave a lasting legacy, however, as its archive of over 3,500 hours of video and more than 20,000 photos was recently digitalized with the aid of a Library of Congress grant providing a valuable historical visual archive of life in Afghanistan during the Soviet occupation.[168]

Conclusion

The genesis of the AMP was in a political action programme developed to undermine the Soviet occupation of Afghanistan and its establishment was 'a major policy objective of the Reagan administration'.[169] The project was authorized by NSDD 166, though mooted earlier by various resistance supporters in Congress, PVOs and the administration as media coverage of Afghanistan waned. Many of the project's advocates were fuelled by the belief that the US position in Vietnam was sabotaged by adverse media opinion and that a similar fate could and should be visited on the Soviets in Afghanistan. In the light of the growth of network news programmes in the early 1980s, obtaining video footage to captivate television audiences was considered essential to this goal. As accessing the battlefields of Afghanistan was so treacherous, training willing *mujahedeen* seemed an enlightened solution. However, it was inevitable that this would lead to accusations of propaganda, as these trainees could hardly be objective under such conditions even if they wished to. Ultimately, as one dissenting BU professor put it:

> Journalism is a process of inquiry and description. It's very different from propaganda. Propaganda is goal oriented. The USIA isn't there [in Pakistan] because they want the *mujahedeen* to learn journalism; they are there to conduct a propaganda effort against the Soviet Union.[170]

Though the controversy surrounding BU's bid for the AMP contract attracted much media commentary, in many cases the media seemed to accept the assertion that a 'news blackout' had been imposed by the Soviets and that such a service was necessary to redress this.[171] The *Washington Post* even called the AMP 'uncensored news for the Western media'.[172] Certainly, the Soviets sought to discourage and make as difficult as possible coverage of events in Afghanistan. However, the lack of coverage reflected the fact that US and European publics were just not that interested in the conflict as it dragged on and on. The administration wished to encourage media interest but not for the sake of Afghanistan. Instead, it hoped to further its aim of damaging the Soviet's international credibility and this was evident from its choice of a training partner in BU that was ideologically compatible.

Although the Smith-Mundt barred distribution of the media project's output in the United States, at least until 'independent', the USIA endeavoured to appear 'hands off' from the outset stating it would 'not try and influence where Afghans distribute their news'.[173] But producing news that was unbiased or even representative of the diverse Afghan community would be difficult due to the power and influence of the resistance groups in Peshawar and the deference which had to be accorded to them to allow the project proceed. Women's voices and experience of the war and the camps were marginalized and sacrificed for the propaganda goals of the project. Furthermore, divisions within the Afghan population were glossed over by the project and an emphasis on Muslim identity or the 'enshallah factor' was encouraged to help transcend tribal differences similar to that encouraged by US education projects in Afghanistan at the time.[174] Later, the Taliban would similarly emphasize Afghan's Muslim identity as transcending tribal mores and ties with ominous results.

The USIA and BU's intentions were to wage a cold war battle with video cameras and pencils and the project was inevitably subject to the intrigues and machinations of Peshawar at that time – a potent mix 'questionable interests' and unfettered funding.[175] However, by choosing Olsson and Daud to take over the AMRC the USIA officials involved did eventually hand the project over to individuals who hoped to capture something other than conflict for future generations. They ultimately managed to circumvent the Cold War imperatives of the Reagan era and document a defining period of Afghanistan's long history and, most importantly, 'help Afghans tell their story to the world'.[176]

6

'The road to Geneva and beyond': The superpower summit, public diplomacy and the Afghan conflict

Concurrent with the genesis of the US AMP in March 1985, the Communist Party of the Soviet Union elected a new leader: Mikhail S. Gorbachev. Gorbachev's agenda for internal reform of the Soviet Union necessitated a more constrained foreign policy for the Eastern superpower, which was buckling under economic stagnation. Younger and more dynamic than previous Kremlin leadership, British Prime Minister and Reagan ally Margaret Thatcher described Gorbachev as a man she could 'do business' with. Soon after the Soviet leaders' assent to power the United States and USSR were engaged in arranging a superpower summit in Geneva, Switzerland, for November 1985. The summit offered hopes of an easing of tensions and an arms reduction treaty that US allies, and their publics, wholeheartedly supported.

While Gorbachev sought an arms treaty to check military spending, the Reagan administration contrived to deflect Soviet scrutiny, and that of international audiences, from its SDI. The challenge for the Reagan administration was to appear to be willing to negotiate a new détente without sacrificing its SDI. To this end, officials developed a propaganda strategy to highlight the Soviets' alleged interference in regional conflicts in the Third World to justify a hawkish stance by Reagan on any arms treaty. The public diplomacy programme around the Geneva summit focused on this goal with the Afghan conflict providing much of the content. It portrayed the battle between the *mujahedeen* and the Afghan and Soviet armies in Manichaean terms while eschewing the more complex political and social ramifications of the conflict in Pakistan and Afghanistan. This policy offered the administration negotiating leverage at the summit but would bestow upon the region a destructive legacy stretching far beyond the Cold War.

The conflict in Afghanistan played a large role in the US public diplomacy surrounding the lead-up to the momentous 1985 meeting; but while the administration publicly backed the *mujahedeen* and used their cause to undermine the Soviets, it was careful to remain aloof from deeper political involvement. This 'hands off' policy served to privilege the most ruthless but militarily effective resistance members favoured by the Pakistanis. More moderate or representative elements who could have offered a more peaceful future to Afghanistan were marginalized. Ultimately, the administration was concerned with damaging the credibility of the Soviet Union not becoming explicitly or inextricably entangled in a conflict many miles from home.

Paradoxically, while the administration rhetorically endorsed the resistance and increased arms supplies to them, it refused to afford the *mujahedeen* leadership political recognition as a government-in-exile. The Reagan administration's preference to remain at a remove from the Afghan conflict encouraged it to extend its creed of privatization to foreign policy. Pro-*mujahedeen* PVOs privately solicited and channelled funds to elements of the Afghan resistance.[1] Some PVOs were particularly influential with links to the administration and Congress. They were adept at raising the profile of the conflict via media punditry, celebrity-glittered dinners or lectures and talks aimed at propagandizing the American public. It is testament to the positive public image the *mujahedeen* enjoyed in the Untied States that a wide range of political and celebrity figures were happy to publicly support their struggle. The administration's policy empowered such organizations and granted them access to Washington's corridors of power. The PVOs publicly pressed the administration into proffering greater assistance and diplomatic recognition to the *mujahedeen* at the cost of other Afghan leaders and groups. Furthermore, they agitated against any Afghan peace talks accusing the State Department of a willingness to 'sell-out' the Afghans as part of a wider understanding with the Soviets. This hard-line rhetoric from the PVOs made any willingness in the administration to pursue a settlement on Afghanistan that did not involve the Peshawar Seven difficult to justify. As a result, it hindered progress and prolonged the conflict.

The roadmap to Geneva

Mikhail Gorbachev's leadership style differed greatly from previous Soviet leaders. He was witty, urbane and suave and soon caught the imagination of the Western media.[2] *Time* magazine described him as 'a vibrant presence' but the Reagan administration characterized the Kremlin's new media-friendly attitude as a more Machiavellian 'charm offensive'.[3] Furthermore, Gorbachev quickly sought to alter the terms of the Cold War stand-off between the United States and USSR calling for a missile freeze just two weeks after taking office leaving the Reagan administration feeling outmanoeuvred.[4] Anti-communist conservatives were also unconvinced by him. The Heritage Foundation warned of misplaced 'tidal waves of optimism in the West' generated by the assent of Gorbachev and aided by a 'new and relatively sophisticated public relations campaign conducted by the Kremlin'.[5] Such a media-savvy Soviet leader challenged US propaganda, which had characterized the Kremlin as greying and grim, by seeking to re-imagine relations between the superpowers and end the 'ice age' between them.[6] Arrangements were soon underway for a superpower summit meeting for the first time in six years and the first time ever for President Reagan. Wary Cold War hawks like Zbigniew Brzezinski cautioned that the summit risked being turned into a 'PR competition' by Gorbachev whose only negotiating strength was his appeal amongst the Western media. This, urged Brzezinski, must be recognized and countered.[7] However, internationally, Gorbachev's appeal extended beyond his worldly charm to the policies he was touting.

While Gorbachev sought to reduce arms spending to allow him to focus on domestic economic recovery, Reagan wished to avoid cuts to the SDI.[8] As world publics rallied in international capitals against nuclear war, the United States did not want to be perceived as ratcheting up military spending while the Soviets offered a freeze. USIA polls showed some European publics were willing to offset SDI development against a nuclear arms treaty at Geneva and were sceptical of the sincerity of US negotiating efforts.[9] Thus, moves by Gorbachev to improve the USSR's image by openly offering to negotiate on such matters threatened to establish the Soviet Union as 'a more formidable adversary to battle in the court of world public opinion' for the United States.[10] The Geneva summit quickly became a focal point for this propaganda clash.

As soon as the summit meeting was announced in July 1985, the USIA mounted a 'major public diplomacy campaign' to publicize US 'hopes and concerns' for the meeting.[11] The administration's 'Road to Geneva' strategy involved a number of orchestrated opportunities to publicly demonstrate American concern for the Third World, human rights and resistance movements in an effort to regain ground earlier lost to the Soviets in the propaganda battle.[12] The administration sought to manage public perceptions of the Geneva summit and unsettle the Soviets by concentrating attention on so-called regional issues, such as the conflicts in Afghanistan and Nicaragua. According to Washington, these conflicts were aggravated by Soviet interference and were the 'roots of tensions' in the international system.[13] This strategy addressed three key audiences: US allies, Congress and the US public.[14] Some in Congress already supported this position particularly *mujahedeen* advocates like Gordon Humphrey. They were already agitating for Soviet human rights violations in Afghanistan to be linked to any arms control initiatives in Geneva.[15] However, at this stage, the Reagan administration was itself divided on the desirability of negotiating with the communists and, by now, the 'dealers' were winning out creating a divergence between propaganda and policy.[16] Afghanistan provided the 'bleeders' with an opportunity to shape the debate by publicly railing for a harder line with the Soviets, which constrained the administration's room to manoeuvre and negotiate.

While European and world publics hoped for progress on an arms reduction treaty, the 'PR battle' gained momentum as Geneva neared. Each superpower began marking out negotiating positions to further their own agendas and undermine those of their rivals. On 9 September 1985, Gorbachev gave an extensive interview to *Time* magazine which lamented the Reagan administration's 'campaign of hatred against the USSR' in the lead-up to the summit and argued that 'abusive words are no help'. Gorbachev argued that 'the objective of [the USSR's] moratorium on nuclear explosions' was to find a solution to the arms limitation deadlock and called on the United States to join them and to 'resume the negotiations on a complete ban on nuclear tests as well as of the proposals regarding peaceful cooperation and the prevention of an arms race in space'.[17]

This, Gorbachev argued, was a genuine proposal and not just an attempt to influence public opinion. He appealed for the United States to respond by suspending the development of one of its strategic missiles. Countering such Soviet 'propaganda' would become a major focus of the Reagan administration public diplomacy programme in the lead-up to the summit.[18] The day Gorbachev's *Time* interview appeared in print, Ben

Elliot, Reagan's conservative head of speechwriting, argued that Reagan's UN General Assembly address later that month should set the stage for Geneva. He recommended putting the Soviets 'on the defensive' and undermining 'State and NSC's treaty-mongering, policy paralysis'. This could be achieved, according to Elliot, by focusing on the 'slaughter' in Afghanistan, the KAL airliner incident and Soviet violation of every treaty it was a signatory to since the Second World War.[19] Ultimately, Reagan's speech proved less inflammatory. However, it did include an impassioned defence of SDI and flagged Soviet involvement in a range of regional conflicts as an issue inciting US mistrust of the USSR.[20] The speech was carried in full on the USIA's Worldnet service and administration officials were readied to provide 'TV/press reinforcement'. The next day a follow-up US UN backgrounder on Afghanistan was distributed to foreign and domestic journalists and the administration called for a debate on the conflict.[21] In his televised address to the nation on 14 November 1985, just before departing for Switzerland, Reagan reiterated that regional conflicts in Afghanistan, Nicaragua, Cambodia, Angola and Ethiopia were the real obstacles to lasting world peace requiring resolution before meaningful arms negotiations could occur.[22]

Of all the named conflicts, Afghanistan was the most problematic for the Soviets and, therefore, an obvious target for particular US attention. NSDD 194 stated that Washington wanted countries to 'stop trying to expand their influence through armed intervention and subversion'. However, the Reagan administration was guilty of subversion and intervention in Afghanistan by arming the resistance, widening the gulf between its rhetoric and the reality of its policies.[23] Reagan publicly advocated for the resolution of this conflict and peace in Afghanistan and castigated the Soviets for the continued warfare. In the meantime, CIA arms deliveries to the region increased tenfold over the course of 1985, and sixty thousand tonnes of company materiel was, at that time, on the loose in Pakistan.[24] The CIA was setting up guerrilla warfare training camps for *mujahedeen*, both foreign and Afghan, in Egypt and elsewhere and seeking ways to co-ordinate with and encourage the participation of the newly arriving international *jihadi* or 'Afghan Arabs' in the conflict.[25]

Considering actual Reagan administration policies towards these regional conflicts, a strong public diplomacy programme was vital to positively shape public perceptions of US actions during the upcoming talks. Communicating alleged Soviet wrongdoings would help cast Washington as Moscow's moral superior as well as ideological opposite. To this end, the USIA sought to produce a 'continuing supply of supporting products'. These included Worldnet broadcasts, Electronic Dialogue programmes, the controversial AmParts programme (selected American speakers sent abroad to advocate US foreign policy),[26] VOA output and pamphlets.[27] VOA editorials would focus on Afghanistan, Soviet disinformation and exploitation of the Western media, human rights, the alleged Soviet manipulation of the peace movement amongst other issues. The USIA promised videotapes in English, Arabic, French, Spanish and Portuguese documenting Soviet atrocities against the Afghan civilian population.[28] A document titled 'The Road to Geneva and Beyond' listed a timetable of proposed public diplomacy events designed to shape public perceptions in the lead-up to the summit. Those centred on Afghanistan included bilaterals with Pakistan's President Zia al-Haq and Prime Minister Rajiv Gandhi of India on 23 October 1985 to emphasize US concern about the region. Another meeting between the President and the *mujahedeen* leadership in a White House 'Rose Garden ceremony' was scheduled for late October 1985.[29]

On site in Geneva, the USIA utilized superior American satellite communications technology to broadcast to a worldwide audience estimated at 1 billion people.[30] 'America Today', its daily news programme, ran for a half hour daily on a thirty-foot screen in the Geneva Press Centre 'to the delight of the journalists and the voiced chagrin of the Soviets'. It reached a million Europeans and in a 'major coup', some of its produce was even replayed on the US networks Sunday talk shows. According to the report, the impact was 'incalculable'.[31]

As well as disseminating interviews and press briefings, the USIA's Worldnet television channel also edited and repackaged previously produced programmes for output at Geneva and distribution to the international press corps. These consisted of a number of Afghan-related programmes including two from the Electronic Dialogue series on Soviet abuses in Afghanistan presented by Zalmay Khalilzad, by now an advisor to the State Department.[32] In these programmes, Khalilzad identified human rights abuse on a 'macro' and 'micro' level in Afghanistan. Those on the 'macro' level involved the denial of self-determination (sidestepping the thorny concept of democracy as it was alien to most *mujahedeen*) and the deliberate targeting of the civilian population and their crops. On a 'micro' level, Khalilzad alleged that Soviet soldiers raped Afghan wives in front of their husbands, tortured children in front of their parents and used 'toy' bombs and chemical weapons on the Afghan population. In an effort to counter widespread convictions in the media about rebel disunity, Khalilzad contended that the *mujahedeen* were now more professional implying some level of coherence. He argued that Soviets were trying to intensify tribal tensions to create divisions.[33] According to Khalilzad, the rebels were not divided; but if they were, it was due to Soviet machinations. Misrepresenting the causes of rebel disunity served to justify the US continued support for the resistance but failed to acknowledge or address the roots of this factionalism in the disparate religious, social and tribal perspectives of Afghans. However, this bubbling cauldron of division would occasionally boil over and, once the Soviets were no longer a common enemy for the resistance to coalesce around, lead to a destructive civil war during the 1990s.

Another Worldnet report featured Senator James Sasser and Deputy Assistant Secretary of State for the Bureau of Near East and South Asian Affairs Arnold Raphel.[34] Sasser was a Democrat who took a more dovish line on other regional conflicts such as Nicaragua, which gave the appearance of balance to the show. However, his views on Afghanistan were more hawkish. He characterized the invasion of Afghanistan as a 'natural progression of Soviet imperialism' and argued the conflict was, unlike Grenada or Vietnam (where the United States had intervened), a 'true war of national liberation'. Sasser, who had recently returned from visiting Pakistani refugee camps with three other Democratic senators, contended that the *mujahedeen* though religious and conservative were not fundamentalists like the Iranians. This distinction was vital considering the fraught relationship between Tehran and Washington following the Iranian Revolution and the subsequent hostage crisis. Sasser views justified support to the Afghan resistance; however, Raphel repeatedly denied that any US weapons were going to the *mujahedeen*.

In another clip, Deputy Assistant Secretary of State Robert Peck outlined the Soviet's 'deliberate genocide' in Afghanistan and the pressure Pakistan was subject to from the Soviet Union. The documentary 'Land on Fire' reviewed 'Soviet massacres of Afghans in Kunduz and Laghman Provinces' and contained graphic descriptions by refugees of brutal attacks on them by Soviet troops.[35] Of the twenty-two film clips put together by the USIA for distribution at Geneva to major international television networks, five focused wholly, and one in part, on Afghanistan. All emphasized Soviet brutality towards non-combatants and their imperial ambitions in Afghanistan. The Afghan rebels, on the other hand, were presented as liberators and although recognized as religiously conservative like many of their US supporters, they were not ideologically fundamentalist. In other words, according to the propaganda, their attributes and values were compatible with American ideals. The administration emphasized the rebels' religious convictions during the lead-up to the summit. The Department of State described the *mujahedeen* as 'holy warriors' whose secret weapon was 'strength of soul'.[36] Similar religious references were echoed in USIA material, which contrasted American and Afghan's shared belief in god with Soviet atheism.[37]

As well as the Worldnet output, the USIA produced a press package, which outlined Reagan's initiative on regional conflicts. In it, the five conflict-torn states of Afghanistan, Angola, Nicaragua, Cambodia and Ethiopia were described as having 'unpopular Soviet-style regimes' (the description implied Soviet involvement). These were opposed by 'struggling democratic resistance forces' (implying compatibility with Western political ideology) though few of these opposition groups were of democratic heritage.[38] This purported ideological association between the United States and peoples striving for democracy and equality was useful for propaganda purposes but not always evident in American foreign policy. Many of the *Contra* rebels in Nicaragua had been members of Nicaraguan dictator Anastasio Somoza's National Guard while UNITA's Savimbi was a former Maoist who went on to reject participation in UN-organized elections in Angola. In Cambodia, the administration supported the opposition force containing facets of the genocidal Khmer Rouge party.

Also included in the USIA programme for Geneva were VOA editorials on Afghanistan and on Gorbachev's 'pre-Geneva propaganda campaign'.[39] These editorials repeated well-worn US allegations: the targeting of civilians by the Soviet military, the deliberate destruction of crops and livestock, the indoctrination of over forty thousand Afghan children taken to the Soviet Union for schooling and the attempted eradication of Afghan cultural and religious practices.[40] The VOA praised *mujahedeen* resilience in the face of all these atrocities and hardships. To bolster pro-US coverage further President Reagan was prepared to conduct interviews with newspapers and magazines 'published by sympathetic European publishers (Goldsmith, Springer, Murdoch)'. These publishers were all previously involved with the Reagan administration promoting INF deployment on European soil, and Axel Springer's Maitre was a key player in the AMP.[41]

Soon after the summit, on the sixth anniversary of the invasion, a USIA report analysing foreign media opinion on Soviet actions in Afghanistan showed many of the themes emphasized and accusations levelled by the United States in its Geneva campaign reflected in press coverage. Evaluation of 150 newspaper editorials, commentaries and news analysis from thirty-five countries revealed that the administration's tactic of using propaganda centred on the Afghan conflict to malign the Soviets at Geneva was effective and found purchase in Western media coverage.[42] Various publications portrayed Soviet tactics as 'genocide' and 'ruthless warfare' while the rebels were characterized as 'holy warriors', 'heroes' or 'patriots'. Ironically, media coverage also condemned the lack of media coverage of this 'forgotten war'. This echoed another administration theme and demonstrated the success of the campaign that managed to get the media to report on how it allegedly was not reporting the conflict.

However, the coverage was not without nuance as the Soviet insistence that it wanted to find a political solution to Afghanistan gained some purchase. So too did Reagan's admission of a positive discussion on the conflict at Geneva.[43] The US President observed that he believed the Soviets were sincere in seeking a negotiated settlement on Afghanistan.[44] This apparent softening of Reagan's stance did not soften administration rhetoric though, as witnessed by Deputy Secretary of State John Whitehead's address before the World Affairs Council just weeks later. Whitehead described the Soviet invasion as 'communist colonialism' and accused the Soviets of seeking to destroy 'everything Afghan – history, culture, tradition, religion, family'. He criticized the Soviet's 'wilful destruction of crops', use of mines and 'toy' bombs, and the policy of sending Afghan children to the USSR for ideological indoctrination.[45] Whitehead did announce, though, that the United States would be willing to serve as guarantor of a peace settlement in Afghanistan. The propaganda battle between the superpowers was far from over, and Afghanistan would continue to be a useful tool of US foreign policy in this respect regardless of negotiations behind closed doors.

The administration successfully conveyed to the world's media its interpretation of the Afghan conflict and its protagonists via its extensive public diplomacy campaign. However, there was ample evidence that this image bore little relation to the political reality in Afghanistan and Pakistan. The Peshawar Seven were neither democratic nor representative instead were often corrupt, repressive and violent. Furthermore, fissures were evident between the United States and its ally Pakistan, and between Pakistan and its Afghan 'guests'. However, these issues and their consequences for the populations of the two states involved were largely ignored by the Reagan administration.

Democracy and human rights in US public diplomacy

While the Reagan administration was castigating the Soviets for their actions in Afghanistan, the situation on the ground on the Pakistan side of the border was more complicated than presented by US propaganda. Growing discontent within Pakistan over the Afghan refugees sheltering along its North Western borderlands threatened the perception of Pakistan's role as a selfless host for its fellow Muslims. NSDD 194 promised to 'defend human rights everywhere' and the Reagan administration sought to shine the spotlight of public opinion on Soviet Union and its satellites' human rights deficiencies. US allies, such as Pakistan, were largely spared such reproach.[46] Tensions were evident too between the Peshawar leadership and the Afghan refugee community, which questioned the alliance's legitimacy and authority to represent the people of

Afghanistan. These complexities did not sit comfortably with the administration's representation of Pakistan or the *mujahedeen* leadership. Washington ignored rather than addressed them and, as a result, these problems festered.

Pakistan's shaky human rights record and the autocratic rule of Zia ul Haq had long made it a target of congressional and media opprobrium. The Reagan administration sought to gloss over such failings in deference to Pakistan's central importance in routing aid to and providing a safe haven for the Afghan resistance. Pakistan's pivotal role in the conflict was highlighted by the 'Road to Geneva' public diplomacy campaign – Reagan's bilateral meeting with Zia two weeks before the summit was arranged to demonstrate the US concern for the Third World and Afghanistan. When Pakistan and India met to discuss the perceived escalation of their nuclear arms race, President Reagan defended his ally stating that the United States had 'no evidence' that Islamabad was developing nuclear weapons capability.[47] In fact, the administration had been aware since 1982 that it was.[48]

Reagan's address to the UN on 24 October 1985 again highlighted US concern for human rights and selected regional conflicts with an emphasis on Soviet misbehaviour in Afghanistan.[49] At the same time, the administration was receiving many letters that highlighted specific human rights abuses in Pakistan, but never publicly commented on them.[50] Since coming to power Zia had sought to shore up conservative Muslim support by introducing the so-called Black Law which suspended women's right to equal status under the constitution as well as codifying discrimination against women and minorities.[51]

Washington, though always ready to condemn the Kabul government for limiting 'self-determination' in Afghanistan, overlooked Islamabad's lukewarm relationship with the democratic process and the issue of self-determination for the people of Pakistan. Reagan welcomed the visit of prime minister of Pakistan, Muhammad Khan Junejo, in 1986, after an election where political parties were banned and Zia contrived to remain in ultimate control as president. On that occasion, the President described Pakistan as a 'peaceful non-aligned nation… making strides towards democracy' in the face of difficult condition imposed by looming Soviet aggression and the Afghan refugee crisis.[52] The administration sought to place blame for Pakistan's shortcomings firmly at Moscow's door.

Meanwhile within Pakistan, though polls still demonstrated support for the *mujahedeen* and reluctance to recognize the Kabul government, undertows of discontent were emerging. The Afghan refugees were increasingly seen by Pakistanis as an economic burden and as infiltrated with saboteurs.[53] The situation in Pakistan's North West Frontier Province refugee camps was uneasy from the early days of the refugees' arrival. In 1981, Pakistani journalist, Ghani Eirabie, raised concerns about 'the economic and security implications of the presence of 2.5 million armed Afghan refugees on Pakistan soil'.[54]

Pakistan had sought to keep the Afghan refugees apart from its indigenous population but this was not always feasible.[55] Pakistanis local to the camps felt that aid enabled the refugees to accept lower remuneration for work, undercutting locals – something the United States endeavoured to redress.[56] The administration looked seriously on the growing disenchantment amongst Pakistanis. It sought to establish programmes to reduce the competition for work and resources between the refugees and locals.⁵⁷ It was vital to keep the peace between these groups.

Conflict between local Pakistanis and Afghan refugees could generate unrest in Pakistan, threatening Zia's ability to continue to act as a conduit for aid and a safe haven for the resistance. Pakistan was the only state bordering Afghanistan that the United States was on friendly terms with, bar perhaps China.⁵⁸ If this route was blocked then materially supporting the rebels would become virtually impossible. To this end, the administration sought to ensure continued economic as well as military assistance to Pakistan to dilute dissent. As one report outlined, 'a critical factor affecting Zia's ability to a bold Afghan program has been the assurance of strong support from Pakistan's key outside security partners – the US, Saudi Arabia, and China'.⁵⁹ It added that the US 'ability to pursue effective policies on Afghanistan depends, for the time being, on Zia's continuing preeminent role'.⁶⁰ The Reagan administration defended its ally at every turn and undertook to secure effective assistance to it; however, public attitudes within Pakistan towards the United States were ambivalent. Even more worryingly for the administration, belief in US military superiority over the USSR had slipped since 1979 potentially undermining its perception as a protector against the Soviet Union.⁶¹ The relationship between the Western superpower and the 'frontline state' was not one built on trust or respect but Cold War imperatives on the US side. For Zia, the arrangement helped him to maintain power, bolstered Pakistan's military capability and, hopefully, would guarantee a friendly regime in Kabul, ultimately. This would offer Pakistan 'strategic depth' in case of a war with India.⁶²

Whatever Pakistan's shortcomings in the areas of human rights and democratic representation these were publicly minimized by the Reagan administration, in the pursuit of its foreign policy goals in Afghanistan. While Reagan's rhetoric portrayed the *mujahedeen* as a coherent 'democratic resistance' that represented the legitimate voice of the Afghan people was also far from true.⁶³ Ted Carpenter's analysis noted that even the more moderate and secular of the Peshawar Seven organizations had 'little enthusiasm for a Western-style pluralistic nation' to be established in Afghanistan. He added that 'a rebel victory in all probability will not bring about a capitalist economic system or a political system based on respect for individual rights. Even if the "moderates" triumphed, the most likely outcome would be a conservative Islamic state similar to Saudi Arabia or Pakistan'.⁶⁴

Even the formation of the Islamic Unity of the Afghan *Mujahedeen* (IUAM) on 16 May 1985 failed to enhance unity. This was evident in the arrangements for a meeting with President Reagan just before the Geneva summit. The 'Road to Geneva' public diplomacy schedule included a White House Rose Garden ceremony with the *mujahedeen* leadership and the President, which was organized by Khalilzad in his then role as President of the Friends of Afghanistan Committee.⁶⁵ Traditionally, the Rose Garden is where United States' presidents welcome visiting heads of state so the ceremony symbolically conferred this status on the resistance leadership. However, the *mujahedeen*'s lack of unity, dubious political credentials and criminal activity created problems for this propaganda exercise. Advisors warned President Reagan to meet all seven leaders together or none at all, so factionalized was the leadership. One commander was allied to Khomeini and so presumably not the right kind of 'holy warrior' for US propaganda purposes.⁶⁶ As well as the palpably strained 'unity' on display, there were a number of media reports alleging involvement of the *mujahedeen* groups in drug trafficking.⁶⁷ Ultimately, the President, who described the Peshawar Seven as the 'true representatives' of the Afghan people during this visit, refused to recognize the leadership as the government-in-exile of Afghanistan. This was not due to *mujahedeen* division, criminality or associations with anti-US regimes like Iran but due to the Cold War imperatives underscoring US foreign policy in the region. The American embassy in Kabul was proving to be a very effective 'listening post' as, since the 'loss' of Iran, it was one of the closest posts to the southern border of the USSR.⁶⁸ Recognizing the *mujahedeen* leadership as a government-in-exile and withdrawing recognition from the PDPA would impel the closure of this embassy.

Some of the Peshawar Seven's traits were undesirable not only to Washington but to many Afghans as well. In truth, these groups were not as representative of the Afghan people as their own and US propaganda portrayed. When refugees arrived at the Pakistan camps, they were obliged to register with one of the seven *mujahedeen* resistance groups in order to access aid which swelled the parties' memberships. When the United States sent aid, it was channelled through these groups to strengthen their institutional capacity and political capital while allowing the United States to maintain a low profile. No elections were ever held amongst the refugees to justify these leaders' privileged positions of power and, in any case, the refugees in the Pakistani camps were not demographically representative of the Afghan population.⁶⁹

A Congressional Research Report from January 1985 described the refugees in Pakistan as mainly Pashtun while the fighters in Afghanistan were mainly Tajiks, Hazaras and from other minorities. It also reported allegations that the Peshawar Seven were selling donated weaponry to the resistance within Afghanistan – demonstrating the mercenary rather than political nature of this 'leadership'.⁷⁰ A poll conducted just sixteen months after the Geneva summit by the Afghan Information Center in the camps showed 72 per cent wished for the former Afghan King Zahir Shah to become head of state while just 0.45 per cent approved of one of the Peshawar Seven assuming this role. Only 12.5 per cent supported the fundamentalists' objective of establishing a 'pure Islamic state'.⁷¹ It is difficult to believe that support for such a fundamental ideal as the desire for an Islamic state had dropped significantly, more likely it had never existed amongst the majority of Afghans. Yet the fundamentalist parties were receiving the bulk of the aid and all that aid was channelled through the Peshawar Seven organizations whose leadership had minimal support amongst the refugees.

A report sent to President Reagan by Dr Mark Sullivan of The Catholic University of America, Washington, DC, told a similar story.⁷² The academic represented the views of certain Afghan resistance groups within Afghanistan and Pakistan who sought to establish a dialogue with Zahir Shah, the United States and the USSR to further peace negotiations. He described the Peshawar Seven as feared and distrusted alleging their corruption, and self-enrichment had alienated ordinary Afghanis who lived in poverty. They were despised for their strong-arm tactics against anyone opposing them, which included assassination, coercion and intimidation. Sullivan claimed that local commanders ran Gulbuddin Hekmatyar out of Kandahar when he urged a military escalation in the battle for the city as it would have caused unacceptably high civilian casualties.⁷³ However, the perception that the Peshawar groups were the 'legitimate representatives' of the Afghan people was constantly reiterated by their US advocates to justify the procurement of aid, arms and international recognition on their behalf. Failure to maintain that illusion would undermine the rebels' cause to the benefit of the Kabul government and ultimately undermine US foreign policy goals too.

While the Peshawar Seven did not always fit their description as representative leaders for the Afghan people, some Afghan 'refugees' did not always fit their designation either, as it is understood by UNHCR and the West. This meant that much of the aid to the refugee camps was also sustaining the conflict within Afghanistan. Many male refugees assumed dual roles as both rebels (*mujahed*) during the fighting season and refugees (*mohajer*) in the winter.⁷⁴ Some madrassas (religious schools) in the camps offered paramilitary training and boys were shipped off to fight once old enough; in a 1982 report Under Secretary of State for Political Affairs Laurence Eagleburger described not finding one male between the ages of fifteen and forty years in the camp he visited. He concluded that they were 'all across the border fighting either the Russians, the Afghan collaborators or – in their off hours – each other'.⁷⁵ US propaganda portrayed the resistance fighters as brave warriors but the refugees as innocent victims of DRA and Soviet aggression. In fact, they were often one and the same, particularly in the case of male Afghans. Although a 'warrior' might be considered a legitimate target by the Soviet military, *mujahedeen* supporters could decry Soviet targeting of Afghans travelling to and from the battlefield as attacks on refugees.

US public diplomacy while fudging the status of male refugees also avoided addressing the plight of female Afghan refugees. The camps, with their dominant fundamentalist ideology, were difficult places for women where purdah was enforced and restrictions imposed by resistance leaders.⁷⁶ While in Afghan's traditional rural society women had few rights they did have somewhat more freedom than in the camps. In their small local communities, many of the men were relatives which enabled the women to socialize with them. In the camps this was not so, leaving the women much more constrained in their movements. Afghan women from the larger cities would have been free to wear Western clothes, work or attend university. In the areas of Afghanistan under the PDPA's control these practices would have continued, but not in the camps. In the refugee camps, male aid workers were obliged to seek permission from the family patriarch before a woman could attend a clinic or hospital appointment. The camp schools, run by international aid agencies, were mainly for boys. There were 486 boys' primary schools versus 76 for girls, 161 boys' middle schools but only 2 for girls and 4 boys' secondary schools and none for girls.⁷⁷ By contrast, in government-controlled regions of Afghanistan, adult literacy programmes were educating approximately 100,000 people yearly of whom 46 per cent were reckoned to be women. In the mid-1980s, 65 per cent of Kabul University students were women.⁷⁸ However, these tensions between the Afghan refugees within the camps were largely ignored by Western aid agencies seeking to respect 'traditional culture' and operating within a religiously conservative Pakistan. Reagan administration propaganda on the *mujahedeen* disregarded uncomfortable truths about its criminality and religious fundamentalist ideology. It ignored the divisions and factionalism. It presented the refugees in Pakistan as supportive of the leadership and this support as representative of the views of all Afghans. The gap between US propaganda and the complex reality of Afghan politics was substantial. This would cloud understanding of the conflict and the anticipation of its predictably bloody aftermath.

Information that the refugees might be victimizing one another or that for many of the rebels the ideology of freedom and self-determination did not extend to Afghan women was ignored as it would undermine US policy goals. Public diplomacy in 'the road to Geneva and beyond' programme offered a simplistic, palatable image of the *mujahedeen* and of the Afghan refugees who were offered no more self-determination in the camps of Peshawar than in the DRA's Afghanistan. Human rights violations were only publicized when committed by the Soviets or their allies while US allies like Pakistan could expect leniency. Ultimately, US public diplomacy relating to Afghanistan and Pakistan selected issues solely based on whether they could damage the USSR rather than out of any concern for justice, democracy or human rights. The administration's strategy of outsourcing the implementation of its foreign policy goals of increased aid and public awareness of the Afghan resistance was driven by similar Cold War imperatives.

Privatizing Reagan Doctrine propaganda: Afghanistan and PVO support

As the conflict dragged on, more and more private individuals and advocacy organizations were actively seeking to increase support and aid to the *mujahedeen*.[79] In 1986, defence policy analyst Ted Carpenter, in an article for the libertarian CATO institute, argued for the benefits of privatizing the Reagan Doctrine – in Afghanistan's case allowing PVOs fund the *mujahedeen* – to avoid embroiling the United States in far-flung conflicts.[80] This not only reflected some aspects of Reagan's political ideology but also kept the administration's involvement at arm's length. This was vital, as overt US backing could undermine the *mujahedeen*'s credibility and international support. Furthermore, some *mujahedeen* were virulently anti-American which could potentially be embarrassing for an administration seeking to portray the rebels as ideological bedfellows. Carpenter warned that should the rebels win, their resulting rule would be unlikely to be compatible with (espoused) US values. He argued that 'there should be considerable reluctance to back the mujaheddin with U.S. influence and tax dollars when there is a significant risk of creating an Iranian-style dictatorship in Afghanistan'.

However, the Afghan PVOs were eager to assume this role. They would be much more than a tool of Reagan administration foreign policy and consisted of hard-line conservative interests touting a wider anti-Soviet agenda along with Hollywood glitterati and former presidents. By the mid-1980s, the Afghans' cause had attracted much attention from conservative and anti-communist groups and individuals in the United States and elsewhere.

This interest dovetailed with administration policy – a Department of State public diplomacy action plan for Afghanistan listed American private sector involvement and support as an important objective.[81] As AmeriCares boss Robert Macauley pointed out to Vice President Bush in 1984 combining US government resources and those of private voluntary organizations to supply aid to Afghanistan would 'maximize dollar impact while minimizing diplomatic fall out'.[82] The administration sought to actively develop this strategy in cooperation with various PVOs. One Afghan Working Group proposal suggested establishing an 'independent' 'Friends of Afghanistan'-style organization. These would fundraise, generate publicity, lobby international leaders and editorial staff from major newspapers to encourage more coverage. They could also assist 'enterprising young journalists in the form of information, funding and channels to the resistance'.[83] The administration hoped to outsource lobbying for the *mujahedeen* cause and increase the coverage of the conflict via these organizations. However, this intimate relationship between the State Department and the Afghan PVOs was, at varying times, sometimes productive, sometimes combative and sometimes acrimonious. The line between private and public efforts was often obscure.

The State Department hosted seminars on Afghanistan for 'prominent Americans' to raise funds for educational opportunities for young Afghans.[84] It encouraged the organization of benefit galas and focused attention on the impact of the war on Afghan women via private organizations such as Freedom House and the Afghan Resistance Relief Center. Other PVOs like the Cooperation of Democratic Countries (which counted Senator Orrin Hatch and Congressman Laurence McDonald amongst its board of trustees) advocated for aggressive action to encourage the spread of insurrection from Afghanistan into Soviet Central Asia.[85]

The Committee for the Free World – a neo-conservative group of writers and political thinkers – argued that the United States could bring about an 'ideological reformation' of the USSR if it could inflict 'small defeats' in regional conflicts such as Afghanistan, shaking the foundations of the communist regime and undermining its legitimacy.[86] According to one member, Irving Kristol, without such a reformation, stability between the superpowers would prove elusive.[87] However, these confrontational ideologies could very well have had the opposite effect by undermining moderates like Gorbachev and privileging Kremlin hardliners who pushed for a more aggressive stance on Afghanistan and in the Cold War.

Other PVOs had more homespun origins such as the Palm Beach Clinic for Afghans (though also linked to the CFA)[88] established by Palm Beach residents Richard and Susan Williams along with Frank Wright, a public relations consultant.[89] Funds were raised in Palm Beach County in the United States, hence the name, which hung above the finished clinic in English as, according to its benefactors, it helped with publicity and most Afghans were illiterate in any case so the language it was in did not matter to them.[90] Located in a 'strategic yet defensible' location close to Kabul to provide medical treatment for *mujahedeen* and locals, the clinic would be run by Dr Khalid Akram whose appearance in a panel before the Palm Beach Round Table in 1984 had prompted the initiative.[91] Dr Akram, the son of an official of the United Islamic Front and a *mujahed* himself, also testified before the Congressional Task Force on Afghanistan in March 1985 about medical conditions within Afghanistan and 'yellow rain'.[92] At one stage, the retired Williams couple visited Peshawar, Pakistan, dressed in local costume and accompanied by armed bodyguards; they were given a tour of guerrilla training camps by *mujahedeen* – a regular occurrence for Americans seeking a flavour of the conflict. Although established with private funds, the clinic founders hoped to secure federal assistance to cover running costs.[93] This template of an 'ordinary' American citizen, inspired by a visiting 'freedom fighter' setting up a private charity, describes many of the pro-*mujahedeen* PVOs which sprang up in the United States during the course of the conflict. As they were privately established they avoided the scrutiny similar official government actions would trigger, but such organizations inevitably sought federal funding to maintain their projects. In this roundabout way, administration funds were funnelled to the Afghan resistance. Yet other organizations, like the CFA, used their contacts in the administration and Congress to promote their activities and validate their propaganda.

The CFA's promotional leaflets boasted of its pro-*mujahedeen* public diplomacy aimed at domestic US audiences. This included a documentary film about the 'heroic freedom fighters' that was shown across America, participation in the establishment of congressional hearings as well as providing testimony to such hearings. CFA staff personally briefed members of Congress and provided them with factsheets and reports on the conflict. Personnel made numerous appearances on TV and radio talk shows, and gave interviews and information reports to the media. They addressed groups in the United States and around the world.[94]

The CFA argued the Afghan *mujahedeen* were 'fighting our war as well' by stopping the 'Soviet encirclement of both Asia and the Persian Gulf'. The organization contended that the Soviets were using Afghanistan as a 'gigantic research and development laboratory' for testing and perfecting chemical and biological weapons. This technology could eventually be turned on American soldiers if it was not stalled. The organization claimed responsibility for exposing the Soviet use of chemical weapons in Afghanistan. It boasted that the media had 'come to count on the Committee for a Free Afghanistan as a reliable information source' and that its film footage, pictures and analysis were widely used.[95] Its leaflets urged supporters to write to local newspapers and radio stations encouraging more coverage of Afghanistan and contact news editors if they had covered the issue to thank them. It directed members to call on congressional representatives and the Reagan administration to offer more support to the *mujahedeen*.[96] It even produced T-shirts with pro-*mujahedeen* and anti-Soviet slogans. In May 1985, the CFA organized a rally of Washington DC high school students from twenty local schools in support of Afghan students allegedly taken to the USSR. This was attended by congressional supporters including Humphrey and Wilson and administration officials.[97] At this time, the CFA was at the zenith of its advocacy power commanding powerful friends to its cause.

The CFA undertook the organization of a major 'black tie' benefit gala in Washington, DC, hoping to raise $800,000, to be held just a week after the Geneva summit to commemorate the sixth anniversary of the Soviet invasion.[98] The organization liaised with White House Communications Director Pat Buchanan to raise awareness and encourage attendance amongst administration officials.[99] Senator Robert Dole and the millionaire and one-time major Nixon campaign supporter W. Clement Stone were honorary sponsors of the evening. The comedian Fred Travalena was master of ceremonies.[100] Its honorary committee read as a who's who of political figures.[101] Richard Allen, Hoover fellow and former National Security Advisor to Reagan, was on the dinner committee along with Reed Irvine of Accuracy in Media, Edwin Feulner and Charles Lichenstein of the Heritage Foundation, Jack Wheeler of the Freedom Research Foundation and John Singlaub.[102] The organization had a number of celebrities lined up to attend the event, including singers Billy Joel, Roy Orbison, Johnny Cash, Michael Jackson and actors Carey Grant and Robert Duvall.[103] Two private jets were donated to transport celebrities from California to the capital as the CFA endeavoured to draw the American entertainment industry in its cause.[104] President Reagan was invited to address the dinner by Congress' *mujahedeen* advocates but was unavailable. Instead, he videotaped a speech for the occasion animated by familiar US propaganda themes on Afghanistan – 'deadly chemicals' and the targeting of civilians and children.[105] As well as his video message, the President provided a letter of endorsement (drafted by the CFA) for the event invitations. Second Lady, Laura Bush, hosted a reception for selected invitees while British conservative MP Winston S. Churchill proffered a letter of endorsement, as did former President Richard Nixon.[106] The dinner showcased the extensive network of powerful political figures and popular entertainers captivated by the CFA's representation of the *mujahedeen*'s cause.

This was not the only time celebrities were involved in promoting the Afghan cause. In 1984, Frank Capra offered to come out of retirement to direct a film about Afghanistan with narration by the President to raise funds for humanitarian assistance. The film director had previously directed a series of propaganda films titled 'Why We Fight' to generate support for US participation in the Second World War. According to Charles Hill at the State Department 'given Capra's reputation, and his stature amongst American and European intellectuals, his film would have an immediate, highly influential audience'.[107] Reagan had served in the Air Corp's First Motion Picture Unit, which had released Capra's wartime propaganda films and had appeared in some of that series though not those directed by Capra. It seems, however, that this project never got off the ground but demonstrates the range of propaganda initiatives engaging the private sector given consideration by the administration. Another such private-sector enterprise to raise funds and awareness endorsed by the administration was the Variety Clubs International Annual Variety Children's Awards dinner in September 1987 held in New York's Waldorf Astoria.[108] In return for a videotaped message of support from President Reagan, a major portion of funds raised on the night would be donated to an organization called Afghan Children's Relief Fund. Charles Wick promised excellent media and Worldnet coverage ensuring a worldwide audience and, at the NSC's request, even arranged for an Afghan child to be present.[109]

The CFA continued its public diplomacy efforts in 1986, organizing the return to Washington of the IUAM with Professor Burhanuddin Rabbani now as acting leader. This time, they met with the President in the Oval Office.[110] Rabbani was a fundamentalist with Muslim Brotherhood links, who had previously opposed the secular reforms of Zahir Shah and felt his successor Douad (who was overthrown during the 1978 coup) too liberal too.[111] The conservative Rabbani, who would put in place strict Islamic code once president of Afghanistan in 1992, required the State Department provide a male interpreter and intern to assist during the visit.[112]

Notwithstanding Rabbani's fundamentalist leanings, the Senate warmly welcomed him and the alliance to the United States and Rabbani met with influential political figures and the media.[113]

As well as meeting the President, Rabbani's itinerary included a reception hosted by Charlie Wilson in Texas, lunch with the Senate Foreign Relations Committee and coffee with the House Foreign Affairs Committee. Attempts were even made to secure an honorary degree for Rabbani from two universities in receipt of administration funding for Afghan programmes – BU (which had won the AMP contract) and UNO (with which the State Department ran education programmes).[114] Interviews were arranged with USIA organs, the US television networks (through State Department connections) and a whole host of print publications.[115] However, not all the media exposure was positive: the *mujahedeen* leadership was forced to refute a *New York Times* article alleging rebel involvement in opium cultivation and trafficking on a grand scale to fund war efforts. The alliance dismissed the accusations as Soviet propaganda.[116] The meeting with the President was not the positive public diplomacy exercise both sides had envisioned either. Tensions developed as the President refused to extend diplomatic relations to the Afghan resistance and, consequently, withdraw them from the Kabul government.[117] The trip descended into a public diplomacy nightmare. Two of the more anti-American members of the alliance refused to travel to meet Reagan, and Rabbani publicly voiced the IUAM's frustration with Washington's refusal to grant it diplomatic recognition and its lifting of the grain embargo.[118] This disenchantment began to infect the relationship between the administration, particularly the State Department, and US *mujahedeen* supporters.

The CFA had links to the administration and was supportive of Reagan Doctrine goals but its relationship with the Department of State deteriorated over time. The PVO publicly accused the State Department as delaying aid to Afghanistan and of undermining the CFA's role in support of the Afghan resistance.[119] Before the *mujahedeen* leadership visit in 1986, Karen McKay wrote to the Secretary Shultz, protesting at the 'underhanded treatment of the Committee for a Free Afghanistan by the State Department'. She accused the State Department of trying 'to neutralize' and 'discredit' the CFA with Congress and the White House and 'waging a nasty little war against us'.[120] Senator Humphrey, suspected by the administration of working hand-in-hand with the CFA, vociferously backed these complaints. He wrote to the President about 'the snail's pace' of State's spending of humanitarian funds allocated to Afghanistan by Congress and appealed for the closure of the Kabul embassy.[121] The senator publicly accused the CIA of lackadaisical monitoring of the arms flow from Pakistan into Afghanistan. This, he alleged, led to unquantifiable leaks in the weapons pipeline. Furthermore, he castigated the State Department's decision to 'reverse course' and guarantee a peace settlement following the Geneva summit calling it a 'sell-out'.[122]

The Heritage Foundation joined this chorus of disapproval. In a report entitled 'Rhetoric versus Reality: How the State Department Betrays the Reagan Vision', the think tank characterized the State Department as 'dragging its heels in providing aid to Afghans fighting the Soviet invasion and occupation of its country' while allowing the Kabul embassy to remain open and Afghanistan to maintain its 'Most Favored Nation' trading status. It charged the State Department with 'deliberately obstructing the will of Congress and stated Reagan policy'.[123] The report denounced the State Department for refusing to allocate funds to a Californian doctor and friend of Charles Fawcett, Robert Simon and his International Medical Corp (IMC) because they wished to send American medical personnel into Afghanistan.[124] This, the State Department feared, would hand the Soviets a propaganda victory if any were apprehended by the Red Army or kidnapped by the *mujahedeen*. State issued a strident rebuttal stating the report was 'filled with misstatement, inaccuracies and false innuendos' leaving relations between the two institutions frosty.[125] The State Department was in a difficult position – allowing the Soviets an easy propaganda coup was to be avoided but much more damaging to the carefully constructed public perceptions about the Afghan conflict was the reality that Americans were not welcome in Afghanistan by some elements of the *mujahedeen*. The administration did not wish to publicly address this uncomfortable fact. In 1985, journalist Charles Thornton was killed in Afghanistan whilst travelling with rebels on a trip organized by Dr Simon. His body was subsequently held for ransom by a local religious leader, Habibullah Akhund, who alleged Dr Simon did not deliver a promised hospital to his area.[126] Lee Shapiro (who had previously made a documentary about the alleged persecution of the Miskito Indians in Nicaragua by the Sandinistas) and Jim Lindelof (who volunteered with IMC and appeared before congressional hearings on Afghanistan and at CFA forums) were also killed in Afghanistan filming a CAUSA-funded documentary most likely by the *mujahedeen* forces they were travelling with.[127]

Simon also received funding from the CFA and addressed forums they organized as well as appeared in a USIA TV Satellite File on Afghanistan.[128] Senators Clairborne Pell, Paul Tsongas, Gary Hart, Edward Zorinsky and Alan Cranston had recommended his organization for funding from USAID back in October 1984.[129] Simon later testified before the Congressional Task Force on Afghanistan's 'Hearing on Medical Conditions in Afghanistan' in March 1985 to appeal for funding for his activities. At the hearing, Simon stated he had a list of over 200 American doctors willing to travel to Afghanistan but the State Department argued it preferred to distribute medical aid via the International Red Cross, which they contended was more efficient.[130] It seems likely that for diplomatic reasons the State Department sought to divert US aid through less controversial channels. Conversely, for the ideological-driven PVOs and their supporters in Congress any controversy which highlighted alleged Soviet misconduct or generated publicity was welcome. Meanwhile other US PVOs were fighting on another ideological battlefield – the education of Afghan children.

Exploration of the establishment and funding of educational programmes in Afghanistan illuminate the propaganda aimed at Afghanis by Western supporters and the Afghan resistance. Soviet 'indoctrination' of Afghan children was a common feature amongst the propaganda issuing from both the Reagan administration and the PVOs. Afghan children were allegedly spirited away from families and communities to be brainwashed in the Soviet Union. While the Soviets no doubt wished to induct young Afghans into communist ideology, the impetus to transfer Afghan children to the USSR for schooling was driven by the *mujahedeen*'s targeting of schools and teachers from the earliest days of the insurgency. Jeri Laber of Human Rights Watch described Afghan children as 'a prize in a contest of ideologies' between the rebels and the Soviets – US supporters of the *mujahedeen* coveted that prize. The administration's

Afghan Interagency Restricted Working Group recommended channelling funds into Afghan education as part of an agenda of increased political action to support the *mujahedeen*. It proposed that the National Endowment for Democracy (NED) work with a US university to respond to these educational needs.

To assist in the 'contest of ideologies' the NED funded PVOs such as MSF's The Friends of the Children of Afghanistan and The American Friends of Afghanistan (AFA) to develop education programmes for Afghanistan. This was despite the gender-bias evident in the educational programmes the *mujahedeen* were willing to provide. In June 1986, the AFA, along with the Cultural Council of the Afghan Resistance, received a grant of $250,000 from the NED to expand an educational programme within Afghanistan. With the aid of an initial NED grant, the project had already set up ten schools and twenty adult literary centres for resistance fighters and provided teachers, textbooks and cassette tapes. Its focus was to promote 'democratic principles and values among the Afghan people'.[131]

Initially this grant proposal had been submitted under the aegis of the UNO (which also submitted an unsuccessful proposal to run the AMP) by Thomas Gouttierre, director of the Center for Afghan Studies at the university. However, this was withdrawn and resubmitted under the auspices of the AFA of which Gouttierre was president and academic Louis Dupree an active member.[132] Video recorders and training would help to document Afghan life and provide video evidence of the impact of the war within Afghanistan.[133] Such documentation would provide valuable propaganda material resulting in 'a real diplomatic and immediate effect on how the global community views Afghanistan's fight for freedom'.[134]

Mostly this programme's propaganda was aimed at Afghans though. Local *mujahedeen* leaders selected teachers, textbooks were printed in Dari and Pashto, and additional material supplied information on current events and explained 'the Afghan jihad'. The cassettes contained news, commentary on the war, current events and historical information along with Afghan stories and music. In total, the UNO received $60 million from USAID over a ten-year period for their educational programmes in Afghanistan. Gouttierre later admitted that the CIA was involved jointly with USAID and the university in the design and implementation of the project though he denied his centre received any money directly from the CIA.[135]

By 1987, the Alliance education project was a major component of the USAID programme for Afghanistan and figured 'prominently in our public diplomacy efforts' designed to increase 'the political, military and economic costs to the Soviets of their occupation of Afghanistan'. The goal of the aid programme was to stem depopulation within resistance areas and strengthen the institutional capacity of the resistance. The administration reasoned that by 'sustaining the Afghan people, who support the resistance, we exact costs on the Soviet occupation'.[136] The programme would facilitate the opening of 1,500 elementary schools within Afghanistan, train teachers and supply 120,000 textbooks to Afghanistan, printed by the UNO.[137] However, these books were more interested in propagandizing than educating Afghans. They were filled with illustrations of tanks, land mines, guns and missiles and violent imagery promoting *jihad*, glorifying martyrdom and anti-Soviet resistance. UNO staff insisted that the textbooks were developed to reflect the 'religious and cultural sensitivities' of

Afghans at that time, that they did not wish to impose American values in the books.[138] Nevertheless, the books did promote the US foreign policy goal of raising the costs of the occupation to the Soviets by encouraging militancy, which was the real objective of this 'political action' programme.

Conclusion

The public diplomacy strategy developed to support US objectives at the Geneva summit demonstrates that, for the Reagan administration, Afghanistan was a useful propaganda tool to be wielded against the Soviets to gain leverage with international publics. Threatened by a more media-friendly Kremlin leader in Mikhail Gorbachev, the USIA offered a comprehensive response. Its superior satellite programming effectively dominated the dispersal of information to the media and public during the summit. The administration orchestrated a co-ordinated support system in the form of VOA editorials, briefings from administration officials and public events designed to showcase US concern for human rights and the Third World.

At Geneva, the Reagan administration ostensibly advocated for peace in 'regional conflicts' to deflect attention from its controversial SDI programme while fomenting unrest by keeping the arms flowing into Afghanistan. This raised the costs to the Soviets of occupying Afghanistan, which serviced the US foreign policy agenda regardless of the long-term outcome. This stance was justified as promoting 'peace through strength' in the Cold War stand-off but it would have terrible consequences for the stability of Afghanistan and its social and political cohesion – issues which were already bubbling to the surface amongst the refugee population and known to the administration.

The United States castigated Soviet human rights record in Afghanistan but it cynically overlooked serious serial abuses under its ally Zia in Pakistan – a woman at that time would have had more freedom and rights in Kabul than Peshawar. It presented the *mujahedeen* as democratic representatives of the Afghan people though it knew this to be far from reality and strengthened the military, economic and political power of many corrupt, vicious and unpopular warlords. This power underpinned these individuals' ability to wreak havoc in Afghanistan following the Soviet withdrawal fighting each other for territory, assassinating intellectuals and imposing strict Islamic codes previously alien to Afghan society. The United States also sought to shape young Afghans' perceptions through educational programmes encouraging violent anti-communism and justifying *jihad* as a reaction to the invasion – attitudes not easily moderated post-withdrawal.

By facilitating the privatization of fund and awareness raising through the Afghan PVOs the administration avoided tainting the *mujahedeen* by association with the United States or justifying Soviet allegations of outside interference fuelling the conflict. The PVOs managed to attract much popular and celebrity support for the Afghan 'freedom fighters'. This demonstrates how effectively the narrative of the *mujahedeen* as romantic rebels fighting a David and Goliath battle against an 'Evil Empire' had rooted in the United States, how compelling it proved to most Americans as it reflected their own deeply held political values. However, these PVOs, who often working closely with congressional supporters of the *mujahedeen*, were not malleable tools of the administration. They pressed effectively for more aid and international recognition for the Peshawar Seven and routinely critiqued administration policy on Afghanistan. The CFA assumed a high-profile role in Washington but clashes with the State Department presaged a divergence between administration policy on Afghanistan and the stance of conservative US elements in these organizations and in Congress. Following Geneva, with the United States now committed to underwriting a peace agreement on Afghanistan, a battle over these accords would erupt between the administration and those warning against 'selling out' the Afghans.

7

The beginning of the end: The Geneva Accords and national reconciliation

In May 1980, the Soviets sought to negotiate their military withdrawal from the tangled dynamics of the Afghan civil war they had so recently involved themselves in.[1] This process would drag on through the first half of the decade with little real progress until Gorbachev's 'new thinking' made it an imperative of Soviet foreign policy.[2] By 1987, a breakthrough looked at hand as significant progress was made by the parties to the proximity talks being held in Geneva under the auspices of the UN.[3]

The Geneva talks were ostensibly between Afghanistan and Pakistan; however, both sides deferred to their superpower backer throughout the negotiations. Meanwhile, the *mujahedeen* leadership was not party to the negotiations nor were any other Afghan opposition groups, and so relied on Pakistan and the Reagan administration to guarantee their interests. This slowed progress in negotiations as the goals and agendas of these parties were often in conflict. The Reagan administration, for its part, engaged with the Geneva process fielding mixed motives and sometimes shifting positions. The administration had the difficult task of straddling the expectations of American *mujahedeen* supporters who were generally anti-accords, hard-line anti-communists within the administration who hoped to inflict a 'reverse Saigon' on the Soviets and the State Department's desire to facilitate an orderly and prompt withdrawal of the Red Army though increasingly on US terms.[4] Although the negotiations were shrouded in secrecy, *mujahedeen* supporters in the United States engaged in a very public debate to express their dissatisfaction and to try to influence the outcome. In 1985, US Secretary of State George Shultz had agreed that America would cease aiding the Afghan *mujahedeen* once the Soviet withdrawal began.[5] *Mujahedeen* supporters roundly denounced this policy and accused the Department of 'appeasement', hoping such loaded terminology would provoke a tougher stance. This public pressure on the administration pushed it, in turn, to undermine Soviet attempts to affect a policy of 'national reconciliation' within Afghanistan during 1987, which aimed to put in place a broad-based interim government before the Red Army departed to prevent the outbreak of civil war.

As the negotiations gained momentum from the end of 1986 onwards and the Afghan conflict entered its endgame, at least within its Cold War context, the Reagan administration pandered to the wishes of anti-communist hardliners delaying the Soviet withdrawal. National Security Decision Directive 270 'Afghanistan' was in its draft stages in early 1987 and was endorsed by the President on 1 May 1987. This directive and its drafts illuminate the complexities of the administration's stance. They demonstrate the various options considered to ensure a negotiated outcome that satisfied domestic critics while not appearing 'routinely dismissive of Soviet initiatives'.[6] The documents indicate that US military strategy towards the conflict trumped diplomacy. The result was increased military aid to the *mujahedeen*, rendering compromise less and less attractive to the rebels.[7]

To augment this strategy, NSDD 270 targeted public diplomacy as one of three main ways to respond to the Soviet 'challenge'. The public diplomacy themes developed in the directive and other public diplomacy action plans around this time illuminate the administration's goals. There were also conflicts of interest on both sides of the negotiating table particularly around the Soviet programme of national reconciliation leading to various intrigues affecting the talks. During negotiations, Afghan PVOs, pro-*mujahedeen* anti-communists and congressional supporters in the United States attempted to influence administration policy using public pressure. The machinations over who would rule the state while it transitioned to democracy meant that 'positive symmetry' prevailed – arms continued to flow from both superpowers to both sides during and after the Soviet withdrawal.

The Geneva Accords and the policy of national reconciliation

In late 1981, Soviet Ambassador to the United States Anatoly Dobrynin informed US Secretary of State Alexander Haig that the 'USSR had made a serious mistake in Afghanistan' and wanted to 'find a basis for getting out'. Though Haig sought to follow this up with expert-level talks between the two superpowers in 1982, this was firmly resisted by some in the administration.[8] At this stage, the 'bleeders' in the administration and Congress were in the ascendant and assistance to the *mujahedeen* was on the increase.[9] Shortly after, the first round of the Geneva talks began in June 1982. Brokered by UN Under-Secretary General, Diego Cordovez of Ecuador, these negotiations consisted of indirect or proximity talks between Pakistan and Afghanistan. During the second round of these talks in 1983, hopes were running high for a settlement but this ultimately faltered when Pakistan, under US guidance, rejected the proposals.[10] The next few years saw little significant progress in the negotiations until Gorbachev's assent to power in 1985. The Soviet leader's superpower summit with Reagan in November of that year saw a softening of the US position and a new willingness on both sides to engage constructively in negotiations. At this stage, the Reagan administration agreed in principle to end aid to the rebels once the Soviets commenced withdrawal.[11] This attracted the ire of *mujahedeen* supporters particularly as the rebels, now receiving more military aid under NSDD 166, had a real opportunity to raise the costs of occupation for the Soviets. However, as Pakistani analyst Ahmed Rashid pointed out, it was by now 'a war of prolonged stalemate. The Russians cannot be humiliated; they are not about to suffer a Dien Bien Phu. At the same time, the guerrillas cannot be crushed'.[12] Escalating the conflict would raise the costs for Afghans as well as Moscow but this was of little consideration to the rebels or to their supporters.

Addressing his Politburo colleagues on 13 November 1986, Gorbachev had promised the Red Army would be out of Afghanistan 'within a year, two years at the most'. He warned Kabul to prepare politically for this eventuality by seeking to broaden the representation of opposition factions in government. However, Moscow's attempt to ensure a government in Afghanistan not ruled by Islamic fundamentalists – the very groups privileged by Pakistan and therefore the United States – slowed progress on this goal. Coupled with this, Gorbachev instigated a process of national reconciliation, fearing a bloodbath in Afghanistan following withdrawal if this was not initiated. The Soviet leader indicated he was open to any formula to bring this about including a transitional government lead by the former king Zahir Shah.[13] The Kremlin approached Reagan administration officials for assistance in affecting this.[14] However, Washington was sceptical about Soviet intentions – US documents use the term 'so called national reconciliation'. Instead, the administration viewed these proposals as a Cold War strategy or ploy on the part of the Soviets, which it needed to counter. This worldview constrained consideration of the ramifications of this policy for domestic Afghan politics post-Soviet withdrawal.

On New Year's Eve, 1986, Afghan leader Najibullah announced a ceasefire. Najibullah's proposal offered an initial six-month ceasefire, dialogue and the creation of a coalition government with opposing factions. It also promised devolution of power on a local level and the recognition of Islam as the state religion.[15] Najibullah's proposal had flaws, the most glaring of which was not delineating a withdrawal time frame. However, from the outset, the Reagan administration decided not to engage or negotiate it at all and instead worked to undermine it publicly and privately. Cordovez reckoned that certain elements within Pakistan and the United States wanted the conflict to continue for political and financial gain. He believed that the Soviet determination to implement a national reconciliation programme before withdrawal offered these groups an opportunity to protract negotiations for a settlement.[16] Examination and analysis of the reactions from Islamabad and Washington bear out the UN diplomat's contention.

Initially, Pakistan negotiator and Minister for Foreign Affairs Yaqub Khan had reacted to the announcement positively raising concerns in Washington that Pakistan may compromise on the withdrawal timescale.[17] Pakistan, at this time, was juggling internal pressures – increased arms and drugs smuggling – blamed by many on the Afghan refugees and strained relations with regional rival India. Furthermore, tensions between Zia and his Prime Minister Junejo gradually increased over the course of 1987, particularly over foreign policy as Junejo favoured signing the accords. However, the ISI in particular were determined to see the conflict through to the fall of Kabul. The installation of a pro-Pakistani regime in Afghanistan would offer Islamabad 'strategic depth' in the event of an outbreak of hostilities with India – a constant anxiety for Pakistan. It could also precipitate the settlement of the decades-old contentious Durand Line border dispute between Afghanistan and Pakistan. These motivations led Pakistan to shift its position in the negotiations a number of times not always in Afghanistan's best interests.

Washington's reaction was also influenced by its own domestic and foreign policy imperatives. The US State Department went on the offensive dismissing Najibullah's offer as a 'propaganda gesture'. Newly appointed National Security Advisor Frank

Carlucci wrote to Khan warning that Soviet proposals were designed to sow 'doubt and dissention' amongst the resistance and their supporters – a 'firm and realistic posture' was required to force the Soviets to withdraw.[18] On 21 January 1987, Under Secretary of State Michael Armacost told Cordovez that a short withdrawal period was the administration's primary concern not national reconciliation. He added that the United States would not make it easy for the Soviets in revenge for the 'assistance' the Soviets afforded to the United States in exiting Vietnam.[19] Around this time, in reaction to Soviet proposals for a reduced withdrawal period in the February-March 1987 round of negotiations, the administration drafted NSDD 270 'Afghanistan'. The document offers insight into Washington's publicly undeclared terms for a settlement and its suspicion of Soviet motivations.[20] A key element of the directive was a propaganda strategy to further US objectives of raising the military and political costs to the Soviets and ensuring continued support for Pakistan and the Afghan resistance leadership.

NSDD 270, 'Afghanistan' – the US strategy on withdrawal

The first paragraph of NSDD 270 described the Soviets' policy of national reconciliation as a 'sophisticated political strategy' and stated that 'we remain sceptical that Moscow has made the hard political decisions necessary to a settlement'. As a result, Pakistan and Washington discouraged Afghan opposition engagement in Kabul's attempts to coordinate a programme around this policy.

NSDD 270 encouraged a hard line in respect to other Soviet proposals too. Moscow's offer in the February/March 1987 Geneva round of talks to reduce its withdrawal period from four years to eighteen months was dismissed as a ploy 'to persuade the world that Moscow is serious in searching for a solution in Afghanistan, yet clearly aimed to allow Soviet military operations against the resistance with decreased external support'. According to an earlier draft from January 1987, 'the most important element of our strategy is to ensure that the Soviets face sharply increasing military pressure on the ground' to be reinforced by a political strategy. This was designed to pressure them into a negotiated settlement 'on terms acceptable to the concerned parties, including the Afghan people, Pakistan, and our cooperating partner governments'.[21] However, the Soviets were already offering a negotiated settlement and its terms were acceptable to some Afghan people and some in Pakistan but not to hardliners in the United States, the ISI or the Peshawar Seven. To counter this 'peace offensive,' the administration unleashed an extensive public diplomacy programme to vilify the Soviets, the DRA and what it described as Kabul's 'so-called national reconciliation proposals'.[22] This involved the administration loudly condemning alleged Soviet atrocities in Afghanistan as well as coercing and cajoling Pakistan to follow US guidelines on negotiations. It also promoted the Peshawar Seven as the 'true representatives' of the Afghan people, though refusing to officially recognize them as a government-in-exile. To implement this programme NSDD 270 recommended the establishment of an Afghanistan Public Diplomacy Working Group chaired by the NSC. This would 'provide continuing, specific direction to USG public diplomacy, coordinating and integrating US overt and covert public diplomacy, international information, and psychological information programs'.²³ Other aspects of this strategy included presidential initiatives and USIA global programming on Soviet actions. It suggested cultural and public affairs resources should be targeted at Afghans, international pressure on the DRA/USSR increased and the Afghan Media Project pursued.²⁴ The USIA was tasked with disseminating the themes developed by the group via Worldnet and the VOA.²⁵ The Department of State would handle domestic output, Afghanistan Situation Report Briefings and its Speaker Programme presentations to academic and civic groups.²⁶ Of these elements only the overt public diplomacy and international information programmes are available for analysis, but these alone are extensive and damning of US underlying intentions during this period of negotiations to resolve, or not, the conflict in Afghanistan.

NSDD 270 outlined administration attitudes to Soviet efforts for a resolution in Afghanistan thus: 'Recent Soviet diplomatic/political initiatives have sharpened the political struggle. We must accept this challenge and escalate our own efforts in the political arena.'²⁷ It warned that the administration was 'entering a critical period and needs to maintain strong pressure on the Soviets if we are to have a chance of a suitable negotiated settlement'. So, for the United States, Soviet proposals were perceived through its Cold War worldview as confrontational rather than a genuine attempt to leave Afghanistan in some semblance of peace or national unity. And the negotiating process was an avenue to press American advantage. Affecting this stance involved raising the political as well as the military costs to the Soviets. NSDD 270 identified raising international public awareness of the conflict as a key component to enable this.²⁸ As with most of the administration's propaganda strategies, President Reagan would be instrumental, delivering speeches and attending orchestrated events to highlight the conflict and the Soviets' malign role.

At a NSPG meeting on 6 March 1987, President Reagan had expressed a desire for more personal involvement in Afghanistan and Pakistan policy. National Security Council staffer Robert Oakley described as 'propitious' in the light of the Soviet 'peace offensive' and the unwelcome publicity around Pakistan's nuclear development capacity.²⁹ In the months leading up to NSDD 270, Reagan's persuasive rhetoric was the administration's chief public diplomacy weapon in the Afghanistan negotiations. Beginning with US commemorations of the seventh anniversary (27 December 1986) of the Soviet Invasion, the administration sought to maintain public pressure on the Soviets. Reagan's address on the day accused the Soviets of atrocities such as bombing villages, maiming and orphaning children and spurning Islam and Afghan culture. He castigated the Soviets' 'sham withdrawal' of some 15,000 troops in October 1986.³⁰ US officials put it out that the Soviets had replaced these troops within days, in any case.³¹ The *New York Times* reflected the administration's analysis describing the October withdrawal as 'token'. It attributed Soviet concern over the possible continuation of the guerrilla war after it had disengaged as being cynically rooted in the negative impact it could have on its own citizens and on its reputation in Muslim countries.³² Another *New York Times*' article referring to the ceasefire announcement cited the analysis of 'Western diplomats' as its source. Not surprisingly, given its source, it adhered closely to administration propaganda. It described the national reconciliation programme as 'a Soviet inspired plan to give Afghanistan at least the appearance of greater autonomy and democracy'. It argued that the Soviets only wanted stability in

Afghanistan to 'smooth the way' for withdrawal and improve its relations with Muslim states.³³ Worldwide media coverage of the seventh anniversary mirrored Washington's accusations and was very critical of the Soviet position. However, some media approval emerged for the Soviet/DRA peace strategy of January 1987.³⁴ This demonstrated increasing difficulties the administration would have in controlling the narrative around the conflict once *glasnost* began to take effect, enabling the media to more independently source information.

It does seem likely that the Soviet's programme, though flawed, was a genuine attempt to bring about some level of national reconciliation. Academic Alex Marshall described it as a 'dramatic shift in official state policy' by Kabul, which laid aside its previous attempts to create a strong centralized state. Instead, he argues, the PDPA and its Soviet advisors attempted to develop a 'radically decentralised state' with extensive regional and ethnic autonomy, for example, offering the Shi'a branch of Islam (largely of the Hazara ethnic group) official recognition for the first time in Afghan history.³⁵ Although Afghanistan is largely Sunni, Shi'a Muslims make up a sizeable minority of up to 20 per cent of the population. Conversely, the Peshawar Seven, lauded by Reagan as the 'true representatives' of the Afghan people, contained no Shi'ites nor did it represent a broad ethnic base of Afghanis.³⁶ The Uzbeks of Northern Afghanistan also joined the national reconciliation effort. However, the policy was soon floundering as the resistance leadership refused to lay down arms. Many of the rebels groups' finances were dependent on continued warfare. Furthermore, they were under no pressure to reach an agreement from Washington for whom continued chaos served the purpose of politically damaging the Soviets. The administration sought to undermine the ceasefire and national reconciliation programme publicly to bolster this objective.

In his State of the Union address, less than a month after Najibullah's ceasefire announcement, Reagan characterized the US position thus:

> The Soviet Union says it wants a peaceful settlement in Afghanistan, yet it continues a brutal war and props up a regime whose days are clearly numbered. We are ready to support a political solution that guarantees the rapid withdrawal of all Soviet troops and genuine self-determination for the Afghan people.³⁷

Reagan was only willing to countenance a solution that involved a hasty retreat of the Red Army, as this would heighten Moscow's humiliation. Efforts at national reconciliation could wait until US objectives were served. The State Department disseminated a list of public themes for Afghanistan in March 1987, which portrayed the national reconciliation programme as little more than 'a cosmetic broadening of the Kabul regime'. Various administration officials gave briefings that reflected this perspective. Michael Armacost also used the term 'cosmetic' on Worldnet to describe the DRA's national reconciliation programme.³⁸ Assistant Secretary of State Richard Murphy on another Worldnet broadcast on 27 March 1987, just after the 'Afghanistan Day' proclamation, contended that there was a dramatic increase in attacks by what he called 'Soviet puppet forces' (i.e. the Afghan army) on refugee camps within Afghanistan. He argued that the Soviet 'peace offensive' was mere propaganda and, in fact, the Soviet's had stepped up military action.³⁹ The 'Afghanistan Day' proclamation of 20 March 1987, designed to offset the Soviet 'peace offensive', decried the Soviets' '7-year reign of terror' and their proposals 'aimed at deceiving world opinion'.[40] To maximize publicity high-profile officials and guests such as the Vice-President, Secretary Shultz, NSA Carlucci and a bipartisan congressional group including Charles Wilson and Senator Humphrey attended the signing ceremony. The USIA guaranteed international coverage of the event via Worldnet.[41] In his comments, the President accused 'communist aircrafts' of striking targets on Pakistani soil. At the same time, the *mujahedeen* were involved in similar transgressions, launching attacks within Soviet territory aided by CIA-supplied satellite photos of Soviet bases but the United States did not publicly acknowledge this.[42] Similar 'presidential initiatives' included an address before the World Affairs Council in April 1987. Here the President stated that

> despite a claimed desire for peaceful settlement of these conflicts, despite announcements of cease-fires and talk of "national reconciliation," Soviet troops continue to wage a terrible war against the people of Afghanistan' and went on to say 'the bleeding wound of Afghanistan must be healed. I challenge the U.S.S.R. to set a date this calendar year when it will begin the withdrawal of Soviet troops on a speedy schedule.[43]

Such presidential utterances were guaranteed to garner media attention and the constant disparagement of the Kabul/Moscow national reconciliation initiative would warn off any rebel groups considering supporting it.

As well as the presidential and State Department public diplomacy initiatives, following a NSPG meeting on 12 March, the USIA produced an 'Action Plan for Agency Initiatives on Afghanistan' to incorporate NSC suggestions into its programming.[44] It hoped to get hold of the infamous 'toy bombs', allegedly dropped by the Soviets in Afghanistan, to display on Worldnet though it acknowledged that this may prove 'impossible' (probably because they only existed in US propaganda). Other propaganda themes included Soviet brutality and the fragility of the DRA government. The agency planned to expose narcotics growing and trafficking by the DRA though it recognized 'opium poppies are a cash crop valued by Afghans of all persuasions'. So, even though US-supported *mujahedeen* were as likely to be cultivating and selling it as the Afghan government, the USIA still hoped to use the issue as propaganda by highlighting transgressions by the communists only.

By April 1987, the DRA admitted the ceasefire was a failure as the rebels stepped up attacks. Furthermore, Najibullah accused the United States and Pakistan of discouraging refugees from returning home from the camps of Peshawar. In the *New York Times* 'Western diplomats' charged that Soviets had continued to fight too.[45] Even as the process faltered, the Reagan administration kept up their efforts to use the conflict to publicly undermine the Soviets. A State Department Public Diplomacy Action Plan produced a month later promised to counter the Soviet 'peace offensive' and keep Afghanistan in the public eye and within 'the context of an East-South (i.e., USSR vs Third World) … confrontation'.[46] The potential damage to Afghan citizens and society from the US-led condemnation of the national reconciliation plan is never considered in these documents.

The administration's efforts yielded results as international media criticism of the Soviet occupation gathered momentum throughout the early summer of 1987. A USIA media analysis report of this period showed the majority of Third World, Western Europe, Canadian and Australian newspapers expressed disapproval of the Soviet position. Furthermore, they linked Soviet credibility and sincerity in other areas, like arms control negotiations, to the Afghan issue. This example from the independent Austrian paper *Profil* was cited in the USIA report as typical: 'The Soviet Union in matters of disarmament deserves confidence only if it behaves like a civilized nation should. This means it should stop waging a war of annihilation in Afghanistan.'[47] Soviet citizens also began to question their state's role in Afghanistan. A poll conducted in Moscow in January 1987 showed one in six interviewed criticizing the conflict and blaming it for creating problems such as drug addiction and juvenile delinquency in Soviet society.[48] In his UN address that September, Reagan accused the DRA of 'pretend compromise' and said their proposals had been rejected by the Afghan people though there was no way of quantifying Afghan's opinion, for or against. Rather the Peshawar Seven had rejected any settlement. And Reagan characterized them as 'an indispensible party in the quest for a negotiated solution'.[49] However, the administration's refusal to recognize the resistance leadership as a government-in-exile was a significant factor in ensuring they did not get representation at Geneva demonstrating, yet again, the gulf between Washington's public stance and its actual policies.

Despite all the negative publicity, the DRA did have some success with the national reconciliation programme as it negotiated 'zones of peace' particularly with groups not politically or ideologically driven but, rather, interested in the localized autonomy on offer.[50] Some refugees began returning though the Reagan administration attempted to discourage the UNHCR from documenting this presumably as it would undermine its position that all the people of Afghanistan were united against the DRA.[51] Najib showed a willingness to negotiate a role for the former king and power-sharing with opposition groups; however, the fundamentalist groups were not interested. Some of the rebels had a history of hostilities with Zahir Shah and others a determination to only accept a solely Islamic polity.[52] By withholding support for national reconciliation, they hoped to gain more politically.

In September 1987, the Soviet Minister of Foreign Affairs Eduard Shevardnadze told his US counterpart Secretary Shultz that the USSR intended to withdraw; however, criticism continued unabated over the following months and little further progress was made at the Geneva round of talks.[53] Gorbachev himself told Reagan in December 1987, at the Washington summit, that the Soviet Union would leave within twelve months with the caveat that the US administration halt military aid to the Afghan resistance and a compromise coalition government could be agreed upon for Kabul.[54] However, it was these very caveats which US and *mujahedeen* opposition to the accords ceased upon and dissent crystallized around. The national reconciliation programme was perceived by three-quarters of newspapers surveyed over fifty countries during this period as Soviet/DRA propaganda. Nowhere was public opinion on the Soviet's side and Gorbachev knew withdrawal was imperative; he would later remark that the US obstructive attitude had strengthened the hand of Moscow hardliners and was a factor in delaying this process.[55]

Following the December summit, widespread enthusiasm in Western Europe for an INF treaty helped raise levels of trust in Gorbachev.[56] Now majorities in most Western European countries, bar France, believed the Kremlin leader was serious about withdrawal from Afghanistan.[57] There was also evidence that Soviet 'disinformation' was having an effect with allegations – that the United States supplied chemical and biological weapons to the *mujahedeen* – surfacing in the media in Pakistan, India and Finland, as well as Moscow. Other Soviet 'propaganda themes' detected by the USIA in 1987 included portraying the *mujahedeen* as bandits and accusing the United States of undermining peace attempts. According to the USIA, Moscow also sought to use propaganda to promote Afghan national reconciliation, a rapprochement with Islam, and to argue that outside interference was prolonging the conflict. The fact that the 1987 Non-Aligned Conference did not condemn Soviet actions in Afghanistan was, the USIA believed, evidence that some of these propaganda measures were having the desired effect.[58]

Ultimately, however, the Reagan administration's public diplomacy seriously undermined efforts by Kabul and Moscow to establish a framework for national reconciliation in Afghanistan in preparation for the Soviet troop withdrawal. Though the Soviets and the DRA hoped such a programme would shore up their own interests, it was undoubtedly still a necessary policy in a country riven by years of war and factionalism. US engagement would have made a positive contribution to establishing the political institutions required for the post-conflict period. However, while the Reagan administration, particularly the State Department, ultimately wished to negotiate a resolution to the Afghan conflict, it was constrained by its pro-*mujahedeen*, hard-line anti-communist supporters, particularly in Congress, who believed the overthrow of Najib, the fall of Kabul and Soviet humiliation were the only satisfactory outcome in Afghanistan. To achieve this, US *mujahedeen* supporters conducted a public diplomacy campaign of their own in an effort to influence the administration's Afghan policy.

Congress and the Geneva Accords

While the Reagan administration took a strong line against the Soviets rhetorically and refused to endorse a programme of national unity before withdrawal, it was, as far as congressional supporters of the *mujahedeen* were concerned, not enough. Congress had always been out in front of the administration in their support for the rebels. It was willing to push the Soviets harder than the administration which needed to negotiate with Moscow on a wide range of issues outside of the Afghan conflict that it did not wish to jeopardize. Congress had no such concerns and warned the administration against 'selling out' the resistance parties. Coupled with the pro-*mujahedeen* advocates in the conservative media and PVOs, this put a lot of pressure on the administration to adopt a tough approach or there 'would be hell to pay from the right'.[59] While Congress pushed the administration to stand firm in their support for the Afghans, it, in turn, did not support Pakistan as firmly as the administration wanted. NSDD 270 emphasized the administration's belief that Pakistan was 'key to our ability to implement a policy of opposition to Soviet aggression in Afghanistan'. It raised concerns that Congress appeared to 'underestimate the relationship of Pakistan to our Afghanistan policy'.⁶⁰ Keeping Congress onside was vital for securing military aid to Pakistan. 'Effective management of congressional concerns' was required and the State Department established a working group to handle this task. However, Pakistan's nuclear ambitions became a source of increasing friction between the administration and Congress through the course of 1987. This was a pressing problem for the administration as authorization for the next tranche of military aid to Pakistan was imminently required. The administration needed to tie Afghan resistance requirements to US aid to Pakistan in the minds of congressional supporters. It also needed to appease hardliners with a seemingly uncompromising stand on Afghanistan whilst at the same time not overly provoking the Soviets. Keeping Congress members informed of developments in Afghanistan and involved in Afghan-related events was considered essential to maintaining interest and support.⁶¹

Some in Congress were sympathetic towards Pakistan and believed the state 'under siege' from the Soviet Union due to its role as a safe haven and a conduit for military supplies to the rebels but others needed to be convinced of the necessity to support the state. Supporters of Pakistan testified at congressional hearings to argue this case and shape a more positive perspective on the state. In 1986, USAID's Charles Greenleaf described to the House Foreign Affairs Committee the generosity and 'steadfast support' Pakistan had shown Afghan refugees allowing them 'complete freedom of movement and employment'.⁶² At the same hearing, Academic Barnett Rubin outlined his concerns about Pakistan and their implications for US foreign policy. He warned that support for the *mujahedeen* was waning in Pakistan as people felt the Pakistani military was using the resistance to strengthen its own position.⁶³ He argued that the United States could not pursue any of its policies in Afghanistan without Pakistani cooperation stating

> all aid to the resistance in landlocked Afghanistan must pass through either Iran or Pakistan; practically speaking, through Pakistan. Neither the United States nor any other power such as China or Saudi Arabia can pursue a policy in Afghanistan except in cooperation with Pakistan. The United States cannot supply Stinger missiles to the Afghan resistance except with the consent and cooperation of Pakistan. We cannot send humanitarian assistance inside Afghanistan except with the consent and cooperation of Pakistan. And we cannot pursue or prevent a negotiated solution unless we do so in close collaboration with Pakistan.⁶⁴

Before the Congressional Task Force on Afghanistan, Charles Wilson refuted allegations that the Pakistani military were purloining weapons destined for the *mujahedeen* and added that maintaining Pakistan's confidence in US support was absolutely vital for US foreign policy objectives in Afghanistan.⁶⁵ Nevertheless, Pakistan remained controversial largely over the issue of its nuclear weapons development programme. In an attempt to counter this, the administration argued that continuing military aid would negate Pakistan's need to develop a nuclear bomb.⁶⁶ Speaking before the Defense Policy Panel in March 1987, Assistant Secretary of State Richard Murphy reiterated the administration position saying, 'We support the *mujahedeen* resistance and of course, integral to that, is our support for Pakistan.' He pointed to the pressures Pakistan faced from the Soviet Union and Afghanistan due to its role in the conflict and tied these to the necessity to renew Pakistan's six-year security assistance programme which, he again argued, would reduce 'Pakistan's need and search for developing nuclear weapons'.[67]

At the House hearing on the provision of AWACS to Pakistan on 21 May 1987, Representative Stephen Solarz described Pakistan as 'under siege' from Afghanistan and the Soviet Union. Bill McCollum stated that 'Pakistan has shouldered a significant burden' in assisting the Afghan resistance and that its troubled relationship with the democratic process was largely due to economic stresses caused by 'massive subversion and sabotage' in the state by the Soviets and the DRA.[68] The administration also focused attention on Soviet violations of Pakistani sovereignty calling it 'the frontier of the free world' when offering justification for the supply of AWACS. The rhetoric was vital to bind Pakistan's military needs within a Cold War framework and distance them from its regional rivalry with India and the AWACS' potential role in this.[69] However, the media recounted a number of tales about Pakistan's uranium enrichment programme which, though denied by the Reagan administration, ultimately provoked Congress into allowing the six-year sanctions waver to run out in the autumn of 1987. It was not reinstated until 17 December that year and then only for two and a half years rather than six as requested.[70]

Beneath the surface, the Reagan administration and Pakistan's relationship were not as friendly and supportive as their rhetoric suggested. Rather it was often marked by distrust and duplicity on both sides. While stridently supporting Zia in front of Congress and the world, privately the administration considered any options which advanced its own interests in the conflict including giving consideration to playing on Pakistani insecurities about its national integrity. One suggestion from the Office of the Secretary of Defense, during the drafting of NSDD 270, submitted that the administration should make official statements that it saw 'disturbing signs that Moscow may be contemplating the attempted dismemberment of Pakistan as an independent state'.[71] Whether it was their intention to inform Pakistan that this was only a propaganda ploy is not clear.

In any case, Zia also sought to use the conflict to pursue his own political agenda and manipulate Cold War superpower rivalry to facilitate his regional interests. He privileged a fundamentalist faction gaining power in Kabul as it would allow him more influence in Afghani domestic politics and would sideline the irredentist aspirations of some Afghans centred on redrawing the Durand Line. To this end, he endeavoured to block the former king, Zahir Shah, from assuming a role in a transitional administration in Afghanistan post-withdrawal, though he enjoyed widespread support from Afghans when polled, by refusing to grant him a visa to enter Pakistan to conduct talks.[72] Zia's alliance with the United States also brought with it internal political problems. Pakistanis grew increasingly distrustful of America following the congressional stop on aid to Pakistan in September 1987 and were overwhelmingly (88 per cent of people polled) in favour of the development of a Pakistani nuclear weapons programme.[73] A draft National Security Study by the United States described

Pakistan's internal security issues as having worsened since 1979 due to the presence of the Afghan refugees, increased availability of arms and a 'burgeoning narcotics trade'. Although the Pakistani public had strongly endorsed Zia's position on the Afghan conflict, 'a generalized latent discontent' was deemed to be developing.[74] A survey of Pakistani media reaction to the December 1987 superpower summit showed general disappointment on the lack of progress towards a solution on Afghanistan.[75] So both 'allies' were suspicious of one another and, in the end of the day, seeking to pursue their own political advantages in negotiations rather than grand humanitarian ideals of freedom and self-determination for Afghanistan. The administration also faced domestic obstacles to its negotiating positions on the peace accords.

The Congressional Task Force on Afghanistan took a characteristically intransigent stance on the Geneva negotiations and sought to publicize its objections via hearings. At these the State Department was subject to much vilification. *Mujahedeen* supporters believed that a disparity existed between State Department policy towards the negotiations and President Reagan's own publicly stated political support for the rebels. This focus on the apparent disunity in the administration and the State Department's alleged disregard for the President's preferences offered an opportunity for members of the CTF to undermine or modify State's stance. Just before the start of the seventh round of Geneva talks in May 1986, the CTF held a hearing on the negotiations. At this, Senator Humphrey described the administration's decision to sanction the negotiations as 'high-handed', 'arrogant' and 'immoral' as the *mujahedeen*, whom he deemed 'the legitimate representatives of the Afghan people', were not a party to them.[76] He argued that 'the State Department has made a very grave error in offering to guarantee the terms of the settlement. And I implore the administration to keep the State Department in hand in the weeks and months ahead'.[77] He labelled the withdrawal terms on offer as a 'sell-out' of the rebels and likened the talks to the Yalta conference in the closing months of the Second World War where the fates of many Eastern European states were decided in their absence.[78] Following on, Democratic Senator William Bradley chided the administration for only 'paying lip service' to the resistance's goals. Bradley called on it to support the Peshawar Seven's aspiration to take Afghanistan's seat at the Islamic Conference and the UN and assist further in developing its institutional capacity.[79] Charles Wilson also denounced the State Department, recalling how it had tried to stymie humanitarian aid his committee had earmarked for the Afghans with the following damning statement:

> 240 million Americans would like to provide humanitarian aid to the Afghan Freedom Fighters, particularly morphine for amputations and such things as that, there are five American who would not like to do this. Unfortunately, those five all are in positions in the State Department where they can cause serious, serious problems.

He reminded the meeting about how he had forced the resignation of Assistant Secretary of State Gerald Helman who had been in charge of the Cross Border Humanitarian Aid Program over the altercation about a grant to Robert Simon's International Medical Corp.[80] Wilson called on the administration to assist the development of the civil and political capacity of the rebel alliance by channelling aid through them and recognizing them as a government-in-exile. However, Wilson's statement demonstrated his awareness, if not acknowledgement, of the deep-seated disunity amongst the alliance and looming future troubles when he admitted that some groups had been squirreling away weapons. This, he alleged, was for two reasons of which 'the least important reason is that when they do drive the Soviet out they plan on having to fight each other for domination – the fundamentalists versus the moderates, etcetera'.[81] The dominant reason, according to Wilson, was because they expected the United States to cut their aid soon. This suggested that administration policy was driving the *mujahedeen*'s hoarding of weapons rather than internecine rivalry.

In February 1987, the Senate passed a resolution, proposed by Byrd and Humphrey, 92–0, condemning the Afghanistan negotiations, describing the Soviet proposals as 'a cynical and hypocritical public relations campaign' and adding that

> the offer by the Soviet puppet regime in Kabul for a cease-fire and amnesty in the name of national reconciliation is a transparent attempt to isolate the democratic resistance (the mujahedin), confuse the populace and accomplish the surrender of the democratic resistance while the Soviet military occupation continues unabated.[82]

Shortly after this vote, on 17 February 1987, the CTF held another hearing this time to review progress at Geneva and publicize the talks' perceived shortcomings.[83] It took testimony from mostly hard-line anti-Soviet commentators including Richard Pipes, Fred Iklé from the Department of Defense and Charles Lichenstein – a controversial former envoy to the UN under Kirkpatrick who, at one stage, had suggested that the UN assembly be moved from New York following a spat with the Soviets.[84] Lichenstein was, at the time of the hearing, a fellow with the Heritage Foundation.[85] Senator Humphrey's opening statement set the tone outlining his belief that the Soviets were hoping to achieve in negotiations at Geneva that which they could not achieve on the battlefields of Afghanistan. He was concerned that a 'sell-out' of the 'Afghan people' was imminent.[86]

Iklé followed on, offering one of the administration's perspectives on the talks – that Soviet offers of a negotiated settlement were little more than an 'attempted deception'.[87] He argued that the Soviets, unlike the United States, would not adhere to the terms of any agreement in any case. Iklé echoed Congress' unwavering support for the *mujahedeen* and confirmed to Humphrey that the administration would not countenance a 'sell-out' of the Afghan resistance. Iklé also used his testimony to highlight the pivotal role of Pakistan in channelling support to the rebels and to stress the importance of congressional approval for Pakistan's second multi-year security assistance programme. Humphrey used the opportunity to warn Iklé that any agreement by the administration to a withdrawal period of longer than four months would be considered a 'breach of faith' by Congress and could potentially threaten congressional support for Pakistan's aid package making clear that their support for Pakistan was dependent on the administration's support for the *mujahedeen*.[88]

Yet another congressional committee, this time the Senate Armed Services Committee hearing on National Security Strategy, sat during this same time period and also strove to focus attention on Afghanistan and influence policy. Senator Humphrey was a member of this committee too and used the hearing to lament the administration's lack of economic sanctions on the Soviet Union over its intervention in Afghanistan.[89] Zbigniew Brzezinski, who gave testimony, agreed with Humphrey and argued for increased public diplomacy to garner more international attention on the war. This publicity would make it more problematic for the Soviets, as Vietnam became for the United States. Brzezinski argued that increased coverage of the conflict could help to exacerbate tensions between the Muslim world and the USSR and exploit 'the internal weakness of the multi-national nature of the Soviet Union itself' which, by its very structure, comprised 'fissures and openings'. Modern communications were instrumental to this strategy.[90] At the hearing, Humphrey warned the committee to 'watch the State Department' in case they agreed a deal with the Soviets which left Afghanistan as 'a de facto Soviet satellite'.[91]

Congressional supporters of the *mujahedeen* used other opportunities besides hearings to seek to influence the Geneva negotiations. A joint resolution designating 21 March 1987 'Afghanistan Day' denounced the Soviets 'deceptive' troop withdrawal in October 1986 along with its national reconciliation and cease-fire proposals.[92] At the Washington summit in December 1987, congressional leaders met with Gorbachev and threatened to hold up ratification of the Intermediate and Short Range Nuclear Arms Treaty unless the Soviets provided a suitable timetable for withdrawal.[93] The INF treaty, which had high public approval ratings, was already the target of anti-communist conservatives, enraged with Reagan's 'neo-detente' with Gorbachev.[94] Impending arms treaties like the INF and the looming START talks set to be negotiated in Moscow in 1988 encouraged Congress' stance. Linking the Soviet's policy on Afghanistan to ratification of the arms treaties was effective on two fronts for hardliners – it delayed withdrawal and so raised the costs for the Soviets further and hindered ratification of these arms agreements which symbolized an unwelcome softening of the administration's attitude towards Moscow.[95]

On 27 January 1988, several members of Congress wrote to Reagan alleging the State Department had agreed to a Geneva peace package on Afghanistan that contravened the President's own policy on the matter. The letter recalled Reagan's past public pledges of support for the *mujahedeen*, which were now under treat from a premature cut-off in aid. They demanded the President increase military aid if the Soviets did not withdraw promptly enough.[96] A couple of months later Representative Lee Hamilton of the House Foreign Affairs Committee wrote to Secretary Shultz querying differences between State's interpretation of the conditions for the aid cut-off to the *mujahedeen* ('irreversible withdrawal') and the President's ('cessation of similar aid').[97] Withdrawal alone was not enough for the Peshawar Seven and their supporters who wanted the fall of the Kabul government along with it and an Islamic government in its stead. Compromise was not an option.

A 'Sense of the Senate' resolution on US policy towards Afghanistan was passed 77–0 on 29 February 1988. It urged continued assistance to the rebels until withdrawal was complete.[98] In March 1988, as the final round of the Geneva talks got underway, the

Senate issued another resolution, again passed 77–0, urging the administration to hold tough in negotiations. Senate Majority Leader Robert Byrd stated he wanted to see a draft of the accords before agreeing to ratify the INF treaty; however, cracks were beginning to appear in the congressional consensus on Afghanistan. Senator Pell and Representative Solarz advocated agreement with Solarz stating 'it's time to take yes for an answer. If the Soviets are willing to leave Afghanistan, let's hold the door open for them'.[99]

Who should rule?

Meanwhile, neither Zia nor the Reagan administration could seem to decide their preferred endgame to the conflict, in particular, whether they wanted an interim government in place in Afghanistan before Soviet withdrawal was completed or not.[100] The Soviets had initially promoted this policy but then seemed poised to side line it for the sake of an agreement – they did not want to delay any longer and face quitting Kabul 'on the struts of helicopters'.[101] The Reagan administration, it seemed, wanted whatever the Soviets did not. Zia was weighing which political structure in Kabul best suited his domestic and regional political interests.[102] Washington was still torn between those determined to delay settlement in order to further 'bleed' the Soviets and those who believed a speedy end to the conflict was now possible and desirable. As the administration dithered, the Afghan resistance and its US supporters protested against the accords and any compromise interim government involving either the Afghan communists or the former king.

The Reagan administration, though going against the resistance's wishes by participating in Geneva without them, sought to ameliorate this somewhat with their public diplomacy and also complicate Soviet efforts to create a consensus on an interim government. To this end, Washington would only recognize the Rebel Alliance in Peshawar as the true representatives of the Afghan.[103] A Department of State document entitled 'Public Themes for Afghanistan' from 28 March 1987 declared that 'the US supports the Afghan Resistance and views the Resistance Alliance as a genuine spokesman of the Afghan people in their struggle for freedom'.[104] It ignored the proposals of those who had the ability and political gravitas to bring about some level of reconciliation within Afghanistan and were willing to negotiate with Najibullah.

The administration and other supporters of the Resistance Alliance were aware of the reputation of some of the fundamentalists as anti-democratic, unpopular and violent towards political opponents and set about glossing over these unpalatable facts. In a set of contingency questions and answers prepared by the State Department in response to the imminent signing of the Geneva Accords and accompanying media interest, it was noted that arms were in fact distributed to the most effective rebel groups not the most popular and that evidence suggested that this was the fundamentalists.[105] So the administration was aware that the resistance groups receiving US military aid were neither representative nor moderate. In the end, 'promoting an effective resistance political front' was part of the political strategy designed to reinforce 'the most important element of our strategy' – increasing military pressure on the Soviets.[106]

In any case, there was widespread belief in Washington and amongst *mujahedeen* supporters that the resistance would quickly topple Najibullah once the Soviets pulled out Kabul, thus rendering a compromise arrangement over a transition administration unnecessary. This would undoubtedly be a bloody, violent confrontation and Afghan's 'self-determination' would arrive on the edge of a sword, but this conviction did have the advantage of relieving Washington of the responsibility of persuading its supporters, allies and the *mujahedeen* to offer any further concessions to the Soviets or DRA. Ultimately, the nature of the political system put in place in Afghanistan post-conflict was of little interest to US Cold War warriors and so they were happy to generate support for Zia's preferred choice – the fundamentalists. To this end, the administration spent the year leading up to the final agreement in Geneva promoting the Peshawar Seven as an effective political front, representing the majority of the Afghan population, so when they violently wrested power from the DRA this could be spun as Afghan 'self-determination'.

The Department of State set to work on this strategy developing a public diplomacy action plan on Afghanistan in May 1987 that recommended setting up an Interagency Afghanistan Public Diplomacy Working Group to provide focus and consistency and increase publicity favourable to the *mujahedeen*. This group would coordinate 'government-wide efforts to maximise media coverage of the war and publicity favorable to the resistance'. It would comprise members drawn from the State Department, USAID, USIA, NSC and the Pentagon.[107] As the plan pointed out, 'the best public diplomacy, of course, emanates from the resistance itself. A major focus of our efforts is to enhance the resistance's capabilities in this area'. One suggestion involved bringing 'a group of Resistance Alliance-affiliated Afghans who are engaged in information work' to the United States via the USIA's International Visitors Program. Once in the United States, they would meet with representatives from the media, academia and the government and 'have opportunities to share their knowledge and insight on the situation in Afghanistan'. Another example of the Afghan-related propaganda was aimed at a domestic audience. In another effort to shape public perception of the *mujahedeen*, Acting Deputy Assistant Secretary of State Herbert Hagerty chided the press for calling the resistance 'rebels' instead of 'resistance fighters' or 'freedom fighters'. He characterized the Peshawar Seven's 'high command' as having evolved from a military alliance to a political one and these 'elder leaders', having 'submerged' their differences, were now 'representatives of the free Afghan people'.[108] Using terms like 'high command' implied a level of cohesion and unity amongst the bickering Peshawar Seven, and the term 'elders' created an air of wisdom and gravitas which was, in reality, not a feature of the leadership.

Human rights, the impact of the conflict on women and alleged war crimes (though not *mujahedeen* ones) all became fodder for public diplomacy exploitation.[109] The State Department would liaise with PVOs Freedom House and ARC to disseminate news articles on the effect of the war on Afghan women and children. The CFA was by now under the directorship of Henry Kriegel who had a history of Republican conservative advocacy – he founded the Young Americans for Freedom chapter at Columbia University, New York, as a student.[110] The CFA initiated a War Crimes Project 'to expose Soviet violations of international law in Afghanistan'.[111] Public

Affairs guidance to Posts advised liaison with local media and human rights groups to 'promote heightened awareness of Afghanistan'. It described the upcoming months as 'providing excellent opportunities to focus public attention on Afghanistan' with an upcoming UNGA debate, the publication of the Ermacora Report on human rights in Afghanistan and the December anniversary of the invasion.[112] Foreign Press Center briefings and VOA programmes would complement these 'opportunities' as well as a speech by Reagan around the time of the anniversary of the invasion.

The administration endeavoured to engage other private interests in their propaganda strategy on Afghanistan around the impending Geneva settlement to add credibility and extra funding. The Department of State Public Diplomacy Action Plan outlined that 'we also seek greater involvement of the private sector in the U.S. and abroad in support of various elements of our Afghanistan policy', though whether outsourcing this to the pro-*mujahedeen* PVOs is what they had in mind is not clear.[113] The Department of State did seek to enlist private sector support in shaping the future leadership of Afghanistan. It proposed a seminar attended by NSC senior staff including Frank Carlucci, Whitehead, Armacost, Murphy, Wick and Shultz to raise private sector funding to educate young Afghans 'who in [sic] their return will be contending with both Russian-trained cadre and Iranian influenced exiles for leadership positions'. A contribution would provide the funder with 'a unique opportunity to affect the values and attitudes of a country which has come out from under the Soviet yoke'.[114] It would also allow the United States a level of influence in Afghanistan post-conflict rather than just leaving Afghanistan to the Afghans as its rhetoric argued.

Private individuals and Congress members did help advocate public diplomacy themes that complemented the administration's agenda such as 'promoting the Afghan resistance alliance as an effective political front'.[115] However, there is no evidence that this was done at the administration's behest. At this time, questions began to surface about the fundamentalist nature of some of the resistance groups in the Alliance. The administration and a number of individuals linked to the PVOs sought to distance Afghani Islam from the fundamentalist radical style of Khomeini and his fevered anti-Americanism. Robert Peck, under questioning at a House hearing from Representative Solarz about the possibility of a fundamentalist regime securing power, argued that 'there are aspects of extremism in Iranian practice which I think would be very unfortunate and very surprising if they emerged in Afghanistan given their cultural traditions'.[116] At the Congressional Task Force hearing in February 1987, Lichenstein, when questioned about the nature of a future political system in Afghanistan, said it would most likely be 'traditionalist' and not like the 'typical democratic political processes' of the United States but it would still be 'representative'.[117] It was a difficult task to appear pro-Islamic but anti-fundamentalist. Even the more 'traditional' Muslim leaders were not likely to embrace the 'democracy' the United States was touting as the next step for Afghanistan post-withdrawal. Whatever the ultimate government in Afghanistan it was unlikely to remotely resemble Western-style democracy. This reality was recognized but downplayed by *mujahedeen* supporters.

Unlike the 'fundamentalists', many of the so-called 'traditional' factions of Afghan society were supporting a compromise with the PDPA to end the conflict, and rallies were held in support of installing the former king as an interim head of state.[118]

Although there was considerable backing for a transitional role for the king from within Afghanistan and the Soviets were willing to accept him as a neutral figurehead, the fundamentalists wanted an Islamic government.[119] Pakistan supported this due to decades-old animosities with Zahir Shah and the United States had little to gain by going against their ally on this matter.[120]

The Peshawar Seven had firmly and vocally rejected the ceasefire and any attempts at national reconciliation, though others within the country and without were willing to negotiate with Najibullah to bring about peace.[121] Younis Khalis, then leading the seven-party alliance, denounced UN interlocutor Diego Cordovez as a 'Soviet puppet' and threats were issued that the *mujahedeen* would shoot down the plane shuttling the Ecuadorean between Kabul and Islamabad for negotiations.[122] Now in possession of US Stinger missiles, this threat was not to be taken lightly. The Resistance Alliance refused to countenance any PDPA involvement in an interim government and turned down a meeting with Cordovez.[123] They also declined to meet Michael Armacost evidence that their relationship with Washington began to fracture in the face of an agreement between the superpowers which did not settle the question of who should rule during the transition period.[124]

The resistance's US supporters backed them on this, determined that the war should not end with any semblance of Soviet influence remaining in place in governing circles. Reinforcing Washington's rhetoric, they publicly promoted the Resistance Alliance as suitable political front and minimized its fundamentalist nature. Theodore Eliot Jr. of ARC took to the papers arguing that the resistance was not dominated by fundamentalists and, in any case if it was, these fundamentalists were not like anti-Western Iranian fundamentalists.[125] This propaganda filtered through to reporting on the *mujahedeen*. One reporter with the *Washington Post* described the civil administration being developed by a *mujahedeen* coalition in the north of Afghanistan where power had shifted into the hands of Islamic fundamentalist leaders who were 'young' and 'modernizing'. He went on to describe the term 'Islamist' as representing 'fundamentalist revolutionaries with modernizing goals' who view Islam as a political ideology as well as a religion. The Islamists even believed in education for girls as 'local conditions permit'.[126] The fact that a march by Afghan refugees in San Francisco following the December 1987 superpower summit was attended by mostly men was excused as 'in keeping with Islamic tradition' women remained at home. This drew no negative commentary from the reporter (who was female). Neither did the appeals from the speakers to the women present to keep to traditional Islamic practices and dress though one woman present stated that this was not expected of her when she had lived in Kabul.[127] Another article noting the hours of Islamic studies and 'ideological training' given to *mujahedeen* at one camp observed that 'the political-religious training was notably devoid of the strident sloganeering and indoctrination associated with Iran's Revolutionary Guards'.[128]

Many of the pro-*mujahedeen* advocacy PVOs and other conservative anti-communist elements were, like the Peshawar Seven, avidly anti-accords. They publicly expressed their disgust at any potential agreement particularly targeting the State Department which, again, was accused of 'appeasement'. The Heritage Foundation argued that Gorbachev's 'new thinking' was stimulated by the damage wrought by

US-supplied Stinger missiles and described the *mujahedeen* as supported by an overwhelming majority of Afghans.[129] Richard Pipes likened Gorbachev to Hitler.[130] Daniel Pipes argued that Soviets' agreement to withdraw was actually 'a sophisticated strategy' to undercut support for the *mujahedeen*, leaving a power vacuum which would provoke a civil war amongst the Afghans allowing the Red Army to re-enter with international backing.[131] William Kling of the Foreign Policy Project of the conservative Free Congress Foundation founded by Paul Weyrich wrote to Reagan requesting the *mujahedeen* not be pressed into a coalition government and that the government continue aid until all Soviet troops had fully withdrawn.[132] Private and congressional supporters pushed for 'positive symmetry' – that is, that the United States continue to supply military aid to the *mujahedeen* until the last Soviet soldier left. Shultz had originally promised to end US aid thirty days after Soviet withdrawal had begun provided this withdrawal was 'front-loaded' – that half of all Soviet troops would retreat within a short period of time but *mujahedeen* supporters pushed for a reversal of this policy.[133]

An editorial in the *Washington Times* reflected these opinions urging the continuation of aid to the resistance until the Soviet withdrawal was complete.[134] Jeane Kirkpatrick took to the papers to describe the *mujahedeen* as feeling 'betrayed' by the Reagan administration that was 'too eager for any agreement'.[135] The CFA had distrusted the UN negotiation process for years.[136] In 1988, Kriegel wrote to Reagan arguing that cutting aid to the *mujahedeen* whilst the Soviets were still supplying the DRA would amount to a 'sell-out' of the rebels and 'contrary to everything you have said regarding your support for the freedom fighters. It is contrary to the principles of the many people who believed in you and voted you into office'.[137] Enclosed with Kriegel's letter were hundreds of petitions signed by CFA supporters calling on the President not to 'let the detentists and appeasers in the State Department and the National Security Council block our critical support of the Afghan resistance!' Kriegel wrote again on 12 April 1988, stating 'you have let down the Afghan resistance' pointing out that the Peshawar Seven had denounced the agreement.[138] Robert H. Krieble, co-founder of the Loctite Corporation and a former vice chairman of the Heritage Foundation, told Reagan 'your Department of State once again fails to accurately carry out your clear definition of your foreign policy' regarding any aid cut-off to the Afghan rebels.[139]

The accords were signed on 14 April 1988 by Afghanistan and Pakistan with the two superpowers as 'international guarantors'. Defiant, the Peshawar Seven held a large rally in Peshawar a few days later. Hekmatyar addressed the crowd surrounded by bodyguards dressed in US combat fatigues. He vowed to continue fighting and urged refugees not to return home yet. Younis Khalis described the United States and other Western states as 'enemies of Islam' while moderate members of the alliance expressed their concern about the domination of fundamentalists at the rally.[140] No interim administration had been established and a tacit policy of 'positive symmetry' meant the arms would continue to flow to both sides while the Soviet troops withdrew.

The administration continued to seek to manage the message following the settlement. This meant promoting more 'themes' for public consumption. These included presenting the accords as a 'triumph' for the *mujahedeen* and a 'watershed' for alleged Soviet expansionary ambitions.[141] However, Kabul did not fall as predicted by the United States. Instead the bloody, protracted civil war continued just without the Soviet presence. As the administration's public diplomacy efforts waned, the media began to reflect the events on the ground more accurately. Articles detailed *mujahedeen* atrocities and their civilian casualties. Unnamed US officials began to offer judgements on the continuing conflict that criticized the 'bearded men' and alleged *mujahedeen* involvement in opium growing.[142] There were revelations of how Arab charities, governments and wealthy individuals funding the resistance had pressed an anti-Western form of fundamentalist Islam on the fighters.[143] In January 1989, as fighting continued to rage across Afghanistan, the CFA held a 'Fall of Kabul' raffle asking for entrants to predict 'when will Kabul fall?' For a five-dollar entry fee, with half the pot going to the winner and half to 'one of several top Mujahid commanders', entrants could submit a guesstimate – flaunting the flippant attitude to Afghans' safety and dignity which defined so much of the United States' engagement with the war-ravaged state and its people.[144]

Conclusion

Negotiations in Geneva on Afghanistan gathered pace from late 1986 on, putting a settlement within sight as the conflict dragged into its eighth year. The withdrawal of the Red Army was proving a sticking point with the Soviets hoping the 'fig leaf' of a UN-brokered resolution would ameliorate the humiliation somewhat. The haggling around a suitable time frame for withdrawal and the political hue of a future Afghanistan bogged the talks down. This provided an 'opportunity' for US hardliners to land a few final punches on their communist adversary. While the US State Department did largely seek to facilitate what the United States had always alleged it desired – a withdrawal of the Red Army from Afghanistan – it appeared that some parties attempted to hamper a resolution for a variety of reasons. These detractors turned to the most effective weapon they had in their arsenal to influence world opinion and Reagan administration policy – propaganda.

Chief amongst the reasons for dissent was a desire to inflict a 'reverse Saigon' on the Soviets. Many Americans involved in Afghanistan seemed still stung by events in Southeast Asia over a decade beforehand. Again and again, Vietnam was evoked to justify anti-Soviet policies. Residual bitterness for the perceived Soviet role in the US entanglement there seemed to drive this sentiment among conservatives. At one stage, while giving testimony on the conflict, Louis Dupree reminded the House Foreign Affairs Committee how the Soviets had escalated the war in Vietnam while the Paris Peace talks were underway. This, he argued, justified the continued supply of weapons to the *mujahedeen* taking 'a leaf from the Vietnam War in doing so'.[145]

Another factor was that some, such as Zia, Afghan arms-trading intermediaries and even the *mujahedeen* themselves stood to gain politically or financially from the continuation of the conflict. A visceral distrust of the Soviets amongst conservative anti-communists in the administration, Congress and private individuals and advocacy organizations influenced their perception of the Geneva process and drove their attempts to scupper it. Pushing for military aid to continue to the *mujahedeen* until withdrawal was complete and all aid stopped to the DRA facilitated the continuation of the conflict long after the superpowers lost interest.

Finally, the actions of the Soviets themselves in seeking to leave a stable and friendly or at the very least neutral neighbour on its southern borders encouraged an impasse to develop. This policy would have benefitted Afghanistan post-conflict and the Reagan administration should have engaged and negotiated this rather than use it to score points off the Soviets and appease its supporters. It justified this approach by promoting the Peshawar Seven, which rejected national reconciliation, as the only true representatives of the Afghan people. While the myriad of differing *mujahedeen* groups throughout Afghanistan and the borderlands of Pakistan taken together could be described as having the overwhelming support of the Afghan population, these groups were splintered by ethnic, tribal, political and religious differences and not a monolithic entity represented by the Peshawar Seven as implied. The US position made any further negotiation on a programme of national reconciliation impossible and invalidated other groups' authority to negotiate in the name of the Afghan people. The divisions, however, remained behind the public diplomacy and would soon become undeniable as Afghanistan descended into civil war.

Conclusion

Public diplomacy and propaganda initiatives were central to the Carter and Reagan administrations' response to the Soviet invasion and occupation of Afghanistan. This reaction was rooted in one of the 'lessons' drawn by conservatives and foreign policy hawks from the Vietnam War experience which argued that shaping domestic and international perceptions was vital to the success of foreign policies. The Vietnam analogy was evoked time and time again by pro-*mujahedeen* activists in the administration, Congress and the PVOs. The Afghan conflict could damage the Soviets politically just as the Vietnam War had done to the United States, if it received enough news coverage internationally. This coverage could also undermine Moscow's military efforts in Afghanistan, just as media coverage was perceived to have frustrated American operations in Vietnam. These strategies relied on robust public diplomacy and propaganda initiatives. Furthermore, Vietnam provided a template for the military morass the Soviets could be entangled in if its resistance – the *mujahedeen* – was adequately supported. Informational strategies would facilitate this outcome by generating support for the resistance.

The Vietnam War had another impact on US foreign policy beyond the provision of 'lessons' and hackneyed analogies: it constrained the options available to Washington in response to Soviet actions. Direct military action was out of the question even for the belligerent Reagan administration. However, hard-line anti-communists in neo-conservative and New Right circles were consumed by the need to challenge the Soviet Union and re-assert American power. This aspiration was gratified, by proxy, on the battlegrounds of Afghanistan where Washington financed the *mujahedeen* to battle the Red Army. This course of action was possible due to the consensus amongst the public, members of Congress and the executive that supporting the rebels was an appropriate, or even commendable, stance for Americans to adopt. It fell on the Reagan administration to maintain this consensus as the conflict facilitated a number of its foreign policy objectives.

As documented here, the seeds of the covert CIA operation to aid the Afghan resistance lay in the Carter era. This was also the case with the decision to channel resources into propaganda initiatives on the conflict. Before the 'loss' of Iran, Afghanistan was of little interest to Washington. However, for the Carter administration, the states' newly found significance was rooted in more than geostrategic imperatives. The Soviet action was triggered by its concerns about spreading Islamic fundamentalism and a desire to maintain influence in a neighbouring state rather than expansive designs on the Persian Gulf; nevertheless, it was bound to provoke a strong reaction in Washington. Hard-line anti-communists like Zbigniew Brzezinski recognized that the invasion and occupation of Afghanistan could be used to damage the USSR politically particularly with Muslim states. The emergent 'crescent of crisis' was going to be a predicament for the United States *or* the USSR; Brzezinski was determined it would be Moscow's problem. US credibility with Muslims was strained due to its involvement with the Shah of Iran and its support for Israel. If the Soviets had protracted problems with Afghan Muslims this could reverberate with other Islamic states and rebalance the situation. To this end the rhetoric and propaganda of the Carter administration sought fissures in Soviet relations with its Islamic minorities and strove to widen them using the Afghan conflict. Brzezinski's scheme to provoke Muslims discontent with the Soviet Union would resonate right through the Reagan years. Afghanistan was an arena to prosecute a Cold War contest for the 'hearts and minds' of Muslim publics, and the context of the Cold War blinded Brzezinski and the Reagan administration officials to its potential short-term impact on Afghan politics and society or the long-term implications for international politics. The deliberate tactic to provoke the conflict made eventual reconciliation more elusive in Afghanistan and further militarized its society. The attacks on the institutions of central governance in Afghanistan, underwritten by the United States, weakened the already-shaky control Kabul exercised outside of its boundaries. It empowered local warlords, encouraged local autonomy and a disregard for central authority. Such conditions enabled Osama bin Laden to establish a 'state within a state' for al Qaeda in Afghanistan in the 1990s. Furthermore, US propaganda played a part in legitimizing the concept of 'holy war' in response to communist expansion. However, for some Islamists this ideology was not limited to battling communism but rather all forms of 'modern' political governance in Muslim states. Eventually, some of its proponents would challenge the sole remaining superpower, the United States, for the 'hearts and minds' of these publics on 9/11.

The Reagan administration would use propaganda around the conflict for a range of other purposes too. The Afghan conflict was one of the chief instruments of the administration's propaganda and public diplomacy that spearheaded its ideological confrontation with the Soviet Union in the final decade of the Cold War. NSDD 32 demonstrated the Reagan administration's determination to challenge the Soviet Union. Officials quickly realized that arming the Afghan resistance could provide the means to do this. Once in power the Reagan administration, through a series of policy directives, used the Afghan conflict to ratchet up pressure on the Soviet Union. Drafted in 1982, NSDD 75 explicitly identified Afghanistan as the Soviet's Achilles heel. NSDD 147 from 1984 asserted the 'heightened' strategic importance of the region to Washington following the fall of the Shah of Iran and the Soviet invasion of Afghanistan. NSDD 166 (1985) dramatically increased funding for the Afghan programme and signalled a more proactive turn in administration policy. Public diplomacy and propaganda enabled these strategies. NSDD 32, NSDD 75, NSDD 77, NSDD 147, NSDD 194, NSDD 166 and NSDD 270 attest to the significance the administration attached to effective propaganda in facilitating its objectives. These goals included more than gaining influence with Muslims.

The administration wanted to project the United States as powerful military and moral force on the international stage. It wanted to regain the authority it believed squandered a few short years before in the retreat from Saigon. Reagan administration initiatives, which were wide-ranging, multi-agency and multi-faceted, often blurred the lines between public diplomacy and propaganda. Such strategies overstretched the parameters of the USIA's remit. They required a CIA propaganda expert, Walter Raymond Jr., to co-ordinate and implement. These programmes and policies had a number of objectives from justifying US rearmament, improving its geostrategic footing in South Asia to undermining Soviet credibility. The Afghan conflict was instrumental to these strategies but the state and its people incidental. All these strategies were rooted in a Cold War worldview where gaining supremacy over the Soviet Union rationalized any policy. Thus, the need to secure congressional approval of a military aid package to Pakistan that the administration perceived as vital to America's strategic security in this region justified the public diplomacy exercise to ameliorate the reputation of Zia al Haq. The 'yellow rain' propaganda programme sought, albeit unsuccessfully, to vindicate the renewal of the US chemical weapon stocks.

The administration used propaganda and public diplomacy to enable its objectives; however, these information strategies had a more central, powerful role than this in the US confrontation with the USSR. Hard-line anti-communists within and without the administration considered that the loss of domestic public support for the war in Vietnam had been instrumental in the US defeat. They resolved to visit the same fate on the USSR. This would both serve US interests and avenge Soviet interference in Vietnam. While the USSR was not subject to the same pressures from domestic public opinion, it was sensitive to the vagaries of international publics particularly those of geostrategically important or resource-rich Middle Eastern or Third World states. Propaganda and public diplomacy were intrinsic to this strategy. The concerted, continued and co-ordinated nature of the administration's commitment to information strategies testifies to this. Propaganda and public diplomacy did not just support the US strategy of arming the *mujahedeen*; the conflict in Afghanistan supported the information strategies, which, the administration was convinced, could considerably undermine the credibility of the Soviet Union. Ensuring the continuation of the conflict was vital to this.

As stated earlier, the administration's propaganda and public diplomacy initiatives deployed to this end were wide-ranging. The administration facilitated Afghan-related commemorations and trips to refugee camps by government officials and even a Hollywood actor, all designed to maintain the pressure on Moscow and maximize the political fall-out from the occupation. The administration decried the occupation and appealed for peace; however, NSDD 166 outlined the administration's conviction that 'regardless of the ultimate outcome' in Afghanistan, US interests would be served if the USSR was isolated from Third World and Islamic states. This was the ultimate objective of these public diplomacy initiatives.

The political machinating that underlay the use of 'public diplomacy' on the Afghan conflict in the run up to, and during, the Geneva superpower summit of 1985 offers further evidence of this. Gorbachev's assent to power heralded the opportunity for a new détente between the United States and USSR and a resolution to the Afghan conflict.

However, the Reagan administration felt threatened by the Soviet leader's charming persona that so engaged European publics. The public diplomacy programme outlined in NSDD 194 focused on using the Afghan conflict to undermine Moscow's negotiating power and promote America's credentials amongst Third World and Muslim states by demonstrating its support for human rights and self-determination. This programme professed administration support for self-determination when, in fact, its public advocacy was little more than an effort to gain leverage in arms deals negotiations.

Such initiatives invariably involved statements justifying the US position by lionizing the Afghan resistance though the administration consistently denied the *mujahedeen* political recognition in order to keep the Kabul embassy open as a listening post. Administration officials, particularly President Reagan, hailed the *mujahedeen* as 'freedom fighters', their political values were conflated with those of Americans and their religious beliefs filtered through a Christian worldview. Their retrogressive attitudes towards the rights of women and mistreatment of minorities were known to the administration but went unacknowledged. Their power struggles, violence and drug trafficking were ignored even while the administration prosecuted a drugs war in Panama and Central America. The strict religious regime in the refugee camps of Peshawar tolerated. It was from these camps and their strict religious schools that the Taliban movement emerged, nurtured on the strict interpretation of Islam tolerated or even encouraged by US supporters during the conflict period.

Accusations levelled against the Red Army about the use of 'toy bombs' or the deliberate massacre of civilians were relentless and pernicious. They included the merciless murder and maiming of children and the rape of Afghan women. The Soviet army was likened to the Nazis, its tactics to Genghis Khan and events in Afghanistan to the Holocaust. Analogies to the Second World War massacres were repeatedly evoked. The Soviet and Afghan armies were undoubtedly guilty of brutality and barbarity and Afghan civilians undoubtedly suffered greatly during the conflict. However, many of the accusations emanating from American pro-*mujahedeen* organizations and the Reagan administration were of dubious provenance or hyperbole, in other words, propaganda. Their primary design was to further US foreign policy not assist the Afghan people. This Manichean portrayal of the Soviets and the DRA as irredeemably brutal and the *mujahedeen* as 'holy warriors' narrowed the potential for reconciliation and negotiation on a resolution in Afghanistan. It polarized the opposing sides, fostered resentments, discouraged compromise and emboldened the *mujahedeen* to continue their warfare.

The Reagan administration was not alone in pursuing an anti-communist agenda through support for the Afghan resistance. Propaganda like the 'yellow rain' programme illustrates how an alliance born of common purpose grew between the administration and private organizations like Freedom House and the CFA. Other works on propaganda and public diplomacy indicate that such public/private 'alliances' have been a feature of US foreign policy initiatives in the post-Second World War period as the Cold War crystallized into an ideological and cultural confrontation. Information and ideas that ostensibly originated within American culture and society distanced US governments from allegations of propagandizing and bestowed legitimacy on the product. However, the actions of private citizens and organizations were not always at the behest of Washington; often they were inspired by a Cold War societal consensus on the existential necessity of confronting communism. This trend was encouraged and given authority and legitimacy by elite organizations like the Committee on the Present Danger; however, more importantly, it was reflected in smaller, more 'grassroots' organizations which took it upon themselves to challenge communism wherever they could.

This period saw the 'coming of age' of a conservative 'civil society' confident of its ability to influence government policy and convey its messages through the power of propaganda. The anti-communist PVOs supporting Afghanistan that were part of this development indicate a growing political autonomy which did not require orchestration by the CIA or the Department of State. These groups had outgrown the shackles of these bureaucracies and the constraints of their agenda. This allowed them the freedom to pursue even more radical courses of action sometimes at odds with government policy. During the Reagan years this movement blossomed into a powerful, decentralized, conservative civil society which now wields considerable influence in the American political system demonstrated today by the power of the minority Tea Party to influence the Republican political agenda.

The creation and development of a sample of these organizations involved with the Afghan conflict are documented here offering an insight into the ideologies driving their agendas which were often more wide-ranging than their stated cause of supporting 'freedom' in Afghanistan. Influencing public opinion as a way of influencing government policy was a central tactic of these groups, and the involvement of private organizations and individuals was a recurring feature of the propaganda and public diplomacy around the Afghan conflict. While the Afghan-specific PVOs are now defunct, individuals involved in these campaigns continue to use public forums to promulgate their calls for action. Bernard-Henri Levy has moved on from supporting Afghan *mujahedeen* via Radio Free Kabul to publicly advocating for support for the Transitional Council which challenged Gadaffi in Libya in 2011. Zalmay Khalilzad became involved in the neo-conservative think tank the Project for a New American Century which called for a more belligerent US engagement in world affairs in the 1990s. He later served as President Bush's ambassador to Afghanistan and Iraq. More widely, this exploration of the Afghan PVOs provides an insight into the fledgling conservative lobby industry of the 1980s which has since developed into a powerful influence in contemporary US politics.

The Afghan Media Project envisaged a media agency funded by the US government but developed and run by the private sector. As with other administration initiatives many of the private individuals and organizations that were involved had links to other right-wing, anti-communist causes or to the Reagan administration. BU's H. Joachim Maitre and John Silber were both supporters of PRODEMCA and had worked with the administration in other capacities. This network of right-wing interests in the 1980s has been explored, particularly in relation to US support for the Nicaraguan *Contras*' cause, and now expanded to include analysis of similar groups and individuals in the Afghan conflict.

The PVOs raised the profile of the conflict and raised funds for the rebels. They liaised with members of Congress to host *mujahedeen* on tours to heighten awareness of their cause in the United States. They were influential 'experts' appeared on USIA output as well as television news programmes and in newspapers. They played a pivotal role in shaping perceptions of the conflict and its protagonists in Congress and in the media by providing information, which was often one-sided and sometimes untrue. At other times, the PVOs vocal advocacy limited the administration's manoeuvrability on the terms of a peace deal in Afghanistan. This divergence of aims increased as in the later years of the administration more moderate elements prevailed in foreign policy.

Some PVOs had links to the administration or other conservative anti-communist causes and further declassification may prove a level of collusion; however, it is clear that a common ideology of virulent, anti-communism compelled many of these groups and individuals. These private interests in conservative and New Right circles had also absorbed the 'lesson' from Vietnam about the importance of influencing public opinion as much as administration officials. This 'lesson' informed the actions of conservative, anti-communist organizations like the Heritage Foundation and the CPD. These groups manipulated the narrative of the Afghan conflict to serve their domestic political purposes. They rushed to portray Soviet actions as aggressive and expansionist. They then used this characterization to rally against détente and to argue for the re-assertion of American military and moral authority. They used it to rail against the Carter presidency and champion Reagan's strident foreign policies.

The 'lesson' of using a conflict like Afghanistan to justify American militarism to the American people would be echoed in the actions of the Project for a New American Century (PNAC) a decade later. Their statement of principles directly referenced this era in its call for a 'Reaganite policy of military strength and moral clarity' for America in the post-Cold War era. Peopled by a number of individuals active in the drive for funding the Afghan *mujahedeen* such as Fred Iklé, Khalilzad, Richard Perle, Elliot Abrams and Paul Wolfowitz, the PNAC recognized the centrality of identifying a 'catastrophic or catalysing event' to enable implementation of their radical policies.[1] The same individuals who lobbied for intervention in Afghanistan in the 1980s would call for similar action in Iraq in the 1990s and, later, use their position in the George W. Bush administration in the 2000s to propagate the propaganda required to ensure these ends. The earlier Afghan programme provided a valuable training ground for these foreign policy hawks.

Congress also played a fundamental role in generating support for the Afghan resistance from the earliest days of the conflict. Charlie Wilson's manoeuvres to channel funds to the *mujahedeen*'s military operations have been the subject of books and even a film while the activities of other members of Congress who utilized their positions to propagandize about the conflict are less well documented. Congressional documents and media analysis detail their efforts. The Tsongas-Ritter Resolution publicized Congress' demand for more administration action to aid the *mujahedeen*. The Congressional Task Force on Afghanistan held numerous hearings to pressurize the administration to send more aid, better arms and improve its propaganda output. Congress set aside the Smith-Mundt Act to allow the distribution of USIA videos within the United States, propagandizing the American public. Members of Congress visited the Peshawar camps, dined with Zia and met with *mujahedeen* in Washington. They had close links to pro-*mujahedeen* PVOs like the CFA and Freedom House that provided testimony to congressional hearings and the Congressional Task Force.

As the Soviet withdrawal from Afghanistan neared and relations between the USSR and the United States warmed, cracks in the *mujahedeen* support base in the United States began to appear. While for a significant period of the conflict, the efforts of these individuals and groups reinforced one another there were divergences between them and even within the administration. The CFA and *mujahedeen* supporters like academic Louis Dupree argued for continued military support to the Afghan resistance during the withdrawal period. The State Department had initially agreed to stop the flow of arms as the Red Army withdrew and some members of Congress who previously had taken a pro-*mujahedeen* stance now felt the Soviet withdrawal should be facilitated. More hawkish administration officials like Fred Iklé in the Pentagon disagreed and were determined to exact political costs from the Soviet Union for as long as possible.

In the end, as a resolution neared, the relentless public campaign of the PVOs against the accords enabled the 'bleeders' within the administration, and without, to gain a final triumph. For the uncompromising Cold War warriors in Congress, the administration and the PVOs, the temptation to ensure the Soviets suffered 'their own Saigon' – run out of Afghanistan in haste and humiliation – trumped all other considerations. As a result, once a resolution was in sight they argued against stopping military aid to the resistance. Their Cold War worldview marginalized any consideration that an orderly withdrawal might be best for Afghanistan. Their propaganda campaign ensured it would not take place. As a result, national reconciliation efforts were sacrificed to Cold War intrigues. A government of national unity was never formed, positive symmetry reigned and the war continued unabated following the Soviet withdrawal. These conditions prevailed in Afghanistan facilitating the rise of the Taliban and enabling al Qaeda to establish a safe haven in the war-torn state from where it would launch its offensive on Western targets from the late 1990s on.

Throughout the conflict, supporting the resistance was a political strategy developed to further US policies by prolonging Soviet involvement in Afghanistan. This strategy burnished American credentials internationally as a champion of 'democratic' revolutionaries. Denying political status as a government-in-exile to the resistance was a political strategy designed to appease American ally, Pakistan, and maintain a valuable Cold War 'listening post' in Kabul. These various policies were designed to serve American interests but, in order to create and maintain support internationally they needed to be presented as serving loftier objectives such as 'freedom' and 'self-determination'. This necessitated concerted propaganda efforts, which promoted these perspectives and in the case of the AMP ensured the conflict remained newsworthy. However, these information policies, like the military aid programme, also had potentially long-term consequences unforeseen at the time. As well as gaining martial expertise, could the *mujahedeen* and other insurgents/terrorists also have learnt important lessons about managing public perceptions from this period? Could the education administered via the AMP about the importance of vivid visual imagery to engage a mass audience have had any influence on the exploits of al Qaeda whose members would have been amongst the 'Afghan Arabs' fighting the Red Army? Or even later on, other '*jihadis*' so enamoured of publicity such as the Islamic State? Perhaps the lesson learnt on the battlefields of Afghanistan about the power of propaganda will prove to be the most potent one of all.

Notes

Introduction

1. The term 'bleeders' is used by a number of authors to describe Reagan administration officials who sought to ensure the Soviets remained in Afghanistan for as long as possible to extract the highest penalty.
2. The administration's commitment to strengthening its public diplomacy infrastructure for this purpose is in evidence in a number of NSDDs, for example, NSDD 45, 'United States International Broadcasting', 15 July 1982; NSDD 77 'Management of Public Diplomacy Relative to National Security', 14 January 1983; NSDD 130, 'US International Information Policy', 6 March 1984; NSDD 170 'Radio Marti', 20 May 1985; NSDD 194, 'Meeting with Soviet Leader in Geneva: Themes and Perceptions', 25 October 1985. All available at 'National Security Decision Directives (NSDDs), 1981–1989', Ronald Reagan Library (RRL): http://www.reagan.utexas.edu/archives/reference/NSDDs.html#.VO4aVfmsVpA
3. Fred Halliday characterized the importance of mobilizing domestic support for US foreign policies as a 'lesson' derived from Vietnam by the Reagan administration and its supporters in *Cold War, Third World*, p. 72.
4. James M. Scott, *Deciding to Intervene: The Reagan Doctrine and American Foreign Policy* (Durham NC: Duke University Press, 1996), p. 21.
5. Steve Coll, *Ghost Wars: The Secret History of the CIA, Afghanistan and Bin Laden, from the Soviet Invasion to September 10, 2001* (New York: Penguin, 2004), p. 91.
6. Coll, *Ghost Wars*; Oliver Roy, *Islam and Resistance in Afghanistan* (Cambridge: Cambridge University Press, 1986); Diego Cordovez and Selig Harrison, *Out of Afghanistan: The Inside Story of the Soviet Withdrawal* (New York: Oxford University Press, 1995).
7. Walter Lippmann, *Public Opinion* (New York: Harcourt, Brace and Co., 1922); Harold Lasswell's *Propaganda Techniques in the World War* (Greenville: Coachwhip Publications, 2015); Edward Bernays, *Propaganda* (New York: Liveright, 1928).
8. William Scott Lucas, *Freedom's War: The US Crusade against the Soviet Union, 1945–56* (Manchester: Manchester University Press, 1999); Frances Stoner Saunders, *Who Paid the Piper? The CIA and the Cultural Cold War* (London: Granta, 1999); Hugh Wilford, *The Mighty Wurlitzer: How the CIA Played America* (Cambridge, MA: Harvard University Press, 2008); Nicholas Cull, *The Cold War and the United States Information Agency, 1945–1989* (New York: Cambridge University Press, 2008); Kenneth Osgood, *Total Cold War: Eisenhower's Secret Propaganda Battle at Home and Abroad* (Lawrence: University of Kansas, 2006); Nancy Bernhard, *US Television News and Cold War Propaganda, 1947–1960* (Cambridge: Cambridge University Press, 2003); Alan Axelrod, *Selling the Great War: The Making of American Propaganda* (New York: Palgrave Macmillan, 2009); Walter L. Hixon, *Parting the Curtain: Propaganda, Culture, and the Cold War* (New York, Palgrave

Macmillan, 1998); Laura A. Belmonte, *Selling the American Way: US Propaganda and the Cold War* (Philadelphia: University of Pennsylvania Press, 2008).
9   Jason Stahl, *Right Moves: The Conservative Think Tank in American Political Culture since 1945* (Chapel Hill: University of North Carolina Press, 2016).
10 Giles Scott-Smith charts Lord's (author of NSDD 77) strong ideological belief in the superiority of Western values of liberal democracy and how he sought to infuse US public diplomacy with this moral conviction. See Giles Scott-Smith, 'Aristotle, US Public Diplomacy, and the Cold War: The Works of Carnes Lord', *Foundations of Science*, Vol. 13 (July 2008), p. 16. Concluding *Selling War in a Media Age*, Robert J. McMahon notes that Reagan used 'the comfortable cloak of American innocence and exceptionalism' to market his SDI, see Robert J. McMahon, 'Conclusion: War, Democracy, and the State', in Kenneth Osgood and Andrew K. Frank (eds.), *Selling War in a Media Age: The Presidency and Public Opinion in the American Century* (Florida: University Press of Florida, 2010), p. 257.
11 Both Saunders, *Who Paid the Piper?* and Wilford's *The Mighty Wurlitzer* examine this area.
12 Peter Kornbluh, 'Reagan's Propaganda Ministry', *Propaganda Review* (Summer 1988), p. 25.
13 Raymond L. Garthoff, *The Great Transition: American-Soviet Relations and the End of the Cold War* (Washington, DC: Brookings Institution, 1994), p. 97.
14 Nancy Snow, 'US Propaganda', in Martin Halliwell and Catherine Morley (eds.), *American Thought and Culture in the 21st Century* (Edinburgh: Edinburgh University Press, 2008), p. 103.
15 The United States Information and Educational Exchange Act of 1948 (Smith-Mundt Act) forbad domestic propagandizing.
16 Jowett and O'Donnell, quoted in David Guth, 'Black, White, and Shades of Gray: The Sixty-Year Debate over Propaganda versus Public Diplomacy', *Journal of Promotion Management*, Vol. 14, Nos. 3–4 (2008), p. 311.
17 Jacques Ellul, *Propaganda: The Formation of Men's Attitudes* (New York: Knopf, 1965); Andrew L. Johns, 'Introduction: Hail to the Salesman in Chief', in Osgood and Frank (eds.), *Selling War in a Media Age*, p. 3.
18 Kenneth Adelman, 'Speaking of America: Public Diplomacy in Our Time', *Foreign Affairs*, Vol. 59, No. 4 (Spring 1981), pp. 913–914.
19 Robert Parry and Peter Kornbluh, 'Iran Contra's Untold Story', *Foreign Policy*, No. 72 (Autumn 1988), p. 8.
20 Noam Chomsky and Edward S. Herman, *Manufacturing Consent: The Political Economy of the Mass Media* (New York: Pantheon Books, 1988), p. 18.
21 Lippman, *Public Opinion*, p. 3.
22 Zbigniew Brzezinski, *Power and Principle: Memoirs of the National Security Advisor, 1977–1981* (London: Weidenfeld and Nicolson, 1983).
23 Halliday, *Cold War, Third World*, p. 72.
24 Julian Vaisse, *Neoconservatism: The Biography of a Movement* (Belknap Press of Harvard University Press, 2010); Micklethwait, *The Right Nation: Conservative Power in America* (New York: Penguin Press, 2004); Gregg Easterbrook, 'Ideas Move Nations', *The Atlantic* (January 1986); Lou Cannon, *President Reagan: Role of a Lifetime* (New York: Putnam, 1982).
25 Jerry Wayne Saunders, *Peddlers of Crisis: The Committee on the Present Danger and the Politics of Containment* (Boston, MA: South End Press, 1983).

26 Lucas, *Freedom's War*, p. 99.
27 George Crile, *Charlie Wilson's War: The Extraordinary Story of the Largest Covert Operation in History* (New York: Atlantic Monthly Press, 2003).

Chapter 1

1   CC CPSU International Department, 'CC CPSU Information for the Leaders of the Progressive Afghan Political Organizations "Parcham" and "Khalq" Concerning the Results of the Visit of Mohammed Daud to the USSR', 21 June 1974, Document No. 112504, *The Soviet Invasion of Afghanistan Collection*, Wilson Center Digital Archive, http://digitalarchive.wilsoncenter.org; Odd Arne Westad, *The Global Cold War : Third World Interventions and the Making of Our Times* (Cambridge; New York : Cambridge University Press, 2007), pp. 301–302, details that the Soviets were largely satisfied with the Daoud regime and encouraged the PDPA to work with it.
2   CC CPSU Politburo Session March 17–18, 1979, Document No. 1, September 11th Sourcebooks, Vol. II: *Afghanistan: Lessons from the Last War*, NSA, Electronic Briefing Book (EEB) No. 57, Part I, The Soviet Experience in Afghanistan: Russian Documents and Memoirs.
3   CC CPSU Politburo Session March 17–18, 1979, *Afghanistan: Lessons from the Last War*, NSA.
4   Westad, *Global Cold War*, p. 316.
5   Transcript of A.N. Kosygin, A.A. Gromyko, D.F. Ustinov, B.N. Ponomarev, N.M. Taraki Conversation, Document No. 3, 20 March 1979, *Afghanistan: Lessons from the Last War*, Part I, The Soviet Experience, NSA.
6   Alexander Lyakhovsky, 'Inside the Soviet Invasion of Afghanistan and the Seizure of Kabul, December 1979', Working Paper No. 51, January 2007, p. 17, Cold War International History Project (CWIHP) Publications, Working Papers Series, Wilson Center Digital Archive.
7   Anatoly Dobrynin, *In Confidence: Moscow's Ambassador to America's Six Cold War Presidents* (New York: Time Books, 1995), p. 437.
8   Alexander Lyakhovsky, *The Tragedy and Valor of Afghan* (Moscow: Iskon, 1995), pp. 109–112, details the Soviet military disagreement over the decision.
9   Jimmy Carter, 'The State of the Union Address Delivered before a Joint Session of the Congress', 23 January1980, State of the Union Addresses and Messages Collection, The American Presidency Project, University of California, Santa Barbara.
10 K. Alan Kronstadt, 'Pakistan-US Relations', *Congressional Research Service*, Issue Brief for Congress, Updated 6 March 2006, Federation of American Scientists (FAS); Dennis Kux, *The United States and Pakistan, 1947–2000: Disenchanted allies* (Baltimore, MD: The Johns Hopkins University Press, 2001), pp. 69–70.
11 John Prados, 'Notes on the CIA's Secret War in Afghanistan', *Journal of American History*, Vol. 89, No. 2 (September 2002), p. 466.
12 Douglas Brinkley, 'Eisenhower in Kabul', *New York Times*, 12 January 2002.
13 Roozbeh Shirazi, 'Islamic Education in Afghanistan: Revisiting the United States' Role', *The New Centennial Review*, Vol. 8, No. 1 (Spring 2008), p. 213.
14 Theodore L. Eliot Jr. retired in 1978 and became dean of the Fletcher School of Law and Diplomacy at Tufts University in Boston. He would help set up the AFA in 1979 and commented in the media and for USICA programmes on the situation in Afghanistan.

15 Fred Halliday, *The Making of the Second Cold War* (London: Verso, 1987), pp. 96–97, argues the United States considered Afghanistan to be within the Soviet sphere of influence and along with other NATO countries had diplomatic relations with the PDPA following the coup.
16 Telegram to the US Secretary of State from the US Embassy, Kabul, 'Six Weeks after Afghanistan's Revolution: A Summing Up', 13 June 1978, Document No. 4, *Towards an International History of the War in Afghanistan, 1979–1989* (April 2002), Vol. 1, US Documents, *CWIHP* Publications, Wilson Center.
17 Telegram to the US Embassy, Kabul from the US Secretary of State 'Assessment of Afghan Developments and US-Afghan Relations', 1 December 1978, Document No. 8, *Towards an International History of the War in Afghanistan*, Vol. 1, CWHIP.
18 Steve Galster, introductory essay to 'Afghanistan: The Making of US Policy, 1973–1990', *Afghanistan: Lessons from the Last War*, Digital National Security Archive (DNSA).
19 Robert Gates, *From the Shadows : The Ultimate Insider's Story of Five Presidents and How they Won the Cold War* (London: Pocket, 2008), p. 130.
20 Memorandum for President Carter from Brzezinski, 'NSC Weekly Report', 28 December 1978, *Presidential Papers of the President* (*PPP*), Zbigniew Brzezinski Collection, sf. Weekly Reports 82–90, 12/78 – 3/79, Box 42, Jimmy Carter Library (JCL).
21 Thomas W. Lippman, 'Afghanistan Rejects US Protest over Ambassador's Death', *Washington Post*, 20 February 1979.
22 No author given, 'Death behind a Keyhole', *Time*, 26 February 1979.
23 Steven Strasser, Chris J. Harper, Lars-Erik Nelson and Ron Moreau, 'Death of an Envoy', *Newsweek*, 26 February 1979.
24 Statement by the White House Press Secretary, 'United States Announcement of Cutbacks in Its Development and Military Assistance Programs in Afghanistan', 22 February 1979, *American Foreign Policy: Basic Documents, 1977–1980* (Washington: US Dept. of State, 1983), p. 807.
25 Telegram for US Embassy, Kabul from US Secretary of State Vance, 'Senate Resolution on Appointment of Ambassador to Afghanistan', 14 May 1979, Document No. AF00550, *Afghanistan: The Making of US Foreign Policy, 1973–1990*, DNSA.
26 Gates, *From the Shadows*, p. 145.
27 Ibid., pp. 145–146.
28 Ibid., p. 146; Charles G. Cogan, 'Partners in Time: The CIA and Afghanistan since 1979', *World Policy Journal*, Vol. 10, No. 2 (Summer 1993), p. 76.
29 Brzezinski, *Power and Principle*, p. 427.
30 Memorandum for Brzezinski from Thomas Thornton, 'What Are the Soviets Doing in Afghanistan', 17 September 1979, Document No. 31, *Towards an International History of the War in Afghanistan*, Vol. 1, *CWIHP*.
31 Ronald Reagan endorsed this 'finding' in 1981 and it duly served US requirements until a major policy shift in 1985.
32 Carter, *Keeping Faith: Memoirs of a President* (New York: Bantam Books, 1982), p. 472.
33 No author listed, 'Russia's Risky Bid to Stake a Claim', *The Globe and Mail* (Toronto), 1 January 1980.
34 Kevin Klose, 'Kabul Coup Seen Advancing Historic Moscow Objectives', *Washington Post*, 30 December 1979.
35 Carter Interview with Frank Reynolds, 'World News Tonight', *ABC*, 31 December 1979, *ABC* News Transcripts, 1978, 1979, Internet Archive, https://archive.org/stream/ABCNews19781979/ABC%20News-1978-1979.txt

36 Brzezinski, *Power and Principle*, p. 430.
37 Memorandum for President Carter from Brzezinski, 'Reflections on Soviet Intervention in Afghanistan', 26 December 1979, Document No. 51, *Towards an International History of the Cold War*, Vol. I. *CWIHP*.
38 Memorandum for Carter from Brzezinski, 'Strategic Reaction to the Afghanistan Problem', 3 January 1980, *PPP*, ZBC, Geographical File SW Asia-PG 12/26/79-1/4/80, Box 17, JCL.
39 President Jimmy Carter, 'State of the Union Address Delivered before a Joint Session of the Congress', 23 January 1980, *Public Papers of the Presidents*, American Presidency Project.
40 Memorandum for Carter from Brzezinski, 'Reflections on Soviet Intervention in Afghanistan', 26 December 1979, *CWIHP*.
41 USICA Report, 'The Soviet Propaganda Campaign on the Afghanistan Invasion and Its Impact: A Preliminary Assessment', 21 February 1980, Box 40, P 160, RG 306; Memorandum for Bray from Stanton H. Burnett, 'Soviet Media Coverage of the US in Iran and Afghanistan Situations', 14 April 1980, USICA Office of Research, Special Reports, Box 42, P 160, RG 306.
42 USICA Report, 'The Soviet Propaganda Campaign on the Afghanistan Invasion and Its Impact'. This report outlines a 'common overriding theme' amongst states of fear the Afghanistan conflict would lead to a superpower confrontation and that the United States had 'over-reacted rhetorically' for domestic political reasons threatening détente.
43 In a memorandum for the President on 12 April 1979, Brzezinski advised that the Carter administration was perceived as 'indecisive' and 'not firm' and argued that Carter should 'say from time to time that the US is willing to use its force to protect its interests and those of our allies', Memorandum for President Carter from Brzezinski, 'Opinion: Foreign Policy and Domestic Politics', 12 April 1979, *Public Papers of the President (PPP)*, Zbigniew Brzezinski Collection, sf Weekly Reports 91–101, 3/79-6/79, Box 42, JCL.
44 Lawrence Martin, 'An Old Refrain: Keep to the Right', *The Globe and Mail* (Toronto), 14 July 1980, quotes polls showing a swing to the right amongst Americans with more people identifying themselves as conservatives than liberals.
45 Paul Nitze came to prominence in the Truman administration authoring the alarmist NSC 68 in 1950. He went on to serve in the Department of Defense under Presidents Kennedy and Johnson but failed to gain a position in the Carter administration though a campaign supporter. Rostow also served under Johnson as Under Secretary of State for Political Affairs and went on to serve the Reagan administration as Director of the Arms Control and Disarmament Agency. James R. Schlesinger served in a number of positions under Nixon most significantly as Director of the CIA and Secretary of Defense and under Carter as Secretary of Energy.
46 Paul H. Nitze, 'Strategy in the Decade of the 1980s', *Foreign Affairs*, Vol. 59, No. 1 (Autumn 1980), pp. 82–101.
47 Ibid., pp. 82–101.
48 Anne Hessing Cahn, 'Team B: The Trillion Dollar Experiment', *Bulletin of Atomic Scientists*, Vol. 49, No. 3 (April 1993), p. 26.
49 Jerry Wayne Saunders, *Peddlers of Crisis: The Committee on the Present Danger and the Politics of Containment* (Cambridge, MA: South End Press, 1983), p. 240.
50 Vaisse, *Neoconservatism*, pp. 133–135.

51 Other Democrats who took positions were Paul Nitze, Gene Rostow, Lane Kirkland, Charles Tyroler, Max Kampelman, Edward Bennett Williams and Myer Rashish.
52 Sean Willentz, *The Age of Reagan: A History, 1974–2008* (New York: Harper, 2008), p. 90. Stahl's *Right Moves* provides in-depth research into the creation and development of the Heritage Foundation.
53 Jacob Weisberg, 'Happy Birthday, Heritage Foundation', *Slate*, 9 January 1998.
54 Lawrence C. Soley, *The News Shapers: The Sources Who Explain the News* (New York: Praeger, 1992), pp. 61–62.
55 No author listed, 'Carter's Defense Budget', Report, Heritage Foundation, 21 June 1977, http://www.heritage.org/research/reports/1977/06/carters-defense-budget
56 Michael B. Donley, 'NATO and the Strategic Nuclear Balance', Report, Heritage Foundation, 17 August 1978, http://www.heritage.org/research/reports/1978/08/nato-and-the-strategic-nuclear-balance. Moynihan was responding to the Team A Team B analyses of the NIE.
57 Donley, 'NATO and the Nuclear Balance'.
58 Samuel T. Francis, 'War in the Horn of Africa', Report, Heritage Foundation, 27 February 1978, http://www.heritage.org/research/reports/1978/02/war-in-the-horn-of-africa. Moynihan was a leading neo-conservative during the Carter presidency. See James Traub, 'Daniel Patrick Moynihan, Liberal? Conservative? Or Just Pat?' *New York Times*, 16 September 1990.
59 James Phillips, 'The Iranian Revolution: Long-Term Implications', Backgrounder No. 89, Heritage Foundation, 15 June 1979, http://www.heritage.org/research/reports/1979/06/the-iranian-revolution-long-term-implications
60 Charles T. Baroch, 'Soviet Style Détente: A Continuing US Dilemma', Backgrounder No. 66, Heritage Foundation, 12 October 1978, http://www.heritage.org/research/reports/1978/10/soviet-style-detente-a-continuing-us-dilemma
61 'Soviet Foreign Policy and SALT', *National Security Record*, November 1979.
62 James Phillips, 'Afghanistan: The Soviet Quagmire', Backgrounder No. 101, Heritage Foundation, 25 October 1979, http://www.heritage.org/research/reports/1979/10/afghanistan-the-soviet-quagmire; James Phillips, 'The Soviet Invasion of Afghanistan', Backgrounder No. 108, Heritage Foundation, 9 January 1980, http://www.heritage.org/research/reports/1980/02/the-soviet-invasion-of-afghanistan
63 Phillips, 'Afghanistan: The Soviet Quagmire'.
64 Phillips, 'Pakistan: The Rising Soviet Threat and Declining US Credibility', Backgrounder No. 122, Heritage Foundation, June 1980, http://www.heritage.org/research/reports/1980/06/pakistan-the-rising-soviet-threat-and-declining-us-credibility
65 'Afghanistan: The US Response', *National Security Record*, February 1980.
66 'Afghanistan: The US Response', *National Security Record*. The term 'tar baby' refers to a situation that is extremely difficult to extricate oneself from.
67 Phillips, 'Afghanistan: The Soviet Quagmire'; Phillips, 'The Soviet Invasion of Afghanistan'; Phillips, 'Pakistan: The Rising Soviet Threat'.
68 J.B. Kelly, 'Islam through the Looking Glass', Lecture No. 2, Heritage Foundation (Summer 1980), http://www.heritage.org/research/reports/1980/11/islam-through-the-looking-glass
69 Kelly, 'Islam through the Looking Glass'.
70 Phillips, 'The Soviet Invasion of Afghanistan', p. 9; Phillips, 'Afghanistan: The Soviet Quagmire', p. 7.
71 Phillips, 'The Soviet Invasion of Afghanistan'.

72 Paige Bryan, 'The Soviet Grain Embargo', Backgrounder No. 130, Heritage Foundation, 2 January 1981, http://www.heritage.org/research/reports/1981/01/the-soviet-grain-embargo
73 Phillips, 'Pakistan: The Rising Soviet Threat'.
74 'Exploiting Soviet Vulnerabilities', *National Security Record*, August 1980, Nexis UK via Boole Library, UCC, Cork.
75 'Congress, Détente and US Leverage', *National Security Record*, August 1980. In November 1980, the Republican Party gained a majority in the Senate for the first time in many years. Halliday, *The Making of the Second Cold War*, p. 118, contends that the Senate had started to take a more hawkish foreign policy aspect before this in the late 1970s.
76 Wilentz, *The Age of Reagan*, p. 91.
77 Andrew Blasko, 'Reagan and Heritage: A Unique Partnership', Heritage Foundation, 7 June 2004, http://www.heritage.org/research/commentary/2004/06/reagan-and-heritage-a-unique-partnership
78 See ODI Study, pp. 47–55. The authors describe international NGOs which were formed to specifically assist Afghanistan following the invasion as political 'solidarity' NGOs on which information about their early operations is difficult to obtain. This is due to a culture of secrecy necessitated partly by the safety considerations for staff within Afghanistan as well as political sensitivity, limited record keeping and consideration of the relationship of their cross-border programmes to international law.
79 Helga Baitenmann, 'NGOs and the Afghan War: The Politicisation of Humanitarian Aid', *Third World Quarterly*, Vol. 12, No. 1 (January 1990), pp. 62–85.
80 Baitenmann, 'NGOs and the Afghan War', p. 80.
81 Michael T. Kaufmann, 'R. G. Neumann, 83, Diplomat Fired by Haig from Saudi Post', *New York Times*, 25 June 1999.
82 Telegram to the Department of State from Douglas Archard, Peshawar Consulate, 'Message for Afghanistan Relief Committee', 6 May 1981. Archard outlines funds raised and administered by his wife, Mary, through the sale of ARC T-shirts and calendars. Document No. AF01184, *Afghanistan: The Making of US Foreign Policy*, DNSA. See State Department telegrams to and from the consul in Peshawar dated 6 May 1981; 12 May 1981; 27 May 1981; 28 May 1981; which discuss accessing ARC funds for treatment for an Afghan refugee with a heart complaint, Documents No. AF 01184, AF01188, AF01193, AF01194, *Afghanistan: The Making of US Foreign Policy*, DNSA.
83 Iona Andronov, Excerpts from broadcast version of *Literaturnaya Gazeta* on 'a so-called Afghan relief centre in the United States', *BBC Summary of World Broadcasts*, 28 June 1980, Nexis UK.
84 Neumann was also a Senior Fellow at the CSIS – the 'home for hardliners', see James Allen Smith, *Strategic Calling: The Center for Strategic and International Studies, 1962–1992* (Washington: Center for Strategic & Intl Studies, 1993), p. 120. The think tank also housed Michael Ledeen who would become a key figure in the Iran-*Contra* affair and former Carter NSA Brzezinski amongst others.
85 Graham Hovey, 'Afghan Refugee Problem Is Compared to Palestinians', *New York Times*, 12 June 1980. Dr Dupree was an expert on Afghan affairs and served variously as a consultant to the State Department, CIA, AID, NSA, UN and the Peace Corps. He was an associate of the American Universities Field Staff and taught at Pennsylvania State University and Duke University as well as published

a number of books on Afghanistan and travelled extensively in the country before being deported by the PDPA government in 1978 amid accusations he was a spy. See Alfonso A. Narvaez, 'Louis Dupree, 63, Anthropologist and Expert on Afghanistan, Dies', *New York Times*, 23 March 1989 and Mark Magnier, 'Afghan Center Is Her Monument to Her Great Love', *Los Angeles Times*, 29 November 2013.

86 Klass testimony before the Congressional Task Force on Afghanistan, 'Hearing on Famine', 25 February 1985, p. 78, Document No. AF01620, 'Afghanistan the Making of US Foreign Policy', DNSA. Diana Barahona, 'The Freedom House Files', *Monthly Review*, 1 March 2007.
87 Barahona, 'The Freedom House Files'; Vaisse, *Neoconservatism*, p. 206.
88 Agency Coordinating Body for Afghan Relief & Development (ACBAR), 'Directory of Members, 1991–1992' (Peshawar: Public Art Press, 1991), p. 107.
89 National Endowment for Democracy Project Proposal, 'Afghanistan Democratic Education Project', c. 1986, p. 1, Document No. 145, EBB No. 78, *US Propaganda in the Middle East*, NSA.
90 Baitenmann, 'NGOs and the Afghan War', p. 81; Sayid Khybar, 'The Afghani Contra Lobby', *Covert Action Information Bulletin*, No. 30 (Summer 1988), pp. 61–65.
91 Khybar, 'The Afghani Contra Lobby', p. 65.
92 Cull, *The Cold War and the United States Information Agency*, p. 391.
93 The 52 per cent of the British public saw the USSR as the most powerful world nation and likely to remain so over the following years. USICA Research Report, 'British Public Favors Strong Response to Soviet Actions in Afghanistan', March 1980, Box 41, P 160, RG 306, NARA. In the United States the 47 per cent public saw the USSR ahead of the US militarily while 32 per cent saw the two states as equal, USICA Research Report, 'European Public Opinion after Afghanistan', 4 April 1980, Box 40, P 160, RG 306, NARA.
94 Memorandum for Bray from Stanton Burnett, 'Post Responses to the Cable: Afghanistan Local Issues', 22 February 1980, Box 40, P 160, RG 306, NARA.
95 USICA Research Report, 'The Afghanistan Problem: Public Awareness and Attitudes in Nine Countries', 31 December 1980, P 160, Box 41, RG 306, NARA.
96 The 70 per cent of Brazilians and Mexicans heard little or nothing of the invasion. USICA Research Report, 'Urban Brazil and Mexico: Low Concern over Afghanistan; Little Support of Anti Soviet Actions', 11 July 1980, Box 36, P 64, RG 396, NARA. A survey of nine countries (Britain, Germany, France, Japan, Australia, Mexico, Brazil, India and Israel) in the spring of 1980 showed economic and domestic issues exercising most and little mention of Afghanistan as an important world issue, USICA Research Report, 'The Afghanistan Problem: Public Awareness and Attitudes in Nine Countries'.
97 Brzezinski, *Power and Principle*, p. 427.
98 'Crescent of Crisis', *Time*, 15 January 1979.
99 Artemy M. Kalinovsky and Craig Daigle (eds.), *The Routledge Handbook of the Cold War* (Oxon: Routledge, 2014), p. 187, state this group was formed in 1979 while Georgie Anne Geyer, 'Soviet Trends Were Predicted', *Sarasota Herald Tribune*, 25 September 1989 and Scott, *The Road to 9/11*, p. 71, amongst others state 1977. The CIA produced a number of research reports with a focus on Soviet and Afghan ethnic groups during this period. See Research Paper, 'Afghanistan: Ethnic Diversity and Dissidence', May 1979, Document No. CIA-RDP81B00401R000600110004-3, National Foreign Assessment Center (NFAC), CIA Freedom of Information Act (FOIA) Electronic Reading Room (ERR), https://www.cia.gov/library/readingroom/

home; Research Paper, 'Muslims in the USSR', February 1980, Document No. 0000969765, NFAC, CIA FOIA ERR; Research Paper, 'National Identity among Soviet Uzbeks', May 1980, NFAC, CIA FOIA ERR; Research Paper, 'Nationalities Trends and Political Stability in the Soviet Union', June 1981, Document No. 0000496726, NFAC, CIA FOIA ERR Reading Room.
100 Gates, *From the Shadows*, p. 177.
101 USICA Special Report, 'Policy Implications of Agency Programming for Soviet Nationalities', 30 January 1979, Box 41, P 160, RG 306, NARA.
102 Memorandum for Schneidman from Stanton Burnett, USICA, 'Soviet Broadcasting to Afghanistan More Than Doubles', 10 January 1979, Box 41, P 160, RG 306, NARA; Memorandum for Brzezinski from Stanford Turner, CIA 'Baluchi Broadcasts', 31 January 1980, Document No. 0000768663, CIA FOIA ERR.
103 USICA Report, 'Some Implications for Communications Policy in Middle East Social and Political Developments', 8 March 1979, Box 41, P 160, RG 306, NARA.
104 Jim Hoagland, 'CIA Will Survey Moslems Worldwide', *Washington Post*, 20 January 1979.
105 Memorandum for President Carter from Brzezinski, 'Islamic Fundamentalism', 2 February 1979, *PPP*, Zbigniew Brzezinski Collection, sf Weekly Reports 82–90, 12/78-3/79, Box 42, JCL.
106 Memorandum for Brzezinski from Paul B. Henze, 'The US and the Islamic World', 27 November 1979, *PPP*, Collection No. 27, National Security Affairs, Staff Material: Horn/Special, Chronological file 8/79-4/80, JCL. At this stage Henze was chair of the NWG. Other members or contributors to this group included Hugh Seton-Watson, Alexandre Bennigsen, S. Enders Wimbush and Jeremy Azrael.
107 Brzezinski, *Power and Principle*, p. 428.
108 'Afghan students' Anti-Taraki Demonstrations in New Delhi', *BBC*, 4 July 1979, *BBC Summary of World Reports*, Nexis UK.
109 CIA telegram describing Anti-Soviet Demonstrations, 28 September 1979, Document No. 139, *US Propaganda in the Middle East*, NSA.
110 Special Coordination Committee Meeting, 'Iran: Summary of Conclusions', 17 December 1979, Document No. 49, *Towards and International History of the Cold War*, Vol. I, *CWIHP*.
111 Brzezinski, *Power and Principle*, p. 428.
112 Hendrick Smith, 'US Is Indirectly Pressing Russians to Halt Afghanistan Intervention', *New York Times*, 3 August 1979.
113 'Interview with Brzezinski on Foreign Policy', *US News & World Report*, 16 April 1979.
114 No author or heading given, *Associated Press*, Washington Dateline, 2 August 1979, Nexis UK.
115 Memorandum for Brzezinski and Aaron from Marshall Brement, 'Response to the Soviets Regarding Afghanistan: A Menu of Possible Actions', 28 December 1979, Document No. 54, *Towards an International History of the Cold War*, Vol. I, *CWIHP*.
116 Memorandum for Brzezinski from Stephen Larrabee, 'Soviet Policy in Afghanistan', 31 December 1979, Document No. 61, *Towards an International History of the Cold War*, Vol. I, *CWIHP*.
117 USICA Research Report, 'The Soviet Propaganda Campaign on the Afghanistan Invasion and Its Impact: A Preliminary Assessment', 21 February 1980, Box 40, P 160, RG 306, NARA.

118 Memorandum for President Carter from Brzezinski, 'Reflections on Soviet Intervention in Afghanistan', 26 December 1979, Document No. 51, *Towards an International History of the Cold War*, Vol. I, CWIHP.
119 Memorandum for Brzezinski and Aaron from Robert Blackwell, 'The President's December 28 Telephone Calls to European Leaders', 28 December 1979, *CWIHP*.
120 Memorandum for Brzezinski from Larrabee, 'Soviet Policy in Afghanistan'.
121 No author listed, 'Moscow versus Islam', *Washington Post*, 26 December 1979.
122 Interview with Brzezinski, *US News & World Report*, 31 December 1979.
123 Stephen J. Lynton, 'Soviets Mass Forces near Afghan Frontier; Carter Rebukes Brezhnev, Assails's 'False Response', *Washington Post*, 1 January 1980.
124 President Jimmy Carter, 'Address to the Nation on the Soviet Invasion of Afghanistan', 4 January 1980, *PPP Collection*, The American Presidency Project.
125 G.G. LaBelle, *Associated Press*, 30 December 1979.
126 Memorandum for Brzezinski from the Department of State, 'Actions Taken to Carry Out NSC Decisions of January 2, 1980', 10 January 1980, Document No. 77, *Towards an International History of the Cold War*, CWIHP.
127 Memorandum for Brzezinski from Peter Tarnoff, 'US Soviet Relations and Afghanistan', 31 December 1979, Document No. 62, *Towards an International History of the Cold War*, Vol. I, CWIHP.
128 Jody Powell in his oral history interview for the Carter Presidency Project, Miller Center, University of Virginia, 17–18 December 1981, p. 52 discusses the difficulties the administration had in generating any domestic interest in Afghanistan. See also Memorandum for Brzezinski from Reinhardt, 'European Public Opinion', 4 April 1980, Box 40, P 160, RG 306, NARA, which indicates waning interest in the conflict in Western Europe and the United States by March 1980.
129 Memorandum for Brzezinski from Stephen Larrabee, 'Soviet Policy in Afghanistan', 31 December 1979, Document No. 61, *Towards an International History of the Cold War*, Vol. 1, CWIHP.
130 Crile, *Charlie Wilson's War*, p. 18.
131 Carter, *Keeping Faith*, p. 475.
132 Barry Lorge, 'Olympics Pullout Eyed; U.S. Decision Set in February', *Washington Post*, 17 January 1980.
133 Memorandum for Brzezinski from Tarnoff, 'US Soviet Relations and Afghanistan'.
134 Jordan Hamilton, *Crisis: The Last Year of the Carter Presidency* (New York, NY: Berkley Books, 1982), pp. 112–113.
135 Carter, *Keeping Faith*, p. 481.
136 Leonard Downie Jr., 'Allies Back Off Olympic Boycott; NATO Nations Backing Away from Boycott of Olympics', *Washington Post*, 3 January 1980.
137 Lloyd Cutler, Exit Interview with Marie Allen, p. 8, 2 March 1981, Exit Interview Project, JCL.
138 Cull, *The Cold War and the United States Information Agency*, pp. 391–392; Christopher R. Hill, *Olympic Politics* (Manchester: Manchester University Press, 1992), p. 145.
139 Allen Guttmann, 'The Cold War and the Olympics', *International Journal*, No. 4 (Autumn 1988), p. 560; Cutler, Exit interview, p. 8.
140 USICA Research Report, 'European Opinion after Afghanistan', attached to memorandum for Brzezinski from John Reinhardt, 4 April 1980, P 160, Box 40, RG 306, NARA. British public opinion stood at 62 per cent opposing the boycott in February 1980 up from 44 per cent in January instead favouring other types of

sanctions. By March 1980 British public support for the boycott stood at only 17 per cent, USICA Research Report, 'British Public Favors Strong Response to Soviet Actions in Afghanistan', April 1980, P 160, Box 41, RG 306, NARA.
141 USICA Research Report, 'French Pubic Distrusts Soviet Motives in Afghanistan but Opposes Sanctions', 24 April 1980, P 160, Box 41, RG 306, NARA.
142 Memorandum for Donald Gregg from Stanton Burnett, 11 April 1980, P 160, Box 42, RG 306, NARA.
143 SCC, 'Iran/Afghanistan: Summary of Conclusions', 20 March 1980, Document No. 93, *Towards an International History of the Cold War*, Vol. 1, *CWIHP*. Many Europeans believed Carter actions were driven by his re-election campaign requirements and the issue would lose impetus once the US primaries were over.
144 USICA Research Report, 'The Soviet Propaganda Campaign on the Afghan Invasion and Its Impact: A Preliminary Assessment', 21 February 1980, P 160, Box 42, RG 306, NARA.
145 Memorandum of Conversation between US Secretary of State Vance and German Chancellor Schmidt, 20 February 1980, Document No. 87, *Towards an International History of the Cold War*, Vol. I, *CWIHP*.
146 Steven Strasser, 'Muhammad Ali, Diplomat', *Newsweek*, 18 February 1980.
147 'Diplomacy: Ali's Whipping', *Time*, 18 February 1980.
148 Frank Cormier, 'Ali's African Diplomacy Giving Administration Heartburn', *Associated Press*, 5 February 1980.
149 Betty Glad, *An Outsider in the White House : Jimmy Carter, His Advisors, and the Making of American Foreign Policy* (Ithaca: Cornell University Press, 2009), p. 209.
150 Nicholas Sarantakes, *Dropping the Torch: Jimmy Carter, the Olympic Boycott, and the Cold War* (Cambridge; New York: Cambridge University Press, 2011), p. 92.

Chapter 2

1 Michael Schaller, *Right Turn: American Life in the Reagan-Bush Era, 1980–1992* (Oxford: Oxford University Press, 2007), p. 79.
2 Lou Cannon, *President Reagan: The Role of a Lifetime* (New York: Simon & Schuster, 1991), p. 334.
3 A checklist of United States Government (USG) responses to the Soviet invasion of Afghanistan prepared for Reagan by the Department of State states that the 'Soviet occupation of Afghanistan remains [an] important emphasis of US foreign broadcasting effort. We intend to counter the Soviet "peace offensive" in Western Europe with a public affairs strategy designed to explain US policy and the need for Western rearmament, and the counter Soviet propaganda', 'Current Status of Afghanistan Measures', undated (estimate early/mid-1981), NSC Executive Secretariat, Country File, Near East and South Asia, 'Afghanistan', Box 34, RRL.
4 The 1976 Symington Amendment to the 1961 Foreign Assistance Act prohibited US assistance to any state delivering or receiving nuclear enrichment equipment, technology or material outside the parameters of international safeguards.
5 Wilentz, *Age of Reagan*, pp. 132–133, names some of these backers as Charles Z. Wick, Justin Dart and Henry Salvatori. In his oral history Wick states that he was 'a very minor, minor part of the wealthy businessmen around him [Reagan]' at the time of Reagan's election as governor of California. Wick adds the Al Bloomingdale to the

above list of names as members of Reagan's early supporters and 'kitchen cabinet'. Interview with Charles Z. Wick, 24–25 April 2003, Ronald Reagan Oral History Project (RROHP), Miller Center of Public Affairs, Virginia.

6 Fifty members of the CPD took up positions in the Reagan administration, including Jeane Kirkpatrick, Paul Nitze, Gene Rostow, Lane Kirkland, Charles Tyroler, Max Kampelman, Edward Bennett Williams and Myer Rashish.

7 Reagan was introduced to the CPD by one of its founding members Richard V. Allen, who was also a co-founder of the think tank the Center for Strategic and International Studies (CSIS) and later National Security Advisor to Reagan from 1981 to 1982. Allen stated that initially CPD members were 'doubtful' about Reagan but Allen sought to build bridges between the two sides so that should Reagan get elected he would have 'a cadre of foreign policy people ready to go at a moment's notice'. Allen introduced Reagan to Jeane Kirkpatrick, Paul Nitze and Eugene Rostow, Interview with Richard V. Allen, 28 May 2002, p. 28, RROHP, Miller Center of Public Affairs, Virginia.

8 Sanders, *Peddlers of Crisis*, pp. 264–265 on the CPDs and other conservative groups' anti-SALT media campaign.

9 Letter to Barton L. Hartzell from Reagan, quoted in Cull, *The Cold War and the United States Information Agency*, p. 399.

10 Adelman was deputy US ambassador to the UN and director of the US Arms Control and Disarmament Agency. He also served on Reagan's foreign policy transition team and was a member of the CPD.

11 Adelman, 'Speaking of America', p. 913.

12 Paul Olkhovsky, 'Mobilizing the Airwaves: The Challenge to the Voice of America and RFE/RL', 13 November 1981, Heritage Foundation, http://www.heritage.org/research/reports/1981/11/mobilizing-the-airwaves-the-challenges-to-the-voice-of-america-and-rfe-rl

13 'Conservative Leaders Find Administration Officials Undermining Reagan Mandate', *Human Events*, 30 January 1982.

14 Parry and Kornbluh in 'Iran-Contra's Untold Story', pp. 8–9, detail how US failures in Vietnam informed decision-making about public diplomacy in relation to Nicaragua particularly to target domestic audiences – Congress, the American public, Foreign Affairs Committees and the US media. Fred Halliday in *Cold War, Third World*, pp. 72–73, puts forward a similar argument stating that 'public diplomacy' was a vital element of the military strategy of LIC, which gained pre-eminence during the Reagan administration. According to Halliday, one of the 'lessons' of Vietnam distilled into the LIC doctrine was that the war effort was damaged by lack of domestic US support. Public diplomacy would ensure the 'domestic constituency – within the US government, in Congress, in the media, and in the public sphere as a whole' – was supportive of the foreign policy objectives of the administration and Reagan's rhetoric was central to this.

15 USIA Agenda Paper for Conference on Communication and Information, 'Developing a Public Affairs Strategy for International Issues in Information and Communication', 17 November 1982, Box 43, P 160, RG 306, NARA.

16 NSDD 32, 'US National Security Strategy', 20 May 1982, NSDDs, 1981–1989, RRL.

17 Memorandum for Mr Michel from Ely Maurer, 'Public Diplomacy Relative to National Security', 7 December 1982, Office of the Assistant Legal Advisor for Educational, Cultural and Public Affairs, Department of State, sf Project Democracy, Box 173, A1 5397, RG 59, NARA.

18 See pp. 286–288 for more on US educational programmes in Afghanistan.
19 Claire Magone, Michael Neuman, and Fabrice Weissman (eds.), *Humanitarian Negotiations Revealed: The MSF Experience* (London: Hurst, 2011), p. 181.
20 Europeans strongly supported détente and arms control negotiations. USIA report for Charles Wick for meeting with Caspar Weinberger, 14 September 1982, Box 43, P 160, RG 306, NARA; USIA Foreign Opinion Note, 'INF Deployment Remains Unpopular; Scepticism over Arms Talks Increases', 23 February 1983, Box 3, P 118, RG 306, NARA. For support for Peace Movement, see 'West Europeans Tend to Approve of the "Peace Movement," but Doubt It Will Help Achieve Peace', USIA Foreign Opinion Note, 30 November 1982, Box 3, P 118, RG 306, NARA.
21 USIA report for Wick for meeting with Weinberger, 14 September 1982; USIA Foreign Opinion Note, 'Post-Summit Europe: Public Opinion Generally Unchanged', 16 August 1982, Box 3, P 118, RG 306, NARA.
22 NSDD 77, 'Management of Public Diplomacy Relative to National Security', 14 January 1983, NSDDs 1981–1989, RRL.
23 Scott-Smith, 'Aristotle, Carnes Lord, and US Foreign Policy', p. 256.
24 Scott-Smith, 'Aristotle, Carnes Lord and US Foreign Policy', pp. 257–258.
25 The agency's name reverted to the original in August 1982.
26 Project Truth was a programme designed to counter Soviet propaganda run by the USIA. Afghanistan was one of its areas of interest. See Cull, *The Cold War and the United States Information Agency*, pp. 408–409.
27 Steve Galster, 'Afghanistan: The Making of US Policy, 1979–1990'.
28 Parry and Kornbluh, 'Iran-Contra's Untold Story', p. 9.
29 Memorandum for Robert McFarlane from Geoffrey Kemp and Walter Raymond, 'Afghanistan', 21 June 1984, WHORM sf, Country Files, CO 119 Pakistan, Boxes 146–147, File No. 400773, RRL.
30 Lou Cannon, 'Reagan Plans Appeal at U.N. on Weapons, Seeks Brezhnev Talks', *Washington Post*, 6 April 1982; According to Hertsgaard, *On Bended Knee*, p. 27, Reagan held less press conferences than other modern presidents and even during his election campaign access to him was tightly controlled in the final two months after he made some 'politically damaging statements'.
31 NSDD 75, 'U.S. Relations with the U.S.S.R', NSDDs, RRL.
32 NSDD 75, 'US Relations with the USSR'.
33 Thomas A. Catherman, a former deputy director of the VOA quoted in Alvin Snyder, *Warriors of Disinformation: American Propaganda, Soviet Lies, and the Winning of the Cold War* (New York: Arcade Publishing, 1995), pp. 10–11; Philip Taubman, 'Casey and His CIA on the Rebound', *New York Times*, 16 January 1983.
34 Snyder, *Warriors of Disinformation*, p. xiii.
35 Richard M. Harley, 'America's Voice; What Does It Say to the World?' *Christian Science Monitor*, 15 April 1982.
36 Harley, 'America's Voice'.
37 Cull, *The Cold War and the United States Information Agency*, pp. 405–406. Wick organized a television extravaganza in support of the striking Polish workers in 1981 and organized the promotion and funding for the programme via a Heritage Foundation organ, the National Center for Public Diplomacy, and a public relations committee consisting of experts from large business organizations such as Exxon and General Motors, see Snyder, *Warriors of Disinformation*, p. 8.
38 USIA, 'Soviet Propaganda Alert', 3 May 1982, Special Reports, 1953–1997, Box 43, P 160, RG 306, NARA.

39 Cull, *The Cold War and the United States Information Agency*, p. 409.
40 Halliday, *The Making of the Second Cold War*, pp. 120–121, cites Congress' push for higher military spending in 1979 and 1980 and its hostility towards the Panama Canal and SALT II Treaties as evidence of this. He argues that 'New Right' lobbyists' gathering power was first applied to Congress during this period before going into battle on behalf of the Reagan campaign.
41 The Symington Amendment to the Foreign Assistance Act of 1961 forbad US aid to states seeking to develop nuclear weapons. Don Oberdorfer, *Washington Post*, 7 April 1979, wrote that the announcement had 'come at an awkward moment for American diplomacy. Washington has been concerned in recent weeks about an increasing flow of Soviet weapons to the pro-Soviet government of Afghanistan, which is a neighbor of Pakistan. U.S. officials would like to show solidarity with Pakistan at this time in the interest of regional stability'. However, Carter had been unable to secure 'the reliable assurances' required by the Symington Amendment from Zia, see Robert B. Cullen, *Associated Press*, 6 April 1979.
42 Stuart Auerbach, 'Delay in Pakistan Rescue Is Criticized', *Washington Post*, 23 November 1979; Coll, *Ghost Wars*, pp. 27–37, gives an account of events in the embassy that day and Pakistani authorities delayed response which endangered the US citizens present. Coll estimated it took Pakistani military five hours to make a thirty-minute journey to the embassy. Following the Soviet invasion of Afghanistan, the still smarting State Department and CIA officials in the Islamabad embassy suggested instead of military aid sending the Pakistanis Russian dictionaries and phrase books in preparation of its own takeover by the Soviets, see Coll, *Ghost Wars*, p. 52.
43 The CIA lost valuable 'listening posts' in Iran following the Shah's ouster increasing the value of the ones established around Peshawar, Pakistan, during the Eisenhower administration. See Dennis Kux, *India and the United States: Estranged Democracies, 1941–1991* (Darby: Diane Publishing, 1992), pp. 160 and 241.
44 No author listed, 'Desire to Help Pakistan May Evoke Revision of Symington Amendment', *Nuclear Fuel*, Vol. 6, No. 3 (2 February 1981), p. 12 quotes a Congressional source saying that there were still many staunch opponents of aid to Pakistan without assurances about its nuclear activity. He stated that 'it would be saying to everybody that as long as you can point to the Russian bug-a-bear as threatening you, you can count on the U.S. for assistance regardless of what you do in terms of violation international norms on nonproliferation'.
45 Don Oberdorfer, 'US Reports Some Progress in Mending Ties to Pakistan', *Washington Post*, 28 March 1981.
46 President's News Conference, 16 June 1981, *PPP*, RRL.
47 Telegram from the Department of State to the US Embassy, Islamabad, 'Buckley Briefing of House Foreign Affairs Committee on Pakistan', 20 July 1981, AFO 1216, *Afghanistan: The Making of US Foreign Policy*, DNSA.
48 US Department of State, Bureau of Intelligence and Research, 'India-Pakistani Views on a Nuclear Weapons Options and Potential Repercussions', Report 169-AR, 25 June 1981, EBB No. 377, *The Nuclear Vault*, NSA.
49 CIA, Directorate of Intelligence, 'Afghanistan Situation Report', 26 October 1982, p. 8, Document No. 0001486830, CIA FOIA ERR.
50 Robert Foelber, 'What Price Defense', Heritage Foundation, 6 October 1982, http://www.heritage.org/research/reports/1982/10/what-price-defense
51 Brad Knickerbocker, 'Great Decisions '82; America's Defense: What Price Security?' *Christian Science Monitor*, 29 January 1982.

52 Gates, *From the Shadows*, p. 319.
53 Leslie H. Gleb, 'US Said to Increase Arms Aid for Afghan Rebels', *New York Times*, 4 May 1983.
54 President Reagan, 'Statement on the Third Anniversary of the Soviet Invasion of Afghanistan', 26 December 1982, *PPP*, RRL.
55 Susan Wright, 'The Military and the New Biology', *Bulletin of the Atomic Scientists*, Vol. 2, No. 9 (May 1985), pp. 12–13. Steven Rose, 'The Case against Chemical Weapons', *New Scientist*, Vol. 89, No. 1244 (12 March 1981). An anthrax epidemic in Sverdlovsk, USSR, in 1979 raised US concerns that the Soviets were still developing CBWs.
56 Rose, 'The Case against Chemical Weapons', pp. 670–671, offers an insight into the Army Chemical Corps desire to 'modernize' US chemical weapon stocks by replacing them with new 'binary' style weapons. President Nixon had halted the US chemical weapon programme back in 1969 and it had not been re-activated though research on new weaponry had continued. The Army Chemical Corps proposed to build and equip a new factory to produce these new 'binary' weapons as well as destroy existing 'old' stocks for $6,000 million dollars. The Reagan administration added these proposals to its military budget request to Congress in March 1981 for financial year 1982 and beyond.
57 USIA polls show most Western European publics 'almost universal' support for a worldwide ban on CBWs and desire to see existing stocks destroyed. See USIA Research Memorandum, 'West Europeans Support Chemical Weapons Ban', 15 August 1984, Box 40, P 64, RG 306, NARA; USIA Research Report, 'British Opinion on Security Issues: 1984', Box 54, P 142, RG 306, NARA.
58 In a letter to the *New York Times*, 12 November 1980, titled 'Before We Spend Billions on Chemical Weapons', Professors Matthew Meselson and Stephen M. Meyer argued that US intelligence had 'no hard evidence' that the Soviets had produced lethal chemical weapons over the past decade and that alleged lethal gas used in Afghanistan was more than likely a riot-control agent. As a result, the authors argued that the United States should not resume its chemical weapon production and instead concentrate on anti-chemical weapon training and equipment. Jonathan B. Tucker's article, 'The "Yellow Rain" Controversy: Lessons for Arms Control Compliance', *The Nonproliferation Review*, Vol. 8, No. 1 (Spring 2001), pp. 25–42, reviews the controversy and the science behind it concluding US allegations were based on inadequate evidence and flawed investigation techniques. The allegations now seem largely discredited. Gates later admitted that the allegation was false, see 'Excerpts from Gates Testimony on His Record at the CIA', *New York Times*, 4 October 1991.
59 Wayne Biddle, 'Restocking the Chemical Arsenal', *New York Times*, 24 May 1981.
60 See excerpts from Haig's speech on the administration's policy on arms control, *New York Times*, 15 July 1981; In West Berlin on 14 September 1981, Secretary Haig publicly accused the USSR of using chemical weapons in Afghanistan announcing that the United States now had 'physical evidence', Bernard Gwertzman, 'US Says Data Shows Toxin Use in Asia Conflict', *New York Times*, 14 September 1981; Two months later Jeane Kirkpatrick reiterated these accusations, see her address before the UN General Assembly, 18 November 1981, Department of State, *American Foreign Policy: Current Documents, 1981* (Washington, DC: US Department of State, 1984).
61 As well as eventually becoming a key figure in the Iran-*Contra* affair Michael Ledeen was involved in disinformation cases such as 'Billygate' which alleged that

President Carter's brother Billy was involved in business dealings with Libyan leader, Muammar Gaddafi and the Palestine Liberation Organisation. These charges considerably damaged Carter's re-election campaign. Ledeen was also connected to claims that the KGB was involved in a plot to assassinate Pope John Paul II. See Garthoff, *The Grand Transition*, pp. 93–94, n27; Craig Unger, 'The War They Wanted, the Lies They Needed', *Vanity Fair*, July 2006. Furthermore, Leeden was linked to the Italian military secret service, SISMI. In 1981, Ledeen role was described as special advisor to Alexander Haig.

62 Project Truth Executive Committee Meetings, 18 November 1981 and 2 December 1981, WHSOF, Carnes Lord, Series II, Subject File, 'Project Truth', Box 3, RRL.
63 Ronald Reagan, 'Remarks on Signing Proclamation 4908, Afghanistan Day', 10 March 1982, *PPP*, RRL.
64 Richard Halloran, 'US Accuses Soviets of Poisoning 3,000', *New York Times*, 9 March 1982.
65 Rear Admiral Jonathan T. Howe (US Navy), Director, Bureau of Politico-Military Affairs, Department of State giving evidence before the HFAC, Subcommittee on International Security and Scientific Affairs, 'Foreign Policy and Arms Control, Implications of Chemical Weapons', 30 March and 13 July 1982, Hathi Trust Digital Library, http://catalog.hathitrust.org. The committee met as the House was shortly to vote on whether or not the United States should resume chemical weapon production after a moratorium of thirteen years. The Soviets had proposed a ban on chemical weapon use to the UN the previous month.
66 HFAC, Subcommittee on International Security and Scientific Affairs, 'Foreign Policy and Arms Control, Implications of Chemical Weapons', Appendix 1, Responses by Mr Burt to Additional Questions Submitted in Writing by Chairman Zabloki and Mr Solarz.
67 HFAC, Subcommittee on International Security and Scientific Affairs, 'Foreign Policy and Arms Control, Implications of Chemical Weapons', Appendix 8, 'Report of the Ninth Pugwash Workshop on Chemical Warfare (Geneva, Switzerland, March 12–14, 1982)'.
68 Project Truth Executive Committee Meeting, 9 December 1981, WHSOF, Carnes Lord files, Series II, Subject File sf, 'Project Truth', Box 3, RRL.
69 Sterling Seagrave, *Yellow Rain: A Journey through the Terror of Chemical Warfare* (New York: M. Evans, 1981).
70 Afghan Digest Number One (1983), 306.9044, RG 306, NARA; Afghan Digest Number Two (1983), 306.9045, RG 306, NARA.
71 See roundtable discussion on 'yellow rain' in Lavea Brachman, 'Bumblebees or the Soviet Union: The Yellow Rain Controversy', *Harvard Crimson*, 10 November 1983.
72 Tom Jory, 'Rain of Terror: An ABC News Close Up', *Telegraph* (London), 21 December 1981.
73 Letters between Ernest W. Lefever and William P. Clarke, 16 November 1982, 10 January 1983, WHORM sf National Security – Defense, ND 017, Warfare, RRL. Lefever was a founder of the Ethics and Public Policy Center which is 'dedicated to applying the Judeo-Christian moral tradition to critical issues of public policy'. See Ethics and Public Policy website: http://eppc.org/about. He was nominated for a position with the Department of State by Reagan but was rejected by the SFRC. He drew a Kirkpatrick-like distinction between US pressure over human rights violation in authoritarian versus totalitarian regimes which generated controversy. See

Douglas Martin, 'Ernest W. Lefever, Rejected as Reagan Nominee, Dies 89', *New York Times*, 4 August 2009.
74 Walter Raymond to William Clark, 'Answer to Ernest Lefever', 3 January 1983, WHORM sf National Security – Defense, ND 017, Warfare, RRL. Equal numbers of West Europeans believed the United States as well as the USSR had used chemical weapons in the past, see USIA Foreign Opinion Note, 'West Europeans Strongly Favor a Chemical Weapons Ban', 5 February 1985, Office of Research, Box 4, P 118, RG 306, NARA.
75 Note to Horace Russell, Cary Lord, George Van Eron, Sven Kraemer from Walter Raymond, 'Yellow Rain', undated but approximately 8/9 December 1982, WHORM sf National Security – Defense, ND 017, Warfare, RRL.
76 Memorandum for Laurence Eagleburger from Robert McFarlane, 'Chemical Warfare: An Update', undated but approximately early December 1982, WHORM sf National Security – Defense, ND 017, Warfare, RRL.
77 Memorandum for Robert McFarlane from Walter Raymond, 'Chemical Warfare', undated but approximately late November/early December 1982, WHORM sf National Security – Defense, ND 017, Warfare, RRL.
78 Dr Frederick Seitz, an eminent physicist in his day, would take a more controversial course on retirement as a consultant for RJ Reynolds Tobacco Company and a climate change denier. See 'Obituary: Frederick Seitz', *Telegraph* (London), 14 March 2008.
79 Memorandum for the President from William Clark, 'Chemical and Toxin Weapon Use', 6 July 1983, WHORM sf National Security – Defense, ND 017, RRL.
80 See Stuart Swartzstein's letter to the editor, 'Chemical Warfare: Misplaced Emphasis', *New York Times*, 3 April 1982.
81 Leo Cherne was Chair of the Executive Committee of Freedom House and Chair of the IRC. He was a lifelong friend and business associate of William Casey and involved in the creation of Team B. See Andrew F. Smith, *Rescuing the World: The Life and Times of Leo Cherne* (New York: State University of New York, 2002), p. 158; Michael T. Kaufman, 'Leo Cherne, Leader of Agency for Refugees, Is Dead at 86', *New York Times*, 14 January 1999.
82 Letters to Walter Raymond from Stuart Schweitzstein, 19 November 1982, National Security – Defense, ND 017, 'Warfare', RRL.
83 Memorandum for Richard G. Stilwell from Walter Raymond, 'Support for CBW Project', undated, WHORM sf National Security – Defense, ND 017, 'Warfare', RRL.
84 Frank Barnett was the founding president of the National Strategy Information Center. He, along with Carnes Lord edited *Political Warfare and Psychological Operations: Rethinking the US Approach* (Darby: Diane Publishing, 1989) which argued that the United States needed to 'upgrade its performance in the political-psychological arena' (i.e. propaganda). See p. ix.
85 Memorandum for William Clark from Walter Raymond, 'War Crimes Grand Jury', 10 August 1982, The Reagan Files, http://www.thereaganfiles.com/19820810-cw.pdf
86 Schedule proposal for William K. Sadleir from William Clark, re 'Brief Call on the President by Six Afghan Witnesses to Soviet Atrocities in Afghanistan', 1 February 1983, WHORM sf, Country File, Afghanistan, Box 36, RRL.
87 Editorial by Theodore L. Eliot Jr., *Boston Globe*, 21 March 1982.
88 James A. Phillips, 'Moscow's Poison War: Mounting Evidence of Battlefield Atrocities', Heritage Foundation Report, 5 February 1982; James A. Phillips, 'Moscow's Poison

War: Update', Heritage Foundation Report, 3 September 1982; Rosanne Klass, 'Afghanistan: Don't Fall for Soviet Tricks', *Los Angeles Times*, 29 December 1982.

89 CFA, Free Afghanistan Report, unnumbered and undated, approximately late 1981/early 1982, WHORM sf, Committee for a Free Afghanistan, Box 17, RRL. Jim Leach, Hearing before the Subcommittee on Arms Control, Oceans, International Operations and Environment, SFRC, 'Yellow Rain and Other Forms of Chemical and Biological Warfare in Asia', 10 November 1981, LoC. Leach outlines that exposure of 'yellow rain' use was 'in no small part due to the efforts of energetic private citizens'.

90 The Council for the Defense of Freedom published the *Washington Inquirer*. See Accuracy in the Media Report, Vol. 12–15.

91 Scott, *Drugs, Oil, and War*, p. 144, n71; Michael Massing, 'Who's Afraid of Reed Irvine? The Rise and Decline of Accuracy in the Media', *Nation*, 13 September 1986, pp. 208–209; Khybar, 'The Afghan Contra Lobby', pp. 61–62, re links to Heritage.

92 Russ Bellant, *Old Nazis, the New Right, and the Republican Party* (Cambridge: South End Press, 1991), pp. 39–45; Letter to Elizabeth Dole, Assistant to the President, from Karen McKay, 24 March 1981, WHSOF, Morton Blackwell Files, Series 1, Afghanistan, Box 1, RRL.

93 According to its letterhead, Singlaub was on its Council of Advisors. Both he and Milnor Roberts, Director of the CFA, were involved with the USCWF, see 'Afghanistan', DNSA. Singlaub was also active in funding the Nicaraguan Contras, see Ted Galen Carpenter, 'U.S. Aid to Anti-Communist Rebels: The "Reagan Doctrine" and Its Pitfalls', Cato Policy Analysis, No. 74, 24 June 1986; Bellant, *Old Nazis*, p. 40. The list of advisors to the CFA included Richard Allen, Arnaud de Borchgrave, Jack Abramoff, Louis Dupree, Thomas Gouttierre and more. See CFA headed paper, WHORM sf, 'Committee for a Free Afghanistan', Box 17, RRL.

94 These allegations were made by John Charles Houston, executive director of Free the Eagle, see No author listed, 'Groups Backing Afghan Rebels Don't Even Speak to Each Other', *National Journal*, 8 February 1986.

95 No author listed, 'Groups Backing Afghan Rebels Don't Even Speak to Each Other'.

96 No author listed, 'Groups Backing Afghan Rebels Don't Even Speak to Each Other'; SFRC, Subcommittee on Arms Control, Oceans, International Operations and Environment, 'Hearing on Yellow Rain', 10 November 1981, LoC, P. 72.

97 Letter to Dole from McKay, 24 March 1981, RRL.

98 SFRC, Subcommittee on Arms Control, Oceans, International Operations and Environment, 'Yellow Rain and Other Forms of Chemical and Biological Warfare in Asia', 10 November 1981, LoC.

99 Committee for a Free Afghanistan brought Gailani over re CBW in March 1981 and in October 1981 Mojaddedi, Segatullah and Izzattullah testified before Senate.

100 Paul Koring, 'Rebels Tell of Soviet Atrocities', *Ottawa Citizen*, 27 January 1983; Department of State Briefing Memorandum for Charles Tyson, 'Brief Call by Six Afghan Witnesses', 1 February 1983, NSC, Near East and South Asia Affairs Directorate, 'Afghan Freedom Fighters Meeting', Box 13, RRL. In *Out of Afghanistan*, p. 188, Harrison and Cordovez describe a Michael Barry being director of the South Asia Analysis branch of the CIA in 1985.

101 Richard Bernstein, 'Afghans, in New York, Tell of a Massacre by the Russian', *New York Times*, 28 January 1983.

102 Ibid.; Schedule Proposal for William K. Sadleir from William P. Clark, 'Brief Call on the President by Six Afghan Witnesses to Soviet Atrocities in Afghanistan',

undated but approximately late January 1983, NSC, Near East and South Asia Affairs Directorate, 'Afghan Freedom Fighters Meeting', Box 13, RRL.
103 See Phillips, 'Moscow's Poison War', which describes Afghan fighters bleeding from the eyes and nose, throwing up blood and writhing in pain before dying. Phillips, 'Moscow's Poison War: Update', reported new evidence by the State Department which detailed a chemical or toxin which caused 'the flesh of its victims to decay extremely rapidly after death. When the bodies of such victims are touched or moved, the skin often peels off in large sheets'.
104 Henry David Rosso, 'A Clandestine War of Chemical Terror', *UPI*, 14 February 1982 outlining the Heritage Foundation report 'Moscow's Poison War'.
105 No author listed, 'New Evidence of Chemical Weapons', *New York Times*, 14 March 1982.
106 Robert L. Bartley and William P. Kucewicz, 'Yellow Rain and the Future of Arms Agreements', *Foreign Affairs*, Vol. 61, No. 4 (Spring 1983). The article outlines some of the press scepticism of the administration's case.
107 Memorandum for William Clark from Robert Sims, 'Bob Bartley – Wall Street Journal', 4 May 1983, WHORM sf National Security – Defense, ND 017, Warfare, RRL.
108 Parade article attached to memorandum for the President from William Clark, 'Chemical and Toxin Weapons Use', 6 July 1983, WHORM sf National Security – Defense, ND 017, Warfare, RRL.
109 Dr Townsend was a retired US Air force colonel and medical co-ordinator for the IRC.
110 Dr B. A. Zikria was an Afghan living in the United States but back in Afghanistan treating *mujahedeen*. He also appeared in ABC's *Rain of Terror*, 21 December 1981, 306.9016, USIA, Motion Picture, Sound, and Video Records, NARA.
111 Memorandum for the President from William Clark, 'Chemical and Toxin Weapons Use', 6 July 1983, WHORM sf National Security – Defense, ND 017, Warfare, RRL.
112 Michael Ledeen, 'Letter to the Editor', *Commentary*, February 1984.
113 Lucio Lami, 'Yellow Rain: The Conspiracy of Closed Mouths', *Commentary*, 1 October 1983.
114 Leon Davico, 'Letter to the Editor', *Commentary*, February 1984.
115 See letter to President Ronald Reagan from fifteen members of Congress, 14 April 1981, 'Afghanistan', DNSA. Amongst the fifteen congressmen were: Larry McDonald; George Hansen; Robert K Dornan; Bill Chappell Jr.; Phil Crane; S. I. Hayawaki; John LeBoutillier; Stan Parris; Donald J. Pease; Joel Pritchard; Steve Symms; Don Ritter and Daniel Crane. The letter stated that 'independent sources' had confirmed to these members that the Soviets had used chemical weapons such as napalm and nerve gas in Afghanistan.
116 See 'Excerpts from Gate's Testimony on His Record at the CIA', *New York Times*, 4 October 1991.
117 Cordovez and Harrison, *Out of Afghanistan*, p. 63.
118 Cordovez and Harrison, *Out of Afghanistan*, pp. 63–65, outlines the negotiations about negotiations that took place in early 1981 between Pakistan, the UN and USSR and between Pakistan and the United States. Kux, *The United States and Pakistan*, p. 257, quotes assistant secretary for the Near East and South Asia, Nicholas Veliotes, stating that the renewed US commitment to Pakistan was in return for 'reciprocal benefits in terms of our regional interest', that is, supporting the *mujahedeen* against the Soviet Union. Steve Galster, 'Destabilising Afghanistan', *Covert Action*

Information Bulletin, No. 30 (Summer 1988), pp. 57–58, offers further details of the scuppering of promising early negotiations on the conflict by the Reagan administration.
119 No author listed, 'High Wire Act at the Khyber Pass', *New York Times*, 10 February 1981.
120 Memorandum for George P. Shultz from Richard Pipes, 'Background of Forthcoming US-Soviet Talks on Afghanistan', undated but approximately late June 1982, WHSOF, NSC Executive Secretariat, Near East and South Asia, Country File, Afghanistan, Box 34, RRL.
121 Memorandum for William P. Clark from Richard Pipes, 'Background of US-Soviet Talks on Afghanistan Scheduled to Open in Moscow July 8', WHSOF, NSC Executive Secretariat, Near East and South Asia, Country File, Afghanistan, Box 34, RRL. These 'expert-level' talks recommended by Alexander Haig were to run alongside scheduled START negotiations.
122 Memorandum for William P. Clark from Richard Pipes, 'Afghanistan', 29 July 1982, WHSOF, NSC Executive Secretariat, Near East and South Asia, Country File, Afghanistan, Box 34, RRL.
123 Telegram to State Department, Washington from Ambassador Spiers, Islamabad, 18 August 1982, WHSOF, NSC Executive Secretariat, Near East and South Asia, Country File, Afghanistan, Box 34, RRL.
124 See article by Poullada written for *Soldier of Fortune*, December 1981, reprinted in the CFA, 'Free Afghanistan Report', No. 2, April 1982, WHORM sf, Committee for a Free Afghanistan, Box 17, RRL; Letter to John LeBoutillier (R – N.Y.) from Morgan Norval, Editor, *Political Gun News*, 'Aid to Afghan Freedom Fighters', 27 April 1981, WHSOF, Morton Blackwell, Series 1, sf Afghanistan, Box 1, RRL.
125 The President was a regular reader of *Human Events*, having it delivered directly to his White House residence when he discovered that staff had been keeping copies delivered to his office from him. Some advisors worried that the president took more notice of articles in the magazine than of national security briefs. See Cannon, *Reagan: The Role of a Lifetime*, pp. 363–364; Richard Allen also says similar in his oral history interview, see Richard V. Allen interview, 28 May 2002, p. 68, Ronald Reagan Oral History Project, Miller Center of Public Affairs, Virginia.
126 'Conservative Leaders Finding Administration's Officials Undermining Reagan's Mandate', *Human Events*, 30 January 1982.
127 Selig S. Harrison, 'A Breakthrough in Afghanistan?', *Foreign Policy*, No. 51 (Summer 1983), pp. 14–16.
128 Harrison and Cordovez, *Out of Afghanistan*, p. 103; Peter Schweizer, *Victory: The Reagan Administration's Secret Strategy That Hastened the Fall of the Soviet Union* (New York: Atlantic Monthly Press, 1996), p. 151.
129 Harrison, 'Inside the Afghan Talks', *Foreign Policy*, No. 72 (Autumn 1988), p. 45.
130 Robert Macauley, 'Afghanistan: A War without Army against Army', *Christian Science Monitor*, 16 August 1983.
131 Kirsten Lundberg, *Politics of a Covert Action: The US, The Mujahideen and the Stinger Missile* (Cambridge, MA: Kennedy School of Government, Case Program, 1999), p. 14.
132 Haig interviewed on French television discussing Afghanistan on 23 February 1981 stated, 'it's clear that overall East-West relationships, progress in various functional areas, including arms control, credits, trade, technology transfer, must be governed

by the overall conduct of the Soviet Union in the international family of nations. And I would say there is room for substantial improvement in that overall conduct', *US Foreign Policy Current Documents*, 1981, p. 836; Halliday, *Cold War, Third World*, p. 79, argues that this was essentially a revival of the Nixon/Kissinger policy of 'linkage' – that the United States would only negotiate on arms talks in return of Soviet withdrawal from regional conflicts. In an interview with Walter Cronkite, *CBS News*, on 3 March 1981, when asked what conditions would have to be met by the Soviets before a summit meeting would be agreed Reagan stated that 'I think it would help bring about such a meeting if the Soviet Union revealed that it is willing to moderate its imperialism, its aggression – Afghanistan would be an example', *PPP*, RRL.

133 An article in *Newsweek*, 'Arming America's Friends', 23 March 1981, commenting on Reagan's $15 billion foreign military aid package describes the funds to Oman necessary, amongst other reasons, to upgrade an airfield near the Straits of Hormuz to accommodate defenders to react against Soviet airstrikes out of Afghanistan. Frank Church (former Democratic Senator for Idaho) accused Weinberger of using the invasion of Afghanistan to justify a return to 'the two-and-a-half wars doctrine – and more'. 'America's New Foreign Policy', *New York Times*, 23 August 1981.

134 Scott, *Deciding to Intervene*, p. 48, presents evidence that Casey, others in the CIA and Senator Malcolm Wallop, a supporter of the Afghan rebels in Congress, all stated at various times up to 1985 that the *mujahedeen* had no chance of defeating the Soviet army.

Chapter 3

1 Andrew Bacevich, *The Limits of Power: The End of American Exceptionalism* (New York: Metropolitan Books, 2008), p. 45.
2 Scott, *Deciding to Intervene*, p. 22, uses the term 'declaratory strategy' to describe attempts by the administration to establish a 'public rationale' for the Reagan Doctrine particularly after 1984 though he lists some before then too.
3 Adelman, 'Speaking of America', p. 924.
4 Politburo Meeting Minutes, 'Assisting the Democratic Republic of Afghanistan in Strengthening the Mass Media', 19 February 1980, *Soviet Invasion of Afghanistan*, CWIHP.
5 Paul Olkhovsky, 'Mobilizing the Airwaves', Heritage Foundation Report, 13 November 1981, p. 6.
6 Scott, *Deciding to Intervene*, p. 20.
7 Memorandum for the director of the CIA from R.T. Curran, State Department, 30 July 1981, AFO 1242, *Afghanistan: The Making of US Foreign Policy*, DNSA.
8 Minutes of the CC CSPU Politburo Meeting Regarding the Burial and Deaths of Soldiers in Afghanistan, 30 July 1981 (attendees included Andropov and Gorbachev), *Soviet Invasion of Afghanistan*, CWIHP; Fred Halliday, 'The UN and Afghanistan', *New York Times*, 14 September 1981, writes that the USSR had stopped bringing dead soldiers back home from Afghanistan for burial.
9 House Foreign Affairs Committee (HFAC), Subcommittee on Human Rights and International Organizations, 'The Phenomenon of Torture', 98th Congress, 2nd Session, 15, 16 May and 6 September 1984, LoC, p. 171.

10 Telegram to the Secretary of State from Gerald B. Helman, UN Mission, Geneva, 'Visit to Washington by ICRC President May', 28 July 1981, *Afghanistan: The Making of US Foreign Policy*, DNSA.
11 Telegram to the Secretary of State from US Embassy, Manila, 'International Red Cross Conference: Commission Resolution on ICRC Access to Armed Conflict in Western Sahara, Ogaden and Afghanistan', 12 November 1981, *Afghanistan: The Making of US Foreign Policy*, DNSA.
12 Jeane Kirkpatrick, 'Address before the UN General Assembly', 18 November 1981, *US Foreign Policy Current Documents, 1981*.
13 Jeane Kirkpatrick, 'Call for Soviet Withdrawal from Afghanistan', 24 November 1982, Current Policy No. 441, Department of State, *Afghanistan: The Making of US Foreign Policy*, DNSA.
14 President Reagan's addresses to the UN General Assembly on both 17 June 1982 and 26 September 1983 accused the Soviets of chemical weapon use on the Afghan 'freedom fighters'. His address to the UN on 24 September 1984 notes US support for Afghan self-determination while his 24 October 1985 address outlines US support for negotiations on Afghanistan. His 22 September 1986 speech spoke of the Soviet Union's 'vicious war against the Afghan people'. His final 26 September 1988 address lauded the Afghan 'freedom fighters' courageous, determined battle and US support for Afghanistan's 'freedom and independence'. The United States also sponsored a number of UN resolutions condemning Soviet action in Afghanistan.
15 Letter to Larry McDonald and other House members from Richard Fairbanks, 24 June 1981, AFO 1212, *Afghanistan: The Making of US Foreign Policy*, DNSA.
16 Memorandum for Robert McFarlane from Donald Fortier and Shirin Tahir-Kheli, 'Approaching the UN Secretary General on Afghanistan', 16 July 1984, NSC, Executive Secretariat, Country File, Afghanistan, Box 34, RRL.
17 Coll, *Ghost Wars*, p. 93.
18 Telegram to the US Embassy, Kabul from the Department of State, 'Presidential Message to Afghan People', 30 July 1981, Executive Secretariat, NSC, Country File, Near East and South Asia Country Files, Afghanistan, Box 34, RRL.
19 Telegram from Deane Hinton, US Embassy, Islamabad to the Office of the Vice President, 31 May 1984, NSC, Crisis Management Center, Afghanistan, Box 8, RRL.
20 Edward Girardet, 'Afghan Resistance: Familiar Pattern?' *Christian Science Monitor*, 26 July 1982.
21 See Parliamentary Assembly, Council of Europe, Resolution 769 (1982), 'On the Commemoration of 21 March 1982 as Afghanistan Day', http://www.assembly.coe.int/nw/xml/XRef/Xref-XML2HTML-EN.asp?fileid=16180&lang=en
22 Letter to Representative Don Ritter from William Clark, 7 January 1982, WHORM sf Country File, Afghanistan, Box 36, RRL.
23 Memorandum for Meese, Baker and Deaver, from Bud Nance, 'Keeping Afghanistan in the News', 18 December 1981, WHSOF, Sven Kraemer Files, NATO, Shaping European Attitudes – Afghanistan, Box 90103, RRL; Department of State, 'Congressional Talking Points on Afghanistan Day', 18 February 1982, Elizabeth Dole sf, 1981–1983, Afghanistan Day, Box 2, RRL.
24 Department of State, 'Congressional Talking Points on Afghanistan Day', 18 February 1982, Elizabeth Dole sf, 1981–1983, Afghanistan Day, Box 2, RRL.
25 Baitenmann, 'NGOs and the Afghan War', p. 78; David B. Ottaway, 'Groups Fostered Atmosphere Conducive to Giving Rebels Modern Weapons', *Washington Post*, 12 February 1989.

26 Memorandum for Elizabeth Dole from William Clark, 15 January 1982, Elizabeth Dole sf, 1981–1983, Afghanistan Day, Box 2, RRL.
27 Draft telegram to all posts from Department of State, 'Afghanistan Day, March 21', Dennis Blair sf Afghanistan, RAC Box 5, WHSOF, RRL.
28 'Partial Timetable for Planning Afghanistan Day', Sven Kraemer Files, Nato – Shaping European Attitudes – Afghanistan, Box 4, RRL.
29 Partial Timetable for Planning Afghanistan Day, Sven Kraemer Files, RRL. Nicholas Bethell was a conservative member of the House of Lords, a member of the European Parliament and a committed anti-communist. He was involved in establishing Radio Free Kabul and a member of Resistance International. See Andrew Roth, Obituary of Lord Bethell, *The Guardian* (London), 11 September 2007.
30 Memorandum for James Baker from Elizabeth Dole, 'Afghanistan Day', 9 February 1982, Elizabeth Dole Files, sf Afghanistan Day, Box 2, RRL.
31 Draft telegram to all posts from the Department of State, 'Afghanistan Day, March 21', Dennis Blair sf Afghanistan, RAC Box 5, WHSOF, RRL; Partial Timetable for Planning Afghanistan Day, Sven Kraemer Files, RRL.
32 'Talking Points for Elizabeth Dole – Afghanistan Day', 23 February 1982, WHSOF sf Elizabeth Dole Files, Afghanistan Day, Box 2, RRL.
33 'Afghan Project: Media Program Overview', Dennis Blair Files, sf Afghanistan, Box 5, RRL. Gray and Company's director, Robert Keith Gray, was a conservative republican associate of Reagan whose firm represented what the *New York Times* described as a 'rogue's gallery of clients' including Reverend Moon, the BCCI and 'Baby Doc' Duvalier, see Stephen Labaton, 'Darth Invader of Lobbyists', *New York Times*, 23 August 1992.
34 'Afghan Project: Media Program Overview'. Television shows to be targeted included *The Today Show, Good Morning, America, CBS Morning, McNeill-Lehrer Report* amongst others.
35 Memorandum for Bill Clark from Elizabeth Dole, 'Afghanistan Day', 22 January 1982, Elizabeth Dole Files, sf Afghanistan Day, Box 2, RRL. James Gerstenzang, 'Reagan Proclaims Afghanistan Day', *Associated Press*, 10 March 1982; Jean M. White, 'Bush Leads Tribute to Freedom Fighters', *Washington Post*, 22 March 1982; Memorandum for Meese, Baker and Deaver, from Nance, 'Keeping Afghanistan in the News', Sven Kraemer Files, RRL.
36 Handwritten notes, 'Afghanistan Day', 12 January 1982, Dennis Blair Files, sf Afghanistan, Box 5, WHSOF, RRL. The 'French doctors' was a widely used nickname for *MSF* doctors at this time.
37 Draft telegram to all posts from Department of State, 'Afghanistan Day, 21 March', undated, Dennis Blair sf Afghanistan, RAC Box 5, WHSOF, RRL.
38 Memorandum for Edwin Meese et al. from Elizabeth Dole, 'Afghanistan Day Update', 4 March 1982, Elizabeth Dole Files, sf Afghanistan Day, Box 2, RRL.
39 David Schneider, Deputy Secretary of State for Near Eastern Affairs, addressed the rally held in Chicago, see Miller, *Associated Press*, 21 March 1982; Memorandum for Baker from Dole, 'Afghanistan Day'.
40 Rae McGrath, *Landmines: Legacy of Conflict: A Manual for Development Workers* (Oxford: Oxfam, 1994), pp. 39–40, states there was no evidence or probability such mines were designed to attract children rather the design was dictated by technical reasons.
41 White, 'Bush Leads Tribute to Freedom Fighters'.

42 Arms Project (Human Rights Watch), Physicians for Human Rights (US), *Landmines: A Deadly Legacy* (New York: Human Rights Watch, 1993), p.17.
43 Madelyn Miller, *Associated Press*, 21 March 1982.
44 Telegram to the Department of State from Alfred Atherton, US Embassy, Egypt, 'Another Afghanistan Day in Egypt', 25 March 1982, AFO 1329, *Afghanistan: The Making of US Foreign Policy*, DNSA.
45 The Captive Nations week commemoration was signed into law under President Dwight Eisenhower (Public Law 86–90, 17 July 1959) and sought to raise awareness of nations 'captive' under communist rule. It fell in the third week of July.
46 Merrill Hartson, 'Reagan Condemns Soviet Actions, Wants Meeting with Brezhnev', *Associated Press*, 5 April 1982.
47 William Casey, 'Anti-Defamation League Dinner Address', 3 June 1982, Document No. 0001446213, CIA FOIA ERR.
48 Telegram to the White House from Secretary Shultz, 'My Visit to Pakistan, July 2–4, 1983', 4 July 1983, Document No. 114, *Towards an International of the War in Afghanistan*, Vol. 1, *CWIHP*.
49 Kux, *The United States and Pakistan*, p. 271.
50 Telegram to the Department of State from US Embassy, Islamabad, 'The Political Dimension of the Afghan Insurgency', 28 June 1981, *Afghanistan: The Making of US Foreign Policy*, DNSA. The telegram is summarizing a 'primer' written on the insurgents by the Peshawar Consul and sent on 24 June 1981.
51 CIA Report, 'Afghanistan: Ethnic Diversity and Dissidence', 1 May 1979, Document No. 0000515454, CIA FOIA ERR.
52 Telegram to Judge William Clark from William Wilson, US Embassy, Rome, Executive Secretariat, NSC, Country File, Afghanistan, Box 34, RRL.
53 CIA Report, 'Afghanistan: Ethnic Diversity and Dissidence'.
54 Memorandum for Robert McFarlane from Donald Fortier, 'Afghanistan Background for Tomorrow's Shultz-Weinberger-McFarlane Breakfast', 21 February 1984, NSC, Executive Secretariat, Country File, Afghanistan, Box 34, RRL.
55 In *Afgantsy*, pp. 233–234, Braithwaite describes *mujahedeen* as well of Soviet atrocities such as rebels cutting off the heads of 'infidels' as well as Soviet soldiers and the selling of Soviet soldiers to Western human rights organizations. The 1985 Amnesty International report raised concerns about reports of summary executions by the *mujahedeen* of captured Soviet and Afghan soldiers and 'spies', Amnesty International Report (London: Amnesty International Publications, 1985), pp. 195–198.
56 CIA Report, 'Afghanistan: Ethnic Diversity and Dissidence'.
57 Roger Fenton and Maggie Gallagher, 'Inside Afghanistan', *New Republic*, 29 August 1983, which quotes a 'Western observer' implying Hekmatyar was in the pocket of Moscow. While it is unproven that Hekmatyar had any links to the KGB there are plenty of first-hand accounts of his relationship with the CIA; for examples see Seth G. Jones, *In the Graveyard of Empires: America's War in Afghanistan* (New York: W. W. Norton, 2009), pp. 31–33; Coll, *Ghost Wars*, p. 120.
58 CIA Report, 'Afghanistan: Ethnic Diversity and Dissidence'.
59 CC CPSU Decree Number 147, 8 July 1983, *Towards an International History of the War in Afghanistan*, Vol. 2, Document No. 105, *CWIHP*. This document details authorities in Iran and Pakistan preventing over 1,700 families from returning to

Afghanistan from various refugee camps and an ensuing battle which left 213 people dead – mostly women, children and old men.

60   Valentine Moghadam, 'Building Human Resources and Women's Capabilities in Afghanistan: A Retrospect and Prospects', *World Development*, Vol. 22, No. 6 (1994), p. 859. Moghadam states that as refugees began to flee to Pakistan in the summer of 1978, they cited the forced literacy programme for Afghan women as one of the major reasons for leaving their homeland, p. 864.
61   Moghadam, 'Building Human Resources', p. 861.
62   Moghadam, 'Building Human Resources', p. 859. A UNICEF report produced from a UNICEF and UNIFEM conference titled 'Planning and Afghan Women', December 1989, by Hanne Christensen and Fay Haffenden, noted that 'the People's Democratic Party of Afghanistan (PDPA) has an explicit and positive policy on women's role in society. Changes in attitude have been observed and a greater participation by women in education, employment and other opportunities has been achieved. Integrating the modernizing perspective of some of the urban population with the perspectives of rural and refugee populations where attitudes about women have remained static or have become restrictive is a daunting task for the rehabilitation period.'
63   Craig Davis, '"A" Is for Allah, "J" Is for Jihad', *World Policy Journal*, Vol. 19, No. 1 (Spring 2001), p. 92.
64   See Davis, '"A" Is for Allah', pp. 90–94; Roozbeh Shirazi, 'Islamic Education in Afghanistan: Revisiting the United States' Role', *The New Centennial Review*, Vol. 8, No. 1 (Spring 2008), pp. 219–224.
65   Central Intelligence Agency, Directorate of Intelligence, Office of Political Analysis, 'The Soviets and the Tribes of Southwest Asia', 23 September 1980, Document No. 2, September 11th Sourcebooks, Vol. II: *Afghanistan: Lessons from the Last War*, NSA, EEB, No. 57, Part II, US Analysis of the Soviet War in Afghanistan: Declassified.
66   Andrei A. Doohovskoy, 'Soviet Counterinsurgency in the Soviet Afghan War Revisited: Analyzing the Effective Aspects of the Counterinsurgency Effort', Master's Thesis (Cambridge, MA: Harvard University, September 2009), pp. 39–42.
67   The VOA was already broadcasting in Dari, another major language of the Afghans.
68   Memorandum for Robert McFarlane from Carnes Lord, Geoffrey Kemp, John Lenczowsky, Walter Raymond, 'VOA Coverage of Afghan War', 9 March 1983, Executive Secretariat, NSC, Country Files, Afghanistan, Box 34, RRL.
69   USICA, 'Afghanistan 1982: The Struggle for Freedom Continues', Motion Picture, Sound, and Video Records, USIA Archives, RG 306, NARA. Available in full on PublicResource.org, YouTube channel, http://www.youtube.com/watch?v=ZJ0PNcxUnaY
70   Michael Barry, 'Afghanistan 1982: The Struggle for Freedom Continues'. Michael Barry also appeared in 'Afghan Digest: Number 1' (1983), 306.9044 and translated for the *mujahedeen* brought to Washington in 1983 to meet with President Reagan on a CFA-sponsored trip. See 'Visit of Afghan Survivors' (1983), 306.9964, all at Motion Picture, Sound, and Video Records, USIA Archives, NARA.
71   'Afghanistan Digest, Number 1'; Memorandum for William Clark from Gilbert Robinson, 'Kirk Douglas's Visit to Pakistan', 9 December 1982, WHORM sf, Country File, Pakistan, Box 146, RRL.
72   Ray Peppers, 'Kirk Douglas Visit to Afghan Refugees in Pakistan, Part 2: Follow Up in the US', WHORM sf, Country File, Pakistan, Box 146, RRL.

73 Ray Peppers, 'Kirk Douglas Visit to Afghan Refugees in Pakistan, Part 1: The Visit', WHORM sf, Country File, Pakistan, Box 146, RRL.
74 'Thanksgiving in Peshawar: With Kirk Douglas, November 1982', 306.9840, Motion Picture, Sound, and Video Records, USIA Archives, NARA.
75 Cull, *The Cold War and the United States Information Agency*, p. 428.
76 Mona Megalli, Washington News segment, *UPI*, 25 August 1983; 'Afghanistan: The Hidden War' (1983), 306.9038, Motion Picture, Sound, and Video Records, USIA Archives, NARA.
77 'TV Satellite File: Number 27' (30 November 1983), 306-TVSF-40, Motion Picture, Sound, and Video Records, USIA Archives, NARA.
78 Robert Kaiser, 'Money, Family Name Shaped Scaife', *Washington Post*, 3 May 1999, described Richard Mellon Scaife as 'the most generous donor to conservative causes in American history' and 'became the leading financial supporter of the movement that reshaped American politics in the last quarter of the 20th century'.
79 See Emily Yoffe, 'De Borchgrave; A Cold Warriors' Battle with a World He Sees Full of Dupes, Deception and Disinformation', *Washington Post Magazine*, 8 July 1984, p. 6, in which she states that De Borchgrave was known for his hyperbolic interpretation of 'the Soviet threat' which eventually led to his dismissal from *Newsweek* in early 1980. Although he briefed, at the invitation of Charles Wick, USIA staff on communist disinformation he was later put on the agency's infamous 'black list' of commentators not to be used for overseas speaking assignments for this same reason. De Borchgrave went on to become editor-in-chief of the *Washington Times* in 1985 and joined CSIS in 1991 as a senior advisor and director of the Global Organized Crime Project known since 9/11 as the Transnational Threats Project. De Borchgrave was also the cousin of Count Alexandre de Marenches, Head of French Intelligence at that time (according to Richard Allen's interview with the Ronald Reagan Oral History Project, p. 62) who, in 1981, advised Reagan and Casey to undermine Soviet morale in Afghanistan by smuggling hard drugs, Bibles in Russian and fake Soviet army newspapers containing subversive articles to Soviet soldiers, see Thomas Sanction, 'Dispatches', *Time*, 24 June 2001. De Borchgrave, De Marenches and Michael Ledeen were also embroiled in the disinformation campaign which alleged a Soviet connection in the plot to kill Pope John Paul II in 1981. See Gartoff, p. 93, n. 27.
80 'Afghanistan: Caught in the Struggle' (1983), 306.9036, Motion Picture, Sound, and Video Records, USIA Archives, NARA.
81 'TV Satellite File: Number 27'.
82 'Afghan Digest: Number 2' (1983), 306.9045, Motion Picture, Sound, and Video Records, USIA Archives NARA; 'TV Satellite File: Number 75' (1984), 306-TVSF-89, USIA, Motion Picture, Sound, and Video Records, NARA.
83 Eleanor Davey, 'Famine, Aid, and Ideology: The Political Activism of Medecins Sans Frontières in the 1980s', *French Historical Studies* (2011), Vol. 34, No. 3, pp. 529–558.
84 *BBC Summary of World Broadcasts*, 'US Television Film on Afghanistan "Blatant, Unbridled Forgery"', *Telegraph Agency of the Soviet Union* (TASS), 29 August 1983. TASS was particularly referring to 'Afghanistan: The Hidden War'.
85 The International Conference on Afghan Alternatives was held at the Monterey Institute of International Studies, California, in November 1983. The papers given were collected into a book edited by Ralph H. Magnus titled *Afghan Alternatives: Issues, Options, and Policies* (New Brunswick, NJ: Transaction Books, 1985).

86 Memorandum for Robert McFarlane from Walter Raymond, 'Afghan Political Action', 30 March 1984, Executive Secretariat, NSC, Country File, Afghanistan, Box 34, RRL; Walter Raymond, 'Restricted Working Group: Afghan Political Action Proposal', Executive Secretariat, NSC, Country File, Afghanistan, Box 34, RRL. Zalmay Khalilzad who would later run an organization called AFA was suggested for this role.
87 Martin Durham and Margaret Power (eds), *New Perspectives on the Transnational Right* (London: Palgrave Macmillan, 2010), pp. 141–142; Vaisse, *Neoconservatism*, p. 214.
88 CFA, 'Free Afghanistan Report, No. 4', November 1982, WHORM sf Committee for a Free Afghanistan, Box 17, RRL.
89 CFA, 'Free Afghanistan Report, No. 2', April 1982, WHORM sf Committee for a Free Afghanistan, Box 17, RRL.
90 Amstutz, *Afghanistan: The First Five Years of Soviet Occupation*, pp. 215–216, outlines the beginnings of Radio Free Kabul in 1981 and records it as having demised in the autumn of 1983.
91 Telegram to Douglas Archard, Peshawar Consulate from State Department 'Message for Archard from Afghanistan Relief Committee', 12 May 1981, AF01193, *Afghanistan: The Making of US Foreign Policy*, DNSA.
92 Crile, *Charlie Wilson's War*, p. 74, gives a description of the making and content of this film which Crile describes as 'less than sophisticated'. pp. 223–224 details Herring's, Fawcett's and Wilson's meetings with Hekmatyar.
93 Ann Marsh, 'AmeriCares' Success Hailed, Criticized; Charity Uses Clout and Connections Political, Economic and Religious Ties Help AmeriCares Connections Help Charity', *Harford Courant*, 11 August 1991.
94 No author listed, 'Private Group to Send Aid to Afghan Refugees', *New York Times*, 21 June 1983.
95 A *Village Voice* investigation of the charity in 1991 accused its advisory committee and benefactors of being 'almost exclusively powerful right-wingers with close ties to the intelligence community, president and ex-CIA director George Bush, and the most conservative elements of the Catholic church' and the foundation itself of resembling 'private foreign-policy operation of the U.S. government'; see Russ W. Baker, 'A Thousand Points of Blight: ArmeriCares, George Bush's Favorite Charity, Dispenses Bitter Medicine around the World', *Village Voice*, 8 January 1991.
96 Letter to George H.W. Bush from Robert Macauley, 17 July 1984, Executive Secretariat, NSC, Near East and South Asia, Country Files, Afghanistan, Box 34, RRL.
97 Memorandum for Robert McFarlane from Charles Hill, 'Medical Assistance for Afghan Victims', 9 May 1984, Executive Secretariat, NSC, Near East and South Asia, Country Files, Afghanistan, Box 34, RRL; 'Review and Outlook', *Wall Street Journal*, 1984 (no further date), Executive Secretariat, NSC, Near East and South Asia, Country Files: Afghanistan, Box 34, RRL.
98 Memorandum for Michael Armacost from John Poindexter, 'Additional Humanitarian Relief for Afghanistan', 6 August 1984, Executive Secretariat, NSC, Near East and South Asia, Country Files, Afghanistan, Box 34, RRL; Memorandum for Robert McFarlane from Walter Raymond, 'Humanitarian Assistance to Afghanistan', 19 July 1984, Executive Secretariat, NSC, Near East and South Asia, Country Files, Afghanistan, Box 34, RRL.
99 Letter to Bush from Macauley, 17 July 1984.

100 Andrew Eiva, 'Biographical Background', Free Afghanistan Alliance newsletter, undated, available at Jezail.org website, http://www.jezail.org/03_Eiva-FAAA/Eiva_2.pdf
101 Crile, *Charlie Wilson's War*, p. 328. Crile describes Free the Eagle as an 'extreme, right-wing Mormon operation'; Joan Mower, 'Peanut Butter Revolutionaries: They Lobby for Distant Uprisings', *Associated Press*, 21 July 1986.
102 No author given, 'Groups Backing Afghan Rebels Don't Even Speak to Each Other', *National Journal*, 8 February 1986. Free the Eagle accused the CFA of being a CIA front while McKay of the CFA said Eiva had threatened to kill her.
103 Letter from Eiva, Free Afghanistan Alliance to Charles Moser, Coalition for America, 11 April 1983, *Afghanistan: The Making of US Foreign Policy*, DNSA.
104 Gelb, 'From One Kind of Army to Another', *New York Times*, 25 May 1983; Paul Weyrich also formed the Committee for the Survival of a Free Congress, lobbied Congress about 'yellow rain' chemical warfare by the Soviets and was against a nuclear freeze.
105 Klass gave testimony at the following Congressional hearings: SFRC, 'Situation in Afghanistan', March 1982, LoC; Congressional Task Force on Afghanistan, 'Hearing on Famine', 25 February 1985, AF0 1620, *Afghanistan: The Making of US Foreign Policy*, DNSA; Congressional Task Force on Afghanistan, 'Hearing on Soviet Strategy and Its Implications for the West', 11 March 1985, AF0 1623, *Afghanistan: The Making of US Foreign Policy*, DNSA; HFAC, Subcommittee on Asian and Pacific Affairs, 'Developments in Afghanistan', February 1988, LoC; The Commission on Security and Cooperation in Europe, US Congress, 'The Situation in Afghanistan', 3 May 1990, AF0 2313, *Afghanistan: The Making of US Foreign Policy*, DNSA.
106 Lundberg, 'Politics of a Covert Action', p. 20.
107 Lundberg, 'Politics of a Covert Action', p. 20; Memorandum for John Poindexter from Ronald K. Sable, 'Tsongas Resolution on Afghanistan "Freedom Fighters"', 29 February 1984, Executive Secretariat, NSC, Country File, Afghanistan, Box 34, RRL.
108 Amstutz, *Afghanistan: The First Five Years of Soviet Occupation*, p. 351.
109 Crile, *Charlie Wilson's War*, p. 324, describes Humphrey as 'a close ideological and political ally of the president'. Paul Weyrich was a supporter of Hatch, see James Conaway, 'Righting Reagan's Revolution; Paul Weyrich, Moral Tactician, at War with Incompetence, Moderates and the GOP', *Washington Post*, 22 March 1983.
110 'Aid for Afghanistan', *National Security Record*, Checklist of Issues Coming before Congress to Watch Out For, Number 50, p. 5, October 1982; 'Afghanistan Rhetoric', *National Security Record*, Checklist of Issues Coming before Congress to Watch Out For, No. 53, p. 5, January 1983.
111 Memorandum for the Secretary of State from Lawrence Eagleburger, 'Pakistan and the Afghan Refugees and Freedom Fighters', 24 November 1982, NSC, Executive Secretariat, Near East and South Asia, Country File, Afghanistan, Box 34, RRL.

Chapter 4

1 Richard Allen assessing the Reagan administration's foreign policy in Afghanistan, Richard Allen Interview, 28 May 2002, Ronald Reagan Oral History Project, Miller Center of Public Affairs, University of Virginia.

2   Brzezinski described the invasion as a 'watershed event' in a *Time* magazine interview on 14 January 1980 as it was the first time since the Second World War that the Soviets had used their military might in a country not within its sphere of influence. A Congressional Research Report for the House of Representatives Committee on Foreign Affairs, 'The Soviet Union in the Third World, 1980–1985: Imperial Burden or Political Asset', 23 September 1985, 99th Congress, 1st Session, LoC, p. 16, argues that Afghanistan 'produced a radical shift in American public opinion, countering the "Vietnam Syndrome," expanding the allowable limits of foreign involvement, and energizing a resurgence of US military power; it marked the beginning of American reentry into the Third World, perhaps even a return to globalism'. See also Westad, *Global Cold War*, p. 354 on the growing belief in the possibility of victory in Afghanistan.
3   Jeane J. Kirkpatrick, 'Doctrine of Moral Equivalence', Current Policy No. 580, 9 April 1984, United States Department of State, Bureau of Public Affairs.
4   Stephen S. Rosenfeld, 'Guns of July', *Foreign Affairs*, Vol. 64, No. 4 (Spring 1986), p. 705. Also see Bob Woodward, *Veil: The Secret Wars of the CIA, 1981–1987* (New York: Simon and Schuster, 1987), pp. 315–318, where he describes Casey's amazement at the money procured for the Afghans while the CIA struggled to secure funding for the Nicaraguan Contras.
5   Coll, *Ghost Wars*, p. 125; Pillsbury quoted in Lundberg, 'Politics of a Covert Action', p. 26.
6   NSC, 'National Security Decision Directive 166: US Policy, Programs and Strategy in Afghanistan', 27 March 1985, p. 3, states 'responding to Pakistan's security requirements arising from their support of the resistance' was 'essential to the program'.
7   Steve Galster, 'The Afghan Pipeline', *Covert Action Information Bulletin*, No. 30 (Summer 1988), pp. 56 and 58, lists the 'bleeders' in the administration as Vincent Cannistraro, Morton Abramowitz, Bert Dunn, Oliver North, Elie Krakowski, Richard Armitage and to some extent William Casey. Westad, *Global Cold War*, p. 353, adds Fred Iklé, Richard Perle, Elliot Abrams and Paul Wolfowitz to this list.
8   Many Western Europeans drew parallels between Soviet actions in Afghanistan and US policy in Central America though were more vague on Grenada, see USIA Research Memorandum, 'Western European Public Opinion on Afghanistan', 26 December 1984, Office of Research and Media Reaction, RG 306, P 64, Box 40, NARA, Washington, DC; USIA Report, 'Public Diplomacy Issues', 17 April 1984, Office of Research, USIA Special Reports 1953–1997, RG 306, P 160, Box 46, NARA. This report states that 'media throughout the world has almost uniformly condemned or negatively reported the US role in mining Nicaragua's harbors'. USIA Research Report, 'Long Term Trends in West European Confidence in US Policies and Defense Assistance', December 1983, USIA Archives, Special Reports, RG 306, P 160, Box 46, NARA, details negative effect of INF deployment on European attitudes to United States.
9   Leo P. Crespi, 'Western European Views of US versus USSR Moral Standing in International Behaviour', 19 September 1984, USIA Special Reports, 1953–1997, RG 306, P 160, Box 46, NARA. In this 'think piece' Crespi outlines that Western Europeans see that the United States was seen as morally superior in the area of human rights and aid but it was considered morally equivalent or inferior to the USSR in areas such as chemical weapon use, intervening in other states, attempting to dominate states economically and use of disinformation. Worryingly, these

negative views were even more prevalent amongst the existing elites and the 'successor generation' who could be expected to become the ruling elite in future years. USIA Research Memorandum, 'Western Europeans Support Chemical Weapons Ban', 15 August 1984, Office of Research and Media Reaction, RG 306, P 64, Box 40, NARA.
10   According to a USIA poll, 59 per cent of Italians and 61 per cent of Germans preferred superpower parity rather than superiority of either, USIA Research Memorandum, 'West European Public Opinion', 13 October 1983, RG 306, P 60, Special Reports 1953–1997, NARA.
11   USIA Briefing Paper, 30 January 1984, Office of Research, RG 306, P 49, Box 2, NARA. This poll shows majorities in Italy and Germany against INF deployment on their soil. Britain, where there was still a plurality in favour (47 per cent), experienced a sharp decline from 75 per cent six months earlier and two thirds of the public stated they lacked confidence in US foreign policy and believed it endangered peace.
12   Jeane J. Kirkpatrick, 'Doctrine of Moral Equivalence', Current Policy No. 580, 9 April 1984, United States Department of State, Bureau of Public Affairs. Kirkpatrick quotes a *Guardian* (London) article from 28 October 1983 and an *Observer* (London) article from 30 October 1983 that compare US actions in Grenada to the Soviet invasion of Afghanistan.
13   As well as Kirkpatrick others attending included Frank Shakespeare (formally head of the USIA, a Heritage Foundation board member and chair of the Board for International Broadcasting); the author Tom Wolfe; *National Review* editor Joseph Sobran; Education Secretary William Bennett; Irving Kristol; Tom Bethnell; Michael Novak. According to the Hillsdale College website archive of its *Imprimis publication* (Hillsdale College), Issue 1, January 1986, articles were generated in over 500 newspapers in the United States including *The Washington Post*, *Time* magazine, *The Wall Street Journal* and *The New York Times*.
14   NSC, 'NSDD 130: US International Information Policy', 6 March 1984, *National Security Decision Directives 1981–1989*, RRL.
15   USIA, 'Afghan Digest No. 2', 1983, 306.9045, RG 306, USIA, Motion Picture, Sound, and Video Records Section, NARA.
16   NSC, 'NSDD 147: US Policy towards India and Pakistan', 11 October 1984, *National Security Decision Directives 1981–1989*, RRL.
17   Memorandum for Robert McFarlane from Charles Hill, 'Marking the Fifth Anniversary of the Soviet Invasion of Afghanistan', 23 October 1984, NSC, Executive Secretariat, Near East and South Asia Country Files, Afghanistan, Box 34, RRL.
18   Ronald Reagan, 'Statement on the Fifth Anniversary of the Soviet Invasion of Afghanistan', 26 December 1984, *PPP*, RRL.
19   Memorandum for John Poindexter from Steven Steiner and Walter Raymond, '5th Anniversary of Soviet Invasion of Afghanistan – Actions Underway', 18 December 1984, NSC, Executive Secretariat, Near East and South Asia Country Files, Afghanistan, Box 34, RRL.
20   Gouttierre had coached Khalilzad in basketball when he was a student in Kabul. Khalilzad worked with Brzezinski at Columbia University. See Joe Stephens and David B. Ottaway, 'Afghan Roots Keep Adviser Firmly in the Inner Circle', *Washington Post*, 23 November 2001.
21   Andrew Chang, 'Who Is Zalmay Khalilzad?', *ABC News*, 6 January 2006. At this stage, Khalilzad was an associate professor of political dcience at Columbia University and

on a Council on Foreign Relations fellowship with the State Department though he would join the State Department in 1985 as Special Adviser to Under Secretary of State for Political Affairs; see Stephens and Ottaway, 'Afghan Roots Keep Adviser Firmly in the Inner Circle'.

22 Khalilzad, 'An Ounce of Prevention', *Washington Post*, 10 October 1979.
23 Joan Mower, 'US Provides $500,000 So Afghan Rebels Can Tell Their Story', *Associated Press*, 16 September 1985; Rosanne Klass, 'In Enemy Hands: One Man Lives to Tell a Tale of the Taliban', *The Weekly Standard*, Vol. 16, No. 5, 18 October 2012; Stephens and Ottaway, 'Afghan Roots Keep Adviser Firmly in the Inner Circle'.
24 Zalmay Khalilzad, 'Foreign Center Briefing on Afghanistan', 17 December 1984, 306-FP-219, RG 306, USIA, Motion Picture, Sound, and Video Records Section, NARA.
25 Rosanne Klass, 'Pushing and Pulling Apart Pakistan', *Wall Street Journal*, 2 October 1984; Klass, 'Afghanistan: Don't Fall for Soviet Tricks', *Los Angeles Times*, 29 December 1982; Klass, 'Afghans Suffer under Soviet Holocaust', *Orlando Sentinel*, 20 October 1985.
26 Eliot was also a former US ambassador to Afghanistan.
27 Dean Theodore Eliot, Fletcher School of Law and Diplomacy, 7 December 1984, Electronic Dialogue Series, 306-ED-37, RG 306, USIA, Motion Picture, Sound, and Video Records Section, NARA.
28 NSC, NSDD 147, 'US Policy towards India and Pakistan', 11 October 1984, *National Security Decision Directives 1981–1989*, RRL.
29 Thomas Thornton, US Department of State, 'Hearings before the Subcommittees on Europe and the Middle East and on Asian and Pacific Affairs of the Committee on Foreign Affairs', House of Representatives, 98th Congress, July, August, September, October 1983. Thornton had been an NSC staffer on South Asia in the Carter administration.
30 USIA Research Memorandum, 13 September 1984, Office of Research and Media Reaction, RG 306, P 64, Box 40, NARA.
31 USIA Research Memorandum, 13 September 1984. See also CIA Research Paper 'Muslims in the USSR', 5 February 1980, National Foreign Assessment Center, CIA FOIA Electronic Reading Room.
32 Coll, *Ghost Wars*, pp. 103–104. This propaganda began to arrive in Pakistan in December 1984 and distribution into Afghanistan began early 1985. Also Gates, *From the Shadows*, p. 177.
33 French intelligence chief, Count Alexandre de Marenches, had also recommended such an action to Casey back in 1981.
34 Project Democracy, FY-84, 'Support for Democratic Concepts among Muslims', Office of the Legal Advisor, Subject Files, 1945–1997, Education and Culture, Department of State, RG 59, AI 5397, Box 173, NARA.
35 Project Democracy, 'Center for Afghan Democratic Studies', Office of the Legal Advisor, Subject Files, 1945–1997, Education and Culture, Department of State, RG 59, AI 5397, Box 173, NARA.
36 USIA Research Memorandum, 13 September 1984.
37 Shultz described the US–Pakistan relationship as 'essential to achieving our strategic objectives in Afghanistan and South Asia and is potentially of major importance to our broader Middle East strategy'. See Department of State memorandum for President Reagan from George P. Shultz, 'How Do We Make Use of the Zia

Visit to Protect Our Strategic Interests in the Face of Pakistan Nuclear Weapons Activities', 26 November 1982, EBB No. 377, *The Nuclear Vault*, NSA.

38   USIA Research Memorandum, 'Pakistani Views on US and USSR, Indo-Pak Relations and Other Issues', 17 September 1986 (though polled in late 1985/early 1986), Office of Research and Media Reaction, RG 306, P 64, Box 40, NARA. On the whole, 63 per cent said they did not trust the United States though even more distrusted the USSR, 54 per cent favoured neutrality and 87 per cent thought that Pakistan should develop an 'atom bomb'.

39   Defense Intelligence Agency cable, 'Pakistan-China Nuclear Weapons Production and Testing', 7 December 1985, EBB 377, *The Nuclear Vault*, NSA.

40   Selig Harrison, 'The Soviets Are Winning in Afghanistan', *Washington Post*, 13 May 1984.

41   Rone Tempest, 'Afghan Rebel Getaway; Peshawar: Many Lured by Intrigue', *Los Angeles Times*, 12 May 1986.

42   US Senate Foreign Relations Committee, Media Notice, 'Senate Report Urges Recognising Afghan Government-in-Exile and Asylum for Soviet Prisoners', 27 March 1984, Document No. AF0 1567, *Afghanistan: The Making of US Foreign Policy*, DNSA.

43   CIA, Directorate of Intelligence Report, 'The Afghan Resistance: The Struggle for Unity', 26 June 1984, CIA FOIA ERR.

44   Alex Alexiev, Statement to the Senate Select Committee on Intelligence, 26 September 1984 based on the Rand Report, 'The War in Afghanistan: Soviet Strategy and the State of the Resistance', November 1984, Document No. AF0 1609, *Afghanistan: The Making of US Foreign Policy*, DNSA.

45   Klass, 'US, Aid the Afghans', *New York Times*, 4 January 1984.

46   The rebels did have some anti-aircraft weapons, but these were ineffective against the armour-coated Hind attack helicopters the Soviets began to deploy in the summer of 1984. Alexiev, 'The War in Afghanistan'. According to his associate Jack Wheeler, Alexiev had done some work for the CIA. See Jack Wheeler, 'The Coming Collapse of the Soviet Union', 17 May 1989, Lecture No. 188, Heritage Foundation, http://www.heritage.org/research/lecture/the-coming-collapse-of-the-soviet-union

47   Daniel F. Gilmore, 'US Military Aid to Afghans Is Woefully Inadequate', *UPI*, 26 December 1984.

48   Don Shannon, 'Reagan Warns Moscow on Afghanistan Policy', *Los Angeles Times*, 27 December 1984. Eiva at the Federation for American-Afghan Action was influential on Humphrey and was said to have stoked the Senator's initial interest in Afghanistan. See Crile, *Charlie Wilson's War*, p. 327.

49   Don Oberdorfer, 'Despite Doubts on Effectiveness, Afghan Rebel Aid Gains Support', *Washington Post*, 8 September 1984.

50   Congressional Task Force on Afghanistan, 'Hearing on Famine', 25 February 1985, p. 7, *Afghanistan: The Making of US Foreign Policy*, DNSA.

51   This information is contained in a later hearing at which Lohbeck testifies – The Commission on Security and Co-Operation in Europe (CSCE aka The Helsinki Commission), Hearing on 'Soviet Violations of Human Rights in Afghanistan', 4 December 1985, p. 40, LoC. Lohbeck had exclusively covered Afghanistan and Nicaragua for CBS from 1984.

52   Congressional Task Force on Afghanistan, 'Hearing on Famine'.

53   Crile, *Charlie Wilson's War*, p. 462; Mary Williams Walsh, 'Mission Afghanistan', *Columbia Journalism Review*, Vol. 28, No. 5 (January/February 1990).

54 Letter to Robert McFarlane from Kurt Lohbeck, 8 March 1985, WHORM sf Speeches, 307886, Box 256, RRL.
55 Mary Williams Walsh, 'Strained Mercy: A Relief Agency Dispenses Propaganda', *Progressive*, Vol. 54, No. 5 (May 1990). Williams cites a State Department cable, which describes Lohbeck as a public relations advisor for Haq. Lohbeck, in his memoirs, *Holy War, Unholy Victory* (Washington: Regnery Gateway, Inc., 1989), writes extensively on his interactions with Haq calling him 'an on-going legend' at one stage (p. 117) and describes putting Haq up in his apartment when visiting Washington, DC, and driving him to appointments and meetings in the capital (pp. 123–124).
56 Walsh, 'Mission: Afghanistan'. Williams originally wrote this article for the *Wall Street Journal* where, at the time, she was a staff reporter but the periodical refused to print allegations that CBS coverage on Afghanistan was biased by its reliance on Lohbeck. The article instead appeared in the *Columbia Journalism Review* though in edited form. See Erwin Knoll, 'Journalistic Jihad: Holes in the Coverage of the Holy War', *Progressive*, Vol. 54, No. 5 (1990), pp. 17–22 for details. Lohbeck, *Holy War, Unholy Victory*, accuses Walsh of pursuing a personal vendetta against him, p. 221.
57 Carpenter, 'US Aid to Anti Communist Rebels', describes Wheeler and his foundation as conservative supporters of anti-Marxist insurgencies. Wheeler wrote a number of articles in support of such insurgencies. According to a *Los Angeles Times* article of 1 August 1985, Soviet newspaper *Izvestia* called Wheeler 'an ideological gangster'. The article catalogues Wheeler's contention he had spent time with the Afghan *mujahedeen*, UNITA in Angola, and guerrilla groups in Cambodia, Nicaragua and Mozambique. Furthermore, he conceived and organized the Democratic International – an alliance of anti-communist guerrillas with financial assistance from Lewis Lehrman, a conservative activist linked to the Heritage Foundation and AEI and his group Citizens for America under whose auspices the conference was held. Jack Abramoff, a lobbyist later convicted on corruption charges, was also involved in organizing this 'Jamboree in Jamba', see Mark Hemingway, 'My Dinner with Jack', *The Weekly Standard*, Vol. 11, No. 27 (3 April 2006).
58 Edward S. Herman and David Peterson, *The Politics of Genocide* (New York: Monthly Review Press, 2010), examines how the term 'genocide' has become politicized and is applied in United States solely to situations involving those who threatened US interests but not to US allies. The term was used again and again in relation to Soviet actions in Afghanistan during the course of the conflict.
59 Congressional Task Force on Afghanistan, 'Hearing on Famine', pp. 78–86. In contrast to this testimony a CIA report suggests that the Soviets were not deliberately targeting crops and that the destruction of crops and farm land due to military operations only affected a small portion of cultivated land. See CIA, Office of Near Eastern and South Asian Analysis and the Office of Soviet Analysis Intelligence Report, 'The Soviet Invasion of Afghanistan: 5 Years After', May 1985, Document No. 0000496704, *The Princeton Collection*, CIA FOIA ERR.
60 Congressional Task Force on Afghanistan, 'Hearing on Famine', pp. 111–114.
61 Lohbeck, *Holy War, Unholy Victory*, pp. 90–92.
62 Crile, *Charlie Wilson's War*, pp. 210–211.
63 Klass, Congressional Task Force on Afghanistan, 'Hearing on Famine', pp. 111–114.
64 See L'Observatoire de L'action Humanitaire (Aid Watch), NGOs, *Medecins Sans Frontières*, 'History, 1980–1989', http://www.observatoire-humanitaire.org/en/index.php?page=fiche-ong.php&part=fiche&id=23

65 Suzanne Garment, 'Afghan People See the Cruel Face of Mother Russia', *Wall Street Journal*, 1 March 1985.
66 Congressional Task Force on Afghanistan, 'Hearing on Medical Conditions in Afghanistan', 4 March 1985, Document No. AF0 1622 and Congressional Task Force on Afghanistan, 'Hearing on Soviet Strategy and Its Implications for the West', 11 March 1985, Document No. AF0 1623, *Afghanistan: The Making of US Foreign Policy*, DNSA.
67 Snyder, *Warriors of Disinformation*, pp. 80–82; Hans N. Tuch, *Communicating with the World: US Public Diplomacy Overseas* (Washington, DC: Institute for the Study of Diplomacy, 1990), has a chapter on the inception and development of Worldnet, pp. 99–106.
68 Snyder, *Warriors of Disinformation*, p. 82.
69 According to a Worldnet report, in less than two years Worldnet had garnered 100 hours of foreign television news air time and reached an estimated audience of 2 billion. See 'Worldnet: A Report, 1985', 19 June 1985, USIA Historical Collection, Research and Reports, RG 306, AI 1070, Box 120, NARA.
70 'Europeans Reluctant to Give Afghanistan High Priority', Foreign Opinion Note, 21 January 1986 (poll conducted in December 1985), Office of Research, USIA, RG 306, P 118, Box 4, NARA.
71 See p. 235 for more on the German Afghan Committee and its links to the German New Right and the CFA.
72 Worldnet, No. 157, 'Human Rights in Afghanistan', 12 December 1985, 306-WNET-181, RG 306, USIA, Motion Picture, Sound, and Video Records Section, NARA.
73 TV Satellite File began to be produced in 1983 and was transmitted by satellite into Europe and to other continents via videotape and designed by Wick to support the administration's foreign policy objectives. See Snyder, *Warriors of Disinformation*, p. 38.
74 TV Satellite File, No. 29, 15 December 1983, 306.TVSF.42, RG 306, USIA, Motion Picture, Sound, and Video Records Section, NARA.
75 TV Satellite File, No. 83, 3 January 1985, 306.TVSF.97, RG 306, USIA, Motion Picture, Sound, and Video Records Section, NARA.
76 'We Are Afghanistan', 1984, 306.9990, RG 306, USIA, Motion Picture, Sound, and Video Records Section, NARA.
77 See House Resolution 2068, 99th Congress, Foreign Relations Authorization Act, Fiscal Years 1986 and 1987, LoC, http://thomas.loc.gov/cgi-bin/bdquery/z?d099:hr2068
78 J. Milnor Roberts, 'Report of the Afghan Resistance Seminar', XVII World Anti-Communist League Conference, 3–7 September 1984, Document No. AF0 1605, *Afghanistan: The Making of US Foreign Policy*, DNSA.
79 No author given, 'Portland Man Organises Boot Lift', *Associated Press*, 27 January 1984.
80 Sue Baker, *UPI*, 18 October 1984.
81 No author given, 'U.S. Aid Not Reaching Afghan Guerrillas, Writer Says', *Associated Press*, 19 November 1984.
82 Daniel F. Gilmore, 'Afghans Short on Money, Arms', *UPI*, 26 December 1984.
83 James A. Phillips, 'US Aid for Afghan Freedom Fighters Overdue', Executive Memorandum, No. 44, Heritage Foundation, 17 February 1984, http://www.heritage.org/research/reports/1984/02/us-aid-for-afghan-freedom-fighters-overdue
84 Phillips, 'US Aid for Afghan Freedom Fighters Overdue'.

85 Roger A. Brooks and James A. Phillips, 'In Afghanistan, Moscow Ridicules the UN', Executive Memorandum, No. 51, Heritage Foundation, 8 May 1984, http://www.heritage.org/research/reports/1984/05/in-afghanistan-moscow-ridicules-the-un

86 James A. Phillips, 'Moscow Stalks the Persian Gulf', Backgrounder No. 333, Heritage Foundation, 27 February 1984, http://www.heritage.org/research/reports/1984/02/moscow-stalks-the-persian-gulf

87 Bill Keller, 'US Aid to Rebels in Nine Countries Suggested by Conservative Group', *New York Times*, 20 November 1984.

88 'News and Views from Washington', *National Security Record*, October 1985; 'News and Views from Washington', *National Security Record*, February 1986; Coll, *Ghost Wars*, pp. 101–102.

89 Lundberg, 'Politics of a Covert Action', p. 52.

90 Lundberg, 'Politics of a Covert Action', p. 28. Lundberg gives a detailed account of how Iklé and Pillsbury set about persuading the various figures on the inter-agency steering committees overseeing the Afghan programme, pp. 29–38. CIA Directorate of Intelligence, 'Afghan Situation Report', 10 January 1984, Document No. 0000535006, FOIA Collection, CIA FOIA EER. This reports that the resistance was at its strongest since the invasion though unable to launch sustained attacks in Kabul. Should the rebels be able to inflict more damage on Kabul this would bring more international attention and donations to their cause and encourage the Soviets to negotiate.

91 Paul Dean, 'Adventurer Helps Rebel Groups Fight Communist Forces', *Los Angeles Times*, 1 August 1985.

92 Free the Eagle also supported the American Angolan Public Affairs Council which lobbied for UNITA. See Ann Cooper, 'Third World Insurgent Groups Learning to Play the Washington Lobbying Game', *National Journal*, 8 February 1986. In 1984, Free the Eagle had the second highest expenditure total (behind the oil industry's lobby group) for lobbying Congress. See (no author given), 'Lobbyists' Spending in the First Quarter Was $11.75 Million', *New York Times*, 4 September 1984. At this stage, Eiva was also the director of another lobby group called 'The American Afghan Education Fund'; see Mark Tran, 'Reagan Meets Afghan Rebels', *Guardian* (London), 17 June 1986.

93 David B. Ottaway, 'Rebel Backers on Hill Press Aid Issue', *Washington Post*, 16 January 1986; Fred Kaplan, 'A CIA Loyalist Who Had Doubts on Arms Transfers', *Boston Globe*, 6 December 1986. According to Crile, *Charlie Wilson's War*, p. 416, Vincent Cannistraro was responsible for pointing the finger at McMahon due to a personal vendetta and that it was Cannistraro who informed Eiva that McMahon, along with Clair George, was blocking the supply of Stingers to the *mujahedeen*.

94 'Groups Backing Afghan Rebels Don't Even Speak to Each Other', *National Journal*, 8 February 1986.

95 Crile, *Charlie Wilson's War*, p. 417.

96 Ottaway, 'Rebels' Backers on Hill Press Aid Issue'. Humphrey appeared on the MacNeil/Lehrer News Hour on 27 December 1985 calling for mine detection equipment and anti-aircraft weapons for the *mujahedeen* as well as the severance of all diplomatic relations with Kabul.

97 Insider Report, 'News and Views from Washington', *National Security Record*, October 1985.

98 Lundberg, 'Politics of a Covert Action', pp. 29–38.

99   Crile, *Charlie Wilson's War*, p. 415. Pillsbury had advised Jesse Helms, Orrin Hatch, Chip Hecht and Malcolm Wallop. Alan J. Kuperman, 'The Stinger Missile and US Intervention in Afghanistan', *Political Science Quarterly*, Vol. 114, No. 2 (1999), p. 226. Kuperman alleges that conservative Senators had machinated to have Pillsbury assigned to the Pentagon.
100 Joan Mower, 'Economic Considerations Influenced CIA Deputy Director's Decision to Resign', *Associated Press*, 5 March 1986; David B. Ottaway and Patrick E. Tyler, 'Departure May Clear Way for More Active Policy in Third World', *Washington Post*, 5 March 1986.
101 Kuperman, 'The Stinger Missile', p. 234.
102 James Kelly, 'Press: Shifting the Attack on Leaks; CIA Director Hints at Prosecution of News Organizations', *Time*, 19 May 1986.
103 Kuperman, 'The Stinger Missile', p. 235.
104 Coll, *Ghost Wars*, p. 150. Galster, 'The Afghan Pipeline', p. 60, writes that ethnic Pashtuns from Pakistani Special Forces disguised as rebels were initially manning the stingers.
105 Yuriy Kornilov, 'Gangsters without Guns', *TASS*, 14 June 1985, from *BBC Summary of World Broadcasts*, 19 June 1985; Vladimir Bolshakov, 'Bridgeheads of Radio Aggression', *Pravda*, 9 March 1985, *BBC Summary of World Broadcasts*, 14 March 1985.
106 Viktor Vinogradov, *Krasnaya Zvezda*, 21 March 1985, *BBC Summary of World Services*, 30 March 1985; Yuriy Kornilov, 'In the Service of Slanderers', *TASS*, 27 March 1985, *BBC Summary of World Services*, 3 April 1985.
107 Satenik Harutyunyan, 'Bringing Afghanistan Home: An Analysis of USSR's Military Involvement in Afghanistan and Its Effects on Soviet Populations and Domestic Policy', *Prospect* (11 November 2011), explains how up to 1984 at least the Soviet media portrayed the Soviet army as merely supporting the Afghan army rather than involved in actual fighting.
108 Kuperman, 'The Stinger Missile', p. 239. Kuperman suggests that Gorbachev sought to put pressure on hardliners in the Politburo and military to agree to a withdrawal, and allowing media coverage and consequent negative Soviet public opinion was a tactic to facilitate this.
109 CIA, Directorate of Intelligence Report, 'Soviet Invasion of Afghanistan: Five Years After', p. 15.
110 Moghadam, 'Building Human Resources and Women's Capabilities', p. 867; Alex Marshall, 'Managing Withdrawal: Afghanistan as the Forgotten Example in Attempting Conflict Resolution and State Reconstruction', *Small Wars and Insurgencies*, Vol. 18, No. 1 (2007), p. 70, reports that the *mujahedeen* targeted schools and teachers.
111 Mohammad Yousaf and Mark Adkin, *The Bear Trap: Afghanistan's Untold Story* (London: L. Cooper, 1992), pp. 146–147. Yousaf states that while the *mujahedeen* did not intentionally target civilians they believed it acceptable in the greater cause of defeating the Soviets. Any Afghan involved in the Kabul regime was considered 'fair game' too. Harrison, *Out of Afghanistan*, pp. 154–155, recounts how Kabul went from being relatively peaceful to becoming a war-zone as CIA-supplied rockets were rained down on it by *mujahedeen* leading to many civilian casualties.
112 A USIA report on foreign media in thirty-five countries following the sixth anniversary of the invasion in January 1986 showed widespread international condemnation of the Soviet intervention in Afghanistan. See USIA Foreign Media

Analysis, 'Foreign Media Condemn USSR on 6th Anniversary of Soviet Invasion of Afghanistan', Office of Research, 21 January 1986, RG 306, FMA 1-21-86, NARA.
113   A USIA poll in early 1986 showed Western Europeans and Canadian largely equated the intentions of Gorbachev and Reagan believing both wanted world peace but were still ready to resort to military force to attain objectives. USIA Briefing Paper, 'Europeans and Canadians Urge Second US-Soviet Summit', Office of Research, 16 April 1986, RG 306, P 49, Box 3, NARA.
114   Kuperman in 'The Stinger Missile' gives details of various reports on the effectiveness of the Stinger and whether it provoked or prolonged Soviet withdrawal and concludes it was unlikely to have precipitated Soviet withdrawal, p. 253; Marshall, 'Managing Withdrawal', p. 75, reaches a similar conclusion pointing out that Gorbachev had already taken the decision to withdraw and was seeking way to implement it politically.

Chapter 5

1   NSC, National Security Decision Directive 166, 'US Policy, Programs and Strategy in Afghanistan', 27 March 1985, National Security Decision Directives, 1981–1989, RRL.
2   Denis Steven Rutkus, 'Television Network Evening News Coverage of Afghanistan: A Perspective after Eight Years of War', Congressional Research Service Report, 4 February 1988, p. 6, AF0 2120, *Afghanistan: The Making of US Foreign Policy*, DNSA. The networks analysed by the report were ABC, CBS and NBC.
3   Orrin Hatch, 'Don't Forget the Afghans', *New York Times*, 22 November 1985.
4   Louis Dupree, 'Tainted News about the War in Afghanistan', *New York Times*, 22 June 1984.
5   Theodore Eliot, Fletcher School of Law and Diplomacy, 7 December 1984, Electronic Dialogue Series, 306-ED-37, RG 306, USIA, Motion Picture, Sound, and Video Records Section, NARA.
6   Letter to Robert McFarlane from Walter Raymond, 'Afghan Political Action', 30 March 1984, NSC, Executive Secretariat, Near East and South Asia, Country File, Afghanistan, Box 34, RRL.
7   Letter to McFarlane from Raymond, 'Afghan Political Action'.
8   Letter to Farlane from Raymond, 'Afghan Political Action'.
9   Thomas Gouttierre, House Foreign Affairs Committee, Subcommittee on Human Rights, 'Hearing on the Phenomenon of Torture', 98th Congress, 2nd Session, 15 May 1984, p. 127, LoC.
10 Dr Jack Wheeler, Congressional Task Force on Afghanistan (CTF), 'Hearing on Famine', 25 February 1985, pp. 92–95, AF0 1620, *Afghanistan: The Making of US Foreign Policy*, DNSA. Wheeler lists the 'big five' as the *New York Times*, *Washington Post*, CBS, ABC and NBC.
11 Wattenberg was a scholar with the American Enterprise Institute and also involved with Midge Decter's Committee for a Free World. See Vaiise, *Neoconservatism*, p. 11; Sara Diamond, *Road to Dominion: Right Wing Movements and Political Power in the United States* (New York: Guilford Press, 1995), pp. 192 and 285.
12 CTF on Afghanistan, 'Hearing on Effective Public Diplomacy', 17 June 1985, LoC.
13 Humphreys, CTF on Afghanistan, 'Hearing on Effective Public Diplomacy', p. 1.
14 Brzezinski, CTF on Afghanistan, 'Hearing on Effective Public Diplomacy', pp. 3–5.

15 Wattenberg, CTF, 'Hearing on Effective Public Diplomacy', pp. 31–32.
16 Wattenberg, CTF on Afghanistan, 'Hearing on Effective Public Diplomacy', pp. 60–61.
17 Dupree, CTF on Afghanistan, 'Hearing on Effective Public Diplomacy', p. 34.
18 Dupree, CTF on Afghanistan, 'Hearing on Effective Public Diplomacy', pp. 37–39.
19 Magnus, CTF on Afghanistan, 'Hearing on Effective Public Diplomacy', p. 40.
20 Magnus, CTF on Afghanistan, 'Hearing on Effective Public Diplomacy', pp. 44–50.
21 Scott, *Deciding to Intervene*, pp. 58–59.
22 Lundberg, 'Politics of a Covert Action', p. 26.
23 Commission on Security and Co-Operation in Europe (CSCE), 'Hearing on Soviet Violations of Human Rights in Afghanistan', 4 December 1985, 99th Congress, 1st Session, p. 12.
24 Congressman Gary Ackerman, CSCE, 'Hearing on Soviet Violations of Human Rights in Afghanistan', p. 19.
25 Lohbeck, CSCE, 'Hearing on Soviet Violations of Human Rights in Afghanistan', pp. 40–48.
26 D'Amato, CSCE, 'Hearing on Soviet Violations of Human Rights in Afghanistan', p. 52.
27 Kirkpatrick, CTF on Afghanistan, 'Hearing on Soviet Strategy and Its Implications for the West', 11 March 1985, p. 33, AF0 1623, *Afghanistan: The Making of US Foreign Policy*, DNSA.
28 Afghan Digest No. 3, 1985, 306.9047, USIA, Motion Picture, Sound, and Video Records Section, NARA.
29 TV Satellite File, No. 34, 26 January 1984, 306.TVSF.47, USIA, Moving Images Relating to US Domestic and International Activities, 1982–1999, NARA.
30 Walter Raymond, Memorandum for Afghan Political Group, 'Summary of Afghan Political Action Meeting (Restricted), 29 March 1984', 30 March 1984, NSC, Executive Secretariat, Country File, Near East and South Asia, Afghanistan 3/30/84–5/18/84, Box 34, RRL.
31 James A. Phillips, 'Afghan Freedom Fighters Still Need US Help', Backgrounder No. 1, Heritage Foundation, 18 December 1985, http://www.heritage.org/research/reports/1985/12/afghan-freedom-fighters-still-need-us-help
32 James A. Phillips, 'Updating US Strategy for Helping Afghan Freedom Fighters', Backgrounder No. 552, Heritage Foundation, 22 December 1986, http://www.heritage.org/research/reports/1986/12/updating-us-strategy-for-helping-afghan-freedom-fighters
33 Phillips, 'Updating US Strategy for Helping Afghan Freedom Fighters'.
34 Elaine Sciolino, 'Four Soviet Deserters Tell of Cruel Afghanistan War', *New York Times*, 3 August, 1984; Phil Gailey, 'Soviet Deserter Is Called Unwilling to Work', *New York Times*, 20 December 1984.
35 Gates, *From the Shadows*, p. 358.
36 J. Milnor Roberts, 'Report of the Afghan Resistance Seminar', XVII World Anti-Communist League Conference, 3–7 September 1984, AF0 1605, *Afghanistan: The Making of US Foreign Policy*, DNSA. The World Anti-Communist League is variously described as 'rightist' and pro-Contra see Opinion, 'Franchising the Reagan Doctrine', *New York Times*, 8 February 1987; Jeff Gerth and Wayne King, 'Private Pipeline to the Contras: A Vast Network', *New York Times*, 22 October 1986; Thomas Bodenheimer and Robert Gould, *Rollback!: Right-Wing Power in U. S. Foreign Policy* (Boston, MA: South End Press, 1989), p. 57.

37 Rone Tempest, 'Afghan Rebel Gateway; Peshawar: Many Lured by Intrigue', *Los Angeles Times*, 12 May 1986.
38 Mary Williams Walsh, 'Mission Afghanistan', *Columbia Journalism Review*, January/February 1990, pp. 27–36.
39 Coll, *Ghost Wars*, p. 167.
40 President Reagan, 'Statement Following a Meeting with Leaders of the Afghan Resistance Alliance', 16 June 1986, *PPP*, RRL; Joan Mower, 'Guerrilla Groups Use Lobbyists to Win US Aid', *Los Angeles Times*, 27 July 1986; Doyle McManus and Sarah Fritz, 'Rebel Lobby Becomes New Growth Industry', *Los Angeles Times*, 2 September 1986.
41 George Shultz, 'New Realities and New Ways of Thinking', *Foreign Affairs*, Vol. 63, No. 4 (Spring 1985), p. 716. re: information technology and the East–West ideological conflict.
42 William J. Casey, 'Remarks at the Hoover Institute', Stanford University, Chicago, 3 April 1984, Document No. 0001446245, *FOIA Collection*, CIA FOIA EER.
43 Snyder, *Warriors of Disinformation*, p. 213; Norman Burger, Memorandum for the file, 'Afghan Media Project – Briefing of Evaluation Panel on Project Status', 11 April 1986, USIA Bureau of Programs, Historical Collection, RG 306, A1 (1061), Box 14, NARA. This memo mentions AP and Reuters interest in photographs as long as they were provided with proper documentation. In an interview with the author Stephen Olsson described travelling to London to establish contacts with Vis News, WTN and Agence France Presse, but he found the print news much harder to find distribution for than the photographs or videos.
44 Charles E. Shutt, Hearst Metronome News, 'The Afghan Media Project: Program Report Period November 1986', USIA Bureau of Programs, RG 306, A1 (1061), Box 15, NARA.
45 From the start of the project the USIA was debating whether output from the AMP would be subject to the restrictions of the Smith-Mundt Act which forbad domestic dissemination of USIA material. See this letter from Merry Lymn, attorney advisor to the project, to Delores Clark, Boston University, 'Copy of Law which Bans Domestic Dissemination of Materials Produced by USIA', 30 June 1986, AF0 1746, *Afghanistan: The Making of US Foreign Policy*, DNSA.
46 Richard Hoagland, Memorandum for the File, 'Agency Documents about the AMP', 8 January 1986, USIA Bureau of Programs, RG 306, A1 (1061), Box 14, NARA.
47 Memorandum to Frank Carlucci from Melvyn Levitsky, 'Afghanistan: PD Action Plan', 12 May 1987, AF0 1988, *Afghanistan: The Making of US Foreign Policy*, DNSA.
48 'Faculty Protests Plan to Teach Afghan Rebels', *Washington Times*, 22 August 1986.
49 Text of commentary, Radio Moscow in English for North America, 'USIA Plans for Afghan Anti Government Media Coverage', 21 December 1985, *BBC Summary of World Broadcasts*, 24 December 1985.
50 Text of Commentary of Bakhtar Political Observer, 'US Intensifying Psychological Warfare against the DRA', *BBC Summary of World Broadcasts*, 22 August 1986; Text of Commentary, 'USIA Plans for Afghan Anti Government Media Coverage', 21 December 1985, *BBC Summary of World Broadcasts*, 24 December 1985.
51 Lundberg, 'Politics of a Covert Action', p. 26.
52 Galster, 'The Afghan Pipeline', *Covert Action Quarterly*, p. 59; Snyder, *Warriors of Disinformation*, p. 206. Snyder writes that he first suggested the idea to Wick on 18 March 1985 just nine days before NSDD 166 was authorized. Lohbeck, *Holy*

War, Unholy Victory, p. 166, also states that Raymond approached Humphrey with the idea for training *mujahedeen* to video the war to increase worldwide coverage.
53 Parry and Kornbluh, 'Iran-Contra's Untold Story', p. 4.
54 See letters to Humphrey from USIA Deputy Director Marvin Stone, 20 March 1986, WHSOF, Vincent Cannistraro Files, Afghanistan 05/15/1986–05/23/1986, Box 1, RRL and again on 17 April 1986, AF0 1699, *Afghanistan: The Making of US Foreign Policy*, DNSA, offering updates on the progress of the AMP and other public diplomacy initiatives.
55 Memorandum to Michael Schneider from Saul Gefter, 'Afghan Media Project Update', 9 October 1985, AF0 1651, *Afghanistan: The Making of US Foreign Policy*, DNSA.
56 According to his obituary Koehler made a number of 'sensitive' reports on the Soviet invasion of Afghanistan for the USIA, the NSC and Congress. A friend of Reagan, in 1987, he was appointed assistant to the president and director of communications. He also served as a consultant and special advisor to Wick. See John O. Koehler, Death Notice, 2 October 2012, Stamfordadvocate.com.
57 Memorandum to Schneider from Gefter, 'Afghan Media Project Update', 9 October 1985, AF0 1651, *Afghanistan: The Making of US Foreign Policy*, DNSA. Koehler was already involved in other work for the USIA's Bureau of Programs; see Letter from Counsel to A/D, 'Re: Consultant for the Afghan Media Center Project', Undated, USIA Bureau of Programs, A1 (1061), Box 14, RG 306, NARA.
58 'FY 85 Supplemental: Congressional Amendment', USIA Bureau of Programs, AI (1061), Box 14, RG 306, NARA.
59 Memorandum to Gefter from Lymn, 'Subject: Request for Guidance', 12 November 1985, USIA Bureau of Programs, A1 (1061), Box 14, RG 306, NARA.
60 Memorandum for the file from Richard Hoagland, 'Questions from Michael Hahn', 8 January 1986, USIA Bureau of Programs, RG306, A1 (1061), Box 14, NARA.
61 The AMP would later become known as the Afghan Media Resource Center (AMRC).
62 Steven Olsson, Interview with Author, 11 February 2013.
63 Olsson interview. The UNO did work with the NED on educational programmes within Afghanistan soon after.
64 Memorandum to Michael Schneider from Saul Gefter, 'PD/H Recommendations Regarding Grant Proposals – Concurrence with Evaluation Panel', 31 December 1985, AF0 1675, *Afghanistan: The Making of US Foreign Policy*, DNSA.
65 Norman Burger, Memorandum for the file, 'Afghan Media Project – Briefing of Evaluation Panel on Project Status', 11 April 1986, USIA Bureau of Programs, RG 306, A1 (1061), Box 14, NARA; Letters to Maitre (BU) and Shutt (King Features) from Gefter, 2 April 1986, USIA Bureau of Programs, RG306, A1 (1061), Box 14, NARA, referred to a list provided by the USIA of individuals who 'expressed an interest in the Afghan Media Project' or who had 'special expertise on Afghanistan'.
66 Charles E. Shutt, Hearst Metronome News, 'Afghan Media Project: Program Report Period November 1986', USIA Bureau of Programs, RG 306, A1 (1061), Box 15, NARA.
67 Memorandum to John Mosher from Saul Gefter, 'Afghan Media Staff: Weekly Report', 18 July 1986, AF0 1764, *Afghanistan: The Making of US Foreign Policy*, DNSA.
68 Richard Bernstein, 'For Journalism Dean, Questions about Objectivity', *New York Times*, 3 November 1987.

69 Richard Hoagland, Memorandum for the file, 'Boston University Withdraws from Project', 22 November 1985, AF0 1657, *Afghanistan: The Making of US Foreign Policy*, DNSA.
70 Various Teachers at BU to Provost Jon Westling, 'Letter of Support for Afghan Media Project', 25 November 1985, AF0 1659, *Afghanistan: The Making of US Foreign Policy*, DNSA.
71 Various Teachers at BU to Westling, 'Letter of Support for Afghan Media Project', 25 November 1985.
72 Debra Ann Hatten and Robin Richardson, 'Boston University Project to Train Afghans Stirs Debate', *Christian Science Monitor*, 30 October 1986.
73 Pat M. Holt, 'Bad Precedents at USIA', *Christian Science Monitor*, 4 September 1985.
74 Professor Bernard Rubin believed the project worthwhile in its objective to expose Soviet atrocities. Bernard was involved previously with USIA and consulted for other government agencies see his obituary 'Bernard Rubin, 64, Professor of Government at BU', 6 October 1991, *Boston Globe*.
75 Art Jahnke, 'Cold Warriors' *Boston Magazine*, February 1987. Attached to memorandum to Joseph O'Connell from Saul Gefter, 5 February 1987, AF0 1907, *Afghanistan: The Making of US Foreign Policy*, DNSA.
76 Bob Drogin, 'Boston U and Government Ties Spur Debate on Ethics', *Los Angeles Times*, 22 November 1986.
77 Richard Bernstein, 'For Journalism Dean, Questions about Objectivity', *New York Times*, 3 November 1987.
78 Ross Glebspan and Jonathan Kaufman, 'BU Appointee Draws Concern of Journalists: Some Fear Ideology Will Color Academics', *Boston Globe*, 13 September 1987. Galster also points out that Maitre, inexplicably, had military clearance and was involved in the debriefing of US pilots following the bombing of Libya. See Galster, 'The Afghan Pipeline', p. 59, n. 58. Oliver North was on the NSC staff and subsequently involved in the Iran-*Contra* affair, which sought to divert funds illegally to the Nicaraguan Contras.
79 'Situation Room List', 21 March 1983, *The Iran-Contra Affair: The Making of a Scandal, 1983–1988*, DNSA. In May 1982 Wick had contacted White House Chief of Staff, James Baker, to invite him to attend lunch with Springer and Maitre when they were visiting Washington see letter to James Baker from Charles Wick, 12 May 1982, WHORM af Wick, Box 77, RRL.
80 'Head of USIA Secretly Taped Reagan Aide', *New York Times*, 4 January 1984.
81 See Alexander Cockburn, 'Four Men in North's Safe: The Use of Intellectuals', *The Nation*, Vol. 244, 21 March 1987, p. 351; Vaisse, *Neoconservatism*, p. 214.
82 International Business Communications was a public relations firm that ran pro-*Contra* ad campaigns funded by the State Department and brought *Contra* rebels to the United States to lobby for funds. See *Associated Press*, 'Secret US Contract for Pro-*Contra* TV Ads', 8 February 1987. Also see Lawrence E. Walsh, independent counsel, *Final Report of the Independent Counsel for Iran/Contra Matters, Volume I: Investigations and Prosecutions*, 4 August 1993, Washington, DC, Chapter Thirteen for IBC's role in the Iran-*Contra* affair.
83 Telegram to the Department of State from the US embassy, Honduras, 'The Visit of Ellie Weisel: The Plight of the Miskito Refugees', 12 January 1984, *The Iran-Contra Affair*, DNSA.
84 Bob Drogin, 'Boston U and Government Ties Spur Debate on Ethics', *Los Angeles Times*, 22 November 1986.

85 'Actions to Generate Support for the Contras', 20 March 1985, *The Iran-Contra Affair*, DNSA.
86 Richard Bernstein, 'For Journalism Dean, Questions about Objectivity', *New York Times*, 3 November 1987.
87 Bernstein, 'For Journalism Dean, Questions about Objectivity'; Fox Butterfield, 'The Storm Center of Boston University', *New York Times*, 12 April 1987; Diamond, *Roads to Dominion*, p. 382.
88 Memorandum to Saul Gefter from Robert Francis Smith, 'Afghan Media Panel Decision', 23 December 1985, AF0 1674, *Afghanistan: The Making of US Foreign Policy*, DNSA; C. B. Groce, Memorandum for the record, 'Afghan Media Project Task Force', 20 December 1985, AF0 1673, *Afghanistan: The Making of US Foreign Policy*, DNSA.
89 Memorandum to Merry Lymn from Thomas Harvey, USIA, 'Afghanistan Project', 25 September 1985, USIA Bureau of Programs, RG 306, A1 (1061), Box 14, NARA.
90 Butterfield, 'The Storm Center of Boston University'.
91 Butterfield, 'The Storm Center of Boston University'. In 1980, the Committee to Save Boston University which consisted of a number of academics at the university wrote to the *New York Review of Books* alleging Silber endorsed 'disorder, harassment, and intimidation of free speech' as well as censorship and the violation of the civil liberties of staff and students. Furthermore, he used his administrative powers to punish critics by denying them tenure or merit raises. See Helen Vendler, Howard Zinn, Shane Hunt, S.M. Miller, Freda Rebelsky, et al., 'Academic Freedom at BU', *New York Review of Books*, 12 June 1980.
92 Butterfield, 'The Storm Center of Boston University'.
93 Fox Butterfield, 'Boston U Focuses on Disinformation', *New York Times*, 18 November 1986.
94 Bernard Redmont, *Risks Worth Taking: Odyssey of a Foreign Correspondent* (Maryland: University Press of America, 1992), p. 201.
95 Jake Smith, *Dinner with Mobutu: A Chronicle of My Life and Times* (Philadelphia: Xlibris Corporation, 2005), pp. 146–153.
96 Memorandum to Charles Z. Wick from Michael Schneider, 'Letter from John R. Silber to the Director', 6 December 1985, AF0 1670, *Afghanistan: The Making of US Foreign Policy*, DNSA.
97 Smith, *Dinner with Mobutu*, p. 143.
98 Lohbeck makes no mention of any involvement in his memoirs but described the project as a blatant attempt to influence the news by the US government and that it was impossible to find objective journalists amongst the *mujahedeen*. See *Holy War, Unholy Victory*, pp. 166–167. However, Saul Gefter, the program director, recommended Lohbeck for the USIA satellite speakers program in October 1986; see 'Afghan Media Staff, Weekly Report', 17 October 1986, DNSA AMP, and in June 1986 was listed to contact Lohbeck to generate media coverage of Rabbani's visit to Washington (see p. 280 for more on this trip). Olsson stated that Lohbeck was 'deeply involved' with the Mercy Fund when it was attempting to assume control of the AMP.
99 'The Afghan Media Project: A Proposal Submitted to the USIA by Boston University', 9 December 1985, AF0 1669, *Afghanistan: The Making of US Foreign Policy*, DNSA. Initially Hearst was charged with developing the news distribution element of the project not BU.
100 Drogin, 'Boston U and Government Ties Spur Debate on Ethics'.

101 'The Afghan Media Project: A Proposal Submitted to the USIA by Boston University', 9 December 1985, AF0 1669, *Afghanistan: The Making of US Foreign Policy*, DNSA.
102 Memorandum to Michael Schneider from Saul Gefter, 'Afghan Media Project Update', 15 January 1986, AF0 1682, *Afghanistan: The Making of US Foreign Policy*, DNSA.
103 Report by John O. Koehler on his Trip to Pakistan and Europe to Assess the Current Situation of Media Coverage about Afghanistan, 6 October 1985, p. 2. This report is attached to a letter to Ronald Goldman from Saul Gefter, 'Reception of Concept Paper for Afghan Media Project', 30 September 1985, AF0 1648, *Afghanistan: The Making of US Foreign Policy*, DNSA.
104 Report by Chullaine O'Reilly on BU's Proposal to Train Personnel in the Afghan News Agency, 30 October 1986, AF0 1841, *Afghanistan: The Making of US Foreign Policy*, DNSA.
105 Oliver Roy, *Islam and Resistance in Afghanistan*, Second Edition (Cambridge: Cambridge University Press, 1990), p. 122. Roy details how the Pakistan military government preferred the resistance remain divided for this reason.
106 Memorandum to Schneider from Gefter, 'Afghan Media Project Update', 15 January 1986, AF0 1682, *Afghanistan: The Making of US Foreign Policy*, DNSA; in this memo Gefter states that Undersecretary of State for Political Affairs, Michael Armacost, will discuss the project with Pakistan officials when visiting the country. In a letter to Senator Humphrey in April 1986, USIA Deputy Director Marvin Stone wrote that 'even after Mike Armacost's visit to Islamabad, we are still receiving mixed signals from the Government of Pakistan on the Afghan Media Project'. See letter to Humphrey from Stone, 'Some Other Initiatives USIA is Pursuing to Focus World Attention on Afghanistan', AF0 1699, *Afghanistan: The Making of US Foreign Policy*, DNSA.
107 Hearst Metronome News, 'Work Plan for Afghan News Service, Peshawar, Pakistan', November 1986, p. 1, RG 306, A1 (1061), Box 16, USIA Bureau of Programs, NARA; Memorandum for the Deputy Director, USIA, from Charles Horner, 'Afghan Media Project: Your Meeting with Ambassador Deane Hinton', 12 November 1986, AF0 1860, *Afghanistan: The Making of US Foreign Policy*, DNSA.
108 USIA Report, 'Afghan Media Project', 1 October 1986, AF0 1805, *Afghanistan: The Making of US Foreign Policy*, DNSA.
109 AMP-BU Training Project Update, 11 March 1987, AF0 1945, *Afghanistan: The Making of US Foreign Policy*, DNSA.
110 Letter to Charles Wick from the CTF on Afghanistan, US Senate, 10 June 1986, USIA Bureau of Programs, RG306, A1 (1061), Box 14, NARA; Letter to Charles Wick from Senator Gordon Humphrey, 17 November 1986, USIA Bureau of Programs, RG 306, A1 (1061), Box 14, NARA.
111 Drogin, 'Boston U and Government Ties Spur Debate on Ethics'. The impetus for King Features' action seemed to be when Michael Gartner, head of the America Society of Newspaper Editors and an editor himself, wrote to King Features saying he, as an editor, could not deal with a news bureau involved in such a project.
112 Norman Burger, Memorandum for the file, 'Afghan Media Project – Briefing of Evaluation Panel on Project Status', 11 April 1986, USIA Bureau of Programs, RG 306, A1 (1061), Box 14, NARA. The McCollum Amendment (H. Amdt. 134) amended the Department of Defense Authorisation Act, 1986 (H. R. 1872) which 'granted the Secretary of Defense permission to provide nonlethal assistance to displaced persons or refugees due to the Soviet invasion of Afghanistan. The Secretary may use excess supplies or items given to the Department for such relief. He may use the

most economical military or commercial air transport available. The assistance is to be given high priority and the U.S. portion of the distribution may not be delegated outside the DOD. International aspects of the distribution is to be done by private volunteer organizations designated by AID or by AID if such suitable organization is not available'.

113   Memorandum to Mosher from Gefter, 'Afghan Media Staff: Weekly Report', 18 July 1986, AF0 1764, *Afghanistan: The Making of US Foreign Policy*, DNSA; Press Guidance Document, 'Status of the Afghan Media Project', 5 February 1987, AF0 1906, *Afghanistan: The Making of US Foreign Policy*, DNSA.
114   Memorandum for the deputy director from Horner, 'Afghan Media Project: Your Meeting with Ambassador Deane Hinton', 12 November 1986; Memorandum for Walter Raymond, NSC, from Stanton Burnett, USIA, 'Afghan Media Project – Operating Funds Requirement', 12 August 1986, USIA Bureau of Programs, RG 306, A1 (1061), Box 14, NARA. Letter to Farzana McCormick from Saul Gefter, USIA, 5 August 1986, USIA Bureau of Programs, RG 306, A1 (1061), Box 14, NARA; M. Feltman, 'Notes of AMP Meeting', 31 October 1986, AF0 1844, *Afghanistan: The Making of US Foreign Policy*, DNSA.
115   David Barboza and Narendra Nandoe, 'University Seeks to Expand Its Role in Afghan Media Project', *Daily Free Press*, 10 December 1986, AF0 1869, *Afghanistan: The Making of US Foreign Policy*, DNSA.
116   Barboza and Nandoe, 'University Seeks to Expand Its Role in Afghan Media Project'.
117   Letter to Gefter from Maitre, 7 November 1986, USIA Bureau of Programs, RG 306, A1 (1061), Box 14, NARA.
118   Memorandum for the deputy director from Horner, 'Afghan Media Project: Your Meeting with Ambassador Deane Hinton'. The Mercy Fund would later change its name to the Council for International Development (CFID), Nigel Nicholds and John Borton, 'The Changing Role of NGOs in the Provision of Relief and Rehabilitation Assistance: Case Study 1 – Afghanistan/Pakistan', Working Paper, No. 74, Oversees Development Institute (January 1994), p. 79. Campaigne, a conservative activist, was also involved with US *Contra* supporters, see Clifford D. May, 'Kemp Gains Favor in His Latin Visit', *New York Times*, 13 September 1987; Jacqueline Huard, 'N.H. Conservative Caucus Plans Political Pressure', *Nashua Telegraph*, 30 August 1975. Campaigne served as a state director on The Conservative Caucus along with Senator Gordon Humphrey, see James C. Roberts, *The Conservative Decade: Emerging Leaders of the 1980s* (Westport, CT: Arlington House, 1980), p. 50.
119   Mary Williams Walsh, 'Strained Mercy', *The Progressive*, Vol. 54, No. 5 (May 1990), pp. 23–26.
120   Erwin Knoll, 'Journalistic Jihad', *The Progressive*, Vol. 54, No. 5 (May 1990), pp. 17–22.
121   Telegram to Kent Obee, US Embassy, Islamabad from Gefter, USIA, 'Afghan Media Project – Implementation', 6 November 1986, AF0 1853, *Afghanistan: The Making of US Foreign Policy*, DNSA.
122   Memorandum to deputy director from Horner, 'Afghan Media Project: Your Meeting with Ambassador Deane Hinton'.
123   Telegram to USIA, Washington from Kent Obee, Islamabad, 'Afghan Media Project, Nick Mills Consultations', 2 December 1986, AF0 1865, *Afghanistan: The Making of US Foreign Policy*, DNSA.
124   Memorandum for Mosher from Gefter, 'Afghan Media Project: Update', 13 February 1987, AF0 1916, *Afghanistan: The Making of US Foreign Policy*, DNSA.

125 Telegram to the USIA, Washington from the US Embassy, Islamabad, 23 February 1987, 'Afghan Media Project: Next Steps', AF0 1925, *Afghanistan: The Making of US Foreign Policy*, DNSA.
126 Olsson became involved in the project around this time – January/February 1987. See telegram to the US Embassy, Islamabad from USIA, Washington, 'Afghan Media Project: Next Steps', 28 February 1987, AF0 1930, *Afghanistan: The Making of US Foreign Policy*, DNSA.
127 Olsson interview.
128 Burger, 'Afghan Media Project – Briefing of Evaluation Panel on Project Status'.
129 Guilde du Raid was one of the largest NGOs involved in Cash-for-Food programmes in Afghanistan. See Nicholds and Borton, 'The Changing Role of NGOs', p. 54.
130 For information on the political affiliations of Marechaux and Edel, see Observatoire de L'action Humanitaire (Aid Watch), http://www.observatoire-humanitaire.org/
131 Letter to Marechaux from Richard Hoagland, 31 January 1986, USIA Bureau of Programs, Box 14, A1 (1061), RG 306, NARA. Hoagland was also the USIS Branch Public Affairs Officer in Peshawar.
132 Telegram to the USIA, Washington from Obee, US Embassy, Islamabad, 'Afghan Media Project: US Consultants' Visit', 30 July 1986, AF0 1775, *Afghanistan: The Making of US Foreign Policy*, DNSA.
133 Richard Hoagland, Memorandum for the file, 'Telcon with Richard Bird', 6 January 1986, USIA Bureau of Programs, Box 14, A1 (1061), RG 306, NARA. The German media project had links to the German Afghan Committee run by Dietrich Kantal who was also involved in an organization called Aid on Want that provided humanitarian aid to UNITA in Angola; see Augusta Conchiglia, *Unita, Myth and Reality* (London: ECASAAMA/UK, 1990), p. 60.
134 Note to Mosher from Hoagland, 'Briefing for Dr. Bruno Heck on 1/16/86 at 10 a.m. in Room 550', 15 January 1986, AF0 1683, *Afghanistan: The Making of US Foreign Policy*, DNSA; Memorandum to Gefter from Hoagland, 'Meeting with Dr. Bruno Heck about German-American Cooperation for the Afghan Media Project', 16 January 1986, USIA Bureau of Programs, Box 14, A1 (1061), RG 306, NARA.
135 Memorandum to Gefter from Hoagland, 'Meeting with Dr. Bruno Heck about German–American Cooperation for the Afghan Media Project'.
136 The DAK had ten members when first formed in 1984, and by 1988 this number stood at only twenty while managing a multi-million dollar annual budget. It carefully vetted any new members and did not allow foreigners, even Afghans, to join. *Der Speigel* likened it to an exclusive super-rich golf club. See 'Reiner Klüngel', *Der Speigel*, 30 October 1988.
137 Baitenmann, 'NGOs and the Afghan War', p. 82.
138 ZDF is a German publicly funded television broadcaster. For the details of the proposed German–US media project cooperation, see this memorandum to Mosher from Gefter, 'Afghan Media Project Implementation – Proposed Cooperation with German Media Project on Alternative Action Plan Status Report', 3 June 1986, AF0 1722, *Afghanistan: The Making of US Foreign Policy*, DNSA. For information on Lowenthal's conservative credentials, see Damir Skenderovic, *The Radical Right in Switzerland: Continuity and Change*, 1945–2000 (Oxford: Berghahn Books, 2009), pp. 204–205; Ciarán Ó Maoláin, *The Radical Right – A World Directory* (London: Longman, 1987), p. 128. For DAK's links to the CFA see No author given, 'Reiner Klüngel'.
139 Burger, 'Afghan Media Project – Briefing of Evaluation Panel on Project Status'.

140 Memorandum for Lois Hermann from Richard Hoagland, 'Press Queries about Afghan Media Project', 8 January 1986, USIA Bureau of Programs, RG 306, A1 (1061), Box 14, NARA.
141 Telegram to the US Embassy, Islamabad from USIA, Washington, 'Afghan Media Project – Exposure', 19 February 1987, AF0 1919, *Afghanistan: The Making of US Foreign Policy*, DNSA. This telegram refers to inquiries from CBS and the *Asian Wall Street Journal*.
142 Telegram to the USIA, Washington from US Embassy, Islamabad, 'Afghan Media Project: Next Steps', 23 February 1987, AF0 1925, *Afghanistan: The Making of US Foreign Policy*, DNSA; Telegram to USIA, Washington from Kent Obee, US Embassy, Islamabad, 'Afghan Media Project: In the Headlines Again', 26 January 1987, AF0 1898, *Afghanistan: The Making of US Foreign Policy*, DNSA.
143 Eloise Salholz and Donna Foote, 'Journalism School for Afghan Rebels', *Newsweek*, 30 March 1987, p. 75.
144 Memorandum for Kent Obee from Saul Gefter, 'Afghan Media Project: Publicity/Atmospherics', 26 February 1987, AF0 1929, *Afghanistan: The Making of US Foreign Policy*, DNSA.
145 Dennis Kux, *The United States and Pakistan, 1947–2000: Disenchanted Allies* (Baltimore: The Johns Hopkins University Press, 2001), pp. 282–286.
146 Memorandum for Richard Bisssell, USAID, from Saul Gefter, 'Boston University Afghan Media Project, Program Reports, January and February 1987', 8 April 1987, AF0 1958, *Afghanistan: The Making of US Foreign Policy*, DNSA; Telegram to US Embassy, Islamabad from USIA, Washington, 'Afghan Media Project: Next Steps', 28 February 1987, AF0 1930, *Afghanistan: The Making of US Foreign Policy*, DNSA; Telegram to USIA, Washington from US Embassy, Islamabad, 'Afghan Media Project: Next Steps', 23 February 1987, AF0 1925, *Afghanistan: The Making of US Foreign Policy*, DNSA.
147 Memorandum for Mosher from Gefter, 'Afghan Media Project: Update', 13 February 1987, AF0 1916, *Afghanistan: The Making of US Foreign Policy*, DNSA.
148 Memorandum for Mosher from Gefter, 'Afghan Media Project: Update Addendum', 4 February 1987, AF0 1905, *Afghanistan: The Making of US Foreign Policy*, DNSA.
149 Telegram to US Embassy, Islamabad from Gefter, USIA, Washington, 'Afghan Media Project: Next Steps', 28 February 1987, AF0 1930, *Afghanistan: The Making of US Foreign Policy*, DNSA.
150 Memorandum for Bisssell from Gefter, 'Boston University, Afghan Media Project Program Reports, January and February 1987'.
151 Memorandum for Mosher from Gefter, 'AMP – BU Training Program Update', 11 March 1987, AF0 1945, *Afghanistan: The Making of US Foreign Policy*, DNSA.
152 Memorandum for Mosher from Gefter, 'AMP – BU Training Program Update'; Memorandum for Michael Pistor, NEA, from Saul Gefter, 'Afghan Media Project – Talking Points for Your Meeting with Senator Humphrey', 29 April 1987, USIA Bureau of Programs, RG 306, A1 (1061), Box 14, NARA.
153 Michael Pistor, 'Action Plan on Afghan Programming Initiatives', 16 March 1987, *Afghanistan: The Making of US Foreign Policy*, DNSA.
154 Smith, *Dinner with Mobutu*, p. 160.
155 Report by Koehler International Limited for Dean Joachim Maitre, BU, 14 November 1987, p. 2, USIA Bureau of Programs, RG 306, A1 (1061), Box 14, NARA.
156 Letter to Michael Pistor, NEA, USIA, from Maitre, BU, 'Subject: Interim Report', 10 December 1987, USIA Bureau of Programs, RG 306, A1 (1061), Box 14, NARA.

157 Report by Koehler International Limited, p. 8.
158 Report by Koehler International Limited, p. 8.
159 Letter to John Dixon, USIA, from Maitre, BU, 7 December 1987, USIA Bureau of Programs, RG 306, A1 (1061), Box 14, NARA; letter to Dixon, USIA, from Maitre, BU, 10 December 1987, USIA Bureau of Programs, RG 306, A1 (1061), Box 14, NARA.
160 Letter to Maitre from Michael Pistor, 11 December 1987, USIA Bureau of Programs, RG 306, A1 (1061), Box 14, NARA.
161 Olsson interview.
162 'BU-launched Afghan Journalism Project Created Historic Treasury That's Now in Demand', *BU Bridge*, Vol. 5, No. 14 (23 November 2001), https://www.bu.edu/bridge/archive/2001/11-23/afghanmedia.htm.
163 Letter to Professor Bluestone et al. from BU Provost Jon Westling, 29 November 1985, AF0 1661, *Afghanistan: The Making of US Foreign Policy*, DNSA.
164 Snyder, *Warriors of Disinformation*, p. 210.
165 Ibid., p. 218.
166 Ibid., p. 215.
167 Department of State, 'Afghanistan: Public Diplomacy Action Plan', 29 April 1987, AF0 1977, *Afghanistan: The Making of US Foreign Policy*, DNSA; Report by Chullaine O'Reilly on Boston University's Proposal to Train Personnel in the Afghan News Agency; Snyder, *Warriors of Disinformation*, p. 215.
168 The AMRC Afghan Media Archiving Project, National Audio Visual Conservation Center, Library of Congress Packard Campus, Culpepper, Virginia, US.
169 Letter to Peter McPherson, USAID, from Marvin L. Stone, deputy director, USIA, November 1986, USIA Bureau of Programs, RG 306, A1 (1061), Box 14, NARA.
170 Bernice Buresh, a former *Newsweek* Boston bureau chief and, at that time, associate professor of journalism at BU quoted in Art Jahnke's 'Cold Warriors', *Boston Magazine*, 5 February 1987, AF0 1907, *Afghanistan: The Making of US Foreign Policy*, DNSA.
171 Drogin, 'Boston U and Government Ties Spur Debate on Ethics'.
172 No Author Listed, 'Radio Free Afghanistan to Air in Pashto', *Washington Post*, 1 September 1987.
173 Memorandum for Gefter from Hoagland, 'Meeting with Dr. Bruno Heck about German-American Cooperation for the Afghan Media Project', 16 January 1986, USIA Bureau of Programs, Box 14, A1 (1061), RG 306.
174 Report by Chullaine O'Reilly on Boston University's Proposal to Train Personnel in the Afghan News Agency.
175 Olsson interview.
176 Michael Pistor, 'Action Plan on Afghan Programming Initiatives', 16 March 1987, *Afghanistan: The Making of US Foreign Policy*, DNSA.

Chapter 6

1 Ted Galen Carpenter, 'U.S. Aid to Anti-Communist Rebels: The "Reagan Doctrine" and Its Pitfalls', Research Report, Cato Institute (24 June 1986).
2 Brzezinski, speaking of the relative strengths of both superpowers approaching the summit, argued 'the only card Gorbachev holds is the one handed him by the mass media', Brzezinski, 'Article for *Chicago Tribune* Op-Ed' attached to a letter to

Patrick J. Buchanan, Assistant to the President and Director of Communications, from Zbigniew Brzezinski, 5 November 1985, WHORM sf FO 006–009, 360094, Box 6, RRL.

3   George J. Church, *Time*, 9 September 1985; USIA Research Memorandum, 'Soviet Vulnerability and World Opinion', 11 December 1986, describes Gorbachev's 'charm offensive' leading up to the Reykjavik summit in October 1986, USIA Archives, RG 306, P 64, NARA.
4   Bernard Gwertzman, 'The Message from Moscow', *New York Times*, 8 April 1985.
5   Mikhail Tsypkin, 'Moscow's Gorbachev: A New Leader in the Old Mold', Backgrounder, No. 451, Heritage Foundation, 29 August 1985.
6   Seth Mydans, 'Gorbachev, Receiving O'Neill, Urges US to End Ice Age', *New York Times*, 11 April 1985.
7   Brzezinski, 'Article for Chicago Tribune Op-Ed', attached to letter to Buchanan.
8   The SDI programme sought to develop an anti-ballistic missile shield to protect the United States and its allies from a nuclear attack. Detractors feared it would undermine the doctrine of mutually assured destruction which was credited with averting war between the superpowers since the development of nuclear weapons. The Soviets were obviously concerned it would neuter their first-strike capability and render them vulnerable to a US attack.
9   According to a USIA briefing paper in September 1985, Western European publics had low expectations for successful arms control negotiations in Geneva. The United States was seen as not making a genuine effort at arms control by many in Britain, Italy and France and most were willing to swop SDI development for a nuclear arms control treaty. See USIA Briefing Paper, 'West Europeans Expect Little from the November Meeting; Have Mixed Views on SDI Research', 21 October 1985, USIA Archives, RG 306, P 49, Box 2, NARA.
10 USIA Office of Research, Research Memorandum, 'Soviet Vulnerability and World Public Opinion', 11 December 1986, USIA Archives, RG 306, P 64, NARA.
11 Memorandum for Ronald Reagan from Charles Wick, 'Report on "Public Diplomacy by the USIA for the Geneva Meetings"', 11 December 1985, WHORM sf FO 006–007, 363372, Box 7, RRL.
12 NSC, Meeting Minutes, 'Soviet Foreign Minister Shevardnadze's Visit', 20 September 1985, Document No. 19850920, *Ronald Reagan Collection, Intelligence, and the End of the Cold War*, CIA FOIA ERR.
13 Memorandum for the President from Donald Regan and Robert McFarlane, 'Approaching Geneva: Current Assessment' (no date but likely early October 1985), WHORM sf FO, 000601–342449, Box 1, RRL. Also NSDD 194, 'Road to Geneva and Beyond: Themes and Perceptions for Public Perceptions', 25 October 1985, WHORM sf FO, 006–009, 354683, Box 5, RRL.
14 NSC, Meeting Minutes 'Soviet Foreign Minister Shevardnadze's Visit', 20 September 1985.
15 Transcript of exchange between Senator Gordon Humphrey and Secretary of State George Shultz before the Senate Armed Services Committee, 26 February 1985 in 'To Talk or Not to Talk with the Soviets', *Wall Street Journal*, 21 March 1985.
16 Secretary of Defense, Casper Weinberger and DCI, William Casey were amongst administration officials who objected to the Geneva summit. See Scoblic, *US vs Them*, p. 143.
17 Special Report, 'An Interview with Gorbachev: Candid Views about U.S.-Soviet Relations and His Goals for His People', *Time*, 9 September 1985.

18 USIA, 'Countering Soviet Propaganda: USIA Activities in the Lead Up to the Geneva Meeting', Undated, WHORM sf FO 006–09, 356574, Box 5, RRL.
19 Memorandum for Pat Buchanan from Ben Elliot, 'Summit', 9 September 1985, WHORM sf FO 006–009, 338112, Box 1, RRL.
20 Ronald Reagan, 'Address to the 40th Session of the United Nations General Assembly', New York, 24 October 1985, *PPP*, RRL. The regional conflicts Reagan spoke of were: Afghanistan, Angola, Cambodia, Ethiopia and Nicaragua.
21 USIA, 'Public Diplomacy Implementation for the Geneva Meeting', 25 September 1985, WHORM sf FO 006–09, 356574, Box 5, RRL.
22 Reagan, 'Address to the Nation on the Upcoming Soviet-United States Summit Meeting in Geneva', 14 November 1985, *PPP*, RRL.
23 NSC, NSDD 194, 'Meeting with Soviet Leader in Geneva: Themes and Perceptions', 25 October 1985, WHORM sf FO, 006–009, 354683, Box 5, RRL.
24 John Prados, *Safe for Democracy: The Secret Wars of the CIA* (Chicago: Ivan R. Dee, 2006), p. 488.
25 Westad, *The Global Cold War*, p. 352; Coll, *Ghost Wars*, p. 155.
26 This programme was mired in controversy during Wick's time due to the discovery that the USIA had developed a 'blacklist' of prominent Americans considered not suitable to advocate US foreign policy abroad.
27 USIA, 'Countering Soviet Propaganda: USIA Activities in the Lead Up to the Geneva Meeting'.
28 USIA, 'Countering Soviet Propaganda: USIA Activities in the Lead Up to the Geneva Meeting'.
29 Memorandum for the President from Regan and McFarlane, 'Approaching Geneva: Current Assessment'.
30 Worldnet, 'Geneva November 19–20, 1985: A Report of Television Activities', Summary, WHORM sf FO 006–09, 353176, Box 4, RRL.
31 Worldnet, 'Geneva November 19–20, 1985: A Report of Television Activities'.
32 Worldnet, 'Geneva November 19–20, 1985: A Report of Television Activities'. Khalilzad was now with the State Department serving on its Policy Planning Staff and as Special Advisor to the Undersecretary of State for Political Affairs.
33 Zalmay Khalilzad, Electronic Dialogue Series, 1985, 306-ED-156, USIA, Motion Picture, Sound, and Video Records Section, NARA; Foreign Press Center, Year End Briefing with Professor Zalmay Khalilzad, 17 December 1984, 306-FP-219, USIA, Motion Picture, Sound, and Video Records Section, NARA.
34 US Policy on Afghanistan with Sasser and Raphel, 31 January 1985, Worldnet No. 66, 306-WNET.90, USIA, Motion Picture, Sound, and Video Records Section, NARA.
35 Worldnet, 'Geneva November 19–20, 1985: A Report of Television Activities'.
36 US Department of State publication *Gist*, September 1985, contained in the USIA press package 'The Meetings of President Reagan and General Secretary Gorbachev', Geneva, November 1985', WHORM sf FO 006–09, 380423, Box 8, RRL.
37 Memorandum for President Reagan from Charles Wick, Report on 'Public Diplomacy Support by the United States Information Agency for the Geneva Meetings, November 19–20, 1985', WHORM sf FO 006–009, 363372, Box 7, RRL.
38 US Department of State publication *Gist*, September 1985.
39 USIA, 'Countering Soviet Propaganda: USIA Activities for the Lead-Up to the Geneva Meeting'.

40   The 'kidnapping' of Afghan children and their 'indoctrination' in the Soviet Union was a repeated theme of pro-*mujahedeen* propaganda during the time of the conflict. Afghan children were taken to the USSR for summer camps and other educational opportunities as a counterinsurgency strategy to 'win hearts and minds'. See Andrei A. Doohovskoy, 'Soviet Counterinsurgency in the Soviet Afghan War Revisited: Analyzing the Effective Aspects of the Counterinsurgency Effort', Master's Thesis (Cambridge, MA: Harvard University, September 2009), pp. 39–42. In 1988, Assistant Secretary of State Robert Peck admitted that the State Department had no evidence to support allegations that the Soviets kidnapped any Afghan children. He could only confirm that Afghan orphans were taken to the USSR to be placed in orphanages there. See HFAC, Subcommittee on Asian and Pacific Affairs, 'Hearing on the Geneva Accords on Afghanistan', 100th Congress, 2nd Session, 19 May 1988, LoC, p. 37.
41   USIA, 'Countering Soviet Propaganda: USIA Activities for the Lead-Up to the Geneva Meeting'.
42   USIA Office of Research, 'Foreign Media Condemn USSR on Sixth Anniversary of Soviet Invasion of Afghanistan', 21 January 1986, USIA, RG 306, P 59, Box 1, NARA. This poll analysed 150 editorials, commentaries and news analysis from thirty-five countries from 10 December 1985 to 17 January 1986.
43   Bernard Weinraub, 'Reagan Continues Private Meetings with Gorbachev', *New York Times*, 21 November 1985; No author, 'A Summary of Geneva Talks', *New York Times*, 22 November 1985.
44   Bernard Gwertzman, 'Reagan Bars Ties to Afghan Rebels', *New York Times*, 17 June 1986.
45   John C. Whitehead, 'Afghanistan's Struggle for Freedom', Address before the World Affairs Council, 13 December 1985, Current Policy No. 776, US Department of State, Bureau of Public Affairs, Situation Support Staff, WHORM, RAC, Box 1, RRL.
46   Human rights was one of the four main themes President Reagan was to emphasize in his address to the US nation days before the summit began. See appendix to a memorandum for the President from Donald T. Regan and Robert McFarlane, 'Proposed Major Presidential Events on the Road to Geneva', 8 October 1985, WHORM sf FO 006–09, 356574, Box 5, RRL. See also President Reagan's speech 'Address to the Nation on the Upcoming Soviet-United States Summit Meeting in Geneva', 14 November 1985, *PPP*, RRL.
47   Don Oberdorfer, 'Two Reportedly Agree on Talks; Gandhi and Zia Seek to Avert Nuclear Weapons Race', *Washington Post*, 24 October 1985.
48   See memorandum for the President from Shultz, 'How Do We Make Use of the Zia Visit to Protect Our Strategic Interests in the Face of Pakistan's Nuclear Weapons Activities', 26 November 1982; *Nuclear Vault Collection*, EBB No. 377, NSA. Shultz stated in this memo that there was 'overwhelming evidence' that Zia was breaking assurances given to the United States that Pakistan would not develop nuclear weapons.
49   President Reagan, 'Address to the 40th Session of the UN General Assembly in New York', 24 October 1985, *PPP*, RRL.
50   Letter to President Reagan from Senator Paul Sarbanes, 7 January 1985, about the detention of lawyer Raza Kazim who had been held in solitary confinement for a full year without charge. The reply from Robert F. Turner to Senator Sarbanes highlights the 'positive developments in Pakistan's human rights situation' in the face of offering refuge to 2 million Afghans whilst under threat from the USSR; WHORM sf CO 119

Pakistan, 271865, Box 146, RRL. Another to Vice President Bush from Dr Thomas Eisner of Cornell University and the American Association for the Advancement of Science, 10 November 1983, which pleaded the case of three university professor imprisoned in Pakistan; WHORM sf CO 119 Pakistan, 83336656, Box 146, RRL.
51 Immigration and Refugee Board of Canada, *Human Rights Briefs: Women in Pakistan*, 1 June 1994, http://www.refworld.org/docid/3ae6a83c18.html; Dorothy Q. Thomas and Patricia Gossman, 'Double Jeopardy: Police Abuse of Women in Pakistan', Human Rights Watch Reports, 1992, Pakistan, http://www.hrw.org/reports/1992/pakistan
52 President's Remarks at the Arrival Ceremony for Prime Minister Junejo of Pakistan, 16 July 1986, WHORM sf CO 119 Pakistan, 400773(2), Box 146, RRL.
53 Department of State, Briefing Paper, 'Majorities of Pakistanis Oppose GoP Recognition of Karmal Afghan Government, Favor Aid to Afghan Refugees', 12 July 1985, USIA, RG 306, P 49, Box 2, NARA.
54 Letter to Peter Teeley, Press Secretary to the Vice President from Ghani Eirabie, 30 July 1981, WHORM sf CO 002 Afghanistan, 8123449, Box 38, RRL.
55 Memorandum for the Secretary (Shultz) from Laurence Eagleburger, 'Pakistan and the Afghan Refugees and the Freedom Fighters', 24 November 1982, WHSOF, Executive Secretariat, NSC, Country File: Near East and South Asia, Afghanistan, 7/29/82–5/2/83, 34629, Box 34, RRL.
56 Executive Secretariat, NSC, 'National Security Study: Afghanistan', Recommendations, March 1987, WHOSF, NSDDS, Box 13, RRL.
57 Executive Secretariat, NSC, 'National Security Study: Afghanistan'.
58 China shares a short boundary (approximately 92 km) with Afghanistan along the remote Wakhan Corridor.
59 NSC, Executive Secretariat, 'National Security Study: Afghanistan'.
60 NSC, Executive Secretariat, 'National Security Study: Afghanistan'.
61 Department of State, Briefing Paper, 'Pakistanis Widely Support US-Pakistan Aid Agreement; Indian Elites Generally See US Aid to Pakistan as an Irritant', 12 July 1985, USIA, RG306, P49, Box 2, NARA. USIA Office of Research, Briefing Paper, 'Majorities of Pakistanis Distrust Both US and USSR; Favor Pak Development of Nuclear Arms', 14 July 1986, USIA, RG 306, P 49, Box 3, NARA.
62 Kux, *The United States and Pakistan*, p. 282.
63 Ronald Reagan, 'Presidential Statement Following a Meeting with Leaders of the Afghan Resistance Alliance', 16 June 1986, WHORM sf CO 002 Afghanistan, 429723, Box 36, RRL.
64 Carpenter, 'US Aid to Anti-Communist Rebels'.
65 'Biographical Notes on Afghanistan Resistance Alliance Delegation', WHORM sf CO 002 Afghanistan, 362000–364999, Box 36, RRL.
66 Memorandum for Walter Raymond from Pat Buchanan, 'Afghan Freedom Movement', 23 October 1985, WHORM sf CO 002 Afghanistan, 351474, Box 36, RRL. This was probably Gulbudhin Hekmatyar who was aided by Iran. See Prados, *Safe for Democracy*, p. 477.
67 Mark Kleiman, 'We Can't Stop Friend or Foe in the Drug Trade', *Wall Street Journal*, 9 April 1985. Mr Kleiman was director of policy analysis in the Criminal Division of the Justice Department early in the Reagan administration and later a drug policy researcher at Harvard University.
68 See Prados, *Safe for Democracy*, p. 483.

69 Christine J. Kielpinski, USIA Office of Research, 'Media Habits among Afghan Refugees in Pakistan's North West Frontier Province Camps', February 1986, USIA, RG 306, P 142, Box 55, NARA. A description of the refugees in the NWFP camps outlines that 'since certain groups of the Afghan population are more likely than others to leave Afghanistan, refugees who have settled in the NWFP camps cannot be considered demographically representative of the Afghan population'. Pierre Centlivres and Micheline Centlivres-Demont, 'The Afghan Refugee in Pakistan: An Ambiguous Identity', *Journal of Refugee Studies*, Vol. 1, No. 2, 1988, point out that the majority of refugees in the camps were Afghan Pashtuns who felt entitled to seek hospitality from their ethnic and tribal kin across the border in Pakistan rather than the helpless, hopeless individuals refugees are normally perceived as.

70 Richard P. Cronin, 'Afghanistan after Five Years: Status of the Conflict, the Afghan Resistance and the US Role', Congressional Report No. 85-20, January 1985, p. 6, LoC.

71 David B. Edwards, *Before the Taliban: Genealogies of the Afghan Jihad* (Berkeley: University of California Press, 2002), Part 3, Chapter 7.

72 Dr. Mark O'Sullivan, 'Afghan Report', Peace and World Order Studies Program, Catholic University of America, Washington, DC, late 1987, WHORM sf CO 002 Afghanistan, 618236, Box 38, RRL.

73 O'Sullivan, 'Afghan Report'.

74 Some refugees identified strongly as *mohajer*, an Islamic term for one who goes into voluntary exile if not allowed to practise Islam in one's homeland, and initially whole villages left under the influence of their religious leader for this reason. As men left the camps to return to Afghanistan to fight they considered themselves *mujahed* and upon return, for rest and refuge, reverted to *mohajer* which caused unease amongst Pakistanis many of whom saw these 'swaggering, armed, aggressive lot' as far from traditional refugees. For example, an Afghan could be a schoolteacher in a refugee camp part of the year (*mohajer*) and return to fight in Afghanistan during the fighting season (*mujahed*). See Centlivres and Centlivres, 'The Afghan Refugee', p. 149.

75 Memorandum for Shultz from Eagleburger, 'Pakistan and the Afghan Refugees and the Freedom Fighters'.

76 Henry Kamm, 'Isolated Afghan Refugee Camp Life Turns Women into "Birds in a Cage"', *New York Times*, 27 March 1988.

77 Kamm, 'Isolated Afghan Refugee Camp Life Turns Women into "Birds in a Cage"'.

78 Moghadam, 'Building Human Resources and Women's Capabilities in Afghanistan', p. 867.

79 In a letter to Brzezinski from Anders Fange of the Swedish Committee for Afghanistan, 23 April 1984, Fange mentions the existence of about fifty other Afghanistan committees throughout Europe, the United States, Canada and Australia. WHORM sf CO 002 Afghanistan, 240000–259999, Box 36, RRL.

80 Carpenter, 'U.S. Aid to Anti-Communist Rebels'.

81 Memorandum for Frank Carlucci from Melvyn Levitsky, Department of State, 'Public Diplomacy Action Plans', 12 May 1987, Document No. 146, EBB 78, *US Propaganda in the Middle East*, NSA.

82 Letter to George HW Bush from Robert McCauley, AmeriCares, 17 July 1984, WHSOF, Executive Secretariat, NSC, Country Files: Near East and South Asia, Afghanistan 7/24/84–9/18/84, Box 34, RRL.

83 Agenda attached to memorandum to Robert McFarlane from Walter Raymond, 'Restricted Working Group: Afghan Political Action Proposal', 30 March 1984,

WHSOF, Executive Secretariat, NSC, Country File: Near East and South Asia, Afghanistan, 13/30/84–5/18/84, Box 34, RRL.
84 Memorandum for Carlucci from Levitsky, Department of State, 'Public Diplomacy Action Plans'.
85 Letter and paper to Robert McFarlane and John Lenczowski from Dr Igor S. Glagolev, Director, Association for Cooperation of Democratic Countries, 22 May 1984. Democratic congressman McDonald who died aboard KAL 007 was a member of the Coalition of Peace through Strength, president of the John Birch Society and a member of the WACL. He was also involved with Singlaub in setting up the Western Goals Foundation, a private intelligence network, which subsequently was implicated in the Iran-*Contra* scandal.
86 Robert Pear, 'Push the Russians, Intellectuals Say', *New York Times*, 25 November 1985. This article lists Irving Kristol, Richard Pipes and Elliot Abrams as attendees at a conference organized by the Committee for the Free World. The organization was formed by Midge Decter the neo-conservative columnist and wife of *Commentary* magazine founder Norman Podhoretz.
87 Robert Pear, 'Push the Russians, Intellectuals Say', *New York Times*, 25 November 1985.
88 Chris Hunter, 'PB Clinic Provides Relief in Afghanistan', *Palm Beach Daily News*, 1 November 1985.
89 Frank Wright and Associates Inc. Mr Wright was also director of the Palm Beach Round Table.
90 Peter Grier, 'Afghan Guerrillas Get Aid from Red Cross, French … and Now Palm Beach', *Christian Science Monitor*, 27 December 1985.
91 Letter to Ken McKinnon from H. Richard Williams, News Director for Congressman Tom Lewis, undated but approximately November 1985, WHORM sf CO 002 Afghanistan, 472520, Box 36, RRL.
92 Congressional Task Force on Afghanistan, 'Hearing on Medical Conditions in Afghanistan', 4 March 1985, p. 3, AFO 1622, *Afghanistan: The Making of US Foreign Policy, 1973–1990*, DNSA. See pp. 29–35 for Dr Akram's testimony where he accuses the Soviets of deploying 'yellow rain' and napalm on fields, hospitals and refugee camps, using toy bombs and executing students who refuse to accept communism. Grier, 'Afghan Guerrillas Get Aid from Red Cross'.
93 Memorandum for William Martin from Frederick J. Ryan, 'Palm Beach Clinic for Afghans', 10 December 1985, WHORM sf CO 002 Afghanistan, 472520, Box 36, RRL.
94 CFA flyer, 'Afghanistan: Freedom's Frontier', WHORM sf Committee for a Free Afghanistan, Box 17, RRL.
95 CFA flyer, 'Afghanistan: Freedom's Frontier'.
96 CFA, *Free Afghanistan Report*, No. 6, March 1984, WHORM sf Committee for a Free Afghanistan, Box 17, RRL.
97 Gordon Humphrey, Charles Wilson, Charles Lichenstein, Steve Symms, Barney Frank, Robert Lagomarsino attended; Memorandum for John Poindexter from Walter Raymond, 'Administration Participation at Capitol Hill Event on Afghanistan, May 14', 10 May 1985, WHORM sf Afghanistan, 322082, Box 36, RRL.
98 Letter to the President from Senators/Representatives Wilson, Ritter, Symms et al., 19 September 1985, WHSOF, Office of Media Relations, 1981–1989, Presidential Taping Sessions, Taping 12/06/1985, Box 43, RRL.
99 Letter to Pat Buchanan from Gale Watlington, 27 November 1985, WHORM sf Committee for a Free Afghanistan, Box 17, RRL.

100 Invitation to CFA 'Dinner for Afghan Relief', WHORM sf Committee for a Free Afghanistan, Box 17, RRL.
101 Invitation to CFA 'Dinner for Afghan Relief'. The honorary committee included a host of congressional members from both houses including Charles Wilson, Orrin Hatch, Gordon Humphrey and Don Ritter. Also on the committee were Jeane Kirkpatrick, Henry Kissinger and former President Richard Nixon and staunchly anti-communist British parliamentarians Lord Nicholas Bethell and Winston Churchill of the British Conservative Party.
102 Leichenstein was also involved in the Nicaraguan Contra's cause; see Durham and Power, *New Perspectives on the Transnational Right*, p. 142.
103 Letter to Pat Buchanan from Gale Watlington, 10 October 1985, Office of Media Relations, 1981–1989, Series IV, TV Office, Presidential Tapings Sessions, Taping 12/06/1985, Box 43, RRL.
104 Letter to President Reagan from Gale Watlington, 6 November 1985, Office of Media Relations, Series IV, TV Office, Presidential Tapings Sessions, Taping 12/06/1985, Box 43, RRL.
105 'Presidential Taping, Afghan Relief Dinner, Friday, December 6 1985', Office of Media Relations, Series IV, TV Office, Presidential Tapings Sessions, Taping 12/06/1985, Box 43, RRL.
106 Memorandum for Pat Buchannan for Gail Watlington, 24 October 1985, WHORM af Max Green Files, 1985–1988, Afghan POTUS Event, Box 2, RRL.
107 Memorandum for Secretary Shultz from McFarlane, 'Humanitarian Assistance for the Afghans', 13 February 1985, Executive Secretariat, NSC, Country File: Near East and South Asia, Afghanistan, Box 34, RRL. Memorandum for McFarlane from Charles Hill, Department of State, 'Food and Medical Assistance for the Afghans', 3 December 1984, Executive Secretariat, NSC, Country File: Near East and South Asia, Afghanistan, Box 34. RRL.
108 NSC, Executive Secretariat, 'Action Plan on Afghan Programming Initiatives', 16 March 1987, 8690474, Box 7, WHSOF, RRL.
109 Memorandum for Walter Raymond from Louise Wheeler, 'Variety Clubs Benefit Afghan Children', 30 June 1987, AFO 2012, *Afghanistan: The Making of US Foreign Policy, 1973–1990*, DNSA; Memorandum for Wick from Wheeler, 'President Reagan's Videotape for Variety Lifeline Dinner in New York on September 22', 11 September 1987, AFO 2046, *Afghanistan: The Making of US Foreign Policy, 1973–1990*, DNSA.
110 Department of State, 'Notes from Meeting about Rabbani Visit Public Diplomacy', 3 June 1986, AFO 1721, *Afghanistan: The Making of US Foreign Policy, 1973–1990*, DNSA.
111 Jonathan Steele, 'Kingmaker with a Taste for Power', *Guardian*, 16 November 2001; Jonathan Steele, 'Burhanuddin Rabbani obituary', *Guardian*, 21 September 2011.
112 Steele, 'Burhanuddin Rabbani obituary'. Rabbani ordered women should wear hijab, closed cinemas, banned alcohol and erected gallows to publicly hang criminals.
113 Senate Joint Resolution 365, 'Welcoming the Afghan Alliance', 1 July 1986, 99th Congress of the United States of America, WHORM sf CO 002 Afghanistan, 403000–429999, Box 36, RRL.
114 Department of State, 'Notes from Meeting about Rabbani Visit Public Diplomacy'.
115 See Department of State, 'Notes from Meeting about Rabbani Visit Public Diplomacy' re Khalizad to contact George Will, Saul Gefter to contact Lohbeck (see Chapter 4 for background on Lohbeck) and Dick Ross to contact Mike Hoover to gain access to Dan Rather.

116 Letter to the editor from Burhanuddin Rabbani, Sebgatullah Mojadedi, Pir Sayed, Ahmed Gailani, Maulavi Mohammed and Nabi Mohammedi, *New York Times*, 2 July 1986; Arthur Bonner, 'Afghan Rebel's Victory Garden: Opium', *New York Times*, 18 June 1986.
117 Gwertzman, 'Reagan Bars Ties to Afghan Rebels'.
118 Bernard Gwertzman, 'Afghans Put Case before All Forums', *New York Times*, 19 June 1986; *Afghan News*, A Fortnightly Bulletin of Jami'at Islami Afghanistan (Rabbani's organization), Vol. 2, No. 16, 15 August 1986, WHSOF, Vincent Cannistraro Files, 08/01/1986–01/15/1987, Box 1, RRL.
119 Letter to President Reagan from Patricia A. Johnson, 14 September 1985, WHSOF, Vincent Cannistraro Files, Afghanistan 10/26/1985–12/19/1985, Box 1, RRL.
120 Letter to George Shultz from Karen McKay, CFA, 23 January 1986, WHSOF, Vincent Cannistraro Files, Afghanistan 12/20/1985–03/03/1986, Box 1, RRL.
121 Note to Walter Raymond from Vincent Cannistraro, WHSOF, Vincent Cannistraro Files, Afghanistan 12/20/1985–03/03/1986, Box 1, RRL; letter to President Reagan from Gordon Humphrey, 18 December 1985, WHORM sf CO 002 Afghanistan, 371157, Box 36, RRL.
122 Letter to McFarlane from Humphrey, 1 October 1985, WHSOF, Vincent Cannistraro Files, Afghanistan 10/02/1985–10/20/1985, Box 1, RRL; Marguerite Johnson, 'Leaks in the Pipeline: Some US Arms Not Getting to Rebels', *Time*, 9 December 1985, in WHSOF, Vincent Cannistraro Files, 'Afghanistan' 10/26/1985–12/19/1985, Box 1, RRL; Letter to President Reagan from Gordon Humphrey, 23 December 1985, WHORM sf CO 002 Afghanistan, 371560, Box 36, RRL.
123 Benjamin Hart, 'Rhetoric vs Reality: How the State Department Betrays the Reagan Vision', Backgrounder No. 484, Heritage Foundation, 31 January 1986. As well as Afghanistan the report criticized administration policy towards Nicaragua, Mozambique, Angola, Cambodia and Eastern Europe.
124 According to Lohbeck, *Holy War, Unholy Victory*, p. 96, Fawcett set up the IMC with Dr Simon and Hasan Nouri – an expat engineer. They received 1 million dollars following a meeting with Raymond and Helman for clinics in Afghanistan but no American allowed to go into the country for fear of kidnap. See also Crile, *Charlie Wilson's War*, pp. 364–365.
125 Sidney Blumenthal, 'A Schism between Heritage and State: Deputy Secretary Say Foundation Trustees Should Quit', *Washington Post*, 11 March 1986.
126 Arthur Bonner, 'An Afghan Tale: An American's Body for Ransom', *New York Times*, 12 April 1986.
127 Nikke Finke, 'Under Fire: An Afghan Odyssey', *Los Angeles Times*, 30 October 1987; Edward Giradet, 'Two US Journalist Reported Killed in Afghanistan; Details Murky', *Christian Science Monitor*, 28 October 1987.
128 Attachment to letter to President Reagan from J. Milnor Roberts, 16 October 1984, WHORM sf Committee for a Free Afghanistan, Box 17, RRL; Flyer for CFA forum featuring Dr Simon discussing his work in Afghanistan, 12 September 1984, WHORM sf Committee for a Free Afghanistan, Box 17, RRL. Senators Clairborne Pell and Steve Symms were also presenting this forum. TV Satellite File No. 83, 3 January 1985, 306.TVSF.97, USIA Motion Picture, Sound, and Video Records Section, NARA.
129 Letter to the President for Senator Pell et al., 4 October 1984, WHORM sf CO 002 Afghanistan, 267545, Box 36, RRL.

130 Congressional Task Force on Afghanistan, 'Hearing on Medical Conditions'; Jack Anderson, 'Afghanistan: Medical Nightmare', *Lawrence Journal-World*, 3 March 1985.
131 Project Proposal, 'Afghan Democratic Education Project', NED, c. 1986, AFO 1678, *Afghanistan: The Making of US Foreign Policy, 1973–1990*, DNSA.
132 Cover Letter from Gouttierre to Yale Richmond, NED, Afghanistan Basic Education Project, 30 January 1986, AFO 1687, *Afghanistan: The Making of US Foreign Policy, 1973–1990*, DNSA.
133 'American Friends of Afghanistan', NED, AFO 1677, *Afghanistan: The Making of US Foreign Policy, 1973–1990*, DNSA.
134 Project Proposal, 'Afghan Democratic Education Project', NED.
135 Kenneth Freed, 'Odd Partners in UNO's Afghan Project War and Turmoil in Afghanistan', *Omaha World Herald*, 26 October 1997.
136 Action Plan attached to Memorandum for Carlucci from Levitsky, 'Public Diplomacy Action Plans'.
137 Memorandum for Carlucci from Levitsky, 'Public Diplomacy Action Plans'.
138 Joe Stephens and David B. Ottaway, 'From the US., The ABC's of Jihad; Violent Soviet-Era Textbooks Complicate Afghan Education Efforts', *Washington Post*, 23 March 2002; Craig Davis, '"A" Is for Allah, "J" is for Jihad', *World Policy Journal*, Vol. 19, No. 1 (Spring 2002), pp. 90–94 for description of the content of these textbooks and some images; Shirazi, 'Islamic Education in Afghanistan', pp. 222–223 for a description of some of the text in the schoolbooks.

Chapter 7

1 Riaz M. Khan, *Untying the Afghan Knot: Negotiating Soviet Withdrawal* (Durham: Duke University Press, 1991), pp. 7–8.
2 Gorbachev's 'new thinking' on foreign policy sought to step back from ideological confrontation between communism and capitalism and instead pursued better diplomatic relations and economic cooperation with the United States and other Western states.
3 Khan, *Untying the Afghan Knot*, p. 185.
4 Roy, *Islam and Resistance*, p. 229, uses the term 'Saigon syndrome' to refer to the ambitions of some US officials involved in Afghan affairs during this period to ensure the Soviets did not exit Afghanistan with dignity.
5 Harrison and Cordovez, *Out of Afghanistan*, pp. 189–191, detail this change of position by the State Department following Gorbachev's assent to power.
6 Memorandum for Frank Carlucci from Robert Oakley, 'Afghanistan NSDD', 15 April 1987, WHSOF, Executive Secretariat, NSC, NSDDs, 'NSDD 270', Box 13, RRL.
7 Roy, *Islam and Resistance*, pp. 208–209.
8 Memorandum for Secretary of State Designate George Shultz from Richard Pipes, 'Background for Forthcoming US-Soviet Talks on Afghanistan', 30 June 1982, NSC, Executive Secretariat, Country File, Near East and South Asia, Box 34, RRL. Richard Pipes, Walter Raymond, Geoffrey Kemp were against any 'fruitless "talks" with the conquerors [the Soviets]' urging instead aid to the *mujahedeen*. See Memorandum for William Clarke from Richard Pipes, 'Afghanistan', 29 July 1982, WHSOF,

Executive Secretariat, NSC, Country File, Near East and South Asia, 29/7/82–2/5/83, Box 34, RRL.
9   Scott, *Deciding to Intervene*, pp. 49–51.
10 In Cordovez and Harrison, *Out of Afghanistan*, pp. 4 and 92. Harrison states that this potentially represented 'a lost opportunity for Soviet withdrawal in 1983', pp. 102–106. Richard Cronin, Congressional Research Report, No. 85-210F, 'Afghanistan: United Nations Sponsored Negotiations, An Annotated Chronology', 22 November 1985, LoC, p. 10, suggests disagreement in both Washington and Islamabad on whether to accept Soviet proposals leads to a step back from the breach.
11 Selig Harrison, Testimony, HFAC, Subcommittee on Asian and Pacific Affairs, 'Hearing on Developments in Afghanistan', February 1988, pp. 4–6, LoC.
12 Ahmed Rashid, 'Can the Russians Find a Way Out', *Nation*, 20 February 1988.
13 Telegram to the US Department of State from the US Mission to the UN, 7 July 1987, about Secretary General Perez de Cuellar's 2 July Meeting with Afghan Ambassador Okun, WHSOF, Nelson Ledsky Files, Afghanistan Cables 1987, RAC Box 1, RRL.
14 On 8 July 1987, Deputy Foreign Minister Yuli Vorontsov met the US Ambassador to the Soviet Union Jack Matlock in Moscow asking 'in a low-key and non-confrontational manner' that the two superpowers could discuss the Soviets' concerns that a rapid withdrawal would precipitate a civil war in Afghanistan which could lead to the death of hundreds of thousands. See Telegram to Secretary of State, US, from US Embassy, Moscow 9 July 1987, WHSOF, Nelson Ledsky Files, Afghanistan 1987 Cables, RAC, Box 1, RRL.
15 Khan, *Untying the Afghan Knot*, pp. 188–190.
16 Harrison and Cordovez, *Out of Afghanistan*, p. 292.
17 Harrison and Cordovez, *Out of Afghanistan*, p. 273.
18 Khan, *Untying the Afghan Knot*, p. 195; Letter to Yaqub Khan from Frank C. Carlucci, 10 January 1987, WHORM sf, CO 119 Pakistan, 494000–489999, RRL.
19 Harrison and Cordovez, *Out of Afghanistan*, pp. 274–275.
20 Executive Secretariat, NSC, National Security Decision Directive 270, 'Afghanistan', 1 May 1987, WHSOF, NSDDS, RAC, Box 11, RRL.
21 Memorandum for Carlucci from Levitsky, 'Draft NSSD/NSDD, National Security Study: Afghanistan', 25 March 1987, NSC, Executive Secretariat, NSDDs, NSDD 270, Box 13, RRL.
22 Department of State, 'Public Themes for Afghanistan', 28 March 1987, WHORM sf, CO 002 Afghanistan, 498142–529799, Box 37, RRL.
23 Memorandum to Grant Green, NSC from Fred Iklé, Department of Defense, 16 April 1987, NSC Executive Secretariat, NSDDs, NSDD 270, Box 13, RRL.
24 NSC, Executive Secretariat, NSDDs, NSDD 270, Box 13, RRL.
25 According to Malcolm S. Forbes Jr., Chairman of the Board for International Broadcasting, in testimony before the Senate Committee on Foreign Relations, 'Foreign Relations Authorization Act', 17 March 1987, 100th Congress, 1st Session, LoC, p. 23, USIA polls of Soviet citizens visiting the West indicated those exposed to Radio Liberty were three times more likely to oppose the war in Afghanistan.
26 Department of State, 'Afghanistan: Public Diplomacy Action Plans', 12 May 1987, AF01988, *Afghanistan: The Making of US Foreign Policy, 1973–1990*, DNSA.
27 Memorandum for Carlucci from Levitsky, 'Draft NSSD/NSDD, National Security Study: Afghanistan'.
28 NSC, Executive Secretariat, NSDD 270.

29 Memorandum for Grant Green from Robert Oakley, 'Afghan Day Proclamation: Request for Presidential Signing Ceremony', 16 March 1987, WHSOF, George 'Mike' Andricos Files, RAC Box 13, RRL.
30 President Reagan, 'Statement on the Seventh Anniversary of the Soviet Invasion of Afghanistan', 27 December 1986, *PPP*, RRL.
31 Philip Taubman, 'Soviet Intentions Cited', *New York Times*, 2 January 1987. Deputy Assistant Secretary of State Hagerty says this on Worldnet, 'Soviet Invasion of Afghanistan', 1987, 306-WNET-327, USIA, Motion Picture, Sound, and Video Records Section, NARA. Prados, *Safe for Democracy*, p. 488, asserts that the Soviets did withdraw 15,000 troops and associated equipment.
32 Bernard Gwertzman, 'Afghanistan to Observe a Cease-Fire', *New York Times*, 2 January 1987.
33 Taubman, 'Soviet Intentions Cited', *New York Times*, 2 January 1987.
34 USIA Office of Research, 'World Press Assails Soviets on Seventh Anniversary of Afghanistan Invasion', 22 January 1987, Box 1, RG 306, P 59, USIA, NARA.
35 Marshall, 'Managing Withdrawal', p. 73.
36 Roy, *Islam and Resistance*, p. 212. Roy is describing the Afghan Interim Government but this was formed from the Peshawar Alliance leaders.
37 President Reagan, 'Address before a Joint Session of Congress on the State of the Union', 27 January 1987, *PPP*, RRL.
38 USIA Worldnet series, 'Soviet Withdrawal from Afghanistan with Michael Armacost', 18 February 1987, 306-WNET-347, USIA, Motion Picture, Sound, and Video Records, NARA.
39 USIA Worldnet series, 'US Policy towards Afghanistan with Richard Murphy', 27 March 1987, 306-WNET-378, USIA, Motion Picture, Sound, and Video Records Section, NARA.
40 Memorandum for Grant Green from Robert Oakley, NSC, 16 March 1987, 'Afghan Day Proclamation: Request for Presidential Signing Ceremony', WHSOF, George Andricos Files, RAC Box 1,3, RRL; President Reagan, 'Proclamation 5621, Afghanistan Day 1987', 20 March 1987, *PPP*, RRL.
41 Memorandum for the President from Frank Carlucci, 'Ceremony for Afghanistan Day', WHSOF, George Andricos Files, RAC Box 1,3, RRL.
42 Prados, *Safe for Democracy*, p. 289; Coll, *Ghost Wars*, pp. 161–162.
43 President Reagan, 'Remarks at the Los Angeles World Affairs Council in California', 10 April 1987, RRL.
44 Memorandum for Robert Bemis, NSC, from Marvin Stone, USIA, 'Action Plan Afghan Programming', 24 March 1987, WHSOF, NSC, Executive Secretariat, 8690474, Box 7, RRL.
45 Steven R. Weisman, 'Afghanistan Admits Cease-fire's Failure and Criticizes US', *New York Times*, 28 April 1987.
46 Memorandum for Carlucci from Levitsky, 'Public Diplomacy Action Plans'.
47 USIA Office of Research, Foreign Media Analysis Report, 'World Press Says if Gorbachev Serious about Peace He Must Withdraw from Afghanistan', 8 July 1987, which examined 300 editorials, commentaries and news stories. USIA, FMA 7-8-87, RG 306, Box 1, NARA.
48 Harrison and Cordovez, *Out of Afghanistan*, p. 247.
49 Ronald Reagan, 'Address to the 42nd Session of the United Nations General Assembly', New York, 21 September 1987, *PPP*, RRL.

50   NSC, Executive Secretariat, Telegram to the Department of State, Washington from the US Embassy, Moscow, 'Soviet Views on Afghanistan Following Najib's Visit', 14 August 1987, WHSOF, Nelson Ledsky Files, RAC, Box 1, RRL.
51   Telegram to US Embassy, Islamabad from Secretary of State Shultz, Washington, 'Afghanistan: Armacost-Cordovez Consultations', 27 July 1987, WHSOF, Nelson Ledsky Files, 'Afghanistan, 1987 Cables', RAC, Box 1, RRL.
52   NSC Executive Secretariat, Telegram to the Department of State, Washington, from US Embassy, Moscow, 'Soviet Views on Afghanistan Following Najib's Visit'. Hekmatyar was jailed by Shah back before 1973 and fled to Pakistan once freed, see Lally Weymouth, 'An Afghan Rebel Chief Tells America No Deal', *Washington Post*, 17 September 1989.
53   USIA, Office of Research, Foreign Media Analysis, 'World Press Criticizes Moscow for Hard Line on Afghanistan, Calls US Aid to Pakistan Vital for Afghan Mujahedeen', 20 November 1987, FMA 11-20-87, RG 306, Box 1, USIA, NARA.
54   Melvyn P. Leffler, *For the Soul of Mankind: The United States, the Soviet Union, and the Cold War* (New York: Hill and Wang, 2007), p. 409.
55   Harrison and Cordovez, *Out of Afghanistan*, p. 245.
56   Majorities, ranging from a low of 52 per cent in France to a high of 82 per cent in Italy, believed the Soviets would not violate the treaty. USIA, Office of Research and Media Reaction, Research Memorandum, Post-Summit Survey, 'West Europeans Laud Summit', 21 December 1987, RG 306, P 64, USIA, NARA.
57   USIA, Office of Research, 'West Europeans Laud Summit'. In Britain two-thirds of those polled believed Gorbachev was serious about withdrawal and US allies Italy, West Germany and the Netherlands also took his claims seriously.
58   US Department of State, 'Soviet Influence Activities: A Report on Active Measures and Propaganda, 1986–1987', August 1987, RG 306, A1 (1061), Box 50, USIA, Bureau of Programs, NARA.
59   Handwritten notes in 'Afghanistan: Negotiations for a Soviet Withdrawal', WHSOF, A. Blair Dorminey Files, Domestic Affairs, Box 1, RRL.
60   NSC, NSDD 270.
61   Department of State, 'Afghanistan: Public Diplomacy Action Plans.
62   Charles W. Greenleaf Jr., Assistant Administrator, Bureau for Asia and Near East, Agency for International Development, Testimony, HFAC, Subcommittee on Asian and Pacific Affairs, 'The Situation in Afghanistan', 99th Congress, 2nd Session, 1 May 1986, pp. 39–55, LoC.
63   Barnett Rubin, Testimony, HFAC, Subcommittee on Asian and Pacific Affairs, 'The Situation in Afghanistan', 99th Congress, 2nd Session, 1 May 1986, p. 83.
64   Rubin, Testimony, HFAC, 'The Situation in Afghanistan', p. 81.
65   Wilson, CTF on Afghanistan, 'Hearing on UN Sponsored Peace Negotiations', April 1986, AFO 1701, *Afghanistan: The Making of US Foreign Policy*, DNSA, p. 29.
66   Kux, *The United States and Pakistan*, p. 286.
67   Richard W. Murphy, Assistant Secretary of State for Near East and South Asian Affairs, Testimony, House Committee on Armed Services, Defense Policy Panel, 'National Security Policy', 100th Congress, 1st Session, March 1987, LoC, p. 167.
68   Stephen Solarz, HFAC, Subcommittee on Asian and Pacific Affairs, 'Hearing on the Provision of Airborne Early Warning System for Pakistan', 100th Congress, 1st Session, 21 May and 11 June 1987, LoC, pp. 1–3.
69   See Peck's testimony HFAC, 'Hearing on the Provision of Airborne Early Warning System for Pakistan', 100th Congress, 1st Session, 21 May and 11 June 1987, LoC,

pp. 13–25, in which he only briefly refers to India and minimizes the effect the supply of AWACS would have on its security.
70 Kux, *The United States and Pakistan*, p. 286.
71 'Additional Suggested OSD Insertions', attached to memorandum to the Executive Secretary, NSC from James Lemon, Executive Secretary, OSD, 6 April 1987, NSC, Executive Secretariat, NSDDs, Box 13, RRL.
72 Selig Harrison, Testimony, HFAC, Subcommittee on Asian and Pacific Affairs, 'Developments in Afghanistan', 100th Congress, 2nd Session, February 1988, LoC, p. 8.
73 USIA Foreign Opinion Note, 18 December 1987, 'Pakistani's Show Increased Distrust of Americans; Majority Would Reject Conditional US Aid', RG 306, P 118, Box 5, USIA, NARA.
74 'National Security Study: Afghanistan' attached to memorandum to Frank Carlucci from Melvyn Levitsky, 25 March 1987, Executive Secretariat, NSC, NSDDs, Box 13, RRL.
75 USIA Foreign Media Analysis Report, 'Near East/South Asia Media Praise INF Treaty, but Regret US Neglect of Regional Issues', 24 February 1988, FMA 2-24-88, RG 306, USIA, NARA.
76 Humphrey, Congressional Task Force (CTF) on Afghanistan, Hearing on UN Sponsored Peace Negotiations, 30 April 1986, LoC, p. 2.
77 Humphrey, CTF, Hearing on UN Sponsored Peace Negotiations, 30 April 1986, p. 3.
78 Humphrey, CTF, Hearing on UN Sponsored Peace Negotiations, 30 April 1986, pp. 3–4.
79 Senator Bradley, CTF, Hearing on UN Sponsored Peace Negotiations, 30 April 1986, LoC, pp. 22–23.
80 Charles Wilson, CTF, Hearing on UN Sponsored Peace Negotiations, 30 April 1986, p. 28. See Crile, *Charlie Wilson's War*, pp. 364–366, for a description of how and why Helman was forced to resign from the State Department's Cross Border Humanitarian Aid Program.
81 Wilson, CTF, Hearing on UN Sponsored Peace Negotiations, p. 29.
82 CTF on Afghanistan, 'Review of UN Sponsored Proximity Talks on Afghanistan', 17 February 1987, AF01918, *Afghanistan: The Making of US Foreign Policy*, DNSA, inserted into p. 2 of Iklé's statement.
83 CTF, 'Review of UN Sponsored Proximity Talks on Afghanistan', 17 February 1987.
84 Paul Lewis, 'Charles M. Lichenstein, 75, American Envoy at the UN', Obituary, *New York Times*, 31 August 2002. Irving Kristol sent Lichenstein a congratulatory telegram following this incident, see Douglas Murray, *Neo Conservatism: Why We Need It* (New York: Encounter Books, 2006), p. 61. Lichenstein was also a member of the dinner committee of the CFA's 'Dinner for Afghan Relief'.
85 Obituary of Charles Lichenstein, *The Day*, 30 August 2002.
86 Gordon Humphrey, CTF on Afghanistan, 'Review of UN-Sponsored Proximity Talks on Afghanistan', 17 February 1987, p. 2.
87 Fred Iklé, Testimony, CTF on Afghanistan, 'Review of UN-Sponsored Proximity Talks on Afghanistan'.
88 Humphrey, CTF on Afghanistan, 'Review of UN-Sponsored Proximity Talks on Afghanistan', p. 13.
89 House Committee on Armed Services, Defense Policy Panel, 'Hearings on National Security Strategy', 100th Congress, 1st Session, January, February, March, April, 1987, LoC.

90 Brzezinski, Testimony, House Committee on Armed Services, Defense Policy Panel, 'Hearings on National Security Strategy', 100th Congress, 1st Session, January, February, March, April, 1987, LoC, pp. 86–87 & p. 97.
91 Humphrey, Testimony, House Committee on Armed Services, Defense Policy Panel, 'Hearings on National Security Strategy', 100th Congress, 1st Session, January, February, March, April, 1987, LoC, p. 464.
92 Senate Joint Resolution 63, 100th Congress, 1st Session, WHSOF, George Andricos Files, RAC, Box 1, 3, RRL.
93 Congressional Quarterly Almanac XLIII (1987), LoC, p. 144.
94 USIA Office of Research, Research Memoranda, 'West Europeans Laud Summit', 21 December 1987, showed 97 per cent of Western Europeans polled approved highly of the treaty.
95 Hedrick Smith, 'The Right against Reagan', *New York Times*, 17 January 1988.
96 Letter to President Reagan from Charles Wilson et al., 27 January 1988, WHSOF, George Andricos Files, RAC, Box 1, 3, RRL.
97 Letter to George Shultz from Lee Hamilton, 18 March 1988, AFO 2170, *Afghanistan: The Making of US Foreign Policy*, DNSA.
98 Senate Resolution 386 (S. Res. 386), 'To express the sense of the Senate on United States Policy toward Afghanistan, especially toward the possibility of a Soviet troop withdrawal', AFO 2175, *Afghanistan: The Making of US Foreign Policy*, DNSA.
99 E. A. Wayne, *Christian Science Monitor*, 3 March 1988.
100 Rashid, 'Can the Russians Find a Way Out?', p. 230.
101 Soviet Official quoted in Jefferson Morley, 'The "Negotiators" vs. the "Bleeders"', *Nation*, 20 February 1988, p. 231.
102 Harrison and Cordovez, *Out of Afghanistan*, pp. 256–259. Zia and the ISI wanted an Islamic government but let Foreign Minister Yaqub Khan believe a government headed by the former king was a compromise option.
103 Harrison and Cordovez, *Out of Afghanistan*, p. 309, list the existence of up to twenty-two opposition groups present at a Loya Jirga in 1980 in Pakistan which had hoped to present a legitimate representation of Afghan society. However, the Pakistanis undermined the process and only offered to recognize the fundamentalist groups.
104 'Public Themes on Afghanistan', attached to memorandum to various State agencies from Melvyn Levitsky, Department of State, 28 March 1987, WHORM sf Country File: Afghanistan, 498142–529799, Box 37, RRL.
105 'Contingency Qs and As', attached to memorandum to Colin Powell from Melvin Levitsky, Department of State, 'Afghanistan: Our Public Affairs Handling of a Signature at Geneva', 13 April 1988, WHORM sf Country File: Afghanistan, 562236, Box 37, RRL.
106 'National Security Study: Afghanistan', attached to memorandum for Carlucci from Levitsky.
107 Department of State, 'Afghanistan: Public Diplomacy Action Plan'.
108 Herbert Hagerty Interview, 'Soviet Invasion of Afghanistan', Worldnet Series, 14 January 1987, 306-WNET-327, USIA, Motion Picture, Sound, and Video Records Section, NARA.
109 Department of State, 'Afghanistan: Public Diplomacy Action Plan'.
110 As of 2012, Kriegel was Deputy Director of Americans for Prosperity, Montana. He also co-founded the Bozeman Tea Party. Kriegel also had extreme religious beliefs as a member of Elizabeth Clare Prophet's Church Universal and Triumphant (CUT) New Age religious organization which believed that the Soviet Union was preparing

to launch a first-strike nuclear attack on the United States leading its members to build a massive fallout shelter in Montana and stockpile weapons. See Timothy Egan, 'Guru's Bomb Shelter Hits Legal Snag', *New York Times*, 24 April 1990.

111 Letter to Linas J Kojelis, Associate Director for Public Liaison, White House, from Henry Kriegel, CFA, 15 May 1987, WHORM sf Committee for a Free Afghanistan, Box 17, RRL.
112 Telegram to All Principle Posts from Charles Wick, USIA, 'Public Affairs Guidance 87-53: Afghanistan', 16 October 1987, AF0 2060, *Afghanistan: The Making of US Foreign Policy*, DNSA; Telegram to All Principle Posts from Marvin Stone, USIA, 'Public Affairs Guidance 87-67: Ermacora Report on Human Rights in Afghanistan', 20 November 1987, AF0 2077, *Afghanistan: The Making of US Foreign Policy*, DNSA.
113 Department of State, 'Afghanistan: Public Diplomacy Action Plan'.
114 Department of State, 'Afghanistan: Public Diplomacy Action Plan'.
115 Department of State, 'Afghanistan: Public Diplomacy Action Plan'.
116 Robert Peck, Testimony, HFAC, Subcommittee on Asian and Pacific Affairs, 'Hearing on the Geneva Accords on Afghanistan', 100th Congress, 2nd Session, 19 May 1988, p. 40.
117 Charles Lichenstein, Testimony, CTF on Afghanistan, 'Review of UN Proximity Talks on Afghanistan', 17 February 1987, AF0 1918, *Afghanistan: The Making of US Foreign Policy*, DNSA, p. 51.
118 See letter to President Reagan from the High Council of the Ulema and Clergymen of the Republic of Afghanistan, 21 December 1987, which stated it accepted the new constitution as Islamic in nature and so was willing to join in a process of national reconciliation. WHORM sf, CO 002 Afghanistan, 575200–578999, Box 37, RRL.
119 Memorandum to Colin Powell from Dana Rohrabacher, 'Afghanistan', 8 December 1987, WHORM sf CO 002, Afghanistan, 568000–575119, Box 37, RRL.
120 See Vaughan Williams's analysis of the ISI's objection to Zahir Shah whom Zia could not cross, WHORM sf CO 002, Afghanistan, 599000–605999, Box 38, RRL; Also Rashid, 'Can the Russians Find a Way Out?', p. 229.
121 Khan, *Untying the Afghan Knot*, pp. 183–185 and p. 189. Marshall, 'Managing Withdrawal', pp. 73–74, outlines ceasefires brokered with ethnic minorities such as the Hazaras and Uzbeks.
122 Rashid, 'Can the Russians Find a Way Out', p. 229; Harrison and Cordovez, *Out of Afghanistan*, p. 334.
123 Harrison and Cordovez, *Out of Afghanistan*, p. 325.
124 Henry Kams, 'Afghan Rebels Reported Furious over Rumors of US-Soviet Deal', *New York Times*, 24 February 1988.
125 Theodore J. Eliot Jr, 'Afghanistan's Future', Letter to the Editor, *New York Times*, 2 June 1987.
126 Anthony Davis, 'Afghan Guerrillas Forge a Civil Administration', *Washington Post*, 30 December 1987.
127 Katy Butler, 'March on Soviet Consulate in San Francisco', *San Francisco Chronicle*, 28 December 1987.
128 Anthony Davis, 'Afghan Guerrillas Creating New Units', *Washington Post*, 26 December 1987.
129 James A. Phillips, 'A US Agenda for an Afghan Peace Settlement', Backgrounder No. 643, Heritage Foundation, 4 April 1988, http://www.heritage.org/research/reports/1988/04/a-us-agenda-for-an-afghan-peace-settlement

130 Richard Pipes, Testimony, CTF on Afghanistan, 'Review of the UN Sponsored Proximity Peace Talks on Afghanistan', p. 63.
131 Daniel Pipes, 'Will the Soviets Get Out to Get Back In?' *Los Angeles Times*, 14 April 1988.
132 Letter to President Reagan from William H. Kling, The Foreign Policy Project, 26 February 1988, WHORM sf CO 002, Afghanistan, 543000–547999, Box 37, RRL.
133 Harrison and Cordovez, *Out of Afghanistan*, pp. 261–265.
134 Editorial, *Washington Times*, 7 March 1988.
135 Jeane J. Kirkpatrick, 'Too Eager for Any Agreement on Afghanistan', *Washington Post*, 29 February 1988.
136 CFA, 'The UN and Afghanistan: Stalemated Peacemaking', Free Afghanistan Report, No. 6, March 1984, WHORM sf Committee for a Free Afghanistan, Box 17, RRL.
137 Letter to President Reagan from Henry S. Kreigel, CFA, 24 February 1988, WHORM sf Committee for a Free Afghanistan, Box 17, RRL.
138 Letter to President Reagan from Henry S. Kreigel, Committee for a Free Afghanistan, 12 April 1988, WHORM sf CO 002, Afghanistan, 583800–598999, Box 38, RRL.
139 Letter to President Reagan from Robert H. Krieble, 1 February 1988, WHORM sf CO 002, Afghanistan, 541000–542999, Box 37, RRL.
140 George Arney, 'Afghan Refugees' Rally Assails Geneva Accord', *Washington Post*, 17 April 1988.
141 'Afghanistan Public Diplomacy Strategy', May 1988, WHORM sf CO 002, Afghanistan, 548000–558849, Box 37, RRL.
142 J.F. Burns, 'Afghans: Now They Blame America', *New York Times*, 4 February 1990.
143 James Rupert, 'Arab Fundamentalists Active in Afghan War', *Washington Post*, 2 March 1989.
144 CFA, Flyer, 'When Will Kabul Fall?' *c*. January 1989, AF0 2251, *Afghanistan: The Making of US Foreign Policy*, DNSA.
145 Louis Dupree, Testimony, HFAC, Subcommittee on Asian and Pacific Affairs, 'Hearing on Developments in Afghanistan', 100th Congress, 2nd Session, February 1988, pp. 37–38.

Conclusion

1 A Report of the Project for a New American Century, September 2000, 'Rebuilding America's Defenses: Strategies, Forces, and Resources for a New Century', p. 51.

Selected bibliography

Archival Sources

Ronald Reagan Presidential Library, Simi Valley, California, USA

White House Staff and Office Files (WHSOF)
White House Office of Records Management (WHORM)
Reagan Administration National Security Decision Directives
Ronald Reagan Statements and Speeches, *PPP*, RRL

National Archives and Records Administration, College Park, Maryland, USA

RG 306, United States Information Agency
Research and Reports Historical Collection
USIA Motion Picture, Sound, and Video Records Section
RG 59, Department of State, Office of the Assistant Legal Advisor for Educational, Cultural and Public Affairs

Library of Congress, Washington, DC

Congressional Hearings

Jimmy Carter Library, Atlanta, Georgia

Presidential Papers of Jimmy Carter, *Zbigniew Brzezinski Collection*, Jimmy Carter Library, Atlanta, Georgia, US.
Presidential Papers of Jimmy Carter, *Collection No. 27*, National Security Affairs, Staff Material: Horn/Special.

Digital Archives and Websites

American Presidency Project, http://www.presidency.ucsb.edu
Americans for Prosperity, http://americansforprosperity.org
AmeriCares, http://www.americares.org
Center for Strategic Studies, http://csis.org
Central Intelligence Agency, Freedom of Information Act, Electronic Reading Room, http://www.foia.cia.gov
Council of Europe Parliamentary Assembly, http://assembly.coe.int/nw/Home-EN.asp
Ethics and Public Policy, http://eppc.org
Hathi Trust Digital Library, http://catalog.hathitrust.org
Heritage Foundation, http://www.heritage.org

Jezail.org, http://www.jezail.org
Lehrman Institute, http://www.lehrmaninstitute.org
Lexis Nexus, www.lexisnexus.com
Miller Center of Public Affairs, http://millercenter.org
National Security Archive, https://nsarchive.gwu.edu
Observatoire de L'action Humanitaire (Aid Watch), http://www.observatoire-humanitaire.org
Reagan Files, http://www.thereaganfiles.com
Ronald Reagan Foundation YouTube Channel,
    https://www.youtube.com/channel/UCEJi23qnygQHE5UeLXoV_JQ
United Nations, General Assembly of the United Nations, http://www.un.org/en/ga/
United States National Archives and Records Collection, Historical Election Results, 1789–2004, http://www.archives.gov/federal-register/electoral-college/historical.html
Wilson Center Digital Archive, http://digitalarchive.wilsoncenter.org

Reports and Working Papers

Accuracy in the Media Report, Vol. 12–15 (Washington, DC: Accuracy in the Media, 1984).
Agency Coordinating Body for Afghan Relief & Development (ACBAR), 'Directory of Members, 1991–1992' (Peshawar: Public Art Press, 1991).
Alexiev, Alex. Rand Report, 'The War in Afghanistan: Soviet Strategy and the State of the Resistance', November 1984, http://www.rand.org/content/dam/rand/pubs/papers/2008/P7038.pdf
Amnesty International, 'The Amnesty International Report, 1985' (London: Amnesty International Publications, 1985).
Arms Project (Human Rights Watch), Physicians for Human Rights (US), 'Landmines: A Deadly Legacy' (Human Rights Watch, 1993).
Christensen, Hanne and Fay Haffenden. 'Planning and Afghan Women', UNICEF report produced from a UNICEF and UNIFEM conference, December 1989, https://archive.org/details/azu_acku_pamphlet_hq1236_5_a3_p636_1989
CIA, National Foreign Assessment Center (NFAC), Research Paper, 'Afghanistan: Ethnic Diversity and Dissidence', May 1979, Document No. CIA-RDP81B00401R000600110004-3, CIA FOIA ERR.
CIA, NFAC, Research Paper, 'Muslims in the USSR', 5 February 1980, Document No. 0000969765, CIA FOIA ERR.
CIA, NFAC, Research Paper, 'National Identity among Soviet Uzbeks', May 1980, Document No. 0000969753, CIA FOIA ERR.
CIA, NFAC, Research Paper, 'Nationalities Trends and Political Stability in the Soviet Union', June 1981, Document No. 0000496726, CIA FOIA ERR.
CIA, Directorate of Intelligence, 'The Afghan Resistance: The Struggle for Unity', 26 June 1984, Document No. 0000535014, CIA FOIA ERR.
CIA, Office of Near Eastern and South Asian Analysis and the Office of Soviet Analysis Intelligence Report, 'The Soviet Invasion of Afghanistan: 5 Years After', May 1985, Document No. 0000496704, CIA FOIA ERR.
Congressional Quarterly Almanac, 98th Congress, 2nd Session (Washington, DC: 1984).
Congressional Quarterly Almanac, 100th Congress, 1st Session (Washington, DC: 1987).
Congressional Research Service Report for the House of Representatives Committee on Foreign Affairs, 'The Soviet Union in the Third World, 1980–1985: Imperial Burden or Political Asset', 99th Congress, 1st Session, 23 September 1985.

Cronin, Richard P. 'Afghanistan after Five Years: Status of the Conflict, the Afghan Resistance and the US Role', Congressional Research Service Report Number 85-20, January 1985.
Cronin, Richard P. 'Afghanistan: United Nations Sponsored Negotiations, an Annotated Chronology', Congressional Research Service Report, No. 85-210F, 22 November 1985.
Kronstadt, K. Alan. 'Pakistan-US Relations', Congressional Research Service, Issue Brief for Congress, Updated 6 March 2006, Federation of American Scientists (FAS), https://fas.org/sgp/crs/row/IB94041.pdf
Immigration and Refugee Board of Canada, Human Rights Briefs: Women in Pakistan, 1 June 1994, http://www.refworld.org/docid/3ae6a83c18.html
Lyakhovsky, Alexander. 'Inside the Soviet Invasion of Afghanistan and the Seizure of Kabul, December 1979', Working Paper, No. 51, January 2007, Wilson Center, Cold War International History Project (CWIHP) Publications, Working Papers Series, http://www.wilsoncenter.org/publication/inside-the-soviet-invasion-afghanistan-and-the-seizure-kabul-december-1979
Nicholds, Nigel and John Borton. 'The Changing Role of NGOs in the Provision of Relief and Rehabilitation Assistance: Case Study 1 – Afghanistan/Pakistan', Working Paper, No. 74, Oversees Development Institute, January 1994, http://www.odi.org/publications/2561-changing-role-ngos-provision-relief-rehabilitation-assistance-1-afghanistan-pakistan
Rutkus, Denis Steven. 'Television Network Evening News Coverage of Afghanistan: A Perspective after Eight Years of War', Congressional Research Service Report, 4 February 1988.
Thomas, Dorothy Q. and Patricia Gossman. 'Double Jeopardy: Police Abuse of Women in Pakistan', Human Rights Watch Reports, 1992, Pakistan, http://www.hrw.org/reports/1992/pakistan
Walsh, Lawrence E. 'Final Report of the Independent Counsel for Iran/Contra Matters', Volume I: Investigations and Prosecutions, 4 August 1993, Washington, DC. Available at The Federation of American Scientist's website page: http://www.fas.org/irp/offdocs/walsh/index.html

Selected Books and Articles

Adelman, Kenneth. 'Speaking of America: Public Diplomacy in Our Time', *Foreign Affairs*, Vol. 59, No. 4 (Spring 1981).
American Foreign Policy: Basic Documents, 1977–1980 (Washington: US Dept of State, 1983).
Amstutz, J. Bruce. *Afghanistan: The First Five Years of Soviet Occupation* (Washington: National Defense University, 1986).
Baitenmann, Helga. 'NGOs and the Afghan War: The Politicisation of Humanitarian Aid', *Third World Quarterly*, Vol. 12, No. 1 (January 1990).
Barahona, Diana. 'The Freedom House Files', *Monthly Review*, 1 March 2007, http://mrzine.monthlyreview.org/2007/barahona030107.html
Barnett, Frank R. and Carnes Lord (eds.), *Political Warfare and Psychological Operations: Rethinking the US Approach* (Darby: Diane Publishing, 1989).
Bartley, Robert L. and William P. Kucewicz. 'Yellow Rain and the Future of Arms Agreements', *Foreign Affairs*, Vol. 61, No. 4 (Spring 1983).

Bellant, Russ. *Old Nazis, the New Right, and the Republican Party* (Cambridge: South End Press, 1991).
Bodenheimer, Thomas and Robert Gould. *Rollback! Right-Wing Power in U. S. Foreign Policy* (New York: South End Press, 1989).
Brzezinski, Zbigniew. *Power and Principle: Memoirs of the National Security Advisor, 1977–1981* (London: Weidenfeld and Nicolson, 1983).
Brzezinski, Zbigniew. *The Grand Chessboard: American Primacy and Its Geostrategic Imperatives* (New York: BasicBooks, 1997).
Cahn, Anne Hessing. 'Team B: The Trillion Dollar Experiment', *Bulletin of Atomic Scientists*, Vol. 49, No. 3 (April 1993).
Cannon, Lou. *President Reagan: Role of a Lifetime* (New York: Putnam, 1982).
Carter, Jimmy. *Keeping Faith: Memoirs of a President* (New York: Bantam Books, 1982).
Carter, Jimmy. *White House Diary* (New York: Farrar, Straus and Giroux, 2010).
Centlivres, Pierre and Micheline Centlivres-Demont. 'The Afghan Refugee in Pakistan: An Ambiguous Identity', *Journal of Refugee Studies*, Vol. 1, No. 2 (1988).
Chomsky, Noam and Edward S. Herman. *Manufacturing Consent: The Political Economy of the Mass Media* (New York: Pantheon Books, 1988).
Cogan, Charles G. 'Partners in Time: The CIA and Afghanistan since 1979', *World Policy Journal*, Vol. 10, No. 2 (Summer 1993).
Coll, Steve. *Ghost Wars: The Secret History of the CIA, Afghanistan and Bin Laden, from the Soviet Invasion to September 10, 2001* (New York: Penguin, 2004).
Cordovez, Diego and Selig Harrison. *Out of Afghanistan: The Inside Story of the Soviet Withdrawal* (New York: Oxford University Press, 1995).
Crile, George. *Charlie Wilson's War: The Extraordinary Story of the Largest Covert Operation in History* (New York: Atlantic Monthly Press, 2003).
Cull, Nicholas J. *The Cold War and the United States Information Agency: American Propaganda and Public Diplomacy, 1945–1989* (Cambridge: Cambridge University Press, 2008).
Cullather, Nick. 'Damming Afghanistan: Modernization in a Buffer State', *Journal of American History*, Vol. 89, No. 2 (September 2002).
Davey, Eleanor. 'Famine, Aid, and Ideology: The Political Activism of Medecins Sans Frontières in the 1980s', *French Historical Studies*, Vol. 34, No. 3 (2011).
Davis, Craig. '"A" Is for Allah, "J" Is for Jihad', *World Policy Journal*, Vol. 19, No. 1 (Spring 2002).
Doohovskoy, Andrei A. *Soviet Counterinsurgency in the Soviet Afghan War Revisited: Analyzing the Effective Aspects of the Counterinsurgency Effort*, Master's Thesis (Cambridge, MA: Harvard University, September 2009).
Durham, Martin and Margaret Power. (eds.), *New Perspectives on the Transnational Right* (London: Palgrave Macmillan, 2010).
Ellul, Jacques. *Propaganda: The Formation of Men's Attitudes* (New York: Knopf, 1965).
Garthoff, Raymond L. *Détente and Confrontation: American-Soviet Relations from Nixon to Reagan* (Washington: Brookings Institute, 1994).
Garthoff, Raymond L. *The Great Transition: American-Soviet Relations and the End of the Cold War* (Washington, DC: Brookings Institution, 1994).
Gates, Robert. *From the Shadows: The Ultimate Insider's Story of Five Presidents and How They Won the Cold War* (New York: Simon and Schuster, 1996).
Glad, Betty. *An Outsider in the White House: Jimmy Carter, His Advisors and the Making of American Foreign Policy* (New York: Cornell University Press, 2009).

Guttmann, Allen. 'The Cold War and the Olympics', *International Journal*, Vol. 4, No. 4 (Autumn 1988).
Halliday, Fred. *The Making of the Second Cold War* (London: Verso, 1989).
Herman, Edward S. and David Peterson. *The Politics of Genocide* (New York: Monthly Review Press, 2010).
Isaacs, John. '20 Year Battle on Chemical Weapons Is Over', *Bulletin of the Atomic Scientists*, Vol. 46, No. 6 (July/August 1990).
Jones, Seth G. *In the Graveyard of Empires: America's War in Afghanistan* (New York: W. W. Norton, 2009).
Jordan, Hamilton. *Crisis: The Last Years of the Carter Presidency* (New York: Putnam, 1982).
Khan, Riaz M. *Untying the Afghan Knot: Negotiating Soviet Withdrawal* (Durham: Duke University Press, 1991).
Khybar, Sayid. 'The Afghani Contra Lobby', *Covert Action Information Bulletin*, No. 30 (Summer 1988).
Knoll, Erwin. 'Journalistic Jihad: Holes in the Coverage of the Holy War', *Progressive*, Vol. 54, No. 5 (1990).
Kuperman, Alan J. 'The Stinger Missile and US Intervention in Afghanistan', *Political Science Quarterly*, Vol. 114, No. 2 (1999).
Lucas, William Scott. *Freedom's War: The US Crusade against the Soviet Union, 1945–56* (Manchester: Manchester University Press, 1999).
Lundberg, Kirsten. 'Politics of a Covert Action: The US, the Mujahideen and the Stinger Missile' (Cambridge, MA: Kennedy School of Government, Case Program, 1999).
Lyakhovsky, Alexander. *The Tragedy and Valor of Afghan* (Moscow: GPI Iskon, 1995).
Magone, Claire, Michael Neuman and Fabrice Weissman. (eds.), *Humanitarian Negotiations Revealed: The MSF Experience* (London: Hurst, 2011).
Marshall, Alex. 'Managing Withdrawal: Afghanistan as the Forgotten Example in Attempting Conflict Resolution and State Reconstruction', *Small Wars and Insurgencies*, Vol. 18, No. 1 (2007).
Meher, Jagmohan. *America's Afghanistan War: The Success That Failed* (New Delhi: Kalpaz Publications, 2004).
Micklethwait, John. *The Right Nation: Conservative Power in America* (New York: Penguin Press, 2004).
Moghadam, Valentine. 'Building Human Resources and Women's Capabilities in Afghanistan: A Retrospect and Prospects', *World Development*, Vol. 22, No. 6 (1994).
Nitze, Paul H. 'Strategy in the Decade of the 1980s', *Foreign Affairs*, Vol. 59, No. 1 (Autumn 1980).
Osgood, Kenneth and Andrew K. Frank (eds.), *Selling War in a Media Age: The Presidency and Public Opinion in the American Century* (Florida: University Press of Florida, 2010).
Parry, Robert and Peter Kornbluh. 'Iran Contra's Untold Story', *Foreign Policy*, No. 72 (Autumn 1988).
Prados, John. 'Notes on the CIA Secret War in Afghanistan', *Journal of American History*, Vol. 89, No. 2 (September 2002).
Reagan, Ronald. *Speaking My Mind – Selected Speeches* (New York: Simon & Schuster, 1989).
Reagan, Ronald. *An American Life* (New York: Simon and Schuster, 1990).
Redmont, Bernard. *Risks Worth Taking: Odyssey of a Foreign Correspondent* (Maryland: University Press of America, 1992).

Roberts, James C. *The Conservative Decade: Emerging Leaders of the 1980s* (Westport, CT: Arlington House, 1980).
Rosenfeld, Stephen. 'Guns of July', *Foreign Affairs*, Vol. 64, No. 4 (Spring 1986).
Roy, Oliver. *Islam and Resistance in Afghanistan* (Cambridge: Cambridge University Press, 1986).
Sarantakes, Nicholas Evan. *Dropping the Torch: Jimmy Carter, the Olympic Boycott and the Cold War* (Cambridge: Cambridge University Press, 2011).
Saunders, Jerry Wayne. *Peddlers of Crisis: The Committee on the Present Danger and the Politics of Containment* (Boston, MA: South End Press, 1983).
Schaller, Michael. *Right Turn: American Life in the Reagan-Bush Era, 1980-1992* (Oxford: Oxford University Press, 2007).
Schweizer, Peter. *Victory: The Reagan Administration's Secret Strategy That Hastened the Fall of the Soviet Union* (New York: Atlantic Monthly Press, 1996).
Scott, James M. *Deciding to Intervene: The Reagan Doctrine and American Foreign Policy* (Durham, NC: Duke University Press, 1996).
Scott-Smith, Giles. 'Aristotle, US Public Diplomacy, and the Cold War: The Works of Carnes Lord', *Foundations of Science*, Vol. 13, Nos. 3-4 (July 2008).
Seagrave, Sterling. *Yellow Rain: A Journey through the Terror of Chemical Warfare* (New York: M. Evans, 1981).
Shirazi, Roozbeh. 'Islamic Education in Afghanistan: Revisiting the United States' Role', *The New Centennial Review*, Vol. 8, No. 1 (Spring 2008).
Shultz, George. 'New Realities and New Ways of Thinking', *Foreign Affairs*, Vol. 63, No. 4 (Spring 1985).
Singh, Robert. *American Government and Politics* (London: Sage, 2003).
Smith, Andrew F. *Rescuing the World: The Life and Times of Leo Cherne* (New York: State University of New York, 2002).
Smith, James Allen. *Strategic Calling: The Center for Strategic and International Studies, 1962-1992* (Washington: Center for Strategic & International Studies, 1993).
Snyder, Alvin. *Warriors of Disinformation: American Propaganda, Soviet Lies, and the Winning of the Cold War* (New York: Arcade Pub., 1995).
Soley, Lawrence C. *The News Shapers: The Sources Who Explain the News* (New York: Praeger, 1992).
Stahl, Jason. *Right Moves: The Conservative Think Tank in American Political Culture since 1945* (Chapel Hill: University of North Carolina Press, 2016).
Tuch, Hans N. *Communicating with the World: US Public Diplomacy Overseas* (Washington: Institute for the Study of Diplomacy, 1990).
Tucker, Jonathan B. 'The "Yellow Rain" Controversy: Lessons for Arms Control Compliance', *The Nonproliferation Review*, Vol. 8, No. 1 (Spring 2001).
Vaisse Julian. *Neoconservatism: The Biography of a Movement* (Cambridge, MA: Belknap Press of Harvard University Press, 2010).
Walsh, Mary Williams. 'Mary Williams Walsh, Mission Afghanistan', *Columbia Journalism Review* (January/February 1990).
Walsh, Mary Williams. 'Strained Mercy', *The Progressive*, Vol. 54, No. 5 (May 1990).
Westad, Odd Arne. *The Global Cold War: Third World Interventions and the Making of Our Times* (Cambridge: Cambridge University Press, 2005).
Willentz, Sean. *The Age of Reagan: A History, 1974-2008* (New York: Harper, 2008).
Woodward, Bob. *Veil: The Secret Wars of the CIA, 1981-1987* (New York: Simon and Schuster, 1987).
Yousaf, Mohammad and Mark Adkin. *The Bear Trap: Afghanistan's Untold Story* (London: L. Cooper, 1992).

Index

A
Abrams, Elliot 55, 152
Accuracy in the Media 24, 46
Adelman, Kenneth 7, 8, 36, 54, 63
Afghan Digest (USIA) 45, 64, 74, 91
Afghan Information Center (Freedom House) 24, 67, 114
Afghan Information and Documentation Center 81
Afghan Media Project 9, 55, 84, 87–104, 129, 151
   Afghan Media Resource Center 101–2
Afghan Mercy Fund 79, 98–100
Afghan Relief Committee (ARC) 4, 65, 75, 88, 140, 142
   Afghan Media Project 94
   CTF 'Hearing on Famine in Afghanistan' 79
   formation, founders and fundraising 23–4, 66
   Sarah Scaife Foundation 64
   sponsorship of mujahedeen trip to US 47
   'yellow rain' allegations 46
Afghan Resistance Relief Center 117
Afghan Task Force (Congressional Task Force on Afghanistan) 68, 72, 73, 117, 134, 152
   and Afghan Media Project 98
   'Afghanistan Day' 57
   Geneva Accords 136–7, 141
   'Hearing on Effective Public Diplomacy' 89, 90
   'Hearing on Famine in Afghanistan' 78–80
   'Hearing on Medical Conditions in Afghanistan' 121
   'supply of anti-aircraft missiles to mujahedeen' 78–80
Afghan Working Group (Interagency Working Group on Afghanistan) 38, 65, 67, 74–5, 88, 117, 122

Afghanistan Day 23, 53, 57–60, 69, 130, 138
Afghanistan Relief Week 23
Allen, Richard V. 35, 119
American Aid for Afghans 81
American Friends of Afghanistan (AFA) 24, 122
AmeriCares 50, 64, 65, 66–7, 89, 117
   AmeriCares for Afghanistan
Amin, Hafizullah 15, 17

B
Barry, Michael 47, 63, 79, 80
Boston University (BU) 87, 94–104, 120, 151
British Afghanistan Support Committee 79
Brzezinski, Zbigniew 75, 81, 106, 138, 148
   anti-Soviet propaganda and Islam 8, 21, 26–8, 32
   appearance before the CTF on Afghanistan 89
   involvement with AmeriCares 64, 66
   reaction to Soviet invasion 2, 16, 18, 29, 31, 71
Buckley, James 41
Bukovsky, Vladimir 63, 65–6, 67

C
Campaigne, Antony 98–9
Carter, James 1, 11, 147–8, 152
   'Afghanistan Day' 58
   Carter Doctrine 15, 18, 32
   Heritage Foundation 20–2
   neo-conservatives 19–20, 32, 35
   Olympic boycott 23, 29–31
   propaganda and public diplomacy on Afghanistan 25–8, 76
   reaction to invasion of Afghanistan 2, 8–10, 13–32
   support for mujahedeen 17–18
   USICA/USIA 36, 40

Casey, William 38, 46, 66, 92
  anti-Soviet propaganda and Islam 55, 56, 76
  Reagan Doctrine and Afghanistan 3, 9, 50, 55, 60
Center for Strategic and International Studies (CSIS) 22, 23
Coalition for a Democratic Majority (CDM) 19, 89
Coalition for Peace through Strength 46–7
Committee for a Free Afghanistan (CFA) 64, 67, 70, 100, 117, 152
  advocacy of military aid to mujahedeen 81
  Afghan Media Project 94
  'Afghanistan Day' 57, 59
  Geneva accords 143–4, 153
  links to other conservative organisations 24
  pro-mujahedeen propaganda efforts 118–19
  Simon, Robert 121
  support for Radio Free Kabul 63, 66
  tensions with US Department of State 120, 124
  'war crimes project' 140
  'yellow rain' allegations 46–7, 150
Committee for the Free World 117
Committee on the Present Danger (CPD) 9–10, 21, 44, 151, 152
  establishment and ideology 19–20
  Reagan 20, 35
Congressional Task Force on Afghanistan (CTF) – See Afghan Task Force
Cooperation of Democratic Countries 117
Cordovez, Diego 5, 126, 127–8, 142
Council for the Defense of Freedom 46
Cranborne, Lord Robert 79, 80

D
Daud, Haji Sayed 102, 104
de Borchgrave, Arnaud 64, 66
Douglas, Kurt 54, 63–4
Dubs, Adolph 'Spike' 16, 17
Dubs, Mary Ann 23
Dupree, Louis 88, 89, 122, 144
  advocacy of military aid to mujahedeen 23, 153
  Afghan Media Project 94
Durand Line 15, 61, 127, 135

E
Eiva, Andrew 67, 82, 83
Electronic Dialogue series (USIA) 109
Eliot, Theodore 16, 24, 46, 75, 88, 142

F
Fawcett, Charles 66, 121
Federation for American-Afghan Action (FAAA) 24, 67, 70, 78, 81, 82
Feulner, Edwin 20, 35, 119
Freedom House 75, 91, 117, 140, 150, 152
  advocacy of military aid to mujahedeen 50, 67
  Afghan Information Center 24
  Afghan Media Project 97
  'Chemical/Biological Weapons Information Project' 45
  CTF 'Hearing on Famine in Afghanistan' 79
  sponsorship of mujahedeen trip to US 47
  'yellow rain' allegations 46
Freedom Research Foundation 79, 119
Free the Eagle 24, 67, 82–3

G
Gates, Robert 8, 16, 48, 91
Geneva peace talks and Accords 48–50, 125–7, 132
  attitude of US congress 11, 133, 136–9, 153
  NSDD 270 128–130
  PVOs 4, 11, 126, 133, 142, 153
German Afghan Committee (DAK) 99, 100
Girardet, Edward 57, 63
Gorbachev, Mikhail 11, 65, 83, 85, 117, 143
  efforts to withdraw from Afghanistan 125, 126–7, 132, 138
  Geneva superpower summit 105–7, 110, 123
Gouttierre, Thomas 24, 65, 75, 80, 88, 94, 122

H

Haig Jr., Alexander 41, 49, 126
Haq, Abdul 79, 92, 99
Hatch, Orrin 69, 88, 117
Hekmatyar, Gulbuddin 61, 66, 114, 143
Helman, Gerald 55, 57, 58, 136
Heritage Foundation 6, 14, 42, 54, 69, 70
   advocacy of military aid to
      mujahedeen 68, 81–2, 83, 120–1
   advocacy of propaganda and public
      diplomacy 36, 91, 152
   Carter 22
   formation and methods 20–1
   Geneva Accords 142, 143
   Gorbachev 106
   links to other PVOs 24, 46, 64, 67, 119, 152
   reaction to Soviet invasion of Afghanistan 4, 82
   Reagan 22, 35
   'yellow rain' allegations 47
Hoover Institute, The 22
Humphrey, Gordon 69, 107, 131, 136, 138
   advocacy of military aid to mujahedeen 83
   advocacy of propaganda and public diplomacy 89
   Afghan Media Project 93–4, 98, 101
   Commission on Security and Co-operation in Europe 90
   CTF on Afghanistan 78
   Geneva Accords 136–8
   PVOs 66, 67, 99, 118, 120
Hurd, Ann 98–9

I

Iklé, Fred 83, 137, 152, 153
Institute of Foreign Policy Analysis 45
Interagency Working Group on Afghanistan 65, 74–5, 122
International Committee of the Red Cross (ICRC) 53, 55–6
International Federation for Human Rights 80
International Rescue Committee 46, 64, 66, 91, 101
Islamic Unity of the Afghan *Mujahedeen* (IUAM) 113, 119–20

K

Khalilzad, Zalmay 113
   Afghan Media Project 94–5
   Interagency Working Group 75
   Project for a New American Century (PNAC) 151, 152
   PVOs 75, 91, 94
   USIA 'Electronic Dialogue' series 109
Khan, Yaqub 50, 127–8
King Features Hearst 93–4, 97–8, 101
Kirkpatrick, Jeane J. 55–6, 64, 73, 80, 90, 143
   Kirkpatrick Doctrine 35, 42, 62
Klass, Rosanne 24, 67–8, 78, 79, 97, 102
Koehler, John O. 94, 97, 102

L

Ledeen, Michael 23, 44, 48
Levy, Bernard-Henri 65, 151
Lohbeck, Kurt 78–9, 92, 97, 98–9, 100
Lord, Carnes 7, 8, 36, 37–8, 63

M

Macauley, Robert C. 50, 66, 117
Magnus, Ralph 65, 66, 89
Maitre, H. Joachim 95–8, 101–2, 110, 151
McFarlane, Robert 45, 79, 88
McKay, Karen 24, 46–7, 120
McMahon, John 82–3
Médecins Sans Frontières (MSF) 37, 64, 79, 122
   'French doctors' 58, 67
   The Friends of the Children of Afghanistan 122
Meselson, Matthew 45, 47
Mills, Nick 99
Mosher, John 94, 99

N

Najibullah, Mohammad 127, 130, 131, 139, 140, 142
National Endowment for Democracy (NED) 37, 122
National Security Council (NSC) 29, 56, 119, 141
   Afghan Media Project 94, 98, 101
   'Afghanistan Day' 58

Interagency Afghanistan Public
  Diplomacy Working Group (NSDD
  270) 140
Interagency Working Group on
  Afghanistan (NSDD 77) 38–9
Raymond Jr., Walter 7, 38
National Security Decision Directive
  (NSDD) 32, 37, 148
NSDD 75 3, 39, 148
NSDD 77 7, 37–40, 64, 148
NSDD 130 73
NSDD 147 75, 76, 77, 148
NSDD 166 10, 71–2, 82, 126, 148, 149
  Afghan Media Project 10, 85, 87, 90,
    93, 103
  Muslim public opinion 76
NSDD 194 108, 111, 148, 150
NSDD 270 11, 125–6, 128–9, 133, 135, 148
Nationalities Working Group 26
Neo-conservatives 3, 117, 147, 151
  Carter administration and 13–15,
    19–20, 23–5, 32
  Reagan administration and 33, 35–9,
    42, 50, 54, 55
Neumann, Robert 23, 24, 65, 66
New Right 20–5, 56, 67, 100, 147, 152
  Carter administration and 13, 14, 15,
    19, 32
  Reagan administration and 2, 9, 33,
    50, 55
Nitze, Paul 9, 19–20

O
Olsson, Stephen 94, 99, 101–4
Olympic boycott 13, 29–31

P
Palm Beach Clinic 117
People's Democratic Party of Afghanistan
  (PDPA) 14–15, 62–3, 115, 130, 141–2
Perle, Richard 35, 49, 90, 152
Pillsbury, Michael 83
Pipes, Richard 35, 36, 39, 49, 143
Poullada, Leon B. 24, 49
Private Voluntary Organizations
  (PVOs) 1–4, 32, 72, 118, 123–4,
  151–3
  Afghan Media Project 92, 94, 98–100,
    103

'Afghanistan Day' 53, 57
Congress 54, 67–8, 78–9
Educational programmes 121–2
Geneva Accords 11, 126, 133, 140–2
Military aid to mujahedeen 72, 78–84
Radio Free Kabul 65
Reagan administration 10, 65–7, 75,
  84, 106, 116–17
Tsongas-Ritter resolution 54, 67
USIA 54, 63–5, 74
'yellow rain' allegations 34, 46–8
Project Democracy 7, 33, 37, 38, 39, 40
  Maitre, Joachim 95
  Muslims and 76
Project Truth 7, 33, 38, 39, 40
  'yellow rain' 40, 44–5, 51
PRODEMCA (Friends of the Democratic
  Center in Central America) 65, 70,
  95, 96, 151

R
Rabbani, Burhanuddin 119–20
Radio Free Kabul 54, 63, 65–6, 67
Radio Liberty 28, 91
Raymond Jr., Walter 7, 63, 79, 88, 93–4, 149
  Afghan public diplomacy programme 38
  'yellow rain' 44–6, 51
Reagan/Reagan administration 1, 94, 119,
  141, 147
  Afghan Media Project 87, 92, 97, 103
  'Afghanistan Day' 57–60
  CPD 35
  Geneva peace negotiations and
    Accords 48–50, 125–33, 139, 143–5
  Geneva superpower summit
    propaganda 107–11, 123
  Heritage Foundation 22
  international perceptions of
    administration 72–3
  neo-conservatives and New Right
    9–10, 20, 22, 35
  Pakistan 34, 41–2, 48–51, 61, 72,
    111–13
  public diplomacy and propaganda 3,
    6–8, 32–9, 54–7
  PVOs 4, 23–4, 65–8, 106, 116–20, 143,
    151–2
  Reagan Doctrine 3, 9–10, 35, 37, 53–4,
    69–70

Muslim public opinion 76, 148, 150
  visit by IUAM 119–20
  'yellow rain' allegations 44–8
Redmont, Bernard 95, 96
Ritter, Don 47, 59, 68, 69, 90
  'Afghanistan Day' 57
  ARC 66
  Tsongas-Ritter Resolution 23, 54, 72, 78, 152
Rostow, Eugene 19, 44

S
Saur (April) Revolution 10, 14–16, 31
Schwartzstein, Stuart 46
Seagrave, Sterling 45, 47, 48
Shultz, George 92, 131, 141
  CFA criticism 120
  Geneva Accords 125, 132, 138, 143
  visit to Afghan refugee camps 60
  'yellow rain' allegations 45
Silber, John R. 95–6, 151
Simon, Robert 64, 66, 121, 136
Singlaub, John K. 47, 119
Smith-Mundt Act 7, 38, 81, 93, 103, 152
Stinger missiles 4, 72, 79, 134, 142, 143
  CIA and 11, 82–5
  PVOs 23, 82–5
Strategic Defense Initiative (SDI) 5, 11, 105, 107, 108, 123

T
Team B 20, 35, 42
Tsongas, Paul 67, 68–9, 78, 121
  Tsongas-Ritter Resolution – see under Ritter
TV Satellite File (USIA) 64, 81, 91, 121

U
United States Information Agency (USICA / USIA) 4, 6–7
  Afghan Media Project 10–11, 87, 90–104
  'Afghanistan Day' 130–1
  domestic dissemination of output 39–40, 81, 103–4, 152
  funding under Reagan 33
  Geneva peace negotiations and Accords 129, 131–3
  Kurt Douglas visit to refugee camps 63–4
  military aid to mujahedeen 78, 80–1
  Muslim public opinion 76
  NSC and 38
  output on Afghanistan 64–5, 74, 91–3, 108–10, 131–2
  'Project Democracy' 39–40
  'Project Truth 40
  PVOs 63, 65, 75, 84, 88, 152
    Afghan Mercy Fund 99
    German Afghan Committee (DAK) 100
    Guilde Europeenne du Raid 99–100
  'roadmap to Geneva' 107–10, 123
  Soviet reaction to propaganda 65, 83
  Use of term 'public diplomacy' 6
  'yellow rain' allegations 45
University of Nebraska at Omaha (UNO) 24, 89, 94, 120, 122

V
Vietnam Syndrome 10, 36, 71
Voice of America (VOA) 28, 36, 63, 88, 91, 129
  criticism 54
  Geneva superpower summit 108, 110, 123
  Project Truth 40
  Public Diplomacy Action Plan on Afghanistan 141
  'yellow rain' allegations 45

W
Wattenberg, Ben 89
Weyrich, Paul 20, 67, 143
Wheeler, Jack 79, 81, 82, 89, 119
Wick, Charles 7, 39–40, 80, 96, 119, 141
Wilson, Charles 68, 69, 71, 79, 137, 152
  'Afghanistan Day' 131
  CFA 118
  criticism of Reagan administration 136
  CTF on Afghanistan 78, 134
  Dan Rather (CBS) report on Afghanistan 29
  Hekmatyar, Gulbuddin 66
  Rabbani, Burhanuddin 120
World Anti-Communism League (WACL) 24, 91, 100
Worldnet (USIA) 80, 129, 130–1
  Geneva superpower summit 108, 109

PVOs 40
Soviet reaction to programme 83
'yellow rain' allegations 45, 51

Y
'Yellow rain' allegations 34, 39, 44–8, 51, 117, 149

Z
Zia ul Haq, Muhammad 61, 68, 113, 127, 144, 152
    Carter and 22
    dinner with George Shultz 60
    dinner with Michael Douglas 54, 63
    Geneva Accords 139–40
    Road to Geneva public diplomacy strategy 108, 112
    tensions with Afghan refugees 135–5
    US military aid to Pakistan 22, 41–2, 51
Zahir Shah, Mohammed 119, 127, 132, 135, 142
    support amongst Afghans 61, 114

www.ingramcontent.com/pod-product-compliance
Lightning Source LLC
Chambersburg PA
CBHW072108010526
44111CB00037B/2050